A RACE TO FREEDOM

A RACE TO FREEDOM

THE MIRA SLOVAK STORY

DAVID WILLIAMS

To David,

Good luck!

AMERICA
THROUGH TIME®
ADDING COLOR TO AMERICAN HISTORY

Once you have tasted flight, you will forever walk the earth with your eyes turned skyward, for there you have been and there you will always long to return.

Leonardo da Vinci

America Through Time® is an imprint of Fonthill Media LLC
www.through-time.com
office@through-time.com
www.fonthill.media

Published by Arcadia Publishing by arrangement with Fonthill Media LLC
For all general information, please contact Arcadia Publishing:
Telephone: 843-853-2070
Fax: 843-853-0044
E-mail: sales@arcadiapublishing.com
For customer service and orders:
Toll-Free 1-888-313-2665

www.arcadiapublishing.com

First published 2018
Reprinted 2019

ISBN 978-1-62545-066-1

Typeset in 11pt on 13pt Minion Pro
Printed and bound in England

Contents

Introduction

By the time he became famous for the second time, Miroslav Slovak had given up trying to get Americans to call him "Miro." They insisted on calling him "Mira," a name that 1950s America found easier to pronounce. Never mind that Mira was a name mostly used by women in his native Czechoslovakia—a communist country he had fled in a harrowing escape that had earned him headlines around the world. Slovak was what was known in those days as a man's man. He was a survivor of the Nazis, an escapee from authoritarian communism, and a refugee who—against all odds—was taken under the protective wing of Seattle's Boeing family. Slovak became a daredevil acrobatic pilot, one of the world's most successful hydroplane racers, and then an airline pilot. Women, from spies to starlets, found him irresistible; so, apparently, did Congress, which passed an act for his sole benefit. Slovak got his way in life, but not quite about everything. He could escape the Iron Curtain with MiG fighters on his tail but he could not escape the name "Mira," so eventually he embraced it.

As the executive director of the Hydroplane and Raceboat Museum in suburban Seattle, I crossed paths with Mira Slovak often. He was a legend. Yet it was not until the fall of 2008 that we became close friends, and it took a monumental clerical error to bring it about.

Some of Mira's biggest success came in the late 1950s while he was driving the *Miss Wahoo* unlimited hydroplane for Bill Boeing, Jr. It was a good time for Bill, too, because it allowed him to be seen as successful in a field that was independent of his father's powerful influence.

When the Hydroplane Museum began to restore and run vintage hydroplanes in the mid-1990s, Bill Jr. and I talked about rebuilding his old

Miss Wahoo. The boat was long gone, having been destroyed in an accident in 1966, but we had the original plans and I told Bill we would be happy to build a replica. He asked about the cost and I prepared a budget, but it never went further than that.

In summer of 2007, the Boeing Company was scrambling to get its first 787 done in time to be unveiled on July 8, 2007 (a date that could be read as 7-8-7). The plane was far from complete and there was a push at all levels of the company to make sure that the plane could be presented to the public on time. A large media event was planned, with dignitaries and politicians from around the globe invited to witness what Boeing hoped would be the biggest aviation event of the new century. In all of the rush to make sure that July 8, 2007 went perfectly, one small detail fell through the cracks. One 41-cent stamp had been left off one beautifully embossed white envelope, and one important guest never received his invitation.

When July 8, 2007 arrived, it was a spectacularly warm, clear day and thousands of Boeing employees beamed with pride and cheered as the blue and white Dreamliner emerged from the factory for the first time. Yet there was one voice missing. In the mad dash to get everything done, no one had checked with Bill Boeing Jr. to see if he had received his invitation. He had not; therefore, for the first time, a brand-new plane was unveiled without a member of the Boeing family being present.

Commercial Aviation president Scott Carson knew that Bill's feelings were hurt. Carson assembled a small group of aviation supporters and approached me with a plan to build a *Miss Wahoo* replica, and use the boat as a tribute to Mr. Boeing to show that he was admired and respected by the entire community, not just the aviation world.[1]

We agreed, and construction on the *Miss Wahoo* replica started on September 13, 2008. Mira was excited by the project and flew to Seattle often to check on our progress. He was present when the boat was launched on July 10, 2009, and I gave him a ride in the boat on August 1.

Over the next few years, Mira came to several of our vintage hydroplane exhibitions and eventually he got a chance to drive the boat on his own in Seattle at eighty-one years old, on August 6, 2011.

Mira and I spent hundreds of hours talking about his past. Many of the conversations took place in quaint restaurants in the resort town of Chelan or standing on the shore of Lake Coeur d'Alene, while we waited for the wind to calm enough that we could run the boat. Eventually we began to talk about putting his stories into book form. At first, Mira was reluctant; he did not want a "hydro book" or an "air race book" or even a "Cold War hero book." He wanted it all woven together. We also discussed how he wanted the story presented. His major instruction was "It must be the truth! No Hollywood BS! Even if we tell the truth, to some people it will sound too fantastical to be believed, so we need to search through the archives and find proof so that if someone says 'That never could have happened,' we will be able to prove that it did!"[2] I have tried to honor Mira's desire to only tell the truth. There are a few names that have been changed for obvious reasons, and I have taken a bit of artistic liberty with some of the dialogue. Time, age, and translation from one language to another mean that a few conversations are not word for word, but the spirit and intent have been kept.

A Note about Names

Mira was born with the name Miroslav Slovak, and his friends and family in Czechoslovakia called him Miro. When he came to the United States, Americans had difficulty saying Miro and insisted on calling him Mira. In Czechoslovakia, Mira is typically a woman's name, and for several years, Mira tried unsuccessfully to get Americans to call him Miro. Eventually, he gave up and accepted his new American name. In early drafts of this book, I tried using the name Miro in chapters taking place in Czechoslovakia and Mira for chapters taking place in the United States, but I felt that it created too much confusion for the reader, so I have reluctantly decided to use the name Mira throughout the entire book.

1

Thou Shalt Not Kill: Prague, 1953

Captain Mira Slovak was twenty-three years old and sat at the controls of a DC-3 that was hurtling through the night at 200 mph. Behind him in the passenger cabin, twenty-three innocents were taking naps, thumbing through magazines, or chatting quietly. Mira took his hand from the control yoke and reached into the right pocket of his Czechoslovakian Air Lines uniform to feel the cold lethal steel of a pistol. Hidden in his pocket, his fingers explored the gun; his thumb rested on the hammer and he was tempted to cock it.

Mira's mind wandered to the passengers in the back of the plane and he wondered how they would react when they found out what he was about to do. Would they panic and rush the cockpit? Would they pray? Cry? Or would they even notice when the plane swung 180 degrees and began to head west, over the "Iron Curtain" and away from the land of prison camps, barbed-wire fences, and secret police?

A childhood memory filled his mind—a Catholic priest in a cold stone church preaching a sermon on the Ten Commandments. As the priest in Mira's memory went through the Commandments, Mira gripped the pistol tighter. At Commandment Six, Mira murmured out loud, "Thou shalt not kill."

Next to him, the co-pilot looked up. "What did you say?"

Mira shook his head. "Nothing, I was just talking to myself." Mira was a man of rigid principles and the same principles that were forcing him to escape the iron fist of Communism were also telling him that he had to make his daring escape without hurting anyone.

Mira had formed his sense of right and wrong at the age of eight, when at his grandmother's urging, his parents sent him to study to be a priest at Saleziánsky Ústav, in the city of Trnava. At the seminary, the boys were required to wear a uniform of short pants and suit coats, white shirts, and dark ties. They sat side-by-side at ancient wooden desks with chairs that were so tall that few of the young student's feet (including Mira's) could even touch the ground. The ceilings were high and vaulted and the rooms never warmed in the cold European winter of 1937. Discipline was often meted out with shovels, rakes, wheel barrows, and back-breaking work on the seminary grounds.

Mira hated the place, and his quiet resentment blossomed into outright rebellion. On one occasion, he was sent out into the grounds to work off his punishment for a minor indiscretion. Instead of working, he found a dense juniper bush and crawled under it to hide. He spent all day under the bush, drawing in the dirt, dreaming of airplanes and how he would fly all over the world when he grew up. When the dinner bell rang, Mira refused to come out of his hiding place. The sun went down and the evening turned cold. He simply pulled his thin jacket tighter around his shoulders, trying to stay warm. Eventually, the headmaster came looking for Mira with a flashlight, and the tired, shivering boy was hauled in to a meal of cold mush, water, and a few lashes with a switch. Yet the next time Mira was sent out to do penitent work on the grounds, he hid again. This second act of rebellion ended much the same way as the first. The contest of wills continued one more day. This time, he waited until no one was looking and climbed a tree near the seminary wall. Leaping from the tree to the wall, and then to the ground, he began to walk the 20 kilometers from Trnava back to his parent's home in Leopoldov.

Mira only made it a short way before a priest, returning to the seminary, recaptured the young fugitive and brought him back to face justice. First, Mira received a stern lecture from the headmaster, and then he was told to wait by himself in his bleak dormitory while his parents were summoned.

Seconds crept by like hours as the terrified yet defiant young Mira sat waiting for his parents' wrath. His dorm window faced the highway, and when the eight-year-old boy stood on his bed, he could see the cars and trucks passing on the road below.

After an eternity of waiting, young Mira fell asleep, only to be awoken by a far-off rumbling. There was something familiar in the growling noise of one of the engines out on the highway. It did not sound like the putt-putt-putt of most of the cars that drove by. This was different; this was the deep rumbling of a powerful engine. Mira was certain it was the sound of his father's fast Aero 30 Roadster winding up the hill towards the seminary. He climbed onto the bed and stretched to catch a glimpse of his father's bright red convertible flashing between hedgerows and fence posts. The car accelerated past a slower moving sedan and then Mira saw something truly amazing. As the sporty car swept through a turn, he saw the flash of a long brunette ponytail flicker behind the driver's goggled head. It was not his father coming to scold him; it was his mother coming to rescue him. He flew out of his room and ran down stairs past the angry headmaster who was yelling "Stop, boy, stop!"

Mira burst out of the seminary door just as his mother slid the sleek Aero 30 to a stop on the cobblestone driveway in front of the building. She stepped out of the car like a lioness protecting her cub. Mira ran across the paving stones, chased by the red-faced headmaster. Maria swept Mira into her arms and turned towards the headmaster and announced, "I'm taking my boy home now." Mother and son climbed into the leather-upholstered front seat and roared away as the Aero 30 kicked up dust at the stunned headmaster. Neither Mira nor Maria ever looked back.

2

Peace in Our Time: Munich, 1938

Miroslav Slovak was born in the small farming town of Cífer, Czechoslovakia on October 24, 1929, the night before the American stock market crashed and threw the world's economy in to a depression that would last for years. His father, Jan Slovak, was a tall man with Clark Gable good looks, thick black hair, and a dapper pencil-thin mustache. His mother was Irma Maria Kramarova, who everybody called Maria.

The family moved east from Cífer to the city of Leopoldov, where Jan took a job managing a grain elevator located alongside the main railway between Leopoldov to Piešťany. Along with the grain elevator came a large, old-fashioned, two-story home with thick walls of ochre-colored stucco and heavy green shutters to keep out the fierce winter cold. There were several tall linden trees in the yard. Jan's Český Fousek hunting dog, Leo, loved to lounge in the cool shade under the trees on warm summer days. The big silver-gray dog was famous for his gentle nature, fierce loyalty, and amazing ability to track game birds. Three large gardens provided the family with fruits and vegetables. A fragrant herb garden smelled of mint, chives, and parsley. There were ducks, geese, hogs, and almost anything else Maria needed for her kitchen. Jan hired a Romani couple to tend the gardens, so there were often Romani wagons, with wildly painted carved wooden panels and curved roofs parked beneath the fragrant linden trees.

The house sat on a corner of two main streets. One side was converted to a saloon where the local farmers who came to sell their grain could enjoy a frothy beer and a thick sandwich of cheese and sausage on rustic bread. They sat in small, friendly groups at the sturdy wooden tables and talked about the weather, crops, and all the latest news. Leo would roam in and out of the saloon at will. He quickly learned which customers would sneak him scraps and would curl up under the friendly tables. Soon, a second son, named Jarda, was born, and the family was complete. As the manager of the grain elevator in a region that was heavily dependent on agriculture, Jan quickly became a respected and powerful figure, and he was able to give his sons an upper-middle-class lifestyle.

When Mira was still quite little, Jan paid a local Romani man to teach the young boy how to play the violin. Mira spent hours sitting on a wicker chair under the linden trees struggling to make his small hands curve around the neck of the violin. No matter how hard he tried, Mira just could not get the tiny violin to make the same beautiful sounds that his teacher could. Eventually, Jan came to the conclusion that music just was not in Mira's blood, and the project was abandoned.

Czechoslovakia was created at the end of World War I, when the Allied powers dismantled the Austro-Hungarian Empire and wanted to create a buffer state in central Europe. Included in this new country were the highly industrialized, Czech-speaking former kingdoms of Bohemia and Moravia, but also the rural, agricultural territory of Slovakia.

To assure Czechoslovakia's safety, England, France, and Italy signed treaties pledging to defend Czechoslovakia from any foreign aggression. Czech patriot Thomas Masaryk was elected the first president of Czechoslovakia on November 14, 1918. Masaryk quickly enacted many progressive reforms, including social security and women's suffrage. Both were adopted in Czechoslovakia before they were adopted in the U.S.

When Maria brought Mira home from the seminary, he was a few weeks shy of his ninth birthday and his parents had to get him back into school quickly. They decided on the Slovak-speaking public school. In the few short years since Jan and Maria had sent Mira to the seminary, the mood in Slovakia had changed dramatically. There was now an open movement for secession from the rest of Czechoslovakia, and Andrej Hlinka's fascist Slovak People's Party was the most powerful political party in Slovakia.

Just as Hitler's Nazi Party had a "Hitler Youth" group where boys and girls wore brown-shirted replicas of the Nazi uniform and saluted with "*Heil* Hitler," Hlinka's Party had the *Hlinkova Mladez* (Hlinka Youth). Jan and Maria's neighbors warned them that "it would be better for Mira if he joined the Hlinka Youth." When Mira entered public school in early September 1938, he, like thousands of other young children in Slovakia, wore the brown military uniform of the fascist Hlinka Youth, complete with a neckerchief, garrison cap, and knee socks with garter tabs. Maria hated it, but she swallowed her anger, believing it was best for Mira.

While the Hlinka fascists called for secession in the east, a much more potent threat was facing Czechoslovakia in the west. At the end of World War I, the Allied powers had awarded the Sudeten Mountains to Czechoslovakia, even though there were large numbers of native Germans living in the region. As early as 1936, Adolf Hitler began to demand that the Sudeten be reunited with Germany. He issued a series of threats and promised war if he was not given the Sudeten region. This led to a "Peace Conference" in Munich in late September 1938. England, France, Italy, and Germany were all invited to attend the conference, but no representatives of the Czech government were allowed into the meeting. Hitler convinced British Prime Minister Neville Chamberlain that his only interest was in protecting the Sudeten Germans, who he claimed were being persecuted by the Czechs. If the Allied powers would allow him to annex the Sudetenland, he would be content that Germany had been restored to its historic borders and would make no other demands in Europe.

Chamberlain quickly agreed to a four-party agreement between England, France, Italy, and Germany that gave the Sudetenland and all its mountain fortifications to Hitler. Chamberlain told a stunned Czechoslovakia that the Allies, who had all promised at the end of World War I to "defend the Czech borders as if they were their own," would in fact do nothing to stop Hitler. Chamberlain returned to England to a hero's welcome. Stepping out of his plane and waving the new treaty over his head, he declared "We have secured peace in our time."

In Prague, the Munich treaty was called "The Munich Diktat" or "The Munich Betrayal." In October 1938, Nazi troops began to cross the Czech borders unopposed. President Edvard Beneš felt it was useless to fight Germany without the help of the Allies. As the Nazis crossed into the Sudetenland, Beneš resigned the presidency and fled to London, where he set up a government in exile.

The Nazis kept Hitler's word for a few months and stopped at the edges of the Sudetenland, but when it was clear that there would be no opposition, they travelled deeper into the countryside; by March 15, 1939, Czechoslovakia was overrun by Germany and officially dissolved, being renamed the Protectorate of Bohemia and Moravia. The Nazis took over the rich Czech industrial base and converted it to produce arms and munitions for the growing German army. Slovakia was now free of the bothersome Czechs and became a client state of Nazi Germany.

Responding to these developments with an act of defiance that would be the first of many, Maria built a bonfire in her backyard and ordered Mira to get his Hlinka Youth uniform from his closet. She then threw it on the fire and burned it while Mira watched.

At first, the Nazi occupation did not seem to make much difference to Mira. The Hlinka fascists and the Nazis cooperated in Slovakia and life seemed to move forward unchanged. At nine, Mira was more interested in building model planes and playing with Leo than in who was in charge of the government.

Eventually, the German soldiers began to frequent Maria's small saloon, enjoying the good food and the friendly atmosphere. Business was brisk. Mira felt that the typical German officer was polite, well-educated, and friendly. Many of the Germans who were far from their homes seemed to form a special bond with Leo as he roamed from table to table, wagging his tail and looking for scraps.

By mid-1939, young Mira could see that things were beginning to change. The Romani couple who worked the garden had disappeared, along with their bright painted wagon. There were now empty desks at his school where children named Schwartz, Goldberg, or Katz once sat. His parents began talking in hushed conversations that stopped as soon as Mira walked into the room.

On September 1, 1939, Germany attacked Poland, and World War II began. As the war raged across Europe, life in Leopoldov continued largely unchanged. Germany needed food for its army, and the Slovak farmers allied quickly with the Nazis, so there was little strife in the quiet community.

Mira turned eleven in October 1940, and for him the most important event was the upcoming Christmas holiday. He had recently joined a model airplane club, where he and other boys his age would build and fly balsa wood airplanes. High on Mira's Christmas list was a Velky Vont glider kit with a 54-inch wing span. This would be the biggest glider in the club.

The European winter of 1940 was cold, and December in Leopoldov saw deep snow, but the Slovak house stayed warm and cozy. Maria spent the days leading up to Christmas Eve cooking, and the house often smelled of roasting duck or goose. Maria made mounds of cakes and cookies. Her specialty was a delicate vanilla-flavored crescent dusted with powdered sugar called "*vanilkové rohlíčky*."

In the Czech tradition, the night of December 24 is the most important time of the holiday. The whole family, including grandparents, and a waitress from the pub named Anicka with her husband Petr, came for dinner—a special meal of roast carp and potato soup. After dinner, as everyone sat in a circle around the Christmas tree, presents were passed out. Mira's heart pounded with anticipation when Jan handed him a long, slim package. He ripped off the bright wrapping paper and was rewarded with the sight of an orange and white box with blue printing that said, "Velky Vont." He was in heaven.

By 10 p.m., it was time to head to church for the midnight mass. The church was a small gothic structure made of whitewashed stone, with the portal arches and bell tower trimmed with yellow stucco. The priest read the Christmas story, followed by a choir singing "*Tichá Noc*" ("Silent Night"). A few minutes before midnight, Jan Slovak took a brightly polished trumpet from a battered black case. The congregation hushed as he approached the front of the church.

Jan took a deep breath and played the first few bars of "Oh Holy Night." The clear, piercing notes of the trumpet solo echoed in the high stone vaults of the church and Mira thought he had never heard anything more beautiful. His father played with a slow and spiritual intensity that brought tears to the eyes of everyone around. Mira was so proud that he could not stop smiling. When the last notes faded to silence, the congregation stood and walked into the cold night. Mira kept looking at his father with pride, and then looked around the streets to make sure that any of his friends who were walking home saw them together and knew that Jan was his father. Halfway home, Mira felt sleep creeping over him and had trouble keeping his eyes open. Jan picked him up and carried him easily on his shoulders. It was one of the happiest days of young Mira's life.[1]

Growing up around a working grain silo, Mira was used to the steam locomotives that pulled long strings of grain cars to his father's silo to fill up on sweet-smelling corn or wheat that was stored there. Mira was even used to the Nazi military trains loaded with troops or tanks or artillery that sped through Leopoldov with red, white, and black swastika flags flashing in the slipstream. In 1941, Mira started to see different trains. They did not look like the clean, bright trains that came to fill their cars with grain. These were dark-gray, dirty trains that had a foul yet somehow vaguely familiar scent.

Mira knew that the fascists did not like Jews or the Romani, and that somehow all the Jews and Romani had disappeared from Leopoldov, but he did not know where they had gone. He was about to find out. The Nazis built concentration camps in Poland. The largest of these camps was Auschwitz, located just a few miles across the Czech border in southern Poland, with gas chambers designed to look like disinfecting showers.

The Nazis brought in "undesirables" from all across Europe to be killed at Auschwitz. Soon, rail cars crammed with "deportees" from Germany,

France, Romania, and Czechoslovakia began to converge on the tiny Polish town. As a twisted symbol of Auschwitz's supposed purpose as a work camp, a metal sign hung over the camps entrance that said: *Arbeit Macht Frei*—"Work Makes You Free."

Leopoldov was a major crossroads for train traffic moving through central Europe, which was why it made such a good location for Jan's grain silo. Jan's business was served by a railroad siding that cut across the property and led right up to the silos. That way, a train could be switched onto the side line to spend as much time as needed loading up without blocking the main line traffic.

On the morning of June 22, 1941, Adolf Hitler sprung a surprise attack on the Soviet Union. Even though he had signed a non-aggression pact with Stalin in 1939, Hitler sent over 5 million soldiers storming into Russia along a 1,000-mile border. The need for food, fuel, and supplies was enormous. Fast express trains were loaded full of war materials and sent streaming towards the Eastern Front. That meant that slower, less-important trains were shuttled off to sidings to be out of the way.

One summer morning, a slow-moving cattle train was moved onto the siding in front of Jan's silo. When Maria saw the train, she sprang into action. She went to the saloon and pulled dozens of packs of cigarettes off the shelves and loaded them into a box. Next, she went into the food locker and got all the bread she could find, filling two big pillow cases with a week's worth of bread from the saloon. She sent Mira to the pump with two big buckets and told him to fill them with water.

When all of the preparations were made, she sat Mira and Jarda down and said, "Listen to me very carefully! Do exactly what I say and you'll be safe. The guards won't hurt children."

The boys exchanged questioning looks as if to say "Safe? What are we getting into?"

Maria continued. "I want you to carefully carry the bread and water as close to the train as you can, but make sure that the guards don't see you. Walk behind the bushes so you can get close enough."

The boys nodded. "Miroslav, carry the water pails. Jarda, take the bread. Once you have the sacks and pails as close as possible, I want Miroslav to come back and get the cigarettes. Now this is the important part. Take the cigarettes to the guards. Offer each one a full pack. Mira, your German is very good, so talk with them. Ask them what their names are. Ask if they have girlfriends. Tell them jokes, get them laughing and once they are laughing, tell them that you work on a farm and are used to feeding animals, and you wonder if they would mind if you fed their cattle. They might tell you to go away, but they might let you feed the people."

Mira's face blanched, "But those are cattle cars, and you said to ask if I could feed the cattle."

Maria looked at Mira with tears in her eyes. "Those cars are full of people, and they are going to a very bad place. It is our duty to make a difference whenever we can, so we must feed as many as we can."

Mira approached the guards with the cigarettes while Jarda hid in the bushes with the food and water. Maria's plan worked perfectly, and Mira asked if he could feed the cattle. One heavy guard with a missing tooth cackled, "*Das sind keine Kuhe, Schweine sind*!" (These are not cattle, these are pigs!)

As the other guards began to laugh, Mira waved to Jarda to meet him at the closest wagon. As the boys approached, they noticed the unmistakable smell of many days' worth of urine, feces, and vomit coming from dozens of unwashed bodies. Clearly, the caged Jews had been denied even the most basic sanitation. The boys approached the door with caution. They could hear sobbing and crying but they also heard prayers. The heavy doors were chained shut, but the chains hung loose and allowed the doors to open five or six inches. The boys warily offered a small loaf of bread through the opening. Instantly, dozens of pairs of hands shot out, each one grasping for bread. Mira found that if he broke the small loaves into quarters, he could feed everyone in the car. Jarda began to dip his ladle into the bucket and carefully handed the dripping ladle up through the gap between the doors. Sometimes, the thirsty Jews were so anxious for a drink that they would jostle one another and spill the precious water. When the first bucket was empty, Jarda ran back to get the second.

Mira had expected the train to be full of soldiers, prisoners of war, or old men. He was shocked to see that many of the hands that reached out for bread and water belonged to mothers and children. One girl who was no more than six or seven was small enough to stick her head through the opening. She had brown eyes and dark olive skin. Her thick black hair had been tied up in green bows that were now frazzled and dirty. She looked right at Mira and in perfect Czech she said, "*Děkuji*! *Děkuji mnohokrát*." (Thank you! Thank you very much.) "You have saved our lives!"

Mira was stunned. These were not strangers from other countries; these were Czechoslovakians. They could have been his friends or neighbors. With a cold shiver, he suddenly understood where the Romani family that tended the garden had gone. He now knew for sure where the girl named

Katz or the boy named Goldberg and all his other missing classmates had disappeared to.

Moments later the whistle screeched and the guards shouted orders. Mira and Jarda stepped back from the train as it slowly began to move away. Mira counted twenty-five cars as the train pulled off. They had been able to feed one car, perhaps 100 people, but in twenty-four other cars, thousands more sat fighting hunger and thirst.[2]

3

Strangers at the Back Door: Leopoldov, 1942

Jan's business consisted of buying grain in the fall when it was plentiful and the price was low, then holding it in silos to sell when the price rose. Sometimes, he would sell to bakers, or brewers, or even the army. The business required a lot of interaction with banks and bankers. Before the war, there had been a large number of Jewish people in the banking industry. Consequently, Jan and Maria knew many Jewish businessmen and their families.

One night in early July 1942, Mira was awoken by loud banging on the back door. Mira lay in the dark thinking that maybe it was just a bad dream, but then he heard the pounding again. Mira crawled from under his covers and tiptoed to his bedroom door in time to see Jan and Maria rushing downstairs. Mira silently followed as closely as he could without being caught.

Jan reached the back door, carefully pulled aside a corner of the lace curtains and peeked out. "*Moj boh*!" (My God!) He exclaimed. "It's the Engels family and Arpad Weiss too!"

Without hesitating, Maria opened the door and said, "Come in, come in! Quickly."

From his hiding place on the stairs, Mira saw a stout, bald man in his fifties that he knew was Arpad Weiss, a businessman from the nearby town of Nitra. With him was a younger, thinner man with long curly sideburns. Next was a young boy just a few years older than Mira, followed by a frightened woman with her dark hair wrapped in a tattered wool shawl.

Weiss turned to Jan, "Do you remember Paul Engels? This is his son Peter and his wife Rika." From deep in the house, Mira heard the grandfather clock start to chime. He counted the gongs so he would know what time it was. It was four in the morning and there were four strangers at the door.

Maria took over, "You must be starving." She paused, "I'm not sure if we have anything kosher."

When Mira heard the word "kosher," another gong, almost as loud as the clock, went off in his head. "If they need kosher food, they must be Jewish. If they are Jewish, they must be hiding, because if the Germans knew about them, they would have been on one of the dark trains to Auschwitz years ago."

Arpad answered, "Yes please, we are famished, but don't worry about kosher. The Talmud says that it is our first duty to stay alive and to starve ourselves for want of kosher food would be wrong."

As Maria hurried around the kitchen warming up a big kettle of chicken soup, Jan asked, "Where have you been? What has happened to you?"

Arpad answered. "Even before Munich, we knew things were getting bad, and we applied for exit visas to go to Yugoslavia, and from there, who knows? But it didn't matter, because the visas never came. When the Nazis took over after Munich, we went into hiding. Remember Mr. Wolfe's wheat farm outside of Nitra? He let us live in the tack room behind the stalls. No one ever came to the farm, and if they did they wouldn't bother with the stables. We were getting along just fine. Last night a bomber flew over. We think that he was looking for the rail yards near Nitra, and maybe he got lost. Maybe he saw the farm wagons and in the dark, thought it was the rail yard, but he unloaded his bombs over the Wolfes' farm."

Maria stifled a shrill gasp, "No! Was anyone hurt?"

"Everyone's gone," Arpad said, "the whole Wolfe family. The barn and stables too. The house took a direct hit, and burning wood from the explosion set the stables on fire. We got out and were able to let most of the horses out too, but everything else is gone."

Rika's sobs crew more intense. "We walked all night! 27 kilometers in the dark and every moment we thought that the Gestapo or the Hlinka Guard would stop us. I've never been so afraid!"

Maria moved to Rika and gave her a hug. "Don't worry. It will be all right, you'll see."

Mira wondered if his mother was just being comforting, or if she really had a plan. A moment later, he got his answer. "Miroslav!" she called. "Stop snooping and go get your brother. I've got work for the two of you." Mira ran upstairs wondering, "How does she always know? I'm sure that I never made a sound. Not even a peep, but she knew I was there." Jarda, who was awake and listening at the top of the stairs, hurried to meet

Mira, and soon they were both standing in front of their mother in the darkened kitchen.

"These nice people are going to be joining us for a while, but we need to keep it a secret from everybody. That's important or we could all end up on the next train north. I want you boys, and Peter too, to go down to the basement and move all of the old tools to the far end. We need to set up beds and we need to make a screen so Mrs. Engels has some privacy. See if that old commode works and take a broom and knock down all of the cobwebs. Jarda, make sure that we have some working light bulbs, but only turn one on, then go outside and walk around the house and make sure that no light shows, and if there is anything, even a little crack of light between boards, we need to find rags or newspapers or some way to block it from the inside."[1] Just like that, the entire Slovak family became outlaws.

Jan and Maria knew that if they got caught hiding Jews, they would all be sent to Auschwitz. Maria told Mira, "If you are ever coming home from school and you see that there is trouble, if you see police or Gestapo at the house, run back to school and grab Jarda and find a way to get to your grandparents in Piešťany. They will take care of you."

Maria quickly worked out a schedule to keep the fugitives hidden. In the day, when the saloon was open (and more often than not full of German soldiers), "our guests" (the family code name for Weiss and the Engels family) had to stay quietly in the basement. Maria suggested they sleep, read, or play chess. Once it was dark, the "guests" could come up and take short walks in the back garden. The "guests" tried to make sure that they were not seen, so they searched out blind spots where they could walk in small circles and not be observed by anyone along the road. Food was the simplest problem to solve. The Slovaks' gardens provided almost everything they needed, and if Maria did have to buy anything extra, she could always say it was for the saloon.

Mira and Jarda were warned not to tell their friends. Mira really only had one friend his own age, named Kamil Luptak. Like Mira, he was crazy about airplanes and did not talk about much else. The two had met at the Model Airplane Club and Kamil was far and away the best model builder in the club. As the war went along, it became harder and harder to find model kits, and balsa wood became impossible to locate. Kamil was the first boy to start building his own models totally from scratch, even using his own plans. His planes flew as well as the kits, or better. Young boys brag, and one day, Kamil said, "I bet I could build a real plane!"

"What do you mean a real plane?" Mira asked.

"I mean a real plane, big enough for us to ride in!" The boys began to form a plan. Kamil sketched out drawings of a high-wing monoplane with a two-person side-by-side cockpit and a hand-cranked propeller. Mira asked his father for permission to use one corner of a large grain-drying shed, and then both boys began to scour the businesses and farms of Leopoldov to collect the tools and materials they would need. They begged leftover wood from the lumber yard to cut out the frames, and they stripped an old bicycle to make the landing gear. They used the chain and sprockets from another bike to drive the propeller. Slowly, the huge model began to take shape. No one seemed to take the project too seriously, least of all the German soldiers heading to or from the saloon. They would often stop to watch as the children's project grew all through 1942.

The summer of 1943 began as the Slovaks quietly celebrated the one-year anniversary of Arpad Weiss and the Engels family living in their basement. It was rare for the "guests" to share a meal with the Slovaks, but on this special occasion, Maria felt it was appropriate. Maria roasted a chicken with fresh vegetables from the garden. At one point, Mr. Engels made a toast that Mira did not understand. He held his glass of wine high and said, "Here is to Herr Hitler. May he win himself to death!"

There was laughter all around the table. Mira and Jarda exchanged puzzled looks with each other. Jan saw the confused expressions on the boys' faces and said, "Hitler has conquered Europe and he now has his sights on Russia and large parts of Africa. Mr. Engels thinks, as do I, that as Hitler's empire grows, the task to govern and protect it becomes more and more difficult, and just like a balloon inflated too far, his empire will pop and disappear into a million little pieces."

As the summer of 1943 turned to fall, Mira and Kamil continued to work on their plane, but they were stumped when it came time to cover the plane's intricate skeleton. They knew that real gliders were covered with a special lightweight fabric, which was impossible to find due to the war, and even if they could find it, there was no way that the two teenage boys could afford it. The model planes they built had been covered with tissue paper which the young aviators knew would be too fragile for their full-sized plane. Eventually, they decided to try butcher paper. It was cheap and easy to find but even when the boys pooled their meager allowances they could not afford it. Mira borrowed two large baskets from Maria and the boys walked into the country side picking fruit to sell on the street corners of Leopoldov. When they raised enough money, they bought the paper from the local butcher and carefully glued it to the gliders delicate frame. Then they covered it with a few coats of paint, hoping it just might be strong enough to fly.[2]

In July and August 1943, Hitler's empire, much like the balloon in Jan's analogy, began to show stress and started to shrink. In the east, the Soviet summer campaign was pushing the Germans back along hundreds of miles of front, and injured soldiers returning from Russia told stories of deep mud, food shortages, and staggering loss of life in the millions. In the south, the Allies invaded Sicily in July and by September 28, the Italians had surrendered. By October 13, the new Italian government had declared war on Germany. In November, the Royal Air Force turned its attention to Berlin, and began a five-month-long bombing campaign to break the will of the German people.

As 1943 turned to 1944, the mood in Europe began to shift. The Nazis, no longer seen as invincible, were falling back on almost every front. The fantastic gains they had made in the first months of the Russian campaign were proving impossibly costly to hold. Across the English Channel, the Allied Powers were planning an invasion to liberate Europe. Hitler was still in firm control of Central Europe, including Slovakia. Yet now, there was a growing partisan movement directed by Edvard Beneš and the Czech government in exile in London.

At dinner one night in the spring as Europe waited for the Allied invasion and eventual liberation, Jan was reading a local flyer printed by an organization called the Slovak National Council. The flyer called for organized resistance to the Nazis. Jan fumed that it had been slipped into his hands by one of his neighbors who had been the same adamant fascist who pressured Jan about making sure that Mira joined the Hlinka Youth in the 1930s. "Well, I see that the rats haven't quite decided to abandon their sinking ship yet, but they are in a hell of a scramble to find their life vests now!"

On June 6, 1944, the Allies launched Operation Overlord. The sheer numbers were staggering: 2,000,000 men, sixty large warships, 1,000 mine sweepers, and 4,000 landing craft. Over 11,000 aircraft and support from over 100,000 partisans who were already behind the German lines.[3]

Hitler did not know it, but the "Thousand Year Reign" he had promised his followers had only 328 days left to live. By midsummer, the Allies had a firm hold on Europe. Paris was liberated on August 25 and the U.S. Army Air Corps was operating bases in liberated France and Italy. For Mira, it meant that there were now daily fly overs by new and exciting airplanes. For most of the war, all he had seen were the four-engine bombers: B-17s and B-24s. Now he would see the famous P-51 Mustang; the stout, pugnacious P-47 Thunderbolt; or his favorite, the twin-tailed P-38 Lightning.

In mid-September 1944, Mira was helping Maria in the saloon and was setting a large mug of beer in front of a farmer from the nearby town of Bojničky who had just sold several carts of grain to Jan. The farmer smiled at Mira and said, "Is your garden haunted?"

Mira was caught off guard and said, "No, not at all, what makes you say that?"

The farmer then traced a series or circles on the table with a finger and said, "I was walking by late last night and I could have sworn that I saw people walking in circles in your garden. I couldn't think of any explanation, so I figured they must have been ghosts."

Mira felt a knot in the pit of his stomach. The farmer must have seen Weiss and the Engels family taking their late-night walks. This was dangerous. If the farmer said anything to the Germans, the whole family would be loaded on the next train to Auschwitz. Mira tried to laugh it off and said, "I've never heard of any ghosts, but I know that the woman that cooked here before mother wasn't very good. Maybe that's where she buried her customers?"

The farmer laughed, but then lowered his voice and said, "I won't tell anyone what I saw, but people are beginning to talk. You need to be careful!" Mira passed the message on to Maria and the next morning, Arpad Weiss and the Engels family were moved to a trusted family friend who lived near Bratislava.[4]

4

Liberation: Leopoldov, 1945

By December 15, 1944, advance units of the Red Army's Fourth Ukrainian Front reached the eastern edge of Slovakia. They were slowed by strong Nazi resistance. Even though the Soviet troops moved slowly, the rumors of what Soviet liberation would bring burned through the country like a fire. "*Znasilenie*" was the bitter word whispered by women when they talked about the Russians. "*Veľa znasilnenie*!"

It was not a word that Mira knew; he knew that "*Veľa*" meant "many," but he did not know what the "many" related to. He asked Maria. She got a pained look on her face and then said, "*Znasilenie* means rape, and it is when a filthy pig rips the clothes from an innocent woman, forces her naked legs apart and tries to make her pregnant! That is what *Znasilenie* means!"

Other rumors made their way to Leopoldov. "The Russians stole food. The Russians burned houses. The Russians stole money. The Russians didn't take prisoners. Captured Germans would be executed."

It was a tense Christmas. The war was coming to an end but it did not look like life would ever return to normal. The only bright spot in the fearful winter was that Anicka and Petr announced with youthful excitement that she was pregnant. She was due to give birth in late May.

Unbeknown to anyone in Czechoslovakia, a secret meeting that would determine the embattled nation's fate for the next 40 years was taking place 1,300 miles to the southeast. By February 1945, it was clear that Germany was going to lose the war. The "Big Three" allies held a meeting at the Black Sea resort of Yalta from February 4 to 11 to discuss how post-war Europe would be reorganized. The U.S., the Soviet Union, and the UK each came into the meeting with their own agendas. Soviet Premier Joseph Stalin wanted to maintain a presence in Europe to act as a buffer to assure that Germany would never again be able to launch an attack on the Soviet Union. U.S. President Franklin Roosevelt wanted the Soviet Union's promise to help in the Pacific with the war against Japan. Roosevelt also wanted Stalin's firm commitment that the USSR would take part in the new United Nations he was advocating. Churchill's ambitions were not nearly so grand. He simply wanted assurances that all the occupied nations would be allowed to hold free and democratic elections.

While the fate of Czechoslovakia was never discussed, Stalin's demand to keep troops in Europe assured that he would have tremendous political sway in the region.

The U.S. military warned Roosevelt that without Soviet help, the war with Japan would last another year and result in half a million U.S. dead. The meeting ended with Roosevelt agreeing to let the Soviet Union keep troops in Europe in exchange for Stalin's promise to join the UN and help with the war in Japan.

In early April 1945, the Germans prepared to evacuate Leopoldov. The Nazis needed all available soldiers to defend Berlin. It was not a hurried or panicked withdrawal. Several officers took the time to stop at the saloon and say goodbye. One officer apologized. "I shouldn't be telling you this, but it will be apparent as soon as we leave. We can't let the Russians follow us. So we will be blowing up the railway bridge. I know that will make life hard at the silos but we are just following orders." That night, the Germans loaded up their trucks and left town. Later, Leopoldov was rocked by loud explosions. In the morning, the bridge lay like a broken toy across the swift-flowing Vah River.

For a day nothing happened. The second day, the far-off clank of approaching tanks sent the town into panic. Young boys ran through the streets yelling "*Rusi sa Blizi*!" (The Russians are coming!) Young girls hacked off their hair, blackened their teeth and stuffed pillows under their clothes in an effort to appear as unattractive as possible. Old men dug holes in their gardens and buried their silver and cash. Food and livestock were hidden in basements or lofts. All across the town people hid in fear, waiting for their "liberators" to arrive.

Jan Slovak was an important man in Leopoldov. He was not an elected official, but he was a successful merchant with a big house and lots of influence. Many people gravitated to his home for protection. Soon the house was crowded with grandmother Kramarova, Anicka, Petr, and a dozen anxious and worried neighbors. Leo, as dogs often do, picked up on the group's agitation and paced nonstop in front of the doors. Anicka, now almost eight months pregnant, sat in a rocking chair holding her swelling belly as if to protect the unborn child. About 2 p.m., they began to hear gunshots on the outskirts of town. There were no Germans left, so the huddled crowd wondered who was shooting, and at what. Someone suggested maybe the Russians were celebrating and shooting their guns into the air. Maria jumped up with a sudden frightening thought. "They're drunk! They are drinking their way through town! Quick, everyone help me move the liquor out of the saloon. We'll hide it in the basement. We'll leave them some beer and wine, but we need to hide the whisky and vodka!" Several men went with Maria and the job was finished quickly. Outside, there was now shouting mixed into the gunshots. The shouting was in a language no one could understand but it seemed to be good natured and not threatening. Still more townspeople people came to the Slovaks' house. Eventually, they were out of room and Jan took Leo by the collar, led him out to the garden, and tied him up near the back door.

A short while later, there was a commotion on the road in front of the house. A loud engine roared and barked as a Soviet T-34 tank rattled and clanked into view. The T-34 was a medium tank, designed for a crew of four or five, but it was covered with a crowd of at least eight ragtag, drunken Soviet infantrymen sitting all over the mud-caked tank. One soldier straddled the tank's barrel, holding on with one hand and waving his other in the air like a Cossack riding a wild horse. With a grinding of gears, the tank stopped near the house. The mud-splattered passengers all climbed off and ran toward the grain silos. Mira quickly stepped back from the window, not wanting to attract any attention.

Inside the house, the gathered neighbors waited nervously. Gunshots near the silos indicated that the Russians were attempting to shoot the locks off the grain bins. They would be disappointed. By this time in April, most of the grain was gone, and the bins where empty.

Leo began to snarl and bark. The Russians had found the gardens. Mira peeked out the kitchen window to see four or five haggard men with long unkempt hair and dirty faces rooting through the garden looking for something edible. One of the soldiers shouted and held up a fist full of early carrots that were quickly divided and eaten. "My God!" Mira thought, "These men are starving!"

Leo continued to bark and snap. There was more shouting and finally there was banging on the back door. Maria, flanked by Jarda and Mira, opened the door a few inches and saw a ragged officer in a tan winter coat wearing a gray fur "trooper's hat." There was a bright red star pinned in the center of the cap and a 9-mm Mauser in his right hand. The officer knew one word in Slovak, "*Jedlo*" (food), and he kept repeating it over and over. Maria nodded, "Yes, yes we can get you food."

The Russian pushed open the door as if he was going to force his way past Maria into the kitchen. Leo barked ferociously and leapt at the end of his rope. With the swift, skilled motion of a practiced killer, the Russian turned towards Leo, aimed the Mauser, and blew a fist-sized hole in the center of the dog's forehead. Leo fell to the ground dead. In the stunned silence after the shot, the Russian turned the still smoking pistol towards Maria and again demanded, "*Jedlo*!"

Jan's face turned red with rage. Maria faced the Russian's cold eyes and knew that he would kill her, or Jan or Mira, just as easily as he had killed Leo. She told Mira and Jarda. "Hold your father back! Don't let him come any closer or they will kill him too!" The boys leapt in front of their angry father and pushed him away from the kitchen door, where some of the other neighbors grabbed him and helped restrain him.[1]

Maria quickly pulled a cold ham, two roast chickens, and a large sack of potatoes from her larder and handed them to the officer. He seemed satisfied and turned away from the door. He shouted to his comrades that he had food to share. The rest of the troopers had broken off the locks on all of the silos and grain sheds. They were standing around Mira's plane trying to figure out what it was. Clearly it was not something that a civilian should have, so they roughly pulled the lightweight plane away from the shed and placed it in the middle of the yard. One of the troopers dug a lighter out of his pocket, flicked it open, and lit the paint-soaked butcher paper on fire. The paper and paint made a flammable combination and the plane instantly burst into angry orange flames while black smoke swirled into the April sky. The Russians stood around the fire, breaking off pieces of chicken or ham, eating, joking, and laughing while several years of Mira's work turned to ash.

Once the fire died down and the food was gone, the Russians scrambled back onto their tank and left. Inside the house, there was silent, seething rage. It was Friday, April 13, 1945, and after almost six-and-a-half years of Nazi occupation, Leopoldov had been liberated.

Jan and Mira went out and silently buried Leo beneath his favorite linden tree. Maria drew down the shades and dimmed the lights, and the worried group spent a nervous night sleeping in chairs, on couches, or even on the floor. They heard more troopers and more tanks clank past in the night but no one stopped. On Saturday, a few of the visitors began to drift home to check on their own belongings. On Sunday, Jan decided he would go to church. He felt that he needed to show his face in town. "Lead by example," he said. He would show the people that he was not afraid. Mira asked to go with him. Maria fixed a hearty breakfast of fried potatoes, eggs, and ham. The two set off for the brief walk to church wearing their Sunday best.

"No sense taking the car." Jan said, "The Russians would just steal it." The service was attended by less than a dozen men and not a single woman. Obviously, people were still hiding from their "liberators." After church, Jan spoke with the other men and learned that most of the Russians had moved on but that a detachment of engineers had been left behind to repair the bridges. Most interestingly, the engineers' brigade was under the command of a woman, Captain Nina Kominski.[2]

When Jan and Mira returned, they found that most of their guests, including Anicka and Petr, had gone back to their own homes. It had been a tense and exhausting few days. Mira and the whole family went to bed early.

Mira was awakened in the middle of the night by the frightening sound of a woman shrieking and pounding violently on the back door. The whole family threw on robes and raced towards the door. Maria got there first and opened it to see a naked bloody Anicka sobbing in the dark. Maria folded her into her arms to hide Anicka's nakedness and told Mira, "Don't look, and go grab a blanket." Maria led the hysterical Anicka to the bathroom where she could close the door and give her privacy.

Mira dashed away for the blanket. When he came back, he was met by his father, standing protectively outside the door. Mira could still hear Anicka sobbing uncontrollably while Maria tried to calm her with soft words. Mira handed the blanket to Jan, who passed it through to Maria. Through the sobs, Mira kept hearing the words "*pat muzov*!" (five men) and "*znasilninl ma*!" (raped me). Mira's stomach turned. The beautiful young Anicka, eight months pregnant with her first baby, had been raped by five Russian soldiers.

Jan rapped quietly on the door. Maria opened it and Jan whispered, "Find out where Petr is."

At the mention of Petr, Anicka shrieked again, "Oh Petr, my poor Petr. They held him by his arms and made him watch. Then they beat him with their rifle butts, He is lying on the floor, he might be.... Oh God he might be *mrtvy*!" (dead). She shrieked again and Jan and Mira dashed out of the house to go search for Petr.

Still not wanting to risk taking a car around the Russians, they ran the 2 kilometers to Anicka and Petr's farm. They found the door broken in and a blood-stained mattress on the floor where the Russians had obviously committed their heinous crimes. Next to the mattress in a crumbled heap, they found the beaten and bloodied Petr. As they came in, they could hear him moaning in pain, but they were relieved to know he was still alive.

Mira got water from the sink and they cleaned and bandaged Petr the best they could. His nose was broken, he was missing several teeth, and his eyes were swollen shut from the beating, but the wounds to his body were nothing compared to the wounds to his soul. He had been held at gunpoint while the woman he loved had been raped, beaten, and sodomized by five drunken, laughing monsters and he had been helpless to protect her. He sobbed that he was worthless and he had failed to protect his wife. How could she ever forgive him?

Jan and Mira helped Petr walk slowly back to the Slovak home. When they arrived, Maria had cleaned and calmed Anicka. She was wearing a modest grey dress that Maria had given her. Anicka had quit sobbing, but when she saw Petr, she ran to him and wrapped her arms around him in a desperate hug like a drowning woman in the ocean clinging to an overturned lifeboat. She let out a heartbreaking wail and Petr howled in shame and grief.

The two held each other and sobbed, while the night sky began to lighten and then brighten into morning. Petr slipped into deep healing sleep. With the coming of the new day a change came over Anicka. Her eyes grew dark and cold; she stood up, straightened her back, and held her chin high with a defiant snarl. She was angry and vengeful and she wanted justice.

Her face was bruised and beaten, her lips were swollen and she had a bandage above her left eye. She placed her hands on her distended belly as if to draw strength from her unborn child. Mira thought that she looked like one of the Furies from the Greek myths he had read in school.

Anicka turned to Maria. "Make sure that Petr sleeps. He fought so hard and they hurt him badly." Then she turned to Jan. "Will you come with me? We need to go talk to Captain Kominski."

Jan started to protest, "I don't think that is wise."

Anicka glared at Jan and said, "As a woman, I have just lost everything that makes me who I am; I have nothing more to lose, so I have nothing to fear. What can they do to me now that is worse than what they have already done?" She headed towards the door. She paused and said, "I'm going. You can stay here or you can come with me, but either way, I am going." Jan grabbed his coat and followed her out the door.

April is a fickle month in Slovakia. Some days are bright and full of the promise of spring; others are dark and wet as if winter were still trying to hang on for a few more days. This was one of the dark days. Rain clouds tumbled over the mountains in the distance and by the time Jan and Anicka reached the Russians' camp, the sky was black and heavy and the wind was beginning to blow.

As one of the town's leaders, Jan had no difficulty getting an interview with Captain Kominski. She sat behind her desk and listened to Anicka's story without saying a word. When Anicka had finished her matter-of-fact description of what had been done to her, Captain Kominski stood up, picked up her gun belt from the table, and buckled it on. She walked silently toward the door, the only sound the clicking of her boot heels on the wooden floor. Then, she turned and commanded Anicka, "Come with me."

Once she was outside Kominski barked an order in Russian and soon, the entire engineering brigade was formed up, standing at attention in rows in front of the Captain. She turned to Anicka and asked in halting Slovak, "These men, can you identify them?"

"Absolutely!" Anicka hissed through clinched teeth. Large, heavy rain drops began to fall as Anicka walked the lines of Russian soldiers. She had fought hard and it was easy to spot five men with fresh scratches on their faces and bite marks on their hands. When Anicka was finished, Captain Kominski commanded that the five men come forward and stand side by side in front of Anicka.

Captain Kominski walked behind the accused rapists and in her broken Slovak she called across them to Anicka. "You are sure of these men?" The rain was coming down harder now. The water was streaming off of the men's hair and running down their necks.

Anicka nodded, "Yes I am sure!"

Captain Kominski unsnapped the flap on her holster and said, "100 percent sure?"

"100 percent sure!" Anicka answered.

Kominski nodded once, pulled the pistol from her belt, and placed the muzzle against the back of the neck of the first soldier. "This one?"

"Yes."

She pulled the trigger, the pistol roared, and the man fell face first into the mud, his blood mingling with the rain. Kominski moved to the next soldier. "This one?'

"Yes." Another shot rang out.

"This one too?"

"Yes." One more body fell to the mud

"And this one?'

"Yes."

There was another shot, and the rain continued to pour down. The last of the five soldiers was crying and shaking. He fell to his knees to beg. Kominski asked again, "This one?" Anicka nodded and the fifth and final shot rang out.

Kominski holstered her pistol and turned to Anicka. She said, "Russian justice, yes?"

Anicka said, "Yes," and she and Jan turned and walked from the camp. The rain continued to pour. Jan placed his hand protectively on Anicka's shoulder. She moved it away and said, "Please don't," and walked a few yards ahead. Jan followed in silence. Halfway home, Anicka stopped, knelt in the rain, and began to vomit. When she was finished, she began to cry. Eventually, the rain stopped, she stood up, carefully wiped her mouth with the hem of her borrowed dress, and continued walking home.

The rain caused the Vah River to swell; it rushed and churned over the broken bridge. The Russians could not wait for good weather. They needed to get the bridge repaired so that they could get their tanks across the river and keep after the retreating Nazis. Kominski conscripted all the men in town, including Jan and Mira, to work alongside the Russian engineers to get the bridge open. The Russians did the skilled labor, cutting, welding, and pouring concrete, while the Slovaks did the drudge work, carrying steel, digging holes, or mixing cement. On the second day, Jan and Mira were on the river bank carrying bags of sand when they heard a shout followed by a splash. One of the Russians had slipped and fallen off the bridge into the swift-moving water. He screamed in fright as he flailed in the frigid water. Jan, Mira, and the rest of the Slovak work crew dropped their bags and ran to the river's edge, shouting, "Get a rope! We can save him!"

Suddenly, gunshots rang out. Mira turned to see a Russian lieutenant firing his gun in the air shouting, "Get back to work. All of you back to work!"

Jan shouted, "But we can save him!"

The lieutenant pointed at the huge crew of workers swarming the bridge and said, "We have millions more in Russia. This one will not be missed, get back to work now!"

That night, as Jan and Maria were getting ready for bed Jan whispered, "This is not good. The Russians are worse than the Nazis; we must send Mira away from here before something horrible happens."

On Monday, April 30, 1945, with Russian forces closing in on the *Führerbunker* located 50 feet below the Chancellery Building in Berlin, Adolf Hitler put a gun in his mouth and committed suicide. One week later, on May 7, German General Alfred Jodi signed an unconditional surrender and World War II, which caused the death of at least 60,000,000 people, was officially over.

While the war was raging around him, it was impossible for Mira to give much thought to what he wanted to do for a living when he was older. With the war over, he could finally begin to dream about his future. What he wanted most of all was to fly, but in 1939, the Nazis had shut down all Czechoslovakian airlines and absorbed the Czech Air Force into the Luftwaffe, so there were not any options for professional flying. Mira decided he wanted to be an engineer. He applied to an engineering school in Prague and was accepted; however, he was told that before he could begin studies he must first prove his aptitude by spending a year working as a lathe operator at the school-run machine shop.

5

The City of 100 Spires: Prague, 1945

Czechoslovakian Airlines resumed operations on September 14, 1945. A few days later, Jan and Mira boarded a Junkers Ju 52 "Tri-Motor" to fly the 200 miles from Bratislava to Prague. It was Mira's first time in an airplane and he was worried—not about his safety, but what if he did not like the experience. Flying had been a fascination for him for as long as he could remember. Now that he was about to experience it, he hoped that it would live up to his expectations.

As Mira and his father walked across the trimmed grass of Bratislava's Vajnory Airport, Mira tried to commit every detail to memory. The angular-looking plane, with corrugated aluminum skin, had two large main wheels and a tiny tail wheel that caused it to sit with its nose high in the air like some proud debutante. Even from a distance, the three BMW radial engines gave off the powerful scent of oil and fuel that pilots around the globe recognized as the perfume of aviation. Mira could see where the black crosses of the Luftwaffe had been painted over with silver paint when the plane had been reclaimed for civilian use. A flight crew of three—pilot, co-pilot, and radio operator—climbed into the plane. Mira thought that their crisp blue outfits, with gold-trimmed sleeves and bright brass buttons, were the most splendid uniforms he had ever seen.

Mira, Jan, and about a dozen other passengers climbed the three small steps just behind the left wing and entered the plane. Jan and Mira both had to duck to avoid bumping their heads on the tiny door frame. Inside the plane was a narrow center aisle with a single row of seats on either side. The stiff metal seats with thin brown upholstery looked more appropriate for a factory lunchroom than an airplane, but Mira did not mind. He was about to fulfill a lifelong dream. Each side of the gray metal fuselage was punctuated with a row of seven large rectangular windows that allowed enough light to enter the narrow cabin to keep it from feeling claustrophobic.

Mira sat on the left side of the plane and Jan was directly across the aisle. The radio operator, doubling as a cabin steward, swung the door closed and turned a lever to lock it in place. He then walked through the cabin reminding the passengers to buckle their seat belts. With the plane at rest, the nose was quite a bit higher than the tail and Mira felt uncomfortable sitting with his head reclined so far. He looked to his right to see that Jan was tense and pale, clutching the armrest so tightly that his fingers were digging into the upholstery. With a shock, Mira realized that his father was scared. It was the first time he saw him as something less than invincible.

One at a time, the big 800-hp engines rumbled to life. The wheel chocks were pulled and the plane began to taxi across the grass apron. On the ground, the Ju 52 bounced and waddled around like an awkward bird. After a few moments, the plane made a hard-left turn and paused at the head of the long concrete runway while the pilots ran the engines to full power. When the noise was almost deafening, the brakes were released and the plane began its takeoff roll. For a moment, Mira thought it seemed slow, but then the speed began to build. Soon the tail lifted, and the plane was level, riding on just its two front wheels. A small bounce and the plane was airborne. Mira felt a hollowness in the pit of his stomach as the plane left the ground; it was not bad, just a new feeling.

The Ju 52 quickly gained speed and altitude. Mira's eyes were glued to the window. The familiar world of buildings, roads, and people quickly shrank to the size of toys as the plane climbed away from the ground. Mira thought that the world was beautiful from up in the air. The plane rocked and swayed easily as it sailed on the currents of wind. The fluffy cumulus clouds became impossibly huge as the plane climbed higher and higher. Mira felt an odd companionship to the rugged plane. It was not a mere machine of aluminum and fabric; it now seemed to be a magical creature come to life. This was nothing like he had imagined it would be, it was so much better.

Autumn is a beautiful time of year in Prague. The city is full of oak, beech, and chestnut trees. By October, when the air is crisp and chilly, the city explodes with autumnal color. With its many bridges and "100 spires," Prague had not been a target for allied bombing during the war, so the city was relatively intact. Czech author Heda Margolius Kovaly described postwar Prague:

> There is no other city like Prague; it is not only the beauty of the buildings, of the towers and bridges, though it is that too. They rise up from the slopes and river banks in such harmony that it seems nature created them alongside its trees and flowers.[1]

Jan and Mira arrived in Prague and started moving Mira into a government-run dormitory near the machine shop and getting the fifteen-year-old ready to live on his own in a strange new city. Once Mira was settled, Jan returned to Leopoldov via train, vowing to never fly in an airplane again.

On October 12, 1945, just a few days after Jan went home and two weeks before Mira's sixteenth birthday, Allied Commander-in-Chief Dwight D. Eisenhower visited Prague. The city came to a standstill as thousands of grateful Czechs, including Mira, poured into the streets to cheer and wave as General Eisenhower paraded through the city, standing and saluting in the back of an open car.

Two days later, Czechoslovakia held its first national elections since the Nazis seized power in 1938. After years of war, forced deportations, and secret police, the people of Czechoslovakia longed for a return to safety and freedom. Much of the electorate, remembering that the Western democracies failed to protect them in Munich in 1938, voted for the Soviet-backed Czechoslovakian Communist Party. With 40 percent of the votes, the Communists were able to force a coalition government, with Communist Party leader Klement Gottwald taking the position of prime minister, while Edvard Beneš held on to the presidency. Unknowingly, the people of Czechoslovakia had taken their first step down a road that would soon lead them back into a dark, frightful world of forced deportations, secret police, and torture like that from which they had just emerged.

Winston Churchill was already regretting the decisions made at Yalta. He saw the Soviet Union's chilling effect on the fragile war-torn countries of Europe. When Harry Truman offered Churchill an opportunity to give a speech at Westminster College in tiny Fulton, Missouri on May 5, 1946, Churchill galvanized the English-speaking world when he described how an "iron curtain had descended" across Europe, trapping behind it "all the capitals of the ancient states of Central and Eastern Europe."

The phrase "Iron Curtain" quickly made its way into the American vocabulary and became synonymous with tyranny and oppression. For many Americans trying to rebuild their lives after five years of war, Churchill's eloquent speech was the first indication that another war was on the horizon, but unlike World War II, this would be a "Cold War," fought with threats, diplomats, and spies.

Mira proved to be a capable lathe operator and the year of training passed quickly. Engineering school started in September 1946, and Mira was a month shy of his seventeenth birthday. Two things happened to distract him from giving his full attention to the tedious engineering classes. First, he met a young woman named Jiřinka Nováková in one of his classes. She was seventeen, with long blonde hair and deep blue eyes. Mira found himself head over heels in love for the first time. The second and bigger distraction came on December 6, when the Czechoslovakian Air Command announced that it was accepting applications for pilot training for the new Czechoslovakian Air Force.[2]

Mira mailed in an application and waited. In the first week of January 1947, he received word to report to a classroom in the Žižkov district of Prague on January 19 to take his air force entrance exam. Mira breezed through the battery of tests, and within two weeks he got a letter notifying him that he was on the short list of candidates and should expect final notification in a few months. In mid-June, the official letter from the Air Force Main Staff Headquarters arrived, telling him to report for training on October 1. In the meantime, all pilot candidates were required to take a four-week glider training course through a local glider club. All costs of the training would be paid by the air force. Mira enrolled in a club 15 miles north of Prague at a grass airfield in the city of Kralupy nad Vlatvou.

Few people find their true calling in life, and fewer still excel at it. Mira did both. More than anything, Mira wanted to fly, and it turned out he was very good at it. After two weeks, Mira was soloing in the agile wood and fabric "Grunau Baby" glider.

After class, Mira would take the train back to Prague and meet Jiřinka for a late dinner at an inexpensive café. He would hardly touch his food as he talked through dinner, describing what he had learned, using his hands to bank, swoop, and dive over the table. Mira graduated from glider school with ninety-six other students and on October 1, 1947, while still only seventeen years old, he began training with the Czechoslovakian Air Force.

As with military training the world over, the first few months consisted of countless hours of marching, cleaning, exercising, and running. It is physically and emotionally challenging. Its primary goal is to teach young recruits to work as a unit for the success of the group, rather than just looking out for themselves. One of the unexpected benefits of this training is that it can foster deep and important friendships. This was true for Mira, who in the early days of training met a young man who would dramatically impact his life, Honza Dolezal. Tall and thin, with dark wavy hair and a thoughtful, piercing gaze, Honza had the ability to see into the heart of any matter.

Mira had struggled in public school and thought of himself as not being too bright. In pilot school he excelled and soon found himself, along with Honza, near the top of his class. The young men fell into a friendly rivalry, each trying to outperform the other. It did not matter what the task was—marching, running, or peeling potatoes; Honza or Mira would do everything they could to beat the other. Mira was so happily immersing himself in school that he (and most of the rest of Czechoslovakia) failed to see the dark stain that was spreading out from the Prime Minister's office.

The Czechoslovakian coalition government depended on President Edvard Beneš and Prime Minister Klement Gottwald being willing to cooperate. Gottwald had other plans. He began replacing officers of the Czech security forces with members of his Communist Party. When Beneš's cabinet learned of the replacements, they demanded that Beneš put a stop to Gottwald's communization of the security forces. When Beneš confronted Gottwald about it, Gottwald told Beneš to back off or Soviet leader Joseph Stalin would send Soviet troops storming across the border. When Beneš failed to take action, a large portion of his cabinet resigned, hoping to force a new election that would remove Gottwald and the Communists from power. Gottwald again threatened Beneš, saying that a call for new elections would also trigger a Soviet invasion. On February 25, 1948, under tremendous pressure from the Soviets, Beneš replaced the resigning cabinet members with a slate of Communists handpicked by Gottwald. In mid-June, Beneš resigned in frustration and the new Communist cabinet repealed the democratic constitution, replacing it with a Communist one.

Mira hardly noticed. He was absorbed in the fascinating world of lift, drag, and speed. He was slightly irritated when the students were pulled out of class one at a time and asked to sign papers joining the Communist Party, but Mira only had one question. "If I don't sign, will I still be allowed to fly?"

The answer was "No!" Mira signed the papers. He was going to fly, politics be damned.

Training consisted of classes in theory of flight, the doctrine of weapons and munitions, military council regulations, Morse code, navigation, metrological theory, and moral political education.[3] On June 20, after nine months of elementary training, the cadets were given a final exam before moving on to flight school. Honza got the highest score and Mira was second.

Flight school started in July and the Czech Air Force was struggling to find enough trainer aircraft. They relied on old-fashioned Bücker Bü 131 "Jungmanns". The Jungmann was a fabric-covered biplane that was designed as a Luftwaffe trainer in 1934. The tiny plane had a wing span of only 24 feet and a top speed of just 115 mph, but they were a dream to fly, and Mira quickly fell in love. He soloed after eight flights and soon learned how to coax the plane into doing anything he wanted. Mira and Honza continued to excel, moving from the Bücker Bü 131, to the deadly Avia S-199 fighter, and eventually the twin-engine Siebel Si 204D bomber.

On one training mission in the Siebel, Mira flew near his parents' farm in Leopoldov. He circled the house a few times until he saw his mother come out into the garden. Then, he flew low, wiggling the plane's wings in a friendly wave to his mother. He returned to base, proud that his family had seen him flying the impressive twin-engine plane. His bubble was burst when he received an angry letter from his mother telling him that his "foolish stunt" had scared the turkeys and two of them had run into a fence and broken their necks. She ended the letter with a stern warning to "Stop the Nonsense!"

Meanwhile, Gottwald was beginning to make drastic changes to Czechoslovakia, including closing the borders to foreign travel and immigration. Mira hardly paid attention to this announcement. He could not know that in just a few years, on both sides of the Iron Curtain, he would become the symbol of the millions of people in Soviet-occupied countries wishing to cross closed borders.

Gottwald pressed forward a process called "agricultural collectivization," turning the thousands of small private farms that dotted Czechoslovakia into one large government-owned institution. Mira received word that the grain silo had fallen victim to collectivism. It had been taken from Jan and was being managed by the government. Maria was allowed to continue running the saloon so they were able to stay in the same house. Collectivism proved to be massively inept and quickly led to food shortages and long lines of hungry workers queuing up for hours to buy bread and meat. In July 1949, final exams were given and Honza and Mira again finished first and second in their class.

6

Like Pebbles Dropped in a River: Havlíčkův Brod, 1949

After graduation, the new officers were divided into fighter pilots and bomber/transport pilots and posted to various air fields around the country. Honza and Mira, as the top two performers in the class, got to choose what they were going to do. Most young men would have jumped at the chance to become fighter pilots. Mira's passion was flying; he did not really care what he flew. So he asked his commander, "Who flew more, the fighters or the transports?" He was told that due to a shortage of planes and fuel, the glamorous fighters only flew one brief training mission a month, but that the transport pilots flew every day. That settled it. Both Mira and Honza volunteered for transport duty and were assigned to fly Siebels from an airfield outside the medieval city of Havlíčkův Brod, in the Bohemian-Moravian highlands. The base was used to train bombardiers and navigators and needed qualified pilots to fly the training missions.

Life outside the military began to take on a sinister tone. Gottwald, under the urgings of Stalin, began a series of purges in 1949 that saw over 130,000 Czechs arrested and sent to prison camps or executed. For the people of Czechoslovakia, it was frightfully reminiscent of the Nazi occupation, where a single misspoken word could lead to the secret police coming in the middle of the night to carry away a mother or father, who would never be heard from again.

When Honza and Mira arrived at Havlíčkův Brod, one of the first people they met was veteran pilot Roberto Rojko. He was tall and dark, with wealthy relatives in Chicago who sent him expensive, custom-tailored uniforms that gave him a rakishly handsome air. Roberto introduced Honza and Mira to another pilot, named Jan Housa, and the four became great friends. They lived on the same floor of an inexpensive, sparse military barracks. The four young pilots flew in the same squadron and after each day's missions they would spend their free time together. Somehow, Jan was able to afford a sporty little yellow Škoda 1102 sedan on his tiny officer's salary, and the four friends often piled into the car and drove deep in to the countryside with the windows down and the wind blowing in their hair. Other times, they would head into town looking for food, beer, and girls.

One of the features of the new Communist military was the "Political Officers" who were members of the special "Enlightenment Branch" of the Czech military. There was a political officer in every unit, but he existed outside the normal chain of command and reported directly to the secret police, the *Státní bezpečnost*, better known as the StB. The political officer could have anyone arrested if they were not supportive enough of the government. The political officer depended on informers, who were his eyes and ears within the unit. The pilots knew that they were being watched, so they chose not to spend much time at the officers' club on base, but preferred to head into town to drink and carouse at local "*krcmy*" (pubs), where the beer was cheap, girls were affectionate, and the pilots could talk privately away from the curious ears of the StB informers.

One night, when they were all sitting in the back of a pub, enjoying a dinner of pork and dumplings, washed down by beer, Jan casually asked, "Have you ever thought of escaping to the West?"

Mira whispered harshly, "Don't talk like that! You could get arrested for even thinking that! Why would we want to escape? We have a good life here. Better than anything the West could give us."

Roberto said, "I'd like to see my uncle in Chicago, I've heard so much about the place."

Jan became animated, "We could do this. It would be easy, I mean we're all pilots and we fly close to the borders all of the time. If we wait until we're on a mission that takes us to the base in Pilsen, it would only take five minutes to fly to the German border and we could be on the ground at a U.S. base before the fighter planes in Pilsen would even be in the air!"

Roberto nodded his head, "You've given this a lot of thought, haven't you?"

"Yes, I have." Jan said.

Mira stood up, "Count me out. I don't want any part of this!" He tossed a few bills on the table to cover his tab. "I think I'll walk back to the base."

Honza slid his chair back and said, "I'm going too. You clowns can figure this out on your own, but I want to stay out of prison." Mira and Honza left the table and walked home in the chilly autumn night, whispering about what they had witnessed.

The next day, as the pilots left their briefing and headed across the field toward their planes, Mira approached Roberto and said, "You're not thinking of doing anything stupid, are you?"

Roberto dismissed Mira's worries with a wave of his hand, "Last night that was just the beer talking."

"Good!" said Mira as he turned toward his plane. "You're a good friend and I would miss you."

A few weeks later, Mira was lying in his room late at night trying to sleep when he heard three or four men march down the hall and bang on a door. He crept across the room and opened his door a few inches to get a look at what was going on.

He was stunned to see Jan and three burly policemen in long green leather coats standing outside Roberto's room. While Mira watched, Roberto's door opened a crack and a sleepy-looking Roberto poked his head out, "What's going on? I'm sleeping."

One of the policemen roughly pushed the door open and shouted, "Comrade Roberto Rojko, you are under arrest for treason!"

"What? That's crazy." Roberto began to protest but one of the policemen delivered a quick punch to the stomach, followed by a right cross to the chin and commanded, "Silence, traitor!" Now doors all along the corridor were swinging open and sleepy pilots were spilling into the hall. The police roughly turned Roberto around, pressed his face against the wall, and cuffed his wrists behind his back.

Mira felt helpless. He could not just stand by and watch as Jan and Roberto were arrested, but at the same time, he could not fight off three armed police officers either. Mira looked down the hall and saw Honza standing in front of his door too. They made brief eye contact and Honza, understanding his friend's emotions, briefly shook his head: "No." Mira knew there was nothing they could do.

The guards turned Roberto around and marched him down the hall. That was when Mira got his first good look at Jan, and his blood ran cold. Jan was in his full uniform walking with one of the police officers and they were both smiling with pride. Roberto's hair was ruffled. He was wearing nothing but undershorts and his hands were cuffed behind his back. His eyes looked frightened and lost.[1]

"My God!" Mira thought with a sick feeling in his stomach. "Jan is in on this. He's an informer!"

As they passed close to him, Mira, whispered, "Jan!"

Jan turned towards Mira and hissed, "Not another word Slovak, or I'll have you arrested too!" Roberto simply disappeared. There were no lawyers or trial dates. Roberto's clothes were boxed up; a new pilot was given Roberto's room and it was as if Roberto had never existed.

One day, when they finally got a chance to talk about it, Honza said, "So do you think that it was a setup? Was Jan trying to get us to agree to his plan just so he could arrest us?"

Mira answered, "I don't like to think something so awful, but yes, that was his goal all along. Can you imagine what would have happened to us if we hadn't left the pub? We'd be in prison too!" Honza and Mira continued to fly during the day and wander into town at night to enjoy private conversations away from base. They no longer asked Jan to join them.

The Communist *coup d'etat* that had toppled President Beneš and replaced him with Klement Gottwald had been relatively bloodless, but not all Communist takeovers were. On mainland China, communist revolutionaries led by Mao Tse-tung ousted Nationalist General Chiang Kai-shek in a bloody civil war that lasted four years and caused over 6 million casualties. On October 1, 1949, Mao declared victory. In the United States, anti-communist sentiment began to grow as it became apparent that the postwar world might not be one of freedom and liberty but might be dominated by totalitarian communist regimes.

A month after Roberto's arrest, Honza and Mira stopped into their favorite pub for dinner and a beer. It was a cold night and the place was nearly empty. They took a table near a large open fireplace. As the fire crackled and popped, an attractive waitress with dark hair and hazel eyes brought over two large pitchers of beer. Honza was immediately attracted to the young woman. He stood up and said, "My name is Lieutenant Honza Dolezal."

The young waitress giggled at Honza's direct approach, set down the beers and said, "I am waitress Tereza Novak." Then she saluted, followed by a flirtatious curtsy. Mira and Honza both broke out in a hearty laugh.

"How long have you been working here?" Honza asked in a desperate attempt to make conversation.

"I've just started this week. Today is my third day."

"Well you are doing very well. Do you live nearby?" Honza asked.

"I live with my parents on a farm near the edge of town." Tereza answered.

"It's dark when you get off work. Would you like me to walk you home?"

"I might like the company, but I'm sure my father would not be happy about it, so I must say no."

"Can I see you again?" Honza asked.

"You are seeing me right now," Tereza teased.

"Listen you two," Mira said, "I'm hungry and I want a plate of wiener schnitzel. Once I've got my food, you two can keep flirting all you want." Honza ordered chicken and dumplings and Tereza headed back to the kitchen to turn in the order.

"Oh my God," Honza whispered, "she is the most beautiful creature God has placed on this earth."

Mira smiled and nodded, "Yes, she is pretty, but God has made an awful lot of pretty girls. I still prefer Jiřinka, but we all have our favorites."

Honza and Tereza continued to flirt throughout the dinner. The two fliers went back to the same pub night after night. Eventually, Honza's persistence won Tereza over and he was allowed to walk her home. Yet she insisted that he come into the house and meet her parents.

The Novaks lived in a two-story stone house with a high gabled roof and a big stone chimney a quarter of a mile from the air base, and Honza could often see Tereza's mother and father working in the garden when he took off in the morning.

One afternoon returning from a mission, Honza circled the Novaks' house and saw Tereza in the garden. He decided to show off a little. He skillfully brought the big twin-engine bomber down to rooftop level and flew at the house. As he got closer, Tereza gave him a cheerful wave with a red scarf. Speeding over Tereza's house, Honza wiggled his wings in what he felt would be a friendly wave. Directly over the house, he felt a sudden bump, and then all hell broke loose. There was a lightning rod sticking up from the Novaks' chimney, and when he wiggled his wings to say hello, he hit the rod with his left propeller and wing. The propeller splintered and the fuel tank ripped open. Honza was at the end of a long day of flying and the tank was nearly empty, so as soon as the tank was ripped, it lost whatever fuel remained, and the left engine quit.

The Siebel began to lose altitude, and since he was already at rooftop level, there was not much to lose. He declared an emergency and headed for the airfield. He did not have time to lower the landing gear and slammed down on a grass apron near the far edge of the field. The plane slid through the grass. The left engine was almost knocked off its mounts, but the main fuselage stayed intact. Fire trucks raced to the scene, but with no fuel, there was no fire and miraculously, there were no injuries. The plane, valued at 1,600,000 Czech Koruny (about $80,000 U.S. in 1949), was a complete write-off.

After being checked out at the infirmary, Honza walked back to the barracks. He was embarrassed at his foolishness, happy to be alive, but worried about his future. Mira told him to get a good night's sleep and everything would look better in the morning.

Mira fell asleep quickly after lights out, but at about 2 a.m., he was awakened by the sound of men marching in the hall and pounding on someone's door, just like the night Roberto had been arrested. Mira crept from his bed and cracked open the door. He saw four police officers in the now familiar green leather trench coats pounding on Honza's door. Honza opened the door, and the police grabbed him. "Comrade Honza Dolezal, you are under arrest for destruction of the people's property!" Mira again felt helpless as he saw one of his very best friends being marched off by the secret police.

Mira opened the door and stepped out into the hall. The guards marched Honza closer and Honza said, "No Mira! Don't! This was my own fault."

The barracks door slammed closed and Honza was gone. As with Roberto, it was as if Honza had never existed. His clothes were packed up, his room was given to a new pilot, and Honza disappeared like a pebble dropped into a river.[2]

7

The Sun Will Rise in the West: Prague, 1950

Gottwald's reforms began to dig deeper into the military. During World War II, 724 members of the Czechoslovakian Air Force escaped the Nazi occupation and fled to England, where they formed the Czechoslovakian Air Force in exile (often called the Free Czech Air Force). Flying with the RAF and consisting of one bomber squadron and three fighter squadrons, the Free Czech Air Force flew thousands of missions over Europe and logged close to 500,000 hours flying time. When its fliers returned to Czechoslovakia at the end of the war, they received a mixed welcome. To the people of Czechoslovakia, they were returning heroes, but to the Communist Government, they were spies and agitators sent by England to interfere with rebuilding Czechoslovakia.

From 1945 to 1948, the military struggled to stay apolitical and saw the veterans of the Free Czech Air Force as having invaluable experience quickly promoting them to positions of power. Veterans who did not want to stay in the military were welcomed into Czechoslovakian Airlines (CSA). After the Communist coup in 1948, Gottwald began to replace the veterans with loyal Communists. By late 1949, Gottwald was frustrated with the pace of change in the air force and insisted that anyone who had contact with England or the RAF should be expelled from the air force and arrested.

Mira was awakened often in late 1949 and early 1950 as his former commanding officers were pulled out of bed and marched off to oblivion by men in green leather trench coats. One unexpected result of the purges was that in early 1950, at the astonishingly early age of twenty, Mira was promoted to captain to fill the leadership void left by the arrest of so many veterans.

Czechoslovakia's once-powerful industrial base was not exempt from Gottwald's reorganization. In the same way that he had nationalized the nation's farms, Gottwald was nationalizing its factories and businesses too. The government seized control of all businesses, imprisoning the owners and appointing new government-approved managers from the Communist Party. In communist-controlled Czechoslovakia, party membership was denied to anyone with a bourgeois background. This meant that anyone with previous management or business experience was not allowed into the Party; membership was reserved exclusively for the proletariat (workers who had never owned anything of significant value apart from their own ability to labor). This led to a topsy-turvy situation where anyone with management experience in a particular industry was denied work in that industry, while the management positions were given to the Party members who had the strongest working-class credentials. In fact, Gottwald's government actually looked for the least educated and least experienced people to put in charge of the nationalized factories in an effort to prove that the bourgeoisie did not contribute anything to society and could easily be replaced by the lowest members of the proletariat.

The food shortages and rationing that followed Gottwald's nationalization of Czechoslovakia's agriculture were soon followed by shortages of manufactured goods, like light bulbs and toilet paper. Rationing had not affected the military yet, and Mira was enjoying the new respect and increased pay that he received as a captain.

One afternoon on a routine training flight from Havlíčkův Brod to Prague, he noticed smoke coming from the left engine of his Siebel. He radioed the tower at Havlíčkův Brod that he was turning around and heading back. There are very few things in an airplane's engine housing (known as a nacelle) that can burn, primarily fuel, oil, and in some cases hydraulic fluid. A fire in the nacelle is usually caused by a mechanical failure in the engine or a break in a line leading to the engine. The standard way of fighting a fire is to turn off the pumps that provide fluids to the engine. If the leak is in between the engine and the pumps, shutting down the pumps will deprive the fire of fuel and it will burn out. If the leak is in the tanks or the lines to the pumps, shutting down the pumps does nothing, and the leak will continue until the tanks are empty. Unfortunately, shutting down the supply of fluids to the engine will also shut down the engine. There was a saying among Siebel pilots that "If you lose one engine, the second engine would keep you flying just long enough to reach the crash site."

Mira could tell from the dark blackish-gray color of the smoke that the fire was being caused by fuel, so the likely culprit was a break in the fuel line. He reacted quickly by feathering the propeller on the port engine, then pulling the fuel mixture back to cutoff, which deprived the carburetor of fuel. Then he shut off the magnetos, which killed the engine. While the spinning propeller slowed to a stop, Mira shut off the fuel pumps. Finally, he turned the selector knob on the fire extinguisher to "port" and pushed a red handle that flooded the nacelle with CO_2.

Mira looked out his port cockpit window as the CO_2 billowed from the nacelle and was quickly carried away by the slipstream. As soon as the CO_2 cleared, he saw that smoke continued to pour out of the nacelle. His heart sank. This meant that shutting down the pumps had not helped at all. It also meant that there was nothing further he could do. His CO_2 was exhausted. The fire was still getting fuel and would keep burning until it reached the fuel tanks, and they exploded. The plane was doomed.

Mira reported his position to the tower at Havlíčkův Brod and then flipped an alarm switch on the cockpit instrument panel that rang alarm bells throughout the plane. He keyed the intercom and, as calmly as he could, announced, "We have an uncontrollable engine fire. Check your parachutes and harnesses and prepare to bail out on my command." He felt a sudden rush of cold air and the loud roar of the slipstream as the escape hatch at the back of the cabin was opened.

The Czech Air Force often operated the Siebel with a crew of two—pilot and co-pilot/navigator. On this flight, there were also three navigation students and an instructor. Mira kept the plane on a steady level course as he flew back towards Havlíčkův Brod. He watched the smoke billowing out of the nacelle and soon saw bright orange tongues of flame dancing behind the smoke. He keyed the intercom and announced, "Bail out now!" The students went first, followed by the instructor. Finally, the co-pilot unfastened his belts, hung his radio headset on its hook, placed his hand on Mira's shoulder, and shouted, "Good luck. See you on the ground."

After a few moments Mira banked the plane slightly to his left and twisted in the seat so that he could get a look behind and below the plane. The first thing he saw was a long black smoke trail. Turning his gaze lower, he counted five white billowing parachutes drifting against the blue sky. He felt a sense of relief. His crew was safe. It was just him, alone in the plane. He looked around at the sturdy little Siebel. It seemed crazy to think that in a few moments the plane might explode into a huge ball of fire.

Mira unfastened his seat belt to jump. His hands were shaking. The thought of jumping from the plane terrified him. He looked at the fire again. He tried to picture the fuel system in his mind. He could almost see the diagrams he had studied as a student. The flames that he saw dancing along the nacelle were several feet from the fuel tank. He decided that he would fly on just a bit longer and see if the flames moved any closer. Mira checked his watch. It had been almost ten minutes since he spotted the fire and turned around. He had covered 25 miles and was now only 35 miles from the base. At this speed, he just needed to keep the plane in the air for another fifteen minutes and he could make it home. He checked the flames again. They had moved maybe 6 inches, but no more. He calculated that at the current rate, the flames probably would not reach the fuel tank, unless of course the flames under the aluminum skin were farther ahead than the flames on the outside. In that case, there would not be any warning; the plane would simply explode in a massive ball of fire and fall from the air. Mira shot another glance out the window at the dancing flames; somehow, he knew that he would be okay.

Time seemed to slow down. Mira tried not to stare at the fire. He concentrated on the instrument panel, moving his gaze slowly to each gauge: the altimeter, air speed, fuel pressure, and engine rpm, but his eyes were constantly drawn back to the fire. He willed the flames to back up, but they would not obey. After another fifteen minutes, Mira saw the green hills give way to a cluster of buildings and long asphalt runways. He was home. He called the tower, declared an emergency, and requested immediate clearance to land. As he made his final approach, he saw the red flashing lights of fire trucks speeding across the field. He banked carefully to the right and side-slipped to line up on the runway. He trimmed his ailerons to keep the lifeless port engine slightly higher than the starboard, just as he had been taught when his instructors drilled him on how to land a Siebel with a dead engine. He brought the plane down and hit the runway faster than he had planned. The plane bounced hard but stayed down. Once both wheels were firmly on the asphalt, he cut power and applied the brakes. As he slowed, he saw the fire trucks begin to race towards him, and by the time he brought the crippled plane to a stop, the veteran fire crews were already rolling out hose. Before he could even get out the cabin door, they were spraying foam on the fire. From the safety of the ground, the fire looked small and hardly threatening at all. Under the heavy spray of foam, the flames died quietly. A small plume of white smoke rose up from the nacelle and was dispersed by the light breeze. With the fire out, the wet foam slid off the soot-stained nacelle like snow melting off a roof. The ground crew swarmed the plane, trying to figure out what had gone wrong and how to repair it.

Mira hitched a ride back to Command Operations with the fire crew. As he neared Command Ops, he noticed a small group of people standing in front of the building. He wondered what they were waiting for. When the fire truck slowed and Mira jumped off, the crowd started to clap. Mira was caught off guard. He looked over his shoulder to see if there was someone else that they might be clapping for. There was not; they were clapping for him. As he walked toward the group, several other pilots came forward and patted him on the back, shouting comments like "Amazing," "Great job," and "I never could have done it." Mira humbly waved back thinking, "If they only knew that they are clapping for a coward. I didn't stay in the burning plane from bravery. I stayed because I was terrified to jump!" A few days later, Mira was notified that he would be given a medal for bravery.[1]

Many veterans of the Free Czech Air Force had found jobs flying for Czechoslovakian Air Lines. CSA flew to a dozen destinations in Czechoslovakia and over thirty cities in Europe and the Middle East. As rationing increased and the prisons filled, it was inevitable that people would begin to flee communism and escape to the west. On the night of March 23, 1950, in what was one of the best-planned escape efforts in history, three Czechoslovakian Airlines DC-3s were hijacked at the same time by eight CSA employees who were all former Free Czech Air Force members. The three airliners took off from three different cities and all were diverted to Erding, outside of Munich, West Germany. When the planes landed the next morning, all eight hijackers and 16 of the 74 passengers asked for and were granted political asylum. The scheme had been born in response to Gottwald's 1949 purge of the Free Czech Air Force. As the Free Czech veterans who were working for CSA watched with horror the arrest and disappearance of their friends and colleagues who had stayed in the Air Force, they knew that their time was limited and they too would soon be imprisoned.

Most of the Free Czech Air Force veterans who were flying for CSA had wives and children; the government knew that the men would not abandon their families, so they kept an eye on the fliers and would not allow family members to fly on the same plane with their husbands or fathers. In that way, the communists were confident that the CSA pilots would never try to escape. In a clever bit of scheduling, the eight CSA officers all arranged to be flying on the same night but on three different planes. Then they each booked their families onto one of the other three planes. At a prearranged time, the officers diverted their planes to West Germany and were able to take themselves and their families to freedom.

The Communist government was furious. All Free Czech veterans working for CSA were fired, and many were arrested. CSA suddenly had a huge need for experienced pilots, and Gottwald's all-powerful government filled the need by "loaning" the most qualified and experienced Air Force pilots to CSA.

As a reward for his outstanding record and perhaps in honor of the citation for bravery, Mira was transferred from the air force to CSA in the fall of 1950, a few weeks before his twenty-first birthday, with a pay raise to 32,000 korunas a month (equal to about $1,600), at a time when the average Czechoslovakian was being paid about 8,000 korunas monthly.

Mira was assigned to fly a U.S.-built DC-3. In the aviation world, the "left seat" is reserved for the pilot or commander and the "right seat" is for the first officer, or co-pilot. For Mira's first month flying for CSA, he was given the left seat, but an experienced DC-3 pilot and instructor rode in the right seat to make sure that young Captain Slovak had a veteran with him in case something went wrong.

In late October, when the chestnut trees that cover the hills of Bohemia had turned bright yellow and the oaks were aflame with red and orange leaves, Mira was piloting CSA flight OK-519, from Brno to Prague. The flight departed Brno at 3.25 p.m. and was scheduled to land in Prague at 4.20 p.m. Mira was in the left seat and an experienced veteran instructor was riding in the right seat on what would turn out to be Mira's final "check ride." As the plane flew due west towards Prague, the sun began to set on the horizon ahead of them. From an altitude of 6,000 feet, the DC-3 slid between huge cumulus clouds glowing with a glorious gold light. Mira and the veteran pilot flew in silence for a while, admiring the beauty and grandeur that surrounded them. Then, the veteran spoke. "For my whole career, I have been taught that the sun will always rise in the East and set in the West, and that has been true for my generation. But for you and your generation, I think that it will be different. For your generation, the sun will rise in the West."

Mira started to protest. The old captain raised a finger to his lips and said, "Shhhh!" Then pointed at the sunset and said again, "For you, the sun will rise in the West!" Suddenly, Mira understood. The veteran was telling him that there was no future in Czechoslovakia.[2]

8

Recalled to Life: Poprad-Tarty, 1951

CSA was based at Prague-Ruzyne Airport. Mira was overjoyed to be returning to Prague, with its famous 100 spires, and the slow-moving Vltava river. His new CSA salary was large enough that he was able to get a bachelor apartment near the center of town and its vibrant nightlife. He slipped easily back into civilian life, flying several days a week, and enjoying nights on the town with Jiřinka.

In the beginning, Mira was assigned domestic flights, shuttling back and forth between Prague and Brno or Bratislava. After a few months, he got assigned occasional international flights. Soon, he was flying into non-communist cities like Copenhagen, Oslo, and Stockholm. One of the perks of being allowed to fly to the "West" was that Mira was allowed to bring home a limited quantity of Western products. His father loved Lucky Strike cigarettes, so on every trip to the West, Mira would bring home two packs of American-manufactured Lucky Strikes. He would give one full pack to his father, keep ten cigarettes for himself, and give ten to the mechanics in Prague who took care of his plane.

Mira loved his job, but he never forgot that his freedom to fly across Europe was dependent on his willingness to toe the party line. Even in CSA, there were still informers and political officers, and a joke about Gottwald, or a complaint about rationing made in front of the wrong people, would bring the serious men in the long green coats knocking on your door in the middle of the night.

In early 1951, Mira was assigned to fly CSA flight 522, from Bratislava to Poprad-Tarty airport, once a week. Poprad is a picturesque resort town in the High Tatra Mountains. Mira's flight arrived at 6.35 p.m. and the flight out did not leave until 7.15 the following morning, so he would spend the night at a hotel near the airport. He found that he had plenty of time to kill. Sometimes, he would go into town and explore the pubs; other times, he would look up old friends. CSA shared the field with the Czech Air Force, and a few of Mira's former classmates were stationed at Poprad-Tatry. One evening, as he was walking across the base enjoying a cigarette, he saw a slow-moving, stooped-shouldered figure in a worn blue uniform shuffle in front of him, carrying a mesh bag full of soccer balls. There was something familiar about the man, so Mira called out, "Comrade, please wait!" He jogged a few steps to catch up with the stranger. As Mira neared, the stranger looked over his shoulder. Mira was shocked. Behind the sunken eyes, broken nose, and defeated posture, he recognized Roberto Rojko, staring at him with a confused look on his face like a ghost recalled to life.

"Roberto! Is it really you?" Mira called as he stepped forward to embrace his old friend.

Roberto held up his hands, "Stop! Don't come near me. They're still watching."

"Don't be ridiculous," Mira said, reaching out to touch Roberto's shoulder. "We're old friends."

"Being my friend will land you in prison." Roberto said, pushing away Mira's hand.

"What happened to you? After they took you away—what happened? We never heard."

"Leave me alone. Can't you see? I'm dangerous to you!"

Mira could tell that there was something broken in Roberto's mind. His eyes darted constantly from side to side. His posture reminded Mira of the way Leo would cower and shake during the Allied bombings. Mira knew that if he was going to reach the real Roberto hiding deep beneath the broken mind, he would have to try something different. On the spur of the moment, Mira reached into his jacket pocket and pulled out a pack of Lucky Strikes. "Do you want a cigarette?

Roberto froze. "Why? Why would you give me something?"

"We're old friends, Roberto. I want to sit down and enjoy a smoke with you."

"These are American. Where did you get them?"

"I bought them in Copenhagen. I'm a pilot for CSA. I go to the West at least once a week."

Roberto shook his head slowly and said, "It's a crazy world. I talked about going to the West one time and they sent me to prison but you fly to the

West once a week and you get paid to do it" He pointed at the cigarettes. "You can even bring back contraband. It doesn't make any sense."

Mira shook out a cigarette and offered it to Roberto. "Take one." Roberto smiled as he reached out to take the cigarette. Mira noticed that several of Roberto's teeth were missing. "They tortured you?"

"I can't talk about that."

"What can you talk about?"

Roberto looked at the bag of soccer balls he was carrying and said, "These. I can talk about soccer balls, and calisthenics and running. I'm a 'Recreation Aide' now."

"What do you mean you're a recreation aide?" Mira asked.

"It's my new job. I can't be trusted to go near a plane ever again. They're afraid I might steal it and try to fly to Germany, so now I hand out towels in the gym and I inflate soccer balls with a hand pump." Roberto's eyes flashed in anger. "No offense to you or anyone else, but I used to be the best damn pilot in this whole damn Air Force and one night I mention that I'd like to see my uncle in Chicago and now I'll spend the rest of my life handing out towels and inflating soccer balls!"

Mira flew to Poprad-Tarty once a week. Each time he came, he brought Roberto a pack of Lucky Strikes and tried to convince him to talk about what had happened after his arrest, but Roberto refused. Finally, in early spring when the snows high in the Tatras were beginning to melt and the beech trees were covered with pale green shoots, Roberto offered to tell Mira the story, but first they had to leave the base and walk into the woods, away from the guards and informers. They found a grassy spot on the banks of a rushing creek, swollen from the fresh melted snow. Mira carried two bottles of beer. They sat in silence while he opened a bottle and handed it to Roberto.

Roberto took a long drink. "I really don't understand how it started. I guess the fact that I had relatives in America must have made the StB suspicious of me, but I never wanted to defect. I loved flying. Then I met that bastard Jan Housa, he must have been with the StB from the beginning." Roberto paused to light one of his Lucky Strikes.

> Didn't you ever wonder how he could afford that car? On our salaries? Well he couldn't. He must have been getting paid by the StB all along. I never wanted to escape. Never! I only talked about it that one time, and Jan brought it up first! You were there, you heard it all and it wasn't serious, it was just talk between friends, at least that's what I thought it was. So the night I was arrested, it was two in the morning when they came for me. They took me to

a small brig that was on the base. I kept thinking this is a mistake, and I can get it all sorted out in the morning. They roughed me up some, hit me with their fists, and kicked me in the stomach. I thought it was bad, but it was nothing compared to what happened later. One of the guys kept yelling at me to "Confess! It will all be over if you just confess." I was angry so I shouted back, "I've got nothing to confess. You've got the wrong guy." That just made them kick me harder. Eventually I wised up and stopped talking. After a while they got bored or hungry or something because they left.

The next morning it was more of the same; Nameless guys punching and kicking me and shouting at me to confess. Around midday they took me to a room with a table and two chairs. A man came in and asked me to join him at the table. He claimed to be my lawyer. He said that he could get me out; all I had to do was sign some papers. He slid the document and a pen across the table. It was a confession. All typed up neat and tidy. "Sign here," the lawyer said. I looked back at him and swore, "You stupid bastards, don't you understand? I didn't do anything!"

After that, the "lawyer" and the guards had a long conversation. I couldn't hear all of it, but I think they began to realize that they made a mistake. They couldn't admit it, so they sent me away.

I was blindfolded and loaded into the back of a truck and taken to an old stone building in the countryside. As cold as it was and the musty way that it smelled, it could have been a medieval fortress. I don't know where it was and I don't think I could recognize it if I saw it. I was blindfolded whenever I was outside and the rest of the time I was in a windowless room. When we got to the prison I was dragged to this small stone room with no food, no lights, and no blankets. Nothing, just a bucket to piss in. I was tossed in and they slammed the door. Then they forgot about me. I don't know how long but it was days! A week, maybe more? No food, just a tin cup of water slid under the door once a day. Nobody explained what in the hell was going on, just me alone in the dark, smelling my own shit and listening to screams coming from deeper in the prison. When I didn't think I could take the hunger anymore, the door opened and a jailer came in with this huge plate of roast pork, sauerkraut, and dumplings. It was the most beautiful thing I've ever seen. He set it down in front of me and left. I was starving. I ate it all as fast as I could. I kept thinking, "Eat it before they take it away." Of course, it was a mistake. If you are starving and eat a huge rich meal, it tears up your insides. It gives you stomach cramps that you think will kill you. Within an hour I was rolling on the floor in agony. It was awful.

It went on that way for two months maybe more. No food for days and then a huge plate piled with all of my favorites. Eventually I learned not to eat

> much, but it was tough. When I stopped eating, they turned me over to the Russian. He was a sick bastard that really seemed to enjoy his work. He used tools, just normal hand tools like a hammer, nails, and pliers or vice grips, all laid out on a work tray like a doctor preparing for surgery. He strapped me to a chair, and then strapped my hands down tight to its arms. He asked me who my accomplices were. I told him I didn't have any accomplices because I hadn't done anything! He flashed a savage grin and said, "Oh, we've all done something." Then he took the hammer and five nails and one at a time pounded the nails under the finger nails of my left hand. The pain burned like fire and I screamed and screamed until I lost my voice. After each nail he would pause and ask, "Who are your accomplices?" The pain was so terrible that I couldn't think, I couldn't speak. All I could do was cry and whimper.[1]

Roberto paused in his story. He raised the beer bottle to his lips and took a long drink. Mira could not help but notice that several of Roberto's fingernails were missing from his left hand. "Roberto, I'm so sorry. That must have been awful."

"Mira, I'm just getting started ... what they did later." Roberto shook his head in disgust.

Roberto set his beer down, lit another cigarette, and returned to his story.

> A few days later they took me back to see 'The Russian.' He strapped me in the chair again. This time he worked on my right hand with vice grips. He slowly crushed each knuckle on my right hand. He paused every now and then to ask about my accomplices. But by this point we both knew it was a farce. I had no information and the Russian was just torturing me for his own twisted enjoyment.[2]

Roberto took a long drag on his cigarette, held it for a few moments, leaned back, and blew the smoke straight up.

> The last time I saw the Russian, he had the guards strip me naked from the waist down, then he tied me in the chair with my legs spread. He took a big pair of pliers from his work tray. You know those big long handled pliers that a plumber might use to loosen a rusted pipe joint? Well the sick bastard put them between my legs and grabbed my testicles with them. He started to squeeze and pull and I knew right then he was going to pull them off. I'm sure of it, and I was helpless. So I began to confess. I don't know what I confessed to, I just started making things up. I said I was an agent for the Americans, that my uncle was sending me money to hire people to kill Gottwald. I

> confessed to anything and everything, just to get that monster to set down the pliers and leave me alone. It all ended very quickly. The Russian left the room and another lawyer came in with a confession for me to sign. I don't have any idea what was in it, but I signed and within hours I was carried to a hospital and they started to patch me back up. I was so thin and bruised that it was months before I was fit to be seen in public, but eventually they told me that I had been 'rehabilitated' and they sent me here.[3]

Roberto went silent as if he was drained and had run out of things to say. Mira was stunned. He had heard rumors that prison was brutal but he had no idea that it could be so awful. They sat in silence; the only sound was Roberto inhaling deeply on his Lucky. Mira's head was spinning. He realized with a shiver that had the conversation in the pub gone just a little different, it would have been Mira in the cold stone room with the bleeding fingernails and broken joints.

Mira flew back to Bratislava but kept thinking about Roberto's story and the veteran CSA pilot who told him that the sun would rise in the West. For the first time, Mira began to think that maybe he did not have to spend his whole life serving the communists; maybe there was another way to go.

Mira continued to fly to Poprad-Tatry and bring Roberto his Lucky Strikes, until one day in the summer when he was making his approach to land, he flew over a gathering of green military trucks forming a semicircle around a smudge of gray smoke rising into the still summer air. He recognized the signs of a plane crash and said a silent prayer for anyone that had been on board the ill-fated plane. After he landed, the ground crew told him that Roberto had stolen one of the Bücker biplanes. He circled the base a few times and put on a breathtaking air show full of loops, rolls, and inverted flying. Then, at the end of his show, he climbed high over the base, nosed the plane over, and flew straight into the ground. The official inquest ruled the death a suicide, but deep in Mira's heart, he knew that Roberto had been murdered by the communists in that dark cold prison, and it just took a few months for the deed to be finished. That night, as Mira lay awake in bed trying to sleep, he thought about Roberto and how young, fresh, and vital he had seemed when they first met. It was hard to imagine him dead. He also thought about Honza Dolezal and wondered if, at that very moment, he was lying on the cold stone floor of a forgotten prison, suffering like Roberto. Sleep never did come for Mira that night.

9

Wenceslas Square: Prague, 1951

Mira continued to fly and rack up hours. As summer came, he learned to deal with the brutal thunderstorms that could spring up suddenly in the towering cumulus clouds around the Tatra Mountains. He still loved his job, and put Roberto and his brutal fate out of his mind. However, when he went into Prague to meet Jiřinka for dinner, he could not help but see the food lines getting longer and longer. Mira had lived through the entire Nazi occupation and never seen a bread line once; now in Prague, he saw them often. One morning, on his way to the airport, he saw a handbill nailed to a tree that said, "Communism: A system perfectly designed to solve all of the problems that could only exist under Communism!" By that night, the handbill had been torn down.

One summer morning, while Mira was doing his preflight inspection on a DC-3, he saw a well-dressed officer approaching from his right. The officer cheerfully called his name, but Mira wanted to finish inspecting the hydraulic hose on the plane's landing gear before he turned. The officer approached closer and his shadow fell across Mira's field of view. Mira turned and could not believe his eyes. There, less than 3 feet away, was Honza Dolezal. He stood almost at attention, tall, proud, and immaculately well-dressed. The two friends embraced. "My God, Honza, it's good to see you!"

Honza smiled and said, "It's good to see you too!"

For a moment, Mira remembered Roberto's broken sprit, his mangled hand, and his tortured soul. "How are you? You look well. What happened after they took you away?"

"I'm fine. Really! It was nothing. Just a little misunderstanding."

"Did they send you to prison?" Mira asked.

"Prison? No, more like school, just a few classes to teach me to take better care of the people's property." There was something about Honza's answer that seemed to echo the party line a little too closely. Deep in the back of Mira's mind, an alarm sounded, but he paid it no attention. Honza was back and he was safe and that was the most important thing.

"So what are you going to do now?" Mira asked.

"I'm going to fly for CSA like you. The air force has loaned me to CSA, but I've come to the party late, so I'm going to be a co-pilot. But I still get to fly!"

Mira and Honza quickly renewed their friendship, and it was not long before Honza was flying as co-pilot on many of Mira's flights. By the end of fall, Honza suggested that the two should become roommates. Honza was friends with the elderly widow of one of the CSA's senior captains. The captain had been quite wealthy and had owned a villa overlooking one of Prague's picturesque parks. The People's Housing Authority had recently discovered that the widow was living alone in a villa that could easily provide shelter for several families. They were about to assign her to new lodgings and turn her villa into an apartment complex. Honza was able to convince the Housing Authority that allowing Mira and Honza to live in the villa's guest quarters would mean that the villa was now housing two air force officers as well as the widow of a respected pilot, and it was serving the needs of the people very well.

With their new rooms, Honza and Mira had the perfect bachelor setup. They had space to entertain, gardens to walk in, and easy access to the streetcar to take them to the airport or downtown Prague. Honza took advantage of the villa to entertain a harem of young women, but Mira was spending more and more time with Jiřinka, and after five years, they were beginning to get very serious.

Prague had not been a major target for Allied bombing, so its entire central area was intact, with buildings dating back to the eleventh century. The addition of electric lights to centuries-old buildings gave them an almost fairytale quality. In early winter, when Christmas decorations go up and the city gets blanketed by snow, downtown Prague feels like its own magical world.

One night in December 1951, Mira took Jiřinka out for dinner. It was dark by the time they finished their meal and as they headed toward their streetcar stop it began to snow. The two lovers decided to keep walking. Soon, they found themselves strolling around Wenceslas Square, which is not a square at all, but a long, narrow street that used to serve as the city's horse market. It is the symbolic center of the city, and a stroll along its famous streets takes you past some of the most beautiful buildings in Prague. Before long, they found themselves standing arm in arm in front of the massive bronze Saint Wenceslas monument, silhouetted against the ornate National Museum. They watched the heavy flakes swirl down and stick to the head and shoulders of the passersby. A gust of wind blew through the square, and Jiřinka shivered. Mira wrapped his arms around her to keep her warm. Mira was overwhelmed by the beauty of the moment. He leaned down and gave Jiřinka a brief kiss on the lips. For an instant, there were no bread lines, no secret police, and no political officers or informers. There were only two young people in love. It was one of the most perfect moments in Mira's life. He decided then that he wanted to marry Jiřinka; now he just needed to ask her.

10

Ice: Kosice, 1951

The winter of 1951 was a joyous time for Mira. He was in love with Jiřinka. He was still getting used to his promotion and the generous salary that came with it. Even more important than the money was the validation of himself as an aviator and the respect from his family and friends.

As fast as Mira's ascent to captain had been, in many ways, he was still just a young man. As soon as he had a little extra cash, he did what countless other young men have done—he bought a motorcycle. It was a black and silver Ogar 350, built by Jawa Moto of Prague. The bike was light and fast, capable of 70 mph. Mira decided to keep it at his parents' house in Leopoldov, where he could use it on holidays, taking long rides through the lush rolling hills of Slovakia. Mira was looking forward to a wonderful holiday with his family and imagined the extravagant gifts he would be able to buy them.

A few days before Christmas, he was assigned to flight OK-506, which was a three-stop flight from Prague to the eastern Czechoslovakian city of Kosice. CSA typically used a DC-3 on this route. If everything went according to plan, the plane would leave Prague at 3.10 p.m., fly to Brno, stop to take on more passengers, continue to Bratislava for another brief stop, and arrive in Kosice by 6.35 p.m. Kosice is nestled in a valley in the Carpathian Mountains and could be difficult to fly into during winter. Mira arrived at the airport about ninety minutes before his scheduled departure to perform a pre-flight inspection on his plane. He was disappointed to find out that the dependable American-built DC-3 had been replaced by a Soviet built Li-2. Douglas Aircraft, had licensed the Soviet Union to build its own version of the DC-3, and the Soviets eventually built 4,937 of them under the name “Li-2”. The Li-2s were stronger and heavier than the DC-3 but fell short in quality and performance.

Mira was irked by the change but knew that there was nothing he could do about it. As the time for the flight drew near, he checked the weather charts. Conditions were good on the Prague to Brno leg and from Brno to Bratislava, but there was a fast-moving warm front carrying a lot of moisture rolling up from the Adriatic that would collide with a stationary cold front over the Carpathians. This was a perfect recipe for snow in the late afternoon. The departure from Bratislava to Kosice would not take place until 5.10 p.m., an hour and a half after sunset, and temperatures were forecast to be below freezing with a good chance of ice the whole way.

At 2.30 p.m., Mira walked through the departure lounge to the security checkpoint. As he crossed the lounge he felt the eyes of every passenger following him. He knew that many were shocked to see how young he was. Mira squared his shoulders and raised his chin. He wanted to convey confidence to the nervous passengers. His gaze swept the lounge and he noted several passengers holding shopping bags bulging with brightly wrapped gifts. “It’s almost Christmas,” Mira thought, “and these must be people flying home to their families in Kosice bringing presents and treats.” Mira noticed an attractive young woman with blonde hair and a navy-blue coat, bouncing a baby in her lap. “Maybe this is a daughter bringing her child home to meet Grandma for the first time?” Mira felt a wave of pride as he realized how all of these people trusted him. It was an awesome responsibility, and he would not let them down.

Mira crossed the field towards the silver-and-blue Li-2. The winter sun was weak and the air felt cold and damp. Mira took his position in the left seat and began going through his pre-flight checklist with his co-pilot, checking off each item on the long pre-printed page. Mira was uneasy about this flight, and he wasn’t sure why.

The first two legs of the flight were uneventful. Shortly before he started the engines to depart from Bratislava, Mira walked through the cabin. It was warm and cheerful, with excited passengers looking forward to spending the holidays with their families. The pretty blonde girl had taken off her coat and was giving a bottle to her baby.

The takeoff from Bratislava was textbook perfect. Mira quickly coaxed the Li-2 to its cruising altitude of 7,000 feet and 152 mph. At this speed, the trip should take about ninety minutes. It was a dark night, with the moon obscured by towering clouds. Some nights, the cloud cover was low enough that he could climb out of it and sail along in a world illuminated by the moon and stars. Tonight was not going to be one of those. The plane was going to be "in the soup" the whole way. Shortly after they reached cruising altitude, Mira noticed ice forming on the windshield. He asked the co-pilot to turn on the anti-icing system in the wings and shoot some alcohol to the windshield and propellers.

One of the significant differences between a DC-3 and its Soviet-built twin was the way the planes dealt with ice. The DC-3 used a de-icing system that depended on black rubber bladders or "boots" installed along the leading edge of the wings. When activated, the de-icing system allowed compressed air to be blown in three-second pulses to the bladders, causing them to expand and contract, breaking off the wing ice. It was a rather primitive system but it worked very well. The Soviets used an anti-icing system that was actually newer and more advanced than the American system. The Soviet system called for the leading edges of the wing to be heated so ice would never have a chance to form. There were two problems with the Soviet system—first, the heater did not always work, and the only way you could tell that it was not working was when the wing iced up and the plane tried to fall out of the sky. The second problem was that the warm leading edge allowed the moisture that collected on the leading edge to get pushed back by the slip steam to the back half of the wing, where it would still freeze, altering the shape of the wings and thus their lifting capabilities. Worse yet, the moisture on the left and right wings could freeze in different ways, so that the wings no longer had equal lift.

About sixty minutes into the flight, Mira noticed that the plane was feeling sluggish. He turned on the landing lights and looked out the cockpit windows. He could see that the leading edge of the wing was clear of ice. That was a good sign, but it also meant that the sluggishness was probably being caused by ice forming on the back side of the wing. He trimmed the plane to fly with its nose a bit higher and tried to add some power. When he advanced the throttles, the engines did not respond. Instead of roaring with more power, their speed actually dropped. This was likely caused by ice forming around the air scoops. There was little that Mira could do. There were heater settings for the carburetors that kept ice from forming on them, but the Soviets had never thought to heat the air scoops. On flights over level terrain, the pilot could try losing altitude and hunt for a band of warmer air to melt the ice, but flying over mountains meant having to keep as much altitude as possible. The plane started to lose altitude, he dropped a few hundred feet, from 7,000 feet to 6,700 feet, but it was an ominous sign. He was flying toward a mountain range whose highest peak was over 8,000 feet and he was going to have to thread the needle and fly in the valleys between the mountains.

When they were twenty minutes away from Kosice, their air speed dropped to 125 mph and they had lost another 1,000 feet. They were now at 5,700 feet. On the approach to Kosice, there were peaks and ridges that were close to 4,500 feet. If they lost much more altitude, they would be in serious trouble. Mira asked his navigator to contact Kosice to get a precise fix on their location. The Li-2 did not have radar; it relied on triangulating radio transmissions to determine its location.

As the navigator struggled to get a fix on the Kosice radio beacon, Mira saw his air speed drop to 110 mph and the altimeter begin to unwind from 5,700 feet to 5,000 and then to 4,500, not stopping until the plane was at 4,000 feet. Mira's pulse was pounding. He was struggling to keep the ice-laden ship in the air and he was now hurtling along in heavy clouds at 110 mph. They were 500 feet below the level of known terrain in the area. He knew that the laws of physics did not care a bit about courage or honor. He knew that his plane weighed 23,589 pounds and he was flying through the night at about 161 feet per second, and if he hit the side of a granite mountain at that speed, everything in the plane including him, the engines, the pretty blonde girl, and her smiling baby, would be instantly ripped into tiny postage stamp-sized pieces of blood, bones, and aluminum.

His radio crackled and the Kosice tower said, "OK-GAC, you've dropped below recommended approach altitude. Please state your intention." The altimeter began to unwind again and airspeed continued to drop. In the best of conditions, the Li-2 would stall and drop out of the air at 67 miles per hour, but with its wings misshapen by ice, there was no way of knowing what the stall speed was. An idea began to form in Mira's mind. He knew there was a solution, but it was dancing in his memory, just out of reach.

The radio crackled again, "OK-GAC, you are below the level of known terrain. Report please!" Mira could imagine the excited families waiting at Kosice. They would be checking their watches and see that the plane was due to arrive in under ten minutes. Soon, they would begin lining up to greet their loved ones as they came off the plane. Mira imagined their pain and anguish if he let the plane slam into a mountain and turned the girl in the blue coat and the brightly wrapped presents and the sleeping baby into senseless rubble on the side of a cold, snowy mountain. His memory cleared and he knew what to do. The radio crackled. "OK-GAC what are you doing?"

Mira grabbed the microphone and snapped, "I'm trying to keep this Russian piece of crap in the air!" Mira then turned to the co-pilot and said, "I need you do exactly what I say. Keep the throttles open, but when I tell you to, I want you to back the fuel mixture on the left engine down from full rich to almost idle cutoff. Don't go to cutoff but get as close as you can, and then when I tell you to, slam it back to full rich."

"That's crazy! We're barely staying in the air and you want me to starve the engine for fuel?"

"Yes!" Mira said with growing confidence, "That's exactly what I want you to do. And while you do that I'm going to keep this ship from falling any further down the well."

As the co-pilot leaned out the left engine, Mira used the ailerons to keep the plane level. As loaded with ice as she was, if the plane dipped too far to one side, she might never recover. The co-pilot continued to lean the engine out and just before the engine was totally starved; it let out an enormous backfire that caused flame to shoot out of the air scoop. The force of the backfire and the heat of the flame blew the ice out of the scoop and Mira shouted, "Now! Give me full rich now!" The co-pilot slammed the mixture control forward and the 1,000-hp motor screamed back to life. The co-pilot cheered. Next, they did the same thing with the right engine, leaning it out until it backfired and cleared out the ice. With two strong engines, the ice-crusted plane was able to claw back enough altitude to clear the mountains and sail on into Kosice. Mira quickly explained that when he was still learning to fly a Siebel he had once tried to cut the mixture control all the way to idle cutoff, while leaving the throttles wide open. The resulting backfire had almost knocked the engines off the wings.

Twenty minutes later, the plane was on the ground and Mira was watching with pride as the passengers hugged their loved ones in the arrival lounge. When he watched the pretty blonde in the blue coat hand the sleeping baby to an older woman, who must have been the baby's grandmother, he had to fight back tears. None of the passengers knew that they had been moments away from death.

As Mira was sitting in the pilots' lounge making some final entries into his log book, he was approached by the Kosice Head of Airline Operations. The airline manager nervously asked Mira if he could have a moment. Mira smiled confidently and agreed. He was still feeling elation at having come through a near-death experience. He followed the airline manager to his tiny office, thinking about the compliments he was sure to be given. This would be much more rewarding than the commendation for bravery he had received for staying on board the burning Siebel, because this had been true bravery. He had done something very special. He had saved twenty-four lives and he was proud of himself. When he entered the airline manager's office, he was surprised to see a gaunt man with a hawk nose and slicked-back hair wearing one of the green leather overcoats of the StB. The police officer turned on Mira and put his hands roughly on Mira's shoulders, pushing him down into a waiting chair. Then he stood over him, shaking a thin nicotine-stained finger in Mira's face.

> Captain Slovak, you are playing a dangerous game, and if I ever hear that you refer to any other fine Russian airplane as a "piece of crap" again, I will arrest you! Russian planes are products of the revolution and to claim that they are inferior to American products is counter-revolutionary, and you know what we do with counter-revolutionaries? We shoot them![1]

Mira was stunned. He knew enough of StB justice to keep his mouth shut. He mumbled an apology and watched in disbelief as the policeman turned on his heel and stormed out of the room.

That night, struggling to sleep, Mira felt the final puzzle piece fall into place. From the moment in 1945, when the Russian troops burned his glider and shot his father's dog, Mira knew that he could not live with the Russians. He thought of Anicka and her bruised face. He thought of Roberto and his crushed spirit. He remembered his mother standing up for what she believed in. In his mind's eye, he saw her burning the Hlinka Guard uniform. He thought of the bread lines in Prague and his father's grain silo being given to strangers. That night when he finally fell asleep he dreamed of the sun that would rise in the West and when he awoke, he knew that he had to leave Czechoslovakia.

11

False Start: Prague, 1952

Mira wanted to tell Honza about his decision to defect, but he knew that it was against Czech law to hear about an escape plan and not report it to the StB. Mira did not think that Honza would turn him in, but he did not want to put him in the position of having to make that choice. Besides, there was something different about Honza since he had been arrested. Mira could not quite name it, but there was something about Honza that was almost too good to be true, like a waxed fruit that looked too perfect. Mira was ashamed to think it, but he just did not trust the "new" Honza.

Mira knew he could not tell Jiřinka about his decision either. She came from a large, close family and there was simply no way that she would leave then behind. If he told her that he was going without her, she would be hurt and there was no telling what she would do.

The more Mira thought about his dilemma, the angrier he got. "What sick minds could possibly create a government that would force a man to choose between the people he loved and his freedom?"

Honza's rehabilitation was not quite complete. He still could not accompany Mira to free countries like Denmark, Norway, or Sweden. Honza's flying was restricted to destinations within the Soviet Bloc. One day, Honza was flying co-pilot for Mira in a DC-3 on a flight from Prague to Brno. As the plane began the final descent, the left engine began to misfire—nothing too alarming, but troubling enough that when they were on the ground, they reported the problem to maintenance. While the ground crew worked on the engine, Mira and Honza sat on a bench alongside the hangar, smoking cigarettes and talking. Honza whispered, "You know, this could be just what I've been waiting for."

Mira had not been paying attention and was not sure what Honza had said. "What do you mean?"

"This could be my chance to get out of here. When the mechanics are done with the plane, we can tell them that we want to make a test flight to make sure everything is working before we load up the next batch of passengers. We are only 25 miles from the Austrian border. At 150 mph; we could be across in about 10 minutes. By the time the Czech Air Force scrambled their interceptors, we'd be on the ground at the U.S. Air Force base in Tulin eating apple pie!"

"Don't even joke like that Honza. Remember what they did to Roberto."

"No one can hear me, and besides, I'm not joking."

"You're serious?" Mira whispered.

Honza nodded his head, "Yes."

"Why would I want to do something this foolish? I fly to Copenhagen every week. If I want out, next time I'm in Copenhagen all I need to do is have a taxi take me to the American Embassy."

"You would never do that." Honza said confidently.

"Why wouldn't I?"

"Because you wouldn't leave me behind to face the StB by myself."

Honza was right, Mira would never abandon him. "Are you really serious about doing this?"

"Very serious."

"So let's think this through. We've got to get this right because there won't be any second chances. As close to the border as we are, they might not let us take a plane up without a guard, so what are we going to do if they put a guard onboard with us? Knock him out? Tie him up?"

"Nothing so dramatic," Honza said. "We'll take the plane up today when they finish their repairs, and if they give us a guard, we'll give him a hell of a ride. Lots of climbing and diving and rolls. We'll make sure this guy gets airsick. Next time we do a test flight, no one will want to ride with us!"

Mira noticed a mechanic heading their way, so he motioned for Honza to be silent. The mechanic, wearing grease-stained gray coveralls, stopped a few paces away and said, "We've got the engine all back together. It looks like there was some corrosion on the points in the distributor. I've cleaned the contacts and re-gapped the points. I think that you will be good to go now."

Mira said, "Thank you. We want to take a quick flight, to make sure that everything is working."

The mechanic was cleaning his hands on a red shop towel and looked up at Mira with an irritated expression, "You don't think I know what I'm doing?"

"No comrade, I just have heard that there might be some important Party members on the flight tonight, and I want to be assured that there won't be any problems."

"Suit yourself," the mechanic growled, "But make sure you get permission before you take off."

"I will, comrade, and thank you for your quick work repairing the distributor." The mechanic turned and walked away without replying.

It was surprisingly easy to get permission to make the test flight, but they were required to take along a young, gray-faced Czech Army guard with a submachine gun. It was clear from the moment the guard climbed into the plane that he did not like flying and didn't want to be onboard.

A DC-3 is not a very acrobatic plane, but within a few minutes of takeoff, Mira and Honza were putting the plane through a series of deeply banked left and right turns, followed by some sudden, steep dives. Mira looked over his shoulder and saw the poor guard throwing up into his helmet. Mira did not want to be cruel but he needed to make sure that when this guard returned to the ground that neither he nor any of his fellow guards would ever want to fly with "crazy Captain Slovak." Mira threw in a few more dives, followed by even sharper turns, as the poor guard continued to retch. When they were back on the ground, Mira and Honza had to carry the guard off the plane and hand him to his buddies.

Back at the villa that night, Mira tossed and turned trying to get to sleep. He knew that he would have to deal with Jiřinka, and the sooner the better. He worried that if they were still dating when he escaped, the StB would suspect her of being involved and might arrest her and interrogate her, or worse. He had to break up with her, he had to do it quickly, and he had to do it in a way that put as much distance between them as possible. He decided that he would take her to dinner the next evening and tell her that he had fallen in love with someone else. It seemed like a cruel lie, and it would certainly be one of the hardest things he would ever have to do, but he did not see any way around it.

They never made it to dinner. He stopped by Jiřinka's house. She met him at the door in a cute blue and white dress that she thought showed her figure off to its full advantage without being suggestive. Jiřinka stood on her tiptoes to give Mira a kiss. He turned his head coldly to avoid her lips. Instantly, she knew something was wrong. "What is it?" she asked, with fear making her voice quiver. Mira opened his mouth but the lie he had practiced would not come. He just stood there speechless. "What is it? You've seemed so different lately. What's wrong?" Her mind leapt ahead to the only conclusion she could come to. "You're leaving me, aren't you?"

Mira still could not speak. He nodded and whispered "Yes," but no sound came from his throat.

Jiřinka's eyes flashed with anger. "It's another woman isn't it? You bastard! I can't believe it." She slapped him hard across the face.

He wanted to tell her the truth—he wanted to tell her that he loved her and had never cheated on her. He wanted to tell her he could not live under the iron hand of the communists any longer, but that he just wanted to be free, and he wanted her to come with him to start a wonderful new life in America. Yet he knew it would not help. He knew she would never leave. So instead he just said, "I'm sorry."

"That's it? After five years, all you can say is, 'I'm sorry'? That is pathetic. And to think, I once thought I loved you!" She slammed the door in Mira's face.

Mira walked slowly back to the villa. It had not gone like he had planned, but it was over now. As he walked, he began to get angry, though not at Jiřinka, who was totally blameless. His anger was directed at Gottwald and the Communists. Why were they making everything so difficult? They were worse than the Nazis. The Nazis were evil and had forced the Czech people to do horrible things, but they did not change the nature of the Czech people. The Communists were evil and committed many of the same atrocities that the Nazis did, but the Communists were destroying the soul of Czechoslovakia.

Two weeks later, Mira was in the pilots' lounge in Prague, looking at the schedule for the next week. He and Honza were scheduled to fly the same flight to Brno. "Well, this is it!" Mira thought, "We're really going to go." Mira saw Honza walking across the lounge and he casually called, "Hey Honza, they've got us working together on the Brno flight next week." Honza caught Mira's eyes and made a tiny shake of the head, "no." Instantly, Mira felt goosebumps rise across his arms. Something was wrong. Something had changed. There was no place to talk privately in the lounge, and the two friends were on different flights for the day, so there was not a chance to find out what had changed.

Later that night, sipping beer on the garden patio at the villa, Honza explained. "I've been contacted by the anti-communist underground. They think that it would be a waste to hijack a DC-3 for only two people to escape. They have twenty-three people that they want us to take with us."

Mira was stunned. "This is insane. It will be suicide. How are we going to get twenty-three people on board the plane? Where would we hide them at the maintenance shop? Do they think we can just give them all mechanics' uniforms? Maybe the guards will sit by and watch as twenty-three people run across the field and line up to get on our flight. And most importantly; I know you and I trust you, I don't know who these other twenty-three people are and I don't trust them. Twenty-three people mean twenty-three more chances to get caught."

"Calm down, Miroslav," Honza said. "I'm not going to do anything to put either of us in danger. None of the twenty-three people know anything about each other. It's all very compartmentalized. They call it 'cells.' Everyone is in their own cell and nobody has contact with anyone else."

Mira was insulted that Honza had made such a huge change to their plan without including him. He remembered the awful torture that Roberto had been through and he vowed he would never let something like that happen to himself. "No Honza, I'm sorry but this is just too much. I won't do it."

Honza pleaded, "They're counting on you. For some, this is their last chance. It's life or death!"

"It's life or death for me too! It may not seem like it, but I'm not a risk taker. I learned early on with flying that you look at the situation and you calculate the risk, and you don't go ahead with a maneuver that is too risky, and by any calculation the risk with twenty-three new people is too much."

"I thought you wanted your freedom," Honza said sullenly.

"I do," snapped Mira, "but remember I fly into free Europe every week. If freedom was the only thing I was after, I would just defect next time I'm in Copenhagen. I was willing to help you escape, but I'm not willing to get myself arrested because someone in the underground came up with a new plan."

"Would you be willing to come up with a different plan? Something that you believed was safer?" After a very long pause, Mira agreed. "Good. Would you be willing to meet with my contact in the anti-communist underground?" Mira agreed to that too. "His name is Jan Furchgot. He used to be a meteorologist for CSA and before that for the Free Czech Air Force. He was fired during the CSA purge in 1951."

Before Honza and Mira had a chance to meet with Furchgot, they ran into a new problem. They were visited by the director of the Prague Housing Authority. She was a heavy middle-aged woman who had allowed the power of her position to turn her arrogant and overbearing. With righteous indignation, she told the pilots that allowing two young men to live in such a huge and splendid villa that could easily house several families was counter-revolutionary and a clear misuse of the people's property. She reassigned Honza and Mira to a much smaller two-bedroom apartment on the second floor of an older building closer to the heart of Prague.

Being young bachelors, Honza and Mira had little to move, and they settled into their new apartment quickly. They soon became aware of how much the mood in Prague had changed since the communists took over. In *Under A Cruel Star, A Life in Prague 1941–1968*, Heda Margolius Kovaly describes the troubling changes:

> The atmosphere in Prague was almost as bad as it had been during the war. No one dared to speak out loud, and hardly a week passed without news of someone's arrest. The worst days were Thursdays and Fridays. The Central Committee met on Thursdays and wherever a doorbell rang on those evenings, everyone turned pale.[1]

Mira watched in frustration as fear worked its way into the heart of Czechoslovakia. With informers everywhere, people who had once been proud and vocal about their beliefs became afraid to talk. Common sense and good judgment were replaced by false platitudes and party slogans.

12

Codeword "Picnic": Prague, 1952

On a warm afternoon in early July, Honza took Mira to meet Furchgot. They rode three different streetcars, jumping off each one at the last moment, to grab a passing trolley heading in the opposite direction. Honza said it was to make sure that they were not being followed. Mira felt a twinge of suspicion. "How did Honza know about this type of 'spy' technique?" The meeting took place in a park in central Prague. Furchgot was, pale, shy, and unremarkable in every way. The three men walked slowly along the winding paths of the park. They talked in whispers and paused whenever anyone came near. Furchgot explained that the underground's current plan included a former Free Czech navigator named Helmut Cermack and a civilian glider pilot who had never flown anything with an engine. Their plan was to book all twenty-three of the conspirators on the same CSA flight. Once the plane was airborne, they would overpower the flight crew, and the glider pilot would take over the controls. With Cermack navigating, the plane would fly to England and attempt a wheels-up crash landing at an abandoned RAF field near Dover.

To Mira, the plan seemed so amateurish that it bordered on suicide. First, if any of the conspirators had raised the least suspicion of the StB, they would never all be allowed to book passage on the same flight. Second, a DC-3 flew with a crew of four and the door to the cockpit was very narrow. One determined officer could easily hold off an army of unarmed civilians in the narrow passage, giving enough time for the radio operator to call the ground and alert the Air Force, which would surely send a squadron of Russian MiG-15 jet fighters to shoot the escaping DC-3 from the sky. Also, if all that went according to plan, there was positively no way that an inexperienced glider pilot could possibly fly a twin-engine airliner 700 miles across Europe and land without killing everyone on board. Furchgot listened politely as Mira pointed out flaw after flaw in the plan and when Mira paused, Furchgot said challengingly, "Really? So how would you do it?"

Mira enthusiastically began to describe the improvements he would make. "First you need experienced pilots like Honza and me; second, we need to get weapons on board so the pilots can subdue the rest of the crew. Then we need to find out the scramble time for the MiG interceptors, and what their radio frequencies are. I can do that, I've got plenty of friends flying MiGs. Then we need a cloudless night with a full moon so I can fly low enough to avoid the Air Force's radar."

"So I guess this means you're going to join us?" Furchgot asked.

Mira nodded and said, "Yes, I guess it does."

"That's great news," Honza said looking at his watch, "but I've got to get back to the airport. I'm flying the Bratislava flight tonight."

"Before you leave we need to do two more things." Furchgot said, "First we need to set the next meeting, and second we need to come up with a codeword for the escape, something that we can say in public without creating any suspicion."

"How about 'picnic'?" Mira said. "We can talk about the picnic in public. We can say when is the picnic? Who shall we invite on the picnic? What is the weather like for the picnic, and no one will be suspicious!"

"Great idea!" Honza said. "We'll call it 'picnic.'"

"So when and where do we meet again?" Furchgot asked. "How about the same time, right here in the first week of August?"

"That could work," Mira answered, "but I'm not sure what my flight load is like next month and I won't know until the Monday after next."

"Don't worry." Furchgot said, "I'll walk by your apartment Monday night. If the meeting is going to work, pull down the window shade on the far-right window, but leave the other ones up. If it isn't going to work, leave all of the shades up."

Mira was taken aback, "You know where I live?"

"You would be surprised by what we know." Furchgot said. Mira felt a shiver run down his spine.

The next day, Mira took a taxi across the city to Kbely Air Force Base. He was still a captain in the Air Force on loan to the CSA, so he had no difficulty getting on base and heading to the officers' club. He sat in a dark corner nursing a beer until he saw a couple of friends from school. Mira headed to the bar, ordered a pitcher of beer and walked to their table. There was a joyous reunion when Mira set the full pitcher on the table.

Both the Air Force men had graduated at the same time as Mira but chose to fly fighters. They had a touch of the typical fighter pilot swagger and teased Mira about working for CSA as a "bus driver in the sky" but Mira could sense that they were also jealous of the salary he was making.

As the beer flowed, the fighter pilots began to brag about the MiG-15s they flew and how much faster they were then Mira's lumbering DC-3. "So really," Mira whispered, "How fast can you guys go?"

Wanting to embarrass Mira, the MiG pilots said, "Tell us about your DC-3. How fast can she fly?"

"With a full load of passengers, we can reach almost 230 knots."

Both MiG pilots burst out laughing, "We can fly almost 650 knots!"

Mira was impressed, "Really? Wow! You know back when I was in training I used to love to fly close to the ground, and follow the terrain. But I was in one of those old S-199s. I can't imagine what that would be like in a jet. Do you ever do that in your MiGs?"

One of the pilots whispered, "The generals are afraid we'll bend up one of their shiny new jets, so we are prohibited from ever flying below 500 feet. The MiGs are fast, but their ground control radars are crap. We can't go below 500 feet or the Soviet radar might lead us into the side of a mountain. We can get away with it in the day, but as soon as it gets dark, we have to stay up at 500 feet."

Mira filled the pilots' mugs again. "You know, I see you guys in the air all the time, zipping past me. I'd love to say 'Hello' but I don't know the radio frequencies that you jet jockeys use."

"Oh hell, Mira, that's easy," one of the pilots said, but before he had a chance to say anything, Mira held up his hand.

"Wait, I've had several beers and I'm not going to remember a damn thing in the morning." He pulled out a copy of his day's flight orders and turned it over. "Would you just write them here? That way I don't have to try to remember." The MiG pilot wrote down the frequencies. Mira folded the paper and stuck it in his pocket.

"A month ago, I had a layover in Copenhagen and I went to the movies. Before the feature I saw this newsreel about the U.S. Air Force and they said there were planes on standby twenty-four hours a day, and they could have their planes in the air and at the border in fifteen minutes. Are we doing the same thing?"

One of the MiG pilots nodded his head. "Yes, that seems about right. We have planes standing by too. It takes me about five minutes to get from the ready room to the plane, start the engine, taxi to the runway and take off. Add maybe ten more minutes to form up and be onsite at the border. The whole thing happens pretty fast, well under twenty minutes so I'd agree that fifteen minutes is right."

Mira continued to nurse his beer and talk for another hour before excusing himself from the table, saying, "I've got to fly a busload of tourists to Brno tomorrow so I better get home. It was great to see you boys again, and next time I see a MiG in the air I'll radio hello."

On the taxi ride home, Mira was amazed at how easy it had been to get all the classified information he needed. He felt guilty about using old friends like that, but he knew that there was no way that the StB would realize where Mira got his information.

When Mira got his schedule on Monday he saw that he was free to make the meeting, but he was disappointed that Honza was not. Honza said, "Go ahead without me. They trust you." So Mira went to the window and pulled down the shade on the far right. It was such a simple act, something that millions of people did every day almost without thinking, but this time the simple act was the first step in a journey that would change Mira's life forever.

The next week, the communists gave Mira a huge honor and proved that he was still above suspicion. He was selected to pilot one of the special charter planes that would carry East Bloc athletes to the 1952 Olympic Games in Helsinki. Mira flew several flights from Prague, Warsaw, and Budapest to ferry members of the Czechoslovakian, Polish, and Hungarian teams to the games in Finland.

After the games closed on August 3, Mira returned to Prague. He was careful to switch streetcars three times, just as Honza had shown him on his way to the park for the second meeting. When he arrived, he was surprised to see that Jan Furchgot was joined by two additional conspirators, Helmut Cermak, and Helmut's wife, Hanna. Helmut was short and dark, with a receding hairline. He was twenty-eight years old and had served in the Free Czech Air Force during World War II. He had been a navigator on the RAF's big four-engine Lancaster bombers. After the war, he had spent five years working as a navigator with CSA, until the purges of 1951. When he left CSA, he was hired by the Skoda Munitions plant.

There was a slight rain coming down, so Helmut and Jan opened umbrellas and the four conspirators had to stand close together as they walked. Helmut took control of the meeting, turning to Mira with a hint of irritation in his voice, saying, "I hear from Jan that you were not impressed with our previous plan. What did you think was wrong with it?"

It was apparent to Mira that Helmut had been the "airplane expert" and the leader of the plot. Mira knew that he was going to have to be very careful in the way that he dealt with Helmut. He did not want to defy him openly, but the original plan had been so foolish that Mira was worried about getting involved with a leader who had such questionable judgment. Mira chose his words carefully, "Perhaps I was careless with my words when I met with Jan last time. What I should have said was, 'Now that you have an experienced DC-3 pilot in your group, it might not be necessary to take all the risks that were involved with the original plan.'"

Helmut's attitude softened, "If you were in charge, what would you do?"

Mira had spent quite a bit of time thinking about this, but had never expected to be asked so directly. "I'd start with three major questions. Where are we going? How do we get there? And who are we taking with us?"

Helmut interrupted and said, "The 'where' is already determined. We need to go to England."

"Why England and not Austria or Germany?" Mira asked.

"First, I flew out of England for the RAF and I know it like the back of my hand, and second, there have been several defections via Germany, but we are hearing that Germany may stop accepting refugees at any moment. If we did escape and were sent back, that would be a death sentence."

Mira nodded thoughtfully and replied, "Most of the other defectors have gone to Munich, which makes sense because it is the closest big German city, but what if we go to Rhein-Main, the U.S. Air Force base in Frankfurt. I'm still a captain in the Czech Air Force, which might make me valuable enough to their intelligence operations that they will take us. Besides, we have to fly right past Frankfurt to get to England, so we might as well ask for permission to land and see what they say."

Helmut saw the logic and said, "All right, but we will only land if they give us clearance to land on the U.S. side. I don't want to land on the civilian side and risk getting sent back." The southern portion of the Frankfurt-Main Airport was controlled by the U.S. Air Force and called Rhein-Main Air Base, but the rest of the airport was under German civilian control. There were nods of agreement all around.

Mira spoke again. "That automatically means we need a DC-3. That's the only plane CSA flies that has enough range to reach London. You may not know this, because things have changed since the purge, but the ground crews are stingy with fuel. They know that some pilots are tempted to defect, so there are only a few flights that they put enough fuel on that you could get to England. One of those flights is the evening flight from Prague to Brno. That flight always gets extra fuel."

"Why?" asked Hanna Cermak, who was thirty years old, with long curly hair and an engaging smile. Mira turned towards her.

> There is a mining operation at Moravská Ostrava, near the Polish border. The bigwigs at the mine like to read the newspapers from Prague. They like their newspapers so much that they have their own print shop. The last flight from Prague to Brno every night carries copies of the printing plates from that day's newspaper packed into a crate with a parachute. After we land in Brno and deplane the passengers, we take off again and fly toward the Polish border. There is no place to land, so we open the rear door and fly low. There is a radio beacon at the mining camp and as soon as we are over Moravská Ostrava, a light goes off on the flight deck and we have a crew member push the package out the door. It all seems a little unnecessary to me, but the bigwigs get their newspaper and we get a hundred extra gallons of fuel.[1]

"Very well, "Helmut said, "How will we take over the plane?"

Mira answered, "I still have my Air Force pistol and I think I can round up at least two more."

"How will we get them through security?" Hanna asked.

"Leave that to me." Mira answered. "The fewer people that know about it, the easier it will be. So the only big question left is who's going with us."

Jan and Helmut exchanged nervous looks. Finally, Helmut broke the awkward silence, "We can't talk about that. The underground won't give us any names. They say it is too dangerous. We are to tell them what flight we are going on, and they will take care of the passengers.

Mira did not like that, but he understood the necessity. "Well," he said, "I understand their reasoning, but it makes me very nervous." He looked at his watch. "I have to get back to the airport.

The conspirators continued to meet every two weeks through the end of summer and into fall. They were ready to go by mid-October, right before Mira's twenty-third birthday. Then, the weather turned against them. For six straight weeks, every time they had a date chosen, the clouds rolled in, the wind picked up, and they had to postpone. In early December, they decided that it would be best to wait until spring.

Honza seemed to have lost interest in "picnic." He rarely attended meetings and never expressed an opinion. Mira felt irritated at Honza's new attitude. He did not need the whole elaborate conspiracy. He could slip off to the U.S. Embassy next time he was in Copenhagen. He was only going along with this scheme so that Honza could get out. Yet now, Honza seemed hardly interested. Mira asked him point blank if he still wanted to be part of the escape. "Yes! Of course! I'm just worried. My mother is getting old and her health is poor. I worry about what will happen to her after I leave."

Mira spent an uneasy winter of lost sleep and self-doubt. He immersed himself in flying, picking up flights from other pilots who wanted to spend the holidays with their families. As February wound to a close, Mira knew that there would be clear weather any day. He wanted to say goodbye to his family, but that would put them in grave danger. Everyone in his family would be questioned by the StB once he was in the West, and he needed to make sure that they could honestly tell the police that they knew nothing of his plans. Yet Mira needed to see them one last time. It was a five-hour train ride from Prague to Leopoldov, with a stop to change trains in Bratislava. Mira left Prague on a cold gray afternoon on Friday, February 27, 1953. He sat in a window seat, with his eyes riveted on the outside world as the train rolled through the rain. He knew this might be the last time he would see his home country, and he wanted to take in every detail. He was struck by how much had changed in the four short years since the communists had come to power. There seemed to be a drab fog that had settled over Czechoslovakia. Inside the train, everyone seemed to be dressed in gray, and most clothes looked old and patched. Passengers refused to make eye contact with each other. No one spoke, and if they did it was always with a hushed whisper behind a raised newspaper or the back of a hand, followed by a quick side-to-side glance to make sure no one could have overheard the comment. Outside the train, rivulets of rain formed on the window as the afternoon melted into twilight and eventually a totally dark night. Electrical shortages meant miles without streetlights. Empty shop windows with no goods to sell meant no neon signs for advertising. As the train traveled deeper into the countryside, Mira saw empty fields and boarded-up buildings. To Mira, it looked like a dying land.

The train arrived at Leopoldov shortly after 8 p.m. Mira grabbed his bag and left the train. He felt guilty that he had not brought gifts for his family, but he knew that if he had, it might tip them off that he was planning to defect.

It was an easy walk from the station to his childhood home. Every tree or bush along the way seemed familiar from the countless times he had walked these streets as a young boy. It seemed incomprehensible that he was looking at them for the last time.

Even though the communists had taken away the silo, they had allowed Jan and Maria to keep the house, although Mira could not help but worry that very soon his parents would get a visit from the Housing Authority and be told to move to a small apartment somewhere in town.

Mira paused in the night as he approached the house. From across the road, he could take in every detail of his old home. He wanted to preserve it in his memory. He had lived in this big house with its thick walls and heavy shutters from age three to fifteen. Yellow lamp light spilled out of the windows and he could see his mother working in the kitchen. He was sure that the house would be filled with some wonderful smell coming from the oven. It might be bread, it might be cake, but he had never once opened the door to this house and not been greeted by the loving arms of his family and a fabulous aroma from the kitchen.

His eyes filled with tears as he watched the house. After a moment, his tears gave way to anger. What type of devilish government makes a child have to choose between his family and his freedom? He pulled out a handkerchief and wiped his eyes, blew his nose, and crossed the road. He rang the bell and waited. He could hear his mother's footsteps echo along the hall as she came to the door. She opened it, while drying her hands on her apron. When she saw Mira, her expression turned to joy and she threw her arms around him, giving him a big hug. "What are you doing here?" she asked.

Mira tried to say, "I just wanted to surprise you and Dad," but the second he opened his mouth, a lump formed in his throat, his eyes welled up with tears and he couldn't speak. He pulled Maria closer and hid his tears in her hair. Eventually he regained his composure enough to say, "I had some time off and I wanted to surprise you."

Maria broke the hug, looked at him with a sad smile and said, "Well let's go find your Papa."

Instantly, Mira thought, "My God, she knows I'm defecting! I don't know how she does this, but she always knows what I'm thinking."

"Have you had dinner?" She asked. "Let me get you a plate of pork and dumplings." Gesturing toward the table where Mira had eaten so many meals, she said, "Sit. Make yourself comfortable. Papa!" She called, "Come to the kitchen, we have a visitor." They all sat and talked for hours, but Mira was careful not to talk about politics. He told his parents that he and Jiřinka had split up. Maria's eyes filled with tears at the news. "Oh, I was sure you two would be getting married."

"Me too!" Mira said while thinking, "Maybe mother will think my tears at the door were because of Jiřinka." He went on to tell stories about his time in the air force. He described his trips to the West. They talked about childhood memories. Eventually, well after midnight, Mira made his way upstairs to the room he had shared with Jarda (who was away at engineering school) and crawled into the tiny bed he had used throughout his childhood. As he tried to sleep, his mind was crowded with memories of life in this room; the blissful childhood days building model airplanes before the Nazis came, waking up on Christmas mornings to smell the wonderful meal Maria was cooking, lying awake fearful nights as bombers flew overhead, sneaking downstairs in the middle of the night to see the Engels family standing at the kitchen door. More than anything else, Mira remembered wanting to fly. He remembered sitting at his desk reading books about flying. He remembered running around the room with his arms out, pretending he was an airplane. He remembered sleepless nights while his mind burned with a feverish passion for flight. As so often happened lately, Mira's strongest emotions turned to anger at the communists. He had achieved his childhood dreams. He was a pilot and he should be happy beyond words, but somehow the regime that he flew for took all of the joy from his life. The government with its long tentacles reached into every corner of his life and robbed him of his freedom, and to Mira, without freedom there could be no joy. After a fitful night trying to sleep, Mira came downstairs to join his parents for breakfast.

"I think I'll take my bike out for a spin," Mira announced. He kissed his mother's forehead and headed towards the garage. For Mira, riding his fast and powerful motorcycle came as close to flying as any earthbound experience he had ever found. He roared away from the house without any real destination in mind. He soon found that he was making a farewell tour of his childhood. He started with a quick spin through the streets of Leopoldov, past friends' houses, the church and school, then on to the highway to race toward Trnava and the Saleziánsky Ústav Seminary feeling the wind in his hair. He rode to remember the beauty of this land, to see the rivers and churches, hills and mountains, to take one last look that would burn them into his memory. Yet he rode to forget too, to erase the Nazis and the death trains to Auschwitz, and the Russians and the communists from his mind. As he swept through the countryside, he was able to imagine his homeland free of the invaders, free of the occupiers, free of purges and political officers, free of Party officials and Housing Authorities. He could see it all clearly in his mind's eye, and someday, he hoped to come back and see it for real. It was dark when he returned home. He parked the bike behind the house and went in to enjoy dinner with his parents, followed by more conversation and a much better night's sleep in his childhood room.

On Sunday March 1, Mira slept late and missed breakfast. He came downstairs and went straight out to the yard to clean his bike. He knew that he was leaving it behind and it would probably be given to Jarda. Mira wondered if he would ever see him again. This bike would be his way of saying goodbye, and he wanted to make sure that it was immaculately prepared as a way to show Jarda that he loved him. Mira spent all day with a bucket of hot soapy water and rags cleaning the bike. When it was spotless, he wheeled it into the garage and covered it with a tarp to keep it clean, waiting for the day that Jarda would take it out and ride.

To catch the train, Mira would have to leave the house at 4 a.m. the next day. After dinner, he kissed his parents goodnight and went up to bed. He tossed and turned all night knowing he would never see them again. He worried that they were going to suffer for the actions he was about to take; not only would they miss him and worry about him, but there was a real chance that they could be arrested and interrogated, maybe even imprisoned. Then he thought, "Aren't they already imprisoned? Isn't the whole country one massive prison? If I can escape, maybe I can tell the world about this awful government and help keep other countries from falling to the Soviets."

Mira intended to get up quietly and leave the house without waking his parents, but when he woke up at 3 a.m., there were cooking noises coming from the kitchen and the house was filled with a wonderful smell. Mira packed his bag and came downstairs to see his mother busy at work making Mira's favorite dish, wiener schnitzel. She carefully lifted each golden-brown cutlet out of the bubbling oil, setting it on a bed of white paper to drain. When she was finished cooking, she took four of the cutlets and wrapped each one carefully in white butcher paper Then she bundled the cutlets into a package tied up with string and handed it to Mira, saying, "I don't want you to get hungry on the train."

Mira hugged his mother and accepted the package. He checked his watch and saw that it was almost 4 a.m. and said, "I guess it's time for me to go."

"Let me get my coat. I'll walk with you to the station."

They left the house together and walked along the deserted road toward the station. The snow was only a few inches deep, but it was fresh and there were no tracks. The night was still and quiet; the only movement came from the falling snow. They made small talk about the houses they passed and the people living inside them. They said nothing important, just enjoying each other's company. They reached the station, and Mira kissed Maria's cheek goodbye. He held back the tears until he was on the train, and then he let them roll down his face in silent streams. He found his seat and looked out the window. He was surprised to see Maria still standing on the platform. She had never done that before. She was much too pragmatic to waste time standing on a train platform waiting for the train to leave, yet here she was standing patiently in the snow. As soon as the train started to move, she raised her hand above her head and began a long slow wave. Mira waved back. They locked eyes and kept waving until the station disappeared into the night.

On March 5, 1953, the entire communist world was shocked by the sudden death of Soviet dictator Joseph Stalin. President Gottwald flew to Moscow to take part in the funeral and, more important, to curry favor with Stalin's successor, Nikita Khrushchev.[2] On March 9, shortly after returning from Stalin's funeral, Gottwald collapsed. He lingered in a coma for five days and died on March 14.[3] He was only fifty-six years old. For Mira, the change in leadership meant nothing. He believed that the entire communist system was corrupt and it did not matter who was at the top of government.

Early on the morning of Sunday, March 22, Mira was in the pilots' ready room at Prague-Ruzyne Airport preparing to fly from Prague to Copenhagen. He was scheduled to take off at 8 a.m., fly to Copenhagen, and return home to Prague by 4 p.m. that same day.

Sunday morning was a slow time for CSA and the ready room was nearly empty, just a few young pilots in dark blue uniforms discussing their routes for the day as well as their hoped-for conquests for the evening. The room smelled of coffee and cigarettes as the pilots drank from large white mugs and chain smoked. Cigarette smoke hung in bluish clouds over each pilot. There was a heavy black Bakelite phone hanging on the wall. It rang with a shrill metallic clang. The pilot nearest the phone picked it up and listened, then called out. "Hey Slovak! There's a call for you."

Mira made his way to the phone. It was odd that anyone would call him in the ready room, especially at such an early hour. "I hope nothing's wrong with my father," he thought as he picked up the phone.

"This is Captain Slovak," Mira said, as he put the handset to his ear.

A muffled voice said, "Miroslav, the Secret Police know about Picnic!" and the line clicked dead.

That was it, a five-second conversation that left Mira's heart pounding and his pulse racing. He slumped against the wall with the handset still against his ear, saying "Hello? Hello?" in the vain hopes that somebody would come back on the line and tell him it was a joke. There was something familiar about the voice. Something in the way the voice had mispronounced his name, stretching the "o" sound just a second too long, making it sound like "Mirooslov". He knew he had heard it before, yet the identity was just out of reach, dancing in the corner of his memory. He looked around the ready room, his eyes searching for Honza. He was not there. He looked at the door, half expecting to see a group of men wearing the green trench coats of the StB come bursting through the door carrying machine guns. "What should I do?" he thought. "Who can I talk to?" Mira watched the door for several more seconds and realized that no one was rushing in to arrest him. For the moment, he was safe. He was scheduled to fly to Copenhagen in less than an hour, and if he was not arrested before the flight took off, he could defect once he got on the ground in Copenhagen. He knew that he would feel safer once he was airborne. He quickly grabbed his coat, put on his captain's hat, and headed for his plane.

The flight to Copenhagen was uneventful. Once he was on the ground and cleared customs, Mira had an important decision to make. He knew that he was safe and he could simply walk out of the airport, catch a taxi to the U.S. Embassy, and ask for asylum, but what would happen to Honza, Hanna, Helmut, and the twenty-three other souls who were counting on him to carry them to freedom? Mira feared that his co-conspirators would be rounded up, tried, and sentenced to immediate execution, or worse yet, to be worked to death in the brutal Jáchymov uranium mine near the German border. Mira paced the corridors of the Kastrup Airport, struggling with his conscience. Eventually, he realized that he had no choice but to return to Czechoslovakia and do everything in his power to get "picnic" moving quickly and everybody out of the country before the StB made its move.

Returning to Prague that afternoon was one of the most stressful flights of Mira's life. He had no idea what would happen when he landed. Would he be stopped and arrested? Would he be beaten like Roberto? Would he be shot? After landing, he parked the plane at the gate and watched his passengers deplane. When all the passengers were gone, Mira took a deep breath, stood up, and left the plane. Nothing happened. There were no police, no guards, nothing unusual. He walked across the apron to the terminal, went inside, and made his way to Airlines Operations. He picked up his orders for the next week. They were printed in blue ink on red teletype paper that was as thin as tissue. The paper was so thin that pilots called these orders "flimsies." He and Honza were scheduled to fly together for two flights to Brno the next day. The first one was early in the morning, and the second was OK-300, with a 7.30 p.m. departure. That flight would carry the newspaper plates and the extra fuel. He checked the weather. It would be a clear, cloudless sky with a bright moon. Walking through the airport, he found a pay phone. He dropped in a coin and dialed Helmut's number.

"Hello?" Helmut answered.

"Hello," said Mira "Does tomorrow look like a good day for a picnic?"

"Yes," replied Helmut, "Tomorrow should be a perfect day for a picnic!"

Mira hung up without saying anything more. He was not sure what the StB was going to do. They would probably not arrest him at the airport now. They might grab him at his apartment, or more likely, they would wait until the plane was full and ready for takeoff and then grab him, all the conspirators, and the twenty-three members of the underground too.

It was a few minutes after 5 p.m. on the 22nd, and the following day's first flight left at 8 a.m. He had fifteen hours to kill. He did not want to go back to his apartment and spend the night lying awake waiting for the StB to knock down the door and drag him away. He decided to take a train out of Prague so he could disappear for a few hours. Whenever Mira flew, he carried his pilot's overnight bag, so he always had a change of clothes with him. Before he left the airport, he slipped into one of the water closets and changed out of his uniform into civilian clothes. Feeling slightly less conspicuous, he boarded a bus that would take him across town to the train station, switching buses twice to make sure he was not being followed.

When he arrived at the station, there was a train leaving for Kralupy nad Vlatvou, where Mira had taken his glider training in 1947. He took the last seat in an empty car at the rear of the train, positioning himself so that he could see the whole aisle in his car and into the next car too. That way, he would have plenty of warning if he saw the police coming. He was not sure what he would do; jumping from a moving train did not sound smart, but it was better than being arrested and tortured. He slumped against the seat, pretending to be asleep, but keeping one eye open to watch for the StB. When he arrived in Kralupy nad Vltavou, he left the train and walked out into the night. The city was so dark that it reminded him of the blackouts during World War II. There were almost no cars on the street and very few street lights. With virtually nothing to sell, most of the shops were closed. Eventually, Mira came to a movie theater. When he saw the name of the movie in huge black letters on the marquee, he let out a nervous laugh. It was *Unos*, Czech for "Hijack." After the mass defection of CSA pilots in 1951, the Communist government had ordered noted Czechoslovakian filmmaker Jan Kadar to produce a dramatization of the fate that awaited the CSA pilots once they arrived in the West. The film had just been released in January 1953 and was playing all across the country. Mira thought, "Well, let's see what I'm in for." He pulled out his wallet, paid for his ticket, and went into the theater.

The moody black-and-white film used ominous music and stark lighting to tell how the escaping pilots were used as puppets by the immoral American government until they outlived their usefulness and were imprisoned in bleak concentration camps. Mira told himself that this was just a propaganda film and that he should not let it influence him, but as he watched, his apprehension began to build. In fact, he started to have second thoughts, "My God!" he thought, "here I am about to do the same thing and maybe that is what is going to happen to me." Leaving the theater in a daze, he walked deep into the chilly night and eventually came to the conclusion that the film was just communist propaganda, not to be taken too seriously.

It was 10 p.m. when Mira caught the next train back to Prague, and rode a streetcar back to his apartment. Arriving at 1 a.m., he approached his apartment building cautiously, keeping to the shadows. He looked carefully for any signs of the StB but did not see a soul. He unlocked the door. The apartment was empty. Honza was apparently spending the night with one of his many girlfriends. Without turning a light on, Mira got into bed and laid down in the dark. The gray flickering images of Jan Kadar's melodramatic film kept passing before his eyes. He may have slept, but if so, it was only for a few moments between 5 a.m. and 6 a.m.

Sometime during the night, there had been a light dusting of snow. Mira awoke to a crisp cold winter morning. Prague was frosted with a powdered sugar coating of white. He got out of bed and fixed a simple breakfast of coffee and a hard roll, put on a clean uniform, and repacked his overnight bag. As much as he wanted to take special mementos, he knew that he could not. If he were stopped and searched, the bag had to appear perfectly normal—no extra money, no extra clothing, no photos of his family, nothing that would give away his true intention.

He locked the door and stepped out into the chilly morning, saying a silent farewell to the apartment and all it contained. He caught a bus to the airport. By 7 a.m., Mira was in the pilots' ready room talking with Honza about their first flight to Brno, which would leave at 8 a.m.

There was an unexpected complication. The Chinese government of Mao Tse-tung had sent a delegation of engineers to Czechoslovakia to study Czech industrial techniques, and they would be onboard the morning flight to Brno. Mira and Honza were asked to host the visiting Chinese and give them a tour of Brno's Textile and Engineering Trade Fair facilities. Inwardly, Mira breathed a sigh of relief. The StB would not dare approach him when he was surrounded by Chinese dignitaries. The morning flight to Brno went smoothly and the dignitaries enjoyed their tour.

They arrived back in Prague shortly after 4 p.m. Honza and Mira let all the passengers deplane before they left the cockpit, walked through the cabin, and headed across the apron towards the terminal. When they were halfway between the plane and the terminal with no one near enough to hear, Honza whispered. "Mira, I can't go with you."

Mira felt a wave of panic. “What?”

“I can’t go. My mother is too sick.”

“What are you saying?” Mira asked in shock.

“I’ve given it a lot of thought. I can’t go. I mean I’ll go on the flight, but I won’t stay, I’ll act like I’m a loyal Communist and I’ll ask them to send me back.”

Mira’s mind was racing. “This won’t work. The StB will arrest you.”

“No, I’ve got it all figured out. Everything goes ahead as planned. When you take over the plane, I’ll pretend to fight you. You have to hit me once really good, and I’ll pretend that you’ve knocked me out. The other crew members will see the fight and vouch for me. I’ll be fine. My mother has cancer; I don’t think she has much longer to live. I’ll stay with her until she goes, then I’ll escape later.” Nothing about Honza’s story made sense, but it was too late to call off the escape. The other conspirators had already booked their flights and were heading to the airport.

“I can’t believe that you are doing this. I could have slipped away to the U.S. Embassy in Copenhagen anytime I wanted to but you said you needed my help.”

“Mirooslav,” Honza said, “Don’t make it sound like …” Mira did not hear the rest of what Honza was saying. The way Honza had just said, “Mirooslav” sounded just like the voice on the phone.

“It was you!” Mira said accusingly. “You’re the voice on the phone!”

“Don’t be ridiculous, Mira. It couldn’t have been me. I was flying to Bratislava at the time.”

Mira nodded in agreement but inwardly he thought, “I never told Honza what time the call came in, so how could he know where he was when I got it?” A mechanic approached to ask Mira about the plane, and Honza used the distraction to break off the conversation and walk to the terminal.

Mondays were hectic at Prague-Ruzyne airport. The busy airport handled more than twenty-five flights from all across Europe. Many flight crews met in the terminal dining room to grab a meal and a quick drink before their flights.

Sitting by himself in the dining room, Mira tried to force down a few bites of dinner while he struggled with the news that Honza had given him. He wondered if Honza was with the StB. Had Honza been subjected to the same horrors in prison as Roberto? Had they forced him to become a spy for the StB? Had he just set Mira up in an ambush that would land him in front of a firing squad?

Mira had been a pilot long enough to trust his instincts, and his instincts told him that Honza would never do anything to hurt him. He made up his mind. He was going to go through with it. He continued to the ready room and checked on his plane. He was relieved to confirm that he was carrying the newspaper plates and the extra fuel that came with them. He checked the passenger manifest and saw Helmut, Hanna, and one other name he recognized. It was Bozidar Medic, a television engineer who had replaced Jan Furchgot in the plot a few weeks ago. Mira looked at the rest of the names and wondered how many of the underground's mysterious twenty-three escapees had made it on board. Who were they? Why were they escaping? Well, Mira concluded, he would have all his answers in a few hours.

Finally, the CSA weatherman gave Mira a briefing. The weather was currently clear, cold, and dry all across Eastern Europe, but a warm, moist front rolling in from the Atlantic would bring dense fog later in the evening. It was now almost 7 p.m. and time for Mira to head to his plane. Tonight, he would be flying an eight-year-old DC-3 with the call sign OK-WDZ.

He picked up his bags and headed for security. Everyone flying in a communist country, including pilots and crew, had to go through security screening, where they were searched for guns. In communist-controlled Czechoslovakia, only Party members were allowed to own guns, but even they could not be trusted to carry their weapons on board an airliner. The pilots were not trusted either, so an ingenious system was devised where party members could carry their guns up to the security checkpoint, then they would empty their guns and place the ammunition clips in their pockets. The empty guns were collected in a canvas bag and given to the pilot. Once the plane had reached its destination, the pilot would return the guns to the party members, and the party members would reload their guns. That way, the guns, ammunition, and party members would all reach their destination together, but at no time were the pilots or party members in a position to take control of the plane.

Mira breezed through security and the gate agent handed him a bag containing five pistols. That meant that there were five Communist Party members on the flight. Mira took the bag thinking, "Boy, are these Party bigwigs going to be surprised when they find out that they are heading to the West!"

Mira hurried to catch up with the rest of his crew as they walked to the plane. That night's crew was Captain Miroslav Slovak, Co-Pilot Honza Dolezal, Radio Operator Jaraslov Hendrich, and Flight Engineer Bohumil Lukousky.

Slovak, Dolezal, and Hendrich boarded the plane and headed to the cockpit to start their preflight checklists. Flight Engineer Lukousky stayed outside, walking around the plane doing a visual inspection for anything that might cause a problem.

Mira sat in the left seat, Honza took the right seat, and Hendrich settled into a small compartment lined with radio gear immediately behind Honza on the right side of the plane. Lukousky finished his inspection and entered the cockpit to take his place on the jump seat between Mira and Honza. Mira stood up and announced, "I'm going to take one more walk around myself." It was clearly the captain's prerogative to make a final inspection of the plane, but Lukousky could not help but feel a bit like his captain doubted his ability. He said nothing as Mira squeezed past him.

Mira was met with a blast of cold night air as he stepped out of the warm plane. He walked quickly behind the plane, and once he was out of sight of anyone in the plane or terminal, he ran toward the chain-link fence that stretched between the main terminal and the hangars to the south. There was a spot on the floodlit fence where a broken light bulb cast several feet into deep shadows. Even more conveniently, there were a few tall shrubs along the darkened section of fence. Once Mira reached the fence, he slipped behind one of the shrubs and stuck the pointed toe of his shoe into one of open links and quickly scaled the eight-foot barrier. Using one of the anchoring posts to help him climb down the other side, he landed softly and took a second to adjust his uniform and catch his breath. He now walked confidently through a side door of the terminal. Once inside, he hurried down to a basement locker where he had stashed three pistols. One was his and the others belonged to two CSA pilots who had loaned them to Mira. He tucked the guns into his jacket pockets and headed back to the fence. He quickly scaled it and began to walk briskly back toward his plane. He had only gone a few steps when a voice behind him barked, "Stop! Who are you? Where are you going?"

Mira turned to see a guard pointing an Sa-23 submachine gun at him. Seeing that the guard was a civilian and knowing that the communists were scrupulously obedient to the military, Mira took an imperious tone and barked back, "I am Captain Miroslav Slovak and I am an instructor for the Czechoslovakian Aero Club, and I am checking on our operations here!"

Mira was still in the shadows, and it was unlikely that the guard could distinguish between Mira's airline captain's uniform and an actual Air Force uniform, but the tone of Mira's voice was enough that the poor guard accepted his story, apologized, and let him go.

Mira hurried back to his plane and scrambled on board just before the first passengers arrived. He returned to the cockpit, and while the rest of the crew was busy attending to their preflight details, he slipped one gun into his pocket and the others into an opening in the upholstery directly behind his seat. He sat down, buckled his canvas seatbelt, and began his preflight check list, going through dozens of items—landing gear pins, which Honza confirmed were onboard; control locks, which had been removed and stowed; and circuit breakers, hydraulic quantity, and hydraulic pressure, all of which had been checked. On and on they went until more than 100 different items had been named and checked. With the checklist completed, Mira asked Honza to call the tower for permission to start the engines.

Honza keyed the microphone and said, "Prague-Ruzyne tower, this is Czechoslovakian Airlines Flight three zero zero requesting permission to start engines."

"Negative," was the tower's shocking response. "Please stand by. Do not start your engines. We have a special message for you."

Mira panicked. He was tempted to ignore the tower's instruction and make a run for it. After a moment's clear thinking, Mira realized that would not work. He knew that the instant he tried to start the engines, the crew would oppose him. He tried to project an outward appearance of nonchalance while inside, his mind was visualizing a dark green military truck roaring out of the night to block the plane's path, the canvas sides of the truck spilling open, and a swarm of submachine gun-toting guards pouring out to surround the plane and drag him off to prison. After five minutes, Mira casually asked Honza to call the tower again. Again, the tower responded, "Do not start your engines. We have received a message from the military. They are heading to your position. Please stand by."

Mira felt his blood pressure surge. He knew it was over. He looked at Honza with anger. It all seemed clear now. Honza must have sold him out. Still, there was nothing he could do. The conspirators had all agreed that they needed guns to take over the plane, but they were never going to shoot anyone in the hijacking. They would wave the guns around. They would threaten, but they would never shoot.

Five more minutes passed. Mira's heart was pounding; sweat was dripping down his back. He stared out through the windscreen trying to see what was happening in the darkness that was keeping him from starting the plane. One more time Mira asked Honza to call the tower. "Prague-Ruzyne this is Czechoslovakian Airlines Flight three zero zero requesting permission to start our engines."

This time, the response was shorter and it sounded angry. "Negative. Stand by."

Ten more minutes passed, and then to Miroslav's disbelieving eyes, his worst nightmare seemed to materialize right in front of him. He watched helplessly through the cockpit windows. Out of the darkness, a green military truck pulled up and blocked the plane's path. Five uniformed guards with submachine guns leapt out of the back of the truck and took up positions surrounding the plane. An airline agent rushed toward the plane. Mira gasped in shock, "My God, this is it!"

The agent pounded on the door. The flight engineer hurried to open it. The agent bounded up the steps and burst into the cockpit. "Captain Slovak," the out-of-breath agent gasped. "Would you please do the Air Force a favor? They have a special shipment that is needed urgently in Brno. I know that you are slightly overloaded but it is most urgent that the Air Force receive this shipment."

Mira felt an overwhelming sense of relief, "Yes, I will take it, even though we are overweight."

With the mysterious military cargo on board and Mira's heart beating so hard he could hardly breath, the tower finally gave CSA flight 300 permission to start its engines.

With his voice raspy from stress, Mira gave the order for Lukousky to engage the starters. Slovak opened the throttle to 1,000 rpm and the right engine coughed, whined, and roared to life. Lukousky pressed the left switch and the left engine clunked, banged, and sprang to life. With each engine putting out 1,200 hp, Mira released the parking brake and taxied CSA flight 300 into position for a southwest takeoff on runway twenty-two. As the plane swung into position Honza radioed, "Flight three zero zero ready for takeoff."

Mira began his final pre-takeoff checks. He reset the parking brake, pulled the control column back almost to his chest, and asked Lukousky to advance the throttles to 2,000 rpm. With the engines roaring, Lukousky adjusted the magneto, fuel mixture, and carburetor heat settings. When Mira was satisfied that everything was working properly, he placed his hands on the twin throttle knobs and pushed them forward to 3,000 rpm; at the same time, he released the brakes.

Mira's DC-3 had polished aluminum skin and dark blue markings on the nose of the plane that looked like a stylized blue bird, with a long blue tail that swept back under the windows, and blue block letters spelling out "Czechoslovakian Aerolines" above the windows.

The sleek plane sped down the runway, yawing slightly from side to side. At a few moments after 7.30 p.m., the plane reached 70 miles an hour and lifted off the runway. Honza gave Mira a sheepish grin at the less than perfect takeoff. "I guess your mind must have been on something else," Honza teased. After picking up speed to 140 miles an hour and climbing to 5,000 feet, Mira adjusted his course heading to 93 degrees. He hoped that everything looked normal to the ground controllers. Inside the cockpit the flight appeared normal too. The plane sped on through the night as the moon crept over the horizon. The rising full moon was an important part in Mira's plan. Once he and his fellow hijackers were in control of the plane, Mira intended to avoid the Air Force radar by dropping down to treetop level and using the bright moonlight to navigate their way to the border.

Mira turned control of the plane over to Honza and got up from his seat. "I have some friends in back I want to go see, and I might bring them forward for a few minutes." Honza shrugged with disinterest as Mira headed toward the back of the plane.

As he left the cabin he spotted Helmut and Hanna seated together halfway down the aisle on the right side of the plane. He greeted the Cermaks and noted that Bozidar was seated directly across the aisle from Helmut. Mira had only meet Bozidar once before, but was still able to recognize him. Mira spent a few moments of friendly conversation with Helmut, asking him how work at the Skoda Munitions plant was going and why he was heading to Brno. Then, he casually said, "Why don't you fellows come up and see the cockpit?"

"Of course," they answered. Helmut and Bozidar got up and followed Mira forward to the cockpit. Honza, Lukousky, and Hendrich were each too absorbed in their own tasks to notice when Mira closed and locked the cabin door. Quickly slipping his hand behind the loose upholstery, he retrieved the pistols, giving one each to Helmut and Bozidar.

While the radio operator was reporting the plane's position to ground control, Mira eased himself back into the pilot's seat. "I'll take it from here," he casually told Honza. Honza's attention was on the plane's instrument panel, and he nodded agreement without looking up.

Helmut and Bozidar stood shoulder to shoulder at the back of the flight deck, blocking the door. Mira announced, "We're taking control of the plane. Do what we ask you to do and no one will get hurt." Honza was expecting this, but Mira did not know how well he was going to play along. Mira was shocked to see Honza's hand dart to the throttle levers and pull them back toward idle. Mira pushed Honza's hand off the controls and was rewarded with a powerful punch to the jaw. He was stunned. What type of game was Honza playing? Was he faking the fight or was he really trying to stop the hijacking? Mira clenched his fist and made a half-hearted swing that connected with Honza's cheek. Meanwhile, Bozidar and flight engineer Lukousky were fighting each other in earnest.

Mira turned in his seat, distracted by the fight going on just inches behind him. In an instant, Honza made a desperate lunge for the switches above the electrical panel that would feather the propellers. This was a serious threat. If the propeller pitch was lowered beyond a critical point, the plane would stall and begin to fall out of the night sky. Mira felt that the struggle had gone on long enough and he drove a forceful left hook into the side of Honza's skull. Honza went limp and fell back into his seat unconscious. As Bozidar and Lukousky continued to struggle behind him, Mira pulled out his pistol and held it above his head so everyone on the flight deck could see it. "We've got guns! Don't move an inch or I'll blow your head off!"

Helmut pulled his gun. Lukousky pleaded, "Don't shoot. I have a wife and children."

In the radio nook, Hendrich could not see the flight deck and his earphones kept him from hearing the heated exchanges. He did not know what was going on, but he sensed that something was wrong, so he began to tap out an SOS on the plane's emergency Morse code transmitter. Bozidar simply picked up a microphone from the radioman's table and clobbered him on the back of the head with its heavy weighted base. Hendrich sprawled forward unconscious across the radio station.

Per the plan, Mira continued to fly the plane while Helmut and Bozidar tied the crew up and dragged them to the tiny baggage compartment at the back of the flight deck. Bozidar stood guard in front of the baggage compartment with his gun drawn. Helmut slipped into Hendrich's seat and took over the radio and navigational chores. The first thing he did was tune one of the receivers to the frequency that, thanks to Mira's barroom espionage, they knew the MiG-15 pilots used to communicate.

Helmut radioed their position to Prague ground control. Prague acknowledged their position and then passed flight 300 off to Brno ground control. While flight 300 was in the seam between the two ground-control centers, Mira turned off all exterior navigational lights. Then he disengaged the autopilot and began a rapid descent from 5,000 to 500 feet. On the way down, he changed course from 93 to 273 degrees and headed towards the West German border.

At 7.45 p.m., Helmut reported that they had dropped off ground control radar and that both Prague and Brno were calling for them. A few minutes later, they flew past the historic city of Pilsen. A sharp-eyed observer from the ground must have called in their location and direction because almost instantly, Helmut called out, "They're sending MiGs up after us."

"Now the race is on!" thought Mira. Pilsen was only about 25 miles east of the West German border. At his current speed, Mira figured that he would reach the border in fifteen minutes. He knew that the high-speed MiG-15s flying out of Pilsen Line could reach the border in about fifteen minutes as well. If luck was on his side, Mira thought he would be safely across the border before the MiGs found him.

A sudden pounding on the door reminded the conspirators that they still had a planeload of passengers. "Block the door with your body so they can't force it," Mira yelled, "and find out what they want."

Bozidar did as he was instructed. Mira heard an angry voice asking, "Hey, you're a civilian, what are you doing in the cockpit?"

"Tell him you're a friend of Captain Slovak and he invited you to watch him fly the plane." Mira said.

The angry communist yelled, "Why did we turn around?"

"Tell him that Brno is fogged in and we have been ordered to return to Prague." Mira looked out the cockpit window at the clear night and doubted that the angry passenger would accept the bogus explanation, but to Mira's shock and surprise, the passenger returned to his seat.

Mira continued to fly as close to the ground as he dared. He knew that the Czech Air Force radar had difficulty with ground clutter below 500 feet and might not be able to distinguish between the plane and the hills and buildings it was skimming above. If ground control could not pinpoint his location, the MiGs would have to depend on the pilot's eyesight to locate the fleeing airliner. Honza continued to monitor the MiGs' radio transmissions and report their progress. A few minutes before 8 p.m., Helmut announced ominous news. "Captain, the MiGs are scrambling their messages!" Mira knew this could only mean one thing. The MiGs had spotted them and were preparing to attack.

The MiG-15 was an extremely fast plane, capable of speeds close to supersonic. The fully loaded DC-3 was, by airplane standards, very slow. Mira knew that the MiGs became unstable at low speed and in fact would stall at about 130 knots. He also knew that the MiGs were prohibited from flying below 500 feet. So if he continued to fly very low and very slow, he set up a difficult targeting problem for the MiG pilots. The MiGs would have to set up their attack from high and to the rear. The pilots had to be able to pick out a dark target moving against the dark earth, calculate a dive angle that would allow their high-speed fighters to intercept the slow, ground-hugging airliner, squeeze off a few shots from the guns mounted in the nose of the plane, and then break off before they dropped below 500 feet. While it may have been a difficult scenario for the MiG pilots, Mira knew they were up to the task. Just two weeks earlier, on March 10, a patrol of MiGs from Pilsen had come across two USAF F-84 Thunderjets that had strayed across the border from West Germany. The MiGs attacked and shot down one of the planes while the other scooted back across the border. The U.S. pilot parachuted to safety.

There is a small Plexiglas bubble in the ceiling of a DC-3, right above the navigator's station. It allows the navigator to take sightings on the stars to help navigate at night. Helmut now stood with his head in the navigator's bubble and looked toward the rear of the plane and narrated what he saw. "There are MiG-15s chasing us! They're sweeping in from 5 o'clock! They're on our tail!"

Mira kept his eyes straight ahead. He knew that from where he sat there was no way he could see what was going on behind him and regardless of what crisis was playing out in the night sky, he had to fly the plane. That was the mantra that had been drilled into him in flight school: "Aviate, Navigate, and Communicate," meaning that whatever is going on around you, you must always fly the plane, keep track of where you are, and when possible stay in touch with the ground. The moment you stop flying the plane to pay attention to anything else, the plane will be doomed. Mira waited to see glowing tracers flash past the cockpit windshield or to feel the thud of bullets striking the plane. Neither happened. Somehow, the DC-3 must have crossed the invisible border into West Germany, and the MiGs had broken off their attack. Mira thought that maybe the incident with the F-84 being shot down for violating Czech airspace made the MiG pilots cautious about getting too close to West German airspace, knowing that the USAF was anxious for payback.

Mira climbed back to a normal cruising altitude. At the same time, he instructed Helmut to tune the radio to 121.5 megacycles (the international frequency that is monitored by all air stations at all times) and began broadcasting in English, "We are a Czechoslovakian airliner escaping from Communist Czechoslovakia. We have refugees on board and are seeking asylum. This is our only purpose."

By this time, the scene on the ground was changing. Electricity was tightly rationed in Czechoslovakia, and homes and businesses turned off their lights at night. From the air, West Germany was strewn with bright lights and neon signs. There was no way the five loyal communists that were on board could believe that they were still over Soviet-controlled Czechoslovakia.

Helmut contacted Rhein-Main ground control and had been given a heading of 255 degrees. Just as he was relaying this information to Mira, there was banging against the cockpit door, followed by cries of "Open up!" The loyal communists were attempting to break down the door. When the conspirators did not respond, one of the loyalists slammed his shoulder forcefully into the door. The flimsy door started to give. Mira worried that one more good run at it and the loyalists might succeed in breaking in.

Mira called to Helmut and Bozidar, "Hold on tight!" Then he pushed the control column roughly forward, putting the plane into a perilously steep dive. Moments later, he pulled back on the stick to slam the plane violently into a steep climb. The five loyalists went tumbling to the back of the plane. After a few seconds, Mira nosed the plane into another fierce dive, slamming the communists forward against the cockpit bulkhead, then another quick climb, sending them sailing to the back of the plane again. On Mira's last dive forward, the stress and flex of the plane caused the baggage compartment door to fly open at the exact instant that Bozidar lost the grip on his pistol and dropped it. Unbelievably, the pistol bounced right into the baggage compartment. When Mira pulled up, the pistol came skidding out again and Bozidar picked it up before the dazed prisoners realized what was happening.

Mira knew that the passengers must be terrified, but he trusted that anyone that was seated and wearing a seat belt would come through the wild ride unscathed. Only the people that were standing, trying to break into the cockpit, would be at risk. Mira returned to level flight and set the heading for Frankfurt.

Before Mira could even think of relaxing, Helmut announced, "We have company." Looking out the cockpit window, Mira saw two USAF F-84 Thunderjets 50 yards off the wing tips on either side of the plane. The moon was bright enough that Mira could see clearly into the cockpits of the F-84s. The pilot on his right was wearing a gray rubber oxygen mask and a white helmet with red lightning bolts. The Thunderjets kept pace with the airliner for a while longer, and once they were confident that it really was an escaping airliner, they peeled off and disappeared into the night.

Mira asked Helmut to contact the tower at Rhein-Main Air Force base and confirm that their request for asylum had been granted. The tower responded, "I'm just a corporal and I don't have the authority to offer asylum. I've been unsuccessful in reaching my commanding officer, so I recommend that you land on the civilian side of the airport and request asylum from the West Germans."[2]

The conspirators had already decided that they would not risk turning themselves over to the West Germans, so they set a new course for London's Heathrow Airport. Shortly after they changed headings, Helmut passed more bad news on to Mira: "Heathrow is reporting zero-zero and is closed to all traffic." Zero-zero is an aviation term that describes fog so heavy that there is no visibility in either vertical or horizontal directions.

Mira shook his head and said, "Very well then, let's try for the emergency field at Manston." The field at Manston was built on the chalk cliffs overlooking the English Channel. During World War II, it had been the closest RAF airfield to the front lines, and countless damaged planes, struggling to stay aloft after being shot up in Europe, made their way across the Channel for emergency landings at Manston.

The crew of OK-WDZ was beginning to run out of options. They still had enough fuel to reach Manston, but once they committed to flying across the English Channel, they did not have enough fuel to come back and land anywhere on the European mainland. So if Manston was fogged in by the time they arrived, they would have no other choice but to try landing in the dense fog.

While Mira was changing the course to head to Manston, the loyal communists made another run at the door. Again, Mira slammed the plane through a series of dives and climbs, hoping that he was forceful enough to discourage the loyalists but not so rough as to injure any of the other passengers. It was now almost 10.15 p.m. The hijackers had flown clear across Germany and were over the city of Liege, Belgium, heading toward the English Channel. They would soon be approaching the point of no return, where lack of fuel would commit them to a landing in the UK.

Helmut let out a jubilant cheer and reported good news to Mira. The persistent corporal at Rhein-Main Air Base had located the base commander and had been instructed to "get that plane down here!"

Mira asked Helmut to ask the corporal to confirm that if they landed at Rhein-Main, they would be granted asylum. The corporal said, "Yes sir."

Mira banked the plane, heading back to Frankfurt, but the defectors were not out of the woods yet. They faced two more obstacles that were as dangerous as anything they had confronted so far. The first obstacle was the weather; fog was now blanketing most of Western Europe, and the longer they were in the air, the thicker the fog was getting. Rhein-Main Airbase did have radar and was capable of providing Mira with a ground control approach (GCA), a landing system where an observer on the ground, watching radar, guides an airplane with limited visibility down to a safe landing. It is a fairly common procedure, but to be successful, the pilot needs to be able to communicate accurately with the controller, and that was the second problem. Mira spoke three languages—Czech, German, and Slovakian—but the young American ground controller only spoke English, so the two could not communicate directly. To complicate matters, Mira had never made a GCA before.

Helmut had flown for the RAF during World War II, so he spoke English and offered to translate, but working as fast as he could, there would still be a ten-second delay between the controller's command and Mira getting the message. The approach speed for landing a DC-3 is 85 knots. At that speed, a plane can travel almost 1,500 feet in ten seconds. For a pilot trying to set his airliner down on a precise spot on a dark night in dense fog, 1,500 feet is a long way. It was going to be a difficult landing.

About fifteen minutes out from Frankfurt, the controller asked Mira to make his "identification turns." This is a process where the controller watches his radar screen and asks the pilot to change headings first one way, then another. If the blip on the radar makes the exact turns the controller requested, he knows that he is watching the correct plane. With the identification turns out of the way, Mira brought OK-WDZ down to 1,500 feet. At this altitude, he was still in the bright moonlight but skimming across the surface of the thick fog bank. The undulating fog looked like a strange unknown world. Mira realized that for him, it really was a foreign world underneath the fog. He had no idea what awaited him. Would he be arrested and sent back to Czechoslovakia? Would he go to America? Mira pushed the control yoke forward. The tips of the spinning propellers dipped into the fog, and he began his descent.

Pilots prefer to land facing into the wind, so planes getting ready to land travel on a "downwind leg," where they fly parallel to the runway but continue well past the runway's end. In a typical landing pattern, the downwind leg is followed by the "base leg," where the plane turns 90 degrees and is then perpendicular to the runway (but significantly downwind) and begins its descent. As the plane approaches the center line of the runway, the controller calls for another 90-degree turn, which lines the plane up on the center of the runway and places the plane on "final approach."

Shrouded in the fog, Mira had to trust the ground controller totally. The downwind leg went smoothly as Mira descended to 1,000 feet. He went through his approach checklist: ignition, altimeter, mixture, fuel, static selectors, and dozens of other items. With the checklist complete, he closed the cowl flaps to protect the engine from the cold, moist air he was flying into. Finally, he lowered and locked the landing gear and extended his wing flaps. At the ground controller's command, Mira banked the DC-3 90 degrees onto the base leg. He slipped to 500 feet. A moment later, he turned onto the final approach and descended through the gloom towards the field.

At 100 feet above the earth, the plane slid out of the fog. Instead of the well-lit runway Mira was expecting to see, he was shocked to see that he was flying over a narrow highway and headed straight for the side of a huge military hangar at 85 knots. Reacting quickly, Mira pulled back on the control column and shoved the throttles forward. The engines howled as the heavy plane clawed its way back into the night, clearing the hangar by inches. As Mira climbed back to 1,500 feet, he knew exactly what had gone wrong. The English-to-Czech translation had caused a delay, and OK-WDZ had stayed on the base leg of the pattern too long. When Mira turned onto final approach, he was not on the center line of the runway. At best, he was about 1,000 feet to the south, heading right into the hangars. The short final approach that the GCA had placed him on did not give ground control enough time to tell Helmut that they had flown past the runway and let Helmut translate the message to Mira. Mira told Helmut to ask the tower for a much longer approach to make sure that there would be plenty of time to make corrections as they came down through the fog.

On the second attempt everything went perfectly, and at 11.45 p.m., Frankfurt time, four hours and fifteen minutes after leaving Prague, OK-WDZ made a flawless landing at the Rhein-Main USAF base. As the plane rolled to the end of the runway, a U.S. Military Police jeep that had been speeding down the runway parallel to the plane pulled ahead and flashed its lights, indicating that Mira should follow. The jeep led the plane to the center of a circle of Police jeeps and fire trucks. A flight lineman with a glowing flashlight in each hand directed Mira to park the plane and shut off the engines.

Mira was exhausted and emotionally spent. He did not even have the strength to set the parking brake or go through the usual cooling-down process with the engines. He simply reached out and pulled the throttles back to cutoff, and then switched off the fuel pumps and magnetos. As the big engines began to wind down, Mira slumped over the control column.

Helmut rushed out of the cockpit and ran down the aisle past the stunned communists to open the cabin door and greet the U.S. MPs. As the MPs stepped through the door, Helmut hurried to Hanna and hugged her shouting, "We made it! We made it! We are free. WE ARE FREE!"

Mira was too exhausted to join in the celebration. His thoughts were with his mother and father and Jiřinka back in Czechoslovakia. "Yes, I have my freedom, but at what cost? To never again see my parents, my family, or the woman I love? Is it worth it?" Once more, the anger and outright hatred of communism surged through Mira and he thought, "Of course Helmut is happy. He brought his wife with him. He left nothing behind. I've brought nothing with me and I've left everything behind."

Military police were waiting to escort Mira off the plane. The red flashing lights of the fire trucks reflected off the plane's aluminum skin as the fog closed in. Mira stood up, hung his headset over the control column, put on his captain's hat, and left the flight deck for the last time.[3]

13

Apples in Winter: Frankfurt, 1953

The American military police wore brown uniforms with wide white belts and black armbands emblazoned with white letters that said "MP." They carried Colt .45 automatics in white holsters. The guards with Mira had stern looks on their faces as they escorted him out of the cockpit. As they walked past Lukousky, he hissed, "You bastard! You didn't tell us! My wife is back in Prague!"

Mira stared stoically ahead as the MPs led him off the plane and across the field. Mira stopped and said in Czech, "I'd like to inspect my plane." The MPs looked at each other, not understanding what Mira had asked. Mira pointed at the plane and then used his fingers to make a walking gesture in a circle. The two guards smiled and nodded. Mira walked towards the plane that was sitting quietly like an obedient dog waiting for its master. Mira was curious to see if there were any bullet holes from the MiGs. He circled the plane, hearing an occasional tick or pop as the hot engines began to cool in the chilly German night. Mira slid his hand along the smooth metal of the fuselage. He did not see any bullet holes but he did see something dark caught in the tail wheel. He got on his knees and crawled under the plane. Twisted in the wheel was a broken branch from a linden tree that offered proof that he really did escape at treetop level. Mira did not know when or where he picked up the branch, but he shuddered to think what would have happened if he had been just a few feet lower.

With Mira's inspection complete, the MPs led him to a waiting car, where he was offered a hot cup of coffee and introduced to a tall, stocky man with short-cropped hair and thick glasses. He was named Nicky Morris and he worked for the U.S. Counter Intelligence Corps. Morris spoke a unique brand of Czech that Mira would eventually learn was Czech with a heavy Texas accent. Morris asked Mira if he was hungry. Mira suddenly realized that he had not eaten a full meal in over twenty-four hours. He nodded in agreement.

Morris reached into his coat pocket and pulled out a strange bundle of purple paper and handed it to Mira, who carefully unwrapped the paper and found that he was holding a red crisp apple. He took a bite and let the sweet juices fill his mouth. At this time of year, there was no fresh fruit in Communist Czechoslovakia. People considered themselves lucky to find a few shriveled potatoes or turnips in the stores, but here in the West, at the tail end of a long cold winter, on a dark foggy runway in the middle of the night, an American with a Texas accent had just handed him the sweetest, ripest, most perfect apple he had ever tasted—what an amazing magical journey he was beginning. As he ate the apple, Mira began to believe that maybe, just maybe, things were going to work out all right for him in the West.

Morris and two of the MPs took Mira to a sparse room with a bed and a sink. "You need to sleep," Morris told Mira. "We're going to post two MPs outside your room tonight, but they're here for your protection, not to keep you in. There is a toilet across the hall. Is there anything you need before I go?"

Mira shook his head "No."

"Okay, I'll come back for you in the morning."

"Thank you, Captain Slovak, *dobrou no* (good night)." Morris said as he left the room.

Mira took off his uniform jacket and hung it on a hook; he slipped off his shoes and trousers and sat on the end of the bed to collect his jumbled thoughts. He realized that he was safe from the StB, and that the cruel men in the long green coats could not reach him here. He relaxed for the first time in months. He closed his eyes and instantly fell deeply asleep. When he awoke the next morning, it took him a few moments to remember where he was. He heard voices outside his door talking in English. His foggy head cleared, and he remembered that he had actually gone through with the escape, and he was at a U.S. base in Frankfurt. He dressed quickly from his overnight bag. When he opened the door from his room, the guards were gone, but Nicky Morris was sitting on a folding chair reading a newspaper.

"*Dobre rano* (good morning), Captain Slovak," Morris said as he folded the paper under his arm and stood up. "I hope you slept well. We have a busy day. But first, would you like to get some breakfast?"

Mira was starving. It was now Tuesday morning, and aside from the apple Morris had given him on the airfield, he had hardly eaten anything since Sunday. "I am very hungry," Mira said.

"Good, follow me," said Morris, giving Mira a slap on the back with one of his huge hands. Everything about Morris was bigger, louder, and friendlier than any other person Mira had met.

Mira followed Morris to the officers' mess hall. He was surprised by how big, bright, and clean it was. He took a stainless-steel tray and followed Morris through the food line. They walked past long steaming tables crowded with pans of freshly scrambled eggs, followed by mounds of fried potatoes, bacon, sausage, then pancakes, toast, and jam. The men in line were helping themselves to as much as they wanted. Mira had never seen such generous portions; there were no scowling cooks in dirty aprons ladling skimpy portions onto your tray. You simply took whatever you wanted. After the hot food, there were fruit bowls overflowing with apples, grapes, pears, and bananas. Finally, they came to chilled glasses of orange juice, apple juice, and milk, and urns of steaming hot coffee. Mira had heard that America was a land of plenty; if this first meal was any indication, the stories were true.

Mira followed Morris to a small white Formica-topped table. They sat across from each other. Before they began to eat, Morris folded his hands and bowed his head in a brief moment of prayer. It had been years since Mira had seen anyone say grace over a meal. In communist Czechoslovakia, Catholics had been persecuted, priests were arrested, and open practice of religious beliefs was very dangerous. Morris's easy, almost casual way of expressing his faith brought a lump to Mira throat. When he finished his silent grace, Morris scooped a large portion of eggs onto his fork and said, "So, tell me everything. Why did you do it? Who helped you?"

Mira had spent years living in a land of lies and secrets. It suddenly struck him that since the Nazis took over Czechoslovakia in 1938, he had needed to self-censor everything he said; every word and every sentence had been crafted to come as close to the truth as possible but not offend the Nazis, the Communists, or whomever held power. In an instant, Mira decided that he was done lying to please the authorities. He trusted Morris and wanted to be totally honest with him. He told Morris everything.

After a few hours, Mira was near the end of his story. Morris looked at his watch and said, "Are you ready to become famous? We have a photographer lined up to take photos for the newspapers and I have to warn you, this is going to be a big story." Morris led Mira outside into a chilly Tuesday morning. There was a small group gathered at the front of the building and Mira recognized Helmut, Hanna, and Bozidar. There were two more men that Mira knew were passengers, but he didn't know their names. A photographer in a blue Air Force uniform, holding a large press camera was waving and pointing like a wedding photographer to line up the group. When Mira got closer, the photographer called out, "Here he is now; let's get Captain Slovak in the center next to the girl!"

Once Mira was positioned next to Hanna, there was a loud pop as the flashbulb went off. "Good. Now let's get one more," the photographer said, as he switched plates in the back of the camera and loaded a new flashbulb. Morris was standing to Mira's left, just out of the frame of the photo. Mira turned toward Morris and started to open his mouth to ask Morris why the rest of the escaping passengers were not here for the photo. There was another flash, and the photographer rushed away.

The second photograph, with Mira standing next to Hanna, turning his head to the left with his mouth slightly open, would appear on the front pages of countless newspapers around the world later that night. The U.S. High Commissioner for Germany, former Harvard University president James B. Conant, was reluctant to release the names of the hijackers until they had been investigated and deemed actual defectors, and not Soviet agents, but the papers were clamoring for photos of "The Freedom Six," as they were now being called. Conant also knew that Mira was still an officer in the Czech Air Force and the Czech government could very well consider him a captured combatant. If he allowed a photo of Mira to appear in the papers without clearly identifying him, the Soviets would claim that the U.S. was using photos of POWs for propaganda purposes. Conant's decision was to allow the story to run and the photo to be published, but the only name that could be used by the reporters was Miroslav Slovak. Around the world that night, Mira's name, and only Mira's, was connected with the daring escape to freedom. Set against the backdrop of the Cold War and the virulent anti-communism in the U.S., Mira became an instant celebrity.[1]

As Morris and Mira walked back into the building, Mira asked, "Where was everyone else? The twenty-three passengers that the underground was putting on the plane."

"I'm sorry Miroslav, there aren't any others, just you, Helmut, Hanna, Bozidar, and two passengers."

"Just two passengers?" Mira asked incredulously.

"Yes, those two men that were with you for the photos—Bohumil Suran and Antonin Valejnicek." Mira was stunned. He felt like he had been betrayed, first by Honza, and now by Helmut and the underground. Yet instead of the anger that had been Mira's constant companion for the last several months before the hijacking, Mira was overwhelmed by the urge to laugh. He was free, and he was starting a brand-new life. He shook his head with a gentle chuckle and said, "Well, I guess Helmut really got into my pocket on this", a Czech expression that means, "He took advantage of me."

They walked towards Morris's office. "I'll be moving you to a safe house in Frankfurt tonight." Mira did not recognize the phrase. "A safe house," explained Morris, "is a secret house that we have in the city. It looks just like a normal house, but we have beefed up the security. You will be much safer there then you are here." Mira did not understand how he could be at risk on an American military base. "We are still an occupying army in a conquered country. Our bombers killed countless Germans during the war. But we can't exist without German help. We hire thousands of locals to run the base. Cooks, janitors, gardeners, you name it. And remember, this is still a divided country. So imagine a German woman that is working here as a cook. Maybe she lost her husband to American bombs during the war. Her son was on the Eastern Front and now is stuck in Dresden or Berlin. One day she gets approached by someone who says, 'We can get your son home, if you just put this pill in Captain Slovak's coffee."

"My God! Am I really in danger?"

"Mira, we're at war with the Soviets and it is just as big, and just as real as World War II." Morris paused to look at his watch, "and in about three hours, when today's papers are delivered in the U.S., you will become the face of that war." Morris laid his big hand on Mira's shoulder. "Yes, you are in danger, but it's my job to keep you safe, and Mira, I am very good at my job!"

Getting the defectors to the safe house was a major undertaking. Each one of the conspirators was taken in a separate car to an underground parking garage in downtown Frankfurt. Once inside the garage, the defectors were moved to a second car and asked to lie down in the back seat while the car was driven to a second underground garage and the process would be repeated. Finally, the third car would deliver the escaping Czechs to the safe house. At the safe house, Mira was greeted by a small staff of Czech-speaking agents who were assigned to assist Mira and the other defectors. The director of the house was named Thomas, and his assistant was a strikingly attractive auburn-haired woman named Anna. To the neighbors, Thomas and Anna masqueraded as a husband and wife who ran a small boarding house, but in reality, they were CIA agents running a Cold War safe house.

Morris explained to Mira that he worked for the U.S. military's Counter Intelligence Corps (CIC), but the safe house was run by the civilian Central

Intelligence Agency. As Mira was still a captain in the Czech Air Force, his interrogation would be handled jointly by the CIC and CIA.

The next morning, March 25, the whole complicated car shuffle was repeated as the six conspirators were taken to the Frankfurt offices of the United States High Commissioner for a press conference. As West Germany was still considered an "occupied country," the highest-ranking U.S. diplomat could not be called an ambassador, but was called high commissioner. High Commissioner Conant decided that it was now safe to release the conspirators' names. They were ushered into a large conference room that was crowded with reporters and cameramen. The moment Mira stepped into the room, flashbulbs began to pop. Mira, still wearing his Czech Air Lines uniform, looked down and shielded his eyes from the bright lights with his right hand. The escapees were seated at a long table at the front of the room. Mira sat at the center of the table in front of a collection of microphones, each carrying the large initials of its network—NBC, ABC, CBS, and VOA (Voice of America).

Speaking through an interpreter, the six escapees described their harrowing escape. The reporters directed most of their questions to Mira. He was careful to answer as honestly as he could, with one exception. He really did not know what Honza's story was, and even though it was looking more and more like Honza was working for the StB, Mira protected him during the interview and claimed that "the co-pilot fought hard to prevent me from taking control of the plane."

At one point, Bohumil Suran made the bold statement that "Given the chance, 95 percent of all Czechs would escape to the west." A reporter followed up asking, "If that is true, how come the other twenty-three passengers have asked to be returned to Czechoslovakia?"

Mira said they were going back because "They are worried about reprisals against their families."[2]

At the same time that the press conference was taking place, 3,000 miles away at the United Nations, Soviet Ambassador Andrey Vyshinsky was complainingly loudly that the United States needed to mind its own business and stop tricking innocent communists into breaking the law and hijacking planes. United States Ambassador Henry Cabot Lodge retorted angrily, "A few of your 'innocents' just held a press conference in Germany, and I don't think that you will like what they had to say!"

On March 26, Czech Deputy Foreign Minister Gertruda Sekaninova demanded that the U.S. "immediately return the aircraft and 25 of its occupants, including the pilot, Miroslav Slovak, and the navigator, Helmut Cermak, who must be punished for their actions."[3]

U.S. diplomats worked over the weekend to arrange a meeting between U.S. Ambassador to Czechoslovakia George Wadsworth and the Premier, Viliam Siroky, for Monday, March 30. At that meeting, the U.S. agreed to the immediate return of all passengers who wanted to go back, but would not return the "Freedom Six" because they had been granted political asylum. The U.S. linked returning the plane to the Czech government issuing an apology and paying damages for shooting down an F-84 Thunderjet over West German earlier in the month. The U.S. also demanded the release of an AP reporter named William Oatis, who had been charged with espionage in 1951.

The returning Czechs were placed on an Air Force bus and driven to the border, where they were transferred to a Czechoslovakian bus and driven to Prague.[4] The communists did not agree to the U.S. demands about the plane, so OK-WDZ sat at Frankfurt while the two sides continued to negotiate.

Morris met with Mira every day and continued his interrogation. One morning in early May, when the gardens around the Rhein-Main Air base were filled with blooming tulips, Morris leaned across his desk and said in almost a whisper, "So tell me about the special military cargo you had onboard."

"I really don't know anything." Mira answered. "The tower delayed us, and the Air Force sent out a truck and loaded a 200-pound package into the cargo hold and told me to fly it to Brno. Aside from the glimpse I got as the crate was taken off the truck and placed into the cargo hold, I never even saw it."

Morris leaned back from his desk, shaking his head, "You aren't going to believe this but the Soviets wanted to replace the airbase in Brno. So the generals in Moscow had a brand new base drawn up and they were sending the blueprints to Brno, except they never made it to Brno, because you brought them to Frankfurt! Yup, you brought us 200 pounds of detailed blueprints for a state-of-the-art Soviet air base. Close to 20,000 pages! Now we know everything about their bases. We know how their security is set up, how deep their bunkers are, where they store their nuclear weapons, heck, and we even know how many urinals they have in the rest rooms in the enlisted men's barracks. We know everything!"

Mira was still struggling to find his voice.[5]

"What's the matter son, you got a dumpling caught in your throat?"

Mira finally stammered, "This is incredible!"

"Well, you know what this means, don't you? It means that Uncle Sam owes you a huge debt, and when you get to the states, you need to be ready to tell them how they can pay you back."

"That is simple," said Mira. "I want to go to Korea and I want fly F-86s and fight the communists."

"I'm sorry Mira, but that just might be the one thing that we can't do. You're an officer in a communist air force and a member of the Communist Party. I don't think that there is any way in heck that we could put you into a combat zone. Think of something else that is a little easier to do."

"Perhaps I can become an airline captain in America?"

"I'll get to work on that."

14

Footsteps in the Night: Frankfurt, 1953

On September 28, the Czechoslovakian news agency announced that five conspirators had been convicted in the hijacking of OK-WDZ and sentenced to prison terms ranging from sixteen to twenty-five years. Mira wondered who had been arrested and convicted because as far as he knew the conspirators were all with him in Germany. Maybe these people were part of the mysterious underground that had failed to deliver the twenty-three escaping passengers that Mira had been told about but had never seen. The news story went on to say that the plot's ringleaders—Miroslav Slovak and Helmut Cermak—were still at large in West Germany and had not been included in this trial. Mira knew that he was not included in the trial because as an air force captain, he had already been charged with desertion, court-martialed *in absentia*, and found guilty and sentenced to death. Mira was not worried. Unless the StB kidnapped him and dragged him back to Czechoslovakia, there was no way he would have to face that sentence.[1]

A real bond of friendship developed between Nicky, Thomas, Anna, and Mira. On October 25, they threw him a small party for his twenty-fourth birthday. Morris gave him several pairs of socks. When Mira had first defected, he had only brought his overnight bag with one change of clothes; he also arrived with only about three dollars in his pocket and could not afford to buy more clothes. He frequently had to wash his socks at night so they would be clean the next day. Thomas gave Mira a couple bottles of good German beer. Anna baked him a cake and brought it to him with twenty-four candles burning. When he blew them all out, she gave him a quick kiss on the cheek. There was something in the spontaneous kiss that made Mira wonder if Anna might be interested in him.

In November, days were short and wet, and darkness settled over Frankfurt by 5 p.m., lasting until almost 8 a.m. One night, Mira found himself waking at 3.30 a.m. with a start. He was not sure what he had heard, but something had bumped into his window. Maybe it was a branch blown by the wind? Maybe it was just a bird or a bat? Maybe it had been something much more ominous? Could it be the communists looking for him to take him back to face his sentence? Mira lay awake for a long time, trying to hear it again. Just before he drifted off to sleep, he heard another sound. This time, it was the unmistakable sound of a foot stepping on gravel. The safe house had a gravel path that wound past Mira's window. He spent a sleepless night listening for more sounds that never came. The next morning, he mentioned it at breakfast. In daylight, he and Helmut went out to the yard and looked for footprints. They did not see any, but they did find a broken branch on a rose bush near Mira's window.

The next night, Mira again awoke with a start, but this time it was Hanna creeping into his room. "I heard footsteps too, right outside my window," she whispered.

"Where's Helmut?"

"He sleeps like the dead. I couldn't wake him up."

Mira put his finger to his lips and made a shushing noise. He slipped out of bed and crept to the window. He listened then nodded, "I hear it, there is someone walking around the house." Mira hurried to Thomas's room and rapped on the door. The door opened and Mira said, "Hanna and I heard footsteps outside our windows.

Thomas picked up a phone from the night stand next to his bed and dialed a number. "We're being cased! Send the cars. Now!" He hung up the phone and sprang into action. "Okay!" He said loudly, "Turn on all of the lights, start packing and make as much noise as you can. Whoever is out there was looking to surprise us. If they know that we are all awake and prepared they will have to re-evaluate their plans and that will take a little time. We will have cars here to move everyone out in less than five minutes." He opened the top drawer of his night stand and pulled out two .45 automatic pistols and said, "If it is a Soviet team out there, it's a good bet that you're the one they're after. Can you protect yourself?" Mira nodded, and Thomas handed him the pistol.

Anna stepped out of her own room just down the hall clutching a purple silk robe to her throat. She saw Mira in the hall wearing nothing but his boxers, with a pistol in his hand. "What is it?" she asked. Mira knew that he was in the middle of a crisis, but the sight of Anna's shapely legs disappearing beneath the short robe stirred a curiosity in him that he had not felt since his break up with Jiřinka.

Thomas said, "Mira and Hanna heard noises outside their windows. I think we are being cased. I've decided not to take any chances and we're moving everyone out tonight." Mira returned to his room and quickly put on pants and a sweater. He saw a couple sets of headlights play across the window shade as cars began to pull into the safe house's driveway. He tossed his few belongings into his bag and headed into the hallway.

Thomas and Anna were directing the evacuation. Thomas was still in his robe, but Anna had covered her silk nightgown with a long, belted raincoat. There were two black Mercedes in the driveway. Thomas, Helmut, Hanna, and Bozidar took the first car. Bohumil climbed into the front seat of the second car, Antonin got in the back seat, Mira sat next to him, and just as he was about to close the door, Anna came dashing out of the dark, across the lawn, and squeezed into the back seat next to him. The cars roared off down the street. Mira felt a wave of relief as the safe house disappeared into the darkness. Anna was breathing hard from running and her breath was warm and sweet against Mira's neck. In the darkness of the car, Mira allowed his gaze to linger on Anna longer than would have been polite in a normal setting. He saw that her rain coat had slipped open almost to her thigh to reveal her legs and the fact that under her coat she was still wearing just her nightgown. After a moment, Mira felt self-conscious and looked up to see that Anna was watching him. He felt like a schoolboy who had been caught being naughty and blushed deeply. He expected Anna to scold him for staring at her legs. She did not say anything, but she did not make a move to cover her legs either.

In a few moments, both cars pulled into an underground parking lot and were met by three new cars. As the escapees got out of their cars, Thomas and Anna crossed to the first of the new cars, got into the back seat, and were driven away. The six escapees divided three apiece into the two remaining cars, which drove slowly out of the garage. After one more car switch, they arrived at a new safe house where they were greeted by Thomas and Anna, who had driven ahead to prepare the house.

A few weeks later, while Mira was talking with Morris, he said, "Nicky, you've been asking me these same questions over and over for eight months now. You have to come up with some new questions, because I can't come up with any different answers."[2]

Morris smiled and said, "You know, you are the only one whose answers have never changed. It's actually something we do on purpose. We ask you the same question several times over a period of months and see if your answer changes. If it changes, then we know that you aren't necessarily telling us the truth, but you are telling us what you think we want to hear.

There is a big difference between the two. You are the only one whose answers have stayed constant. So we know we can trust you."[3]

"Thank you," Mira replied humbly.

"So are you ready to go to America?" Morris asked.

"Yes, I think I am!"

When Mira returned to the safe house that night, he could tell that someone had already broken the news to the others. They were all excited about taking the next step in their amazing journey.

Over a dinner of boiled potatoes with sausage, Hanna said, "We have to promise to keep in touch. We've been through so much together that we must keep in touch once we get settled in America."

Helmut poured wine for everybody and raised his glass, "To the Freedom Six! May we stay strong in each other's hearts forever!" All around the table, there were answers of "*Na zdravie*!" (The traditional Czech toast "To your health!") as each diner made eye contact and they clinked their glasses together.

Later, in the deepest, most private part of the night, Mira was again awakened by a noise. He opened his eyes to see Anna standing by his bed, wearing only her thin purple night gown. "You are leaving soon," she said softly. "I saw the way that you looked at me in the car." She bent over and gave Mira the lightest brush of a kiss. "I know that you desire me." She brushed his lips with another kiss. "And I desire you too." She sat down on the bed. "But we both work for the CIA. There are rules for people like us." Anna said as she slid off one shoulder strap, "We can never meet again. Never! Even if you think that you see me, or a girl that looks like me, someday in a faraway place, it will not be me. You must walk on past without blinking or smiling or doing anything that could blow her cover."[4]

Mira nodded. Anna stood up and gave a slight shake to her hips; the silk gown fell to her feet. She carefully stepped out of the gown, pointing her delicate toes like a young girl stepping out of her bath. She was now completely naked and she said, "You must never think of this as something cheap or easy. A woman's heart is fragile and complicated. Even though I will never see you again, you must know that my affection is pure. The communists took my husband and they took my innocence, and I hate them like you do. I will spend the rest of my life working to destroy them."

When Mira woke the next morning, Anna was gone. It was not just that she had left his room; she was gone from the safe house. Thomas told him that she had been assigned to another case.

It took about a week for the USAF to arrange transportation to the U.S. for the escapees. There would only be five travelers. Bozidan Medic had decided to stay in Europe. The remaining five were picked up by two cars a little after 4 a.m. on a cold, dark morning in December. The cars drove them through a depressing drizzle, straight to Wiesbaden Air Force Base, 26 miles west of Frankfurt. There, they boarded an Air Force DC-6. As Mira walked up the steps into the plane, he could see that there was a ring of armed security guards around the plane. He smiled to himself, thinking, "Here the guns are pointed away from me. Back in Czechoslovakia it felt like the guns were always pointing at me."

A DC-6 was a four-engine airliner built by Douglas Aircraft, capable of carrying seventy passengers 4,000 miles at a cruising speed of just over 300 miles per hour. As Mira settled into the plush first-class seats, he looked around and counted: there were three crewmembers, the five escapees, five MPs in uniform, and two CIA handlers. "This is a big, beautiful plane for such a small group. There must be some big shot flying with us. I wonder when he will get here."

A few moments later, the doors were closed, Mira thought. "I guess mister big missed his flight." It was a strange feeling for Mira to be riding in the passenger cabin. He had gotten used to being an airline captain and he suddenly realized he might never pilot an airliner again.

The plane took off and headed west, flying across Germany, France, Spain, and eventually the open ocean. The cockpit door opened and the Air Force captain made his way down the aisle, talking politely with Helmut and Hanna. When he reached Mira's seat, he was joined by one of the CIA handlers, who also worked as a translator. Speaking through the translator, the captain said, "So you must be our guest of honor." Mira was not quite sure what "guest of honor" meant so he nodded politely. The captain continued, "This plane has been under a 24-hour armed guard. On the inbound flight this weekend the radar was acting up, so I came out yesterday afternoon and tried to come on board to check to see if it had been repaired. The guards wouldn't even let me get within 100 feet of the plane."[5]

Mira smiled sheepishly and said, "Well, I hope the radar is working now."

The Air Force captain smiled, "Everything is fine. If you don't mind my asking, what is your name?"

"I am Miroslav Slovak."

"Oh sure, well now this makes sense. You stole that DC-3 from the commies and flew it to Frankfurt. No wonder the plane has been under guard. I bet the Reds would love to get a shot at you!" The captain returned to the cockpit and the plane flew on across the Atlantic.

The DC-6 was flying at 21,000 feet over a heavy bank of clouds when they made landfall on the U.S. Soon, the plane was descending through the thick gray clouds and broke into the clear at about 5,000 feet above the Maryland countryside. Mira was surprised that from this height, the U.S. looked an awful lot like Europe.

The plane was cleared to land at Anacostia Naval Air Base. Mira was disappointed because from his side of the plane, he could not see any of the famous Washington buildings he had seen in newsreels during the war. He had hoped for a grand entrance into his new country, but it was not to be. As the plane sailed out of the afternoon sky, he caught a few glimpses of the muddy Potomac River. Mira could not have imagined what an amazing part in his life that dirty river would play.

As the plane touched down on Anacostia's long main runway, Mira felt the seat belts tug on his hips as the pilot firmly applied the brakes. The plane slowed, taxied to the end of the runway, and started to turn. Mira saw a cluster of buildings come into view and was confident that the plane would taxi towards one of them, shut down the motors, and let the refugees get off, but the plane taxied right past the buildings. It made two more turns, and suddenly, Mira realized they were headed back toward the main runway. The DC-6 reached the head of the runway. If the plane were to turn to the right, it would be back in position to take off, but shockingly, the plane turned to the left, toward a narrow taxiway that led off into waist-high grass and overgrown brush. After a few moments, the narrow taxiway spilled out into a massive, totally abandoned U.S. Air Force base.

The strip of land at the confluence of the Potomac and Anacostia Rivers, known in 1953 as "Naval Air Station Anacostia," had started life as two separate military installations—Bolling Field (an Army Air Corps base) and Anacostia Experimental Flying Field (a Navy base). After World War II, the two operations were combined, and "old" Bolling was shut down. In 1947, a new Bolling base was built farther to the south, but the old, abandoned Bolling still sat waiting for demolition. There was a small taxiway that connected Anacostia to the "old" Bolling runways. Occasionally, there was the need for a totally clandestine air base, and apparently this was one of those occasions. The end of one of the abandoned runways was overgrown by tall shrubs. The DC-6 taxied toward the dark shrubs. As the plane got closer, Mira could see that there were three dark-colored sedans parked against the bushes. As soon as the plane stopped moving, one of the plane's crew members came out of the cockpit and said, "Please stay seated until I tell you to get up." He opened the cabin door just as two men emerged from the shadows carrying what looked like an old-fashioned painter's ladder. They placed the ladder against the side of the plane. The crew member gestured toward Helmut and Hanna. As the Cermaks climbed down, Mira watched one of the sedans move from the bushes to the front of the plane. The instant they were on the ground, the sedan doors swung open, Helmut and Hanna climbed in, and the car gunned its engine and drove away. The crewman pointed to Suran and Valejnicek, and in an instant, they too were down the ladder, climbing into their own dark car. Finally, it was Mira's turn. Quickly, he and the CIA handler were down and pulling away from the plane. Mira watched out of the sedan's rear window as the two men with the ladder disappeared back into the bushes and the DC-6 swung around to head down the taxiway towards Anacostia. The whole process was over in a blink of an eye, and suddenly, the sedan carrying Mira was out into D.C. rush hour traffic. After about an hour of winding through crowded streets past more cars than Mira had ever seen, the sedan arrived at a classic brownstone house in a neighborhood that the handler told Mira was called Georgetown. This was his new safe house in Washington, D.C.

The Georgetown house was beautiful, with hardwood floors, bay windows, and expensive oriental carpets. There was a married couple that ran the house, and unlike in Frankfurt, this couple really was married. The husband served as a security officer and driver, while the wife worked as the cook and housekeeper. Mira and his handler would be sharing the house with a young Polish defector named Jerzy Jawinski, age twenty-two. He had stolen a MiG-15 from the Polish Air Force in May 1953 and flown it to Denmark. The field Jerzy chose to land on was rougher than he had expected, and the plane was badly damaged upon landing, but the U.S. military was still thrilled to get its hands on a MiG-15. Jerzy, like Mira, had left behind his family and a young fiancée. Mira's handler spoke fluent Polish as well as English and Czech, so he was able to help the two fliers communicate with each other and with the America couple. By all accounts, Mira and Jerzy had so much in common that they should have become fast friends, but somehow the two never connected. Mira felt that perhaps it was just a typical fighter pilot's disdain for "airborne bus drivers." Yet the people of the Polish community in the United States loved Jerzy and showered him with gifts. One of the most exciting was a brand-new RCA color TV. Unfortunately, in December 1953, when Mira moved into the Georgetown house, the TV sat unused because most stations were only broadcasting in black and white.

It took a few days for Mira to settle into his new home. On Friday, December 18, he was called to the Pentagon, and when he arrived, he was surprised to be joined by Helmut, Hanna, Antonin, and Bohumil. Soon, a photographer showed up and began to arrange the refugees in front of an American flag. Then, an American general swept in and announced that on behalf of the U.S. government, he wanted to welcome them all to the United States of America, and he was proud to announce that they had all been granted political asylum. People cheered, flashbulbs flared, and once more, Mira's photo appeared in newspapers across the country.[6]

As the Christmas holidays approached, Mira was amazed at the extent to which Americans went to decorate their homes. Electricity was still rationed in Czechoslovakia, so outdoor decorations were limited to pine wreaths on front doors and occasionally, pine boughs draped above the windows. In America, houses were outlined in bright colored lights. Trees in the yard were draped in tiny white lights, and manger scenes with the Madonna and the Christ child were spot-lit in people's front lawns. Mira was not sure if he was impressed or mortified. The only thing that he knew for sure was that he was lonely and he missed his family, as well as Jiřinka and Anna. Christmas passed with a sad little celebration in the Georgetown safe house. It was so different than Christmas at home that Mira almost wished they had just skipped the whole thing.

New Year's Eve was the same. There were several Georgetown parties, but Mira elected to stay home. On New Year's Day, Mira and Jerzy sat in front of the new TV and watched the Tournament of Roses Parade on NBC. It was the first coast-to-coast color broadcast by any network. The parade and the colors where fascinating, but Mira could not understand the English-language commentary, and the Rose Bowl game featuring American college football that followed was complete beyond Jerzy and Mira's comprehension.

Mira continued to go into the Pentagon every day to answer questions for the CIA. Yet Washington, D.C. was a lonely place for Mira. He never connected with his new handler the way he had with Morris, so he spent much of his time thinking about his family and everything that he had left behind. He found a certain peace of mind in walking the quiet streets of Georgetown and its surrounding neighborhoods. His handler felt that as long as he wore civilian clothes and stayed to well-traveled streets, he would be perfectly safe.

Washington neighborhoods had an eclectic array of architecture. On an afternoon late in March, when the sky was blue and the crisp fresh air smelled of cherry blossoms, Mira left the safe house and walked along streets lined with various fruit trees just opening their buds. He turned east along "Q" Street and then left on Massachusetts, following it to DuPont Circle. Along the way, he passed couples strolling hand in hand. He watched with an ache in his heart as a young man playfully picked a bright collection of tulips and daffodils and gathered them into a bouquet that he offered to his girlfriend. The girl took the makeshift bouquet and gave the lucky fellow a kiss that was deep and passionate. Mira rounded DuPont Circle and continued along Massachusetts, enjoying the afternoon. He had no idea where he was going; he just let his feet take him where ever they wanted. Seeing the girl kissing her lover made him think longingly of Jiřinka, but surely, she must have found a new love by now. His thoughts wandered on to Anna and their one night together. Massachusetts Avenue led to Scott Circle, and for reasons he could never explain, halfway around the circle, he turned right onto 16th NW and continued to wander. A block and a half down 16th, on the left side of the street, was an older mansion surrounded by a tall fence. There was a bright red flag flying from a pole in the yard. For just a moment, Mira thought that it was odd that someone would fly a red flag in Washington, D.C., and then with a gunshot bang of realization, he understood that he had found the Soviet Embassy.[7] An unreasonable panic hit him, and he had to leave. He had to get as far away as possible as quickly as possible. Pivoting on his heel to hurry back in the other direction, he turned so fast that he almost ran headlong in to another couple out on a stroll. The man was older and stocky and wearing a gray overcoat with padded shoulders that made him look like a Soviet general. The girl was young and thin, with wonderful legs and auburn hair. It took only a second, but Mira knew he was face-to-face with Anna. He saw a flash of recognition on her face, but then she turned and pointed at a tree covered with bright pink blossoms across the street, a clear effort to divert her companion's attention. Mira's head cleared and in his mind, he could hear Anna's voice from their night together saying, "We can never meet again. Never! Even if you think that you see me, or a girl that looks like me, someday in a faraway place. It will not be me. You must walk past without blinking or smiling or doing anything that could blow her cover." Mira hurried back to his safe house. The next morning, he knew it was time to leave D.C.

It took the CIA a few weeks to figure out what to do with Mira, but by the second week in April, he and his handler flew to Seattle. When the plane landed, they were met by Seattle's CIA station chief, Wayne Richardson, who was short, overweight, and balding. Mira thought that Richardson looked more like a mailman than a CIA agent.[8]

Richardson was a well-known and well-liked personality in the Seattle social scene. He kept an office on the ground floor of the Federal Court House in Seattle. The office consisted of two rooms with a connecting door. One room was occupied by a receptionist who was a female Air Force intelligence officer in plain clothes, and the other was occupied by Richardson. The only marking on either door was the number "12" in

3-inch-tall black letters. Anyone who knew Richardson well knew that his "real" office was across the street in the big circular booth at the back of the bar at the Kennedy Hotel. The Kennedy was one of Seattle's few luxury hotels and its bar was dark, quiet, and popular. Most days, Richardson would head over to the Kennedy at lunchtime, order a steak and a couple of cocktails, and hold court in his booth until 5 p.m.

Richardson brought Mira and his handler to the office in the courthouse. He asked Mira to take a seat while he signed a form that officially made Mira his responsibility. He thanked the handler from DC and told him that there was a car waiting to take him back to the airport; once the agent left, Richardson became friendlier. He sat on the corner of his desk and talked slowly and carefully to make sure that Mira could grasp what he was being told. "Okay, I know that you want to fly an airliner again. And I'm going to do all I can to help make that happen, but we have three problems. One," and Richardson held up a single finger, "your English isn't very good and you must speak English to get a commercial pilot's license in the U.S. So, we will send you to school to learn English. Two," holding up two fingers, "to be an airline pilot, you have to have a radio operator's license, and you can't get a radio license if you aren't a U.S. citizen. Don't worry, I have a U.S. senator named Warren Magnuson working on getting an exemption through Congress. It may take a while but I think that I can get that done. Three, you can't be an airline pilot if you aren't a U.S. citizen, and you can't become a U.S. citizen if you are a member of the Communist Party."

Mira protested, "But I only agreed to join the party so I could fly!"

Richardson nodded and agreed, "Believe me son, I understand, but we have a lot of folks that are really scared of the Reds right now, and it's just going to take a little while to convince them that you are one of the good guys. Normally you have to live in the U.S. five years before you can become a citizen. With this extra hurdle it might take us six or seven, but we're going to get there. I know that you want to fly, and I've looked into it and as far as I can tell, there is only one flying job you can get without a radio license or having to speak English. It's crop dusting. You know, flying low and spraying fertilizer or insecticide on farmers' fields."

Mira cheered up, "I want to fly. If you say you can get me a job as a crop duster, I'll take it."

"It's not quite that easy," Richardson said, "You need a license to crop dust and you have to go to school to get the license. I've found a school that will take you. Of course, we'll pay all of the costs."

"And this school, it is here in Seattle?" Mira asked with his broken English.

"No. It is about 100 miles east of here, in Yakima, Washington. It is called Central Airways and its run by Al Baxter. I'll drive you over tomorrow. But now let's get you a place to sleep and a decent meal. Do you like steak? The Kennedy Hotel serves an amazing rib eye. Let's go grab a bite."

The next morning, Richardson picked up Mira from his hotel and they headed across the state to Yakima. The weather was bright but chilly. Richardson kept looking at the sky, worrying aloud about the weather in the mountains. They took U.S. Highway 410 over Chinook Pass through the Cascades. The pass sits close to Mount Rainier and at 5,430 feet, it gets plenty of snow, even in late spring. The scenery was dramatic as they wound up into the mountains. It had snowed a few days earlier, but plows had cleared the road, piling up several feet of snow next to the guardrails. Coming out of the mountains, Mira was surprised at how quickly the alpine scenery gave way to an arid desert landscape. The road to Yakima cut through fields of sagebrush and windswept mesas.

Yakima was a small city, with a population of about 35,000 people, serving as a transportation center in the heart of the state's agriculture lands. Surrounded by fields of hops, cattle ranches, and orchards, Yakima was a convenient place for farmers to ship their goods to the rest of the state. Yakima only had one tall building, the fourteen-story ultra-modern Chinook Hotel. The Chinook was one of the first buildings in the nation clad with polished aluminum panels, and it stood out against the rest of the long, low, two-story brick buildings in the center of town along Yakima Avenue. Richardson and Mira checked into the Chinook, and after dropping off their luggage in their respective rooms, they met in the hotel's coffee shop for dinner. Richardson told Mira to get a good night's sleep because the next day would be busy, meeting with Al Baxter to enroll in school and searching for an apartment.

Central Airways had been founded in 1939, and despite all the progress that was made in the rest of the aviation world, Central remained faithful to the barnstorming days of the past, when planes were made of wood and cloth and flew off grass runways. Central's fleet consisted of twenty to thirty planes, including a dozen bright yellow and silver WACO UPF-7 biplanes. The company occupied a small collection of clapboard buildings and Quonset huts near the airport. Baxter, the company's founder, had developed a lucrative business, alternating between crop dusting and teaching, depending on the season.

Richardson and Mira arrived at Central Airways a little before 10 a.m. on Friday, April 9. They climbed out of Richardson's car and walked across the dirt parking lot toward the open door of Central Airways. Al Baxter was a big, good-natured whirlwind of a man, and they heard him before they saw him. He was laughing loudly at some joke that one of his pilots had just told.

Baxter sat at a desk crowded with stacks of flying magazines. An off-balance ceiling fan spun over his head with a wobble that made it look like it might crash to the floor any moment. Richardson knocked on the door frame before sticking his head through the opening and calling out, "How you doing Al?"

Al stood up to shake Mira's hand, "Who is this skinny young fellow? Is he that Russian spy you've been talking about?"

With Richardson's help, Mira had practiced his introduction to make sure that he got all his words right. He stuck out his hand, saying, "I am Miroslav Slovak, from Czechoslovakia. I am, I mean I was captain in Czech Air Force. For three years I have been captain too for Czechoslovakian Airlines flying DC-3 from Prague to Copenhagen. I would like to learn from you to dust the crops."

Baxter shook Mira's hand, and then with a loud, easy laugh he said, "Son, we normally want to work with pilots that have a bit more experience than you do." Mira's English was not strong enough for him to understand that Baxter was joking. He thought that Baxter was going to refuse to take him. The crestfallen look on his face was enough to elicit another burst of laughter from Baxter. "Oh hell, Mira, don't take me so seriously, I was just kidding with you!" Mira smiled, beginning to understand that he would be accepted here. "Classes start Monday at 8 a.m. There will be three parts to your training. First, we have to teach you about the chemicals. We'll teach you all about pesticides and fungicides and defoliants: what they do and how to handle them safely. Next, we'll teach you some basics of farming, what the growing seasons for certain crops are, when they need fertilizer, what type of pests they attract, and what the life cycles of these pests are, so we know when to go after them. Finally, we get to the flying. How to apply the chemicals, how to make low fast turns, how to avoid obstacles, and how to fly a pattern to make sure you get good coverage on the field." Baxter paused. "Any questions?"

"No sir."

"All right, your schedule is going to be tight; from 8 until 10, we teach the class on chemicals, then 10 to noon we do the agriculture class. Then you get a half hour for lunch. 12.30 to 2 we do ground school and finally from 2 to 5 we do flight school. You think you can handle this?"

Mira nodded, "Yes, sir."

"Okay then, I think that we're all set. Wayne here has covered all the costs. We'll give you the study materials when you show up on Monday, so that's about everything. Do you have a place to live?"

"Not yet. That's next on our to do list." Richardson said.

"You don't have a car, son, do you?" Mira shook his head. "Then you need someplace that you can walk from, but I think that we're in luck." Baxter turned and yelled, "Dick! Hey Dickey come in here." Baxter's son, Dick Baxter, who was a carbon copy of his father but a few inches shorter, thirty pounds lighter, and at least twenty years younger, came into the tiny office. Al barked, "Do you know if there are any apartments left above the garage?"

"I think the one on the end is empty."

Al turned to Mira, "Well it's nothing fancy, but about three blocks from here there is an old garage that fixes cars and tractors. They have a few studio apartments built over the garage. My students get a deal on the rent. It's cheap and clean, perfect for a bachelor."

"Sounds great!" Richardson said.

"That settles it then. Dick, walk Mira over to the garage and get him settled in there. Wayne and I have a few papers to sign, and Mira, I'll see you back here at 8 a.m. Monday morning."

15

Stick and Rudder Man: Yakima, 1954

Mira was wide awake and staring at the ceiling by 4 a.m. Monday, April 12, 1954. He was excited to finally be starting his new life in America. He was anxious to get his license so he could begin flying again. He had not been at the controls of anything for almost thirteen months, which was the longest that he had gone without flying since he started glider school in 1947.

He left his apartment early and was waiting outside Central Airways' main classroom by 7.30 a.m. when Dick and Al came in together, carrying their lunches in brown paper sacks. Al slapped Mira on the shoulder and said, "You're an eager one, I like that."

There were twelve students in Mira's class. All were men in their mid-to late-twenties and were experienced fliers. Most were Korean War veterans, using their GI benefits to learn a new career. The chemical and agricultural classes were rough for Mira. The language barrier was a huge obstacle, but luckily there were textbooks that covered the subjects, and Wayne had given Mira an English–Czechoslovakian dictionary, so Mira could translate the writings at night, back at his apartment.

Al Baxter taught the ground school. He started his first class by pointing out the window toward the sky and saying, "I know that you are all good pilots up there, but the problem is, you aren't going to be flying 'up there.'" He pointed at the floor, "You're going to be flying down here. You are going to be making passes a few feet off the ground, and then when you get to the end of your pass you'll have to climb to clear a six-foot barbed-wire fence, but not too far, because you still need to fit under a 20-foot-tall telephone line. There is no room for error, no time to think about what to do next."

"Up there," Al pointed to the sky again, "you have to be smooth and gentle. You make nice sweeping turns so you don't spill the passengers' cocktails, and you have plenty of time to recover from a stall, or pull out of a spin. Down here, you have to think fast and act fast! You're going to be flying 100 mph five feet off the ground. If you make a mistake at that speed there is simply no way to recover. You'll be dead in 1/100th of a second. The only way to survive a mistake is never to make a mistake."

"It's going to be tough, and a few of you will wash out, but if you stay with me, I promise you, I will turn you into the best damn stick-and-rudder men in the sky."

There is a common misconception that Orville and Wilbur Wright invented the airplane. That is not quite true; at the turn of the century, there were dozens of people experimenting with airplanes. What the Wright brothers did was invent an ingenious method of controlling an airplane, which allowed them to make the first-ever controlled, powered flight. The Wrights used wires stretching from a control stick to the plane's wing tips to warp the wing tips up or down to get the plane to do what they wanted it to do. The technique was so successful that the Wright brothers quickly patented the idea. One of Alexander Graham Bell's former employees, a man named Glenn Curtis, who was also an aviation pioneer, tried to work around the Wrights' patent by creating small hinged panels called ailerons on the trailing edge of the wings and using wire from a control stick to move the panels rather than warp the wings. The idea worked well and in a short time all airplanes were being maneuvered by a "control stick" that moved either ailerons on the wings or the elevator on the horizontal stabilizer.

In the specialized vocabulary of the aviation world in the 1950s, anyone who could fly a plane was called a pilot. The best pilots were called "flyers," and the best flyers were called "stick and rudder men" because of their uncanny ability to use the control stick to get their planes to do anything they wanted. It was a common belief that most people could be taught to fly, and with enough practice a pilot could become a "flyer," but it took a special talent to become a real "stick and rudder man." Yet here was Al Baxter, standing in front of a classroom of students saying that he could teach them to become stick-and-rudder men. To Mira, this was exciting and inspirational.

Baxter continued his lesson. "I'm going to tell you the most important thing you've ever heard about flying, and it's also the simplest thing that you've ever heard." He paused to make sure that he had everyone's attention.

> Airplanes don't crash! Let me say that again. Airplanes don't crash. Pilots crash, and more often than not, pilots crash because they're trying to make

> the airplane do something that it doesn't want to do. Learn to listen to your plane, and if she starts to tell you that she's unhappy, stop whatever it is that you're doing and she'll get happy again. Let me give you an example. If you're pulling up from a pass to make your turnaround, and you use too much elevator, you're going to stall. Now just before you stall, the plane is going to talk to you. She is going to tell you that she isn't happy. Just before you stall, she is going to start to vibrate. When you feel that vibration, don't try to fix it by applying more power. Don't panic and shove the stick forward. Just ease up your grip on the stick and let it slide through your fingers until it finds neutral. The stall will stop and you can finish your turnaround like nothing happened.[1]

To Mira, it made so much sense. Baxter had an uncanny way of putting things into words that made them clear and easy to follow.

"Now here is something else that you need to think about," said Baxter, holding up a large but crude model of an airplane, and pointing toward the rear of the plane. "You have this vertical stabilizer sticking up into the air." He pointed at the part of the plane that most laymen would call the tail. "And then you have this horizontal stabilizer that sits back here, pretty much parallel to the horizon. Now for most of the flying that you've ever done, the plane stays nice and level like this." He walked forward with the plane. "And if you want to go up you give it some up elevator, right? And if the plane begins to yaw to the right, you give a bit of left rudder. But when you're crop dusting, and you get to the end of a pass and you need to do a tight turnaround, and you are banking close to 90 degrees." He turned the model on its side and used his hands to point at the control surfaces. "Now, your vertical stabilizer isn't sticking up, but it's pointing off to the side, and your horizontal stabilizer is pretty much vertical. As far as their effect on your motion, they have traded places, and if you gave the controls the same input now as you would in a level flight, you'd pile drive it into the ground so fast that there wouldn't be enough left of you to send home to your mother in a shoe box."

"There is another thing I want you to know about flying, and I can promise you that it is going to save your life someday." Baxter looked around to make sure all of his students were listening. "Do less, but do it sooner." He paused to see if his class understood what he was saying. "I'm going to say that again. "Do less, but DO IT SOONER! I've read too many accident reports about pilots who get their planes into trouble and then have to take drastic action to try to save them. If you are paying attention to your plane, really listening to her, it is much easier to make a minor correction to avoid a problem instead of waiting to make a major correction after things have started to go really bad."

The lecture continued until 2 p.m., when it was time to go out to the flight line to get a close-up look at the planes. Central had a fleet of WACO UPF-7s. The UPF-7 was a biplane with fabric-covered wings that looked like it hailed from the 1920s, but most of Central's planes had been built in the early 1940s. The Weaver Aircraft Company of Ohio (WACO) had gambled and built a rugged twin-cockpit biplane trainer with the hope that the U.S. Army Air Corps would buy them in large quantities as it began to train pilots for the war in Europe. The Air Corps switched to monoplane trainers in the 1930s, and of the 600 UPF-7s that were built, only a few found their way into military service. The rest wound up at civilian aviation schools, flying air mail, or crop dusting.

Mira liked the look of the UPF-7. It was an open-cockpit tail dragger like a slightly larger version of his favorite plane, the Bücker Jungmann. When it was his turn to look at the plane, Mira stepped onto the wing and looked into the sparse cockpit. "Hey, you guys," he called out, "where are the instruments?"

Baxter laughed and said, "We don't use instruments. Everything you need to know about is outside of the plane. If you take even a second to look at something inside the plane, you'll end up dead."

The first week of class passed quickly, and Mira was beginning to feel like he was fitting into this new world. When he arrived at Central Airways on Friday morning, April 16, there was a short redheaded stranger in a rumpled blue suit coat waiting outside Central's office. As Mira approached, the stranger pulled a note pad out of his coat pocket and said, "Are you Miroslav Slovak?" Mira was instantly on guard. Could this be a StB agent? No, of course not, how could the StB find him in Yakima?

"Yes, I'm Miroslav."

"I'm from the *Associated Press* and I'd like to ask you a few questions."

"What is the *Associated Press*?"

"I'm a reporter for the newspaper."

"How did you find me?"

"One of your classmates called our office in Seattle and told me about you."

"So there are informers, even in America?"

"Well we won't be sending you to prison. We're just going to make you famous."

"But I don't want to be famous."

"Well you're news, Captain Slovak. People are interested in you. They're going to want to know what you're doing in Yakima."

Mira said, "I wanted to join the Air Force and fight communists, but now I'm going to fight bugs."

The reporter asked Mira a few more questions, writing the answers down in his small spiral-bound notebook. Baxter stuck his head out of the door and yelled, "Mira, we're waiting for you!"

The reporter climbed into a rental car and drove off. On the following Sunday, an AP story with the headline "Czech Escapee Now Flying Crop Dusting Planes" ran in papers across the U.S.[2]

Mira continued to learn new flying techniques. During his military and airline training, he had been taught to avoid "cross control" at all costs. Cross control was a situation where you were using your hands on the stick to tell the plane to go in one direction, while you used your feet on the rudder pedals to tell the plane to go in the opposite direction. The military wanted pilots to avoid it, because it can cause a dramatic drop in airspeed, which could lead to a stall-induced crash. Baxter explained that in crop dusting, there are times when the pilot needs to slide the plane down into a tight space. Being able to reduce airspeed momentarily without reducing power was an advantage, so he taught all his pilots how to use cross controls effectively. Toward the end of June, Mira graduated from the UPF-7 trainer to a Boeing-Stearman 75 Kaydet. The planes looked almost identical, but to a pilot like Mira, the Stearman was from a whole different world. The Stearman had a larger wing, and somehow completed with ease the same maneuvers that a UPF-7 struggled through. Mira was thrilled with the upgrade.

A couple of weeks later, another reporter showed up outside Central's classrooms. This reporter carried a camera and said that he was from *Life*. He asked to spend time with Mira taking photos. Baxter was thrilled that Central was getting the attention of one of the nation's most prominent magazines and said, "Of course!"

The photographer took dozens of color slides of every aspect of Mira's day, including some breathtaking air-to-air shots from the back seat of Dick Baxter's plane, looking down on Mira as he flew his yellow-and-silver Stearman 75 over lush green fields. Unfortunately, at the end of the day, as Mira was landing, the brake calipers on the landing gear locked up. The plane slowly nosed over and ended up balanced in the grass with its tail in the air and its nose sticking into the ground. Mira climbed out of the cockpit and stood with his hands in his pockets, shaking his head and looking at his plane. The photographer snapped a humorous photo of the tall, lanky pilot looking forlornly at his airplane, and that is the photo that found its way into the magazine.

By July, Mira had graduated from school. He was now a proud holder of an Agricultural Pilot's Registration, and he was quickly hired by Central Airways for $150 per month. Even though the pay was less than a tenth of what he had been getting at CSA, Mira was proud that he had been able to come to a new country, learn a new career, and start making his own way. He was also surprised to find that he enjoyed flying crop dusters much more than he had liked flying an airliner. The high-speed, low-level flying of a crop duster was challenging, rewarding, and in some ways purer and freer than spending hours on straight and level flight at 10,000 feet in a CSA DC-3.

Crop dusting has it seasons, and summer to fall was the cotton season in Mexico. In August, Al Baxter loaned Mira to Farmers Air Services of Klamath Falls. Mira headed to Oregon, where he met up with a couple of pilots to ferry three Stearmans down to the Mexicali Valley. It was a warm summer morning when the three fabric-covered biplanes lifted off from a grass runway and headed south. Visibility was unlimited and snow-capped Mount Shasta, perched 90 miles away at the end of the Klamath Valley, acted like a beacon guiding Mira south. With the wind in his hair, sunlight glinting from the spinning disc of the propeller, and a new adventure ahead, Mira could not have been more content. The tiny formation of biplanes soared through cloudless blue sky for several hours until they set down at Dos Palos, in central California, to spend the night and have their luggage bins converted to jump seats to carry their loader boys out to the job sites. Loader boys were young Mexican field hands who mixed the chemicals and dumped them into the planes' hoppers. It had been a tradition for the loader boys to ride to the job sites on the wings of the planes, two to a plane, with one on each side of the lower wing, holding on to the "N" struts while their legs dangled over the front spar. In 1955, Farmer's Air Service felt this was too dangerous and opted to have new jump seats installed in each of its Stearmans.

The next day, they flew to the arid border town of Calexico, California and landed on a dusty airstrip that's only attraction was that it was within walking distance to the DeAnza Hotel. With its palm-lined patios, tall stucco walls, and red terracotta tiles, the DeAnza was like nothing Mira had seen. It had been built in the 1930s when gambling had just been legalized and Hollywood's rich and famous would make the 200-mile journey into the desert to try their luck at blackjack, poker, or roulette.

The afternoon sun was bright and hot. The dusty air seemed to shimmer from dry heat waves coming off the pavement, but behind the thick walls of the DeAnza, shaded rooms with high ceilings and polished tile floors offered a cool retreat. The three flyers checked into the DeAnza and would use it as their base of operations for all their Mexico business.

A typical day in Calexico would start well before daylight, with Mira waking up with a warm cup of cinnamon-flavored hot chocolate delivered to his room. Then, he and the other pilots would walk to their planes, whispering quietly in the pre-dawn stillness. The DeAnza Hotel was one of the few air-conditioned hotels in town, and it took Mira a while to get used to the 80- or 90-degree summer heat that slapped him in the face when he would walk out of the cool hotel lobby each morning.

There were no lights on the primitive airfield, and no running lights on the crop dusters' planes either, so like a World War I dawn patrol, the planes would take off into the dark morning sky aided only by starlight. The pilots hoped that by the time they reached their destination, there would be enough light to land. There were a dozen crop-dusting operations in the Mexicali Valley, and between them, they flew more than 150 planes. As Mira headed south in the purple twilight, he was joined by dozens of other planes, lit only by the flames of their exhausts, lifting off from dark dirt runways called "*pistas*" as they all headed south to the cotton fields. Dozens of biplanes, many of them still carrying their loader boys perched on their bottom wings, skimming 50 feet above the Mexican desert at 150 miles per hour as the sunrise began to streak the sky orange was a sight Mira would never forget.

Somehow Mira would find "his" *pista* and set the plane down on a rough dirt track just outside a chain-link fence surrounding a cotton gin. At the *pista*, Mira would get instructions from a representative of Farmer's Air Service, while a young loader boy in sandals, cut-off jeans, and a red bandana tied over his nose filled his plane. Once the plane was loaded, Mira would take off and fly to a field, usually marked by another young boy with a flag on a long pole. On a good day, working quickly, Mira could get in seven or eight flights.[3,4]

The fields in Mexico were big and flat, with few obstacles, and it was a good way for Mira to practice low-level passes, quick turnarounds, and all the other skills he had learned in Yakima. Mira had flirted briefly with acrobatic flying in Czechoslovakia, but his meteoric rise to captain and his busy schedule flying for CSA had not given him the opportunity to practice enough to get skilled at it. Above the stark, desolate Mexican countryside, flying the nimble Stearman 75, Mira began to feel the open sky calling to him to practice a few simple maneuvers, maybe a quick four-point roll or a loop after delivering his load of chemicals, before landing to refill his tank with pesticides.

Each night, when Mira returned to the DeAnza, he would be greeted by the new smells of Mexican food: hot peppers, onions, and garlic combined in ways that he never could have dreamed of back in Czechoslovakia. He would sit in the deep leather upholstered chairs beneath the tall beamed ceiling and listen to the exotic sounds of a Mexican guitar as he sipped an icy margarita and ate a plate of sizzling *carne asada*. The cold gray of Europe and the fear of communist informers in long green leather coats seemed to belong to a different planet.

For the next year and a half, Mira traveled the western U.S. and Mexico, flying for Baxter or Farmer's or anyone that needed him. In April and May, he sprayed insecticides on newly sprouted wheat in the gentle rolling hills of Washington's Palouse. In June, it was gypsy moths and pine beetles over the rugged forests of Wyoming and Montana. In July, he switched to the corn crops in Colorado for ear worm, then down to Mexico again in August and September to tend to the cotton. His life, flying from city to city day after day, was as close to the old-fashioned barnstorming lifestyle of the 1920s as could be. He flew every day in all kinds of weather. He had more takeoffs and landings in a single week then he would have had in a month of airline flying. He kept getting better and better, developing an instinctive feel for what the plane was doing and why. Central was growing and Baxter seemed to have a fatherly affection for Mira; his superb flying skills, matched with confidence in the air and humility on the ground, quickly earned Mira a special spot in Baxter's heart. He used Mira to ferry his new purchases to Yakima, including a B-17, a B-18, and a B-25.

During a trip to spray for gypsy moths, Mira and a dozen other pilots flew their Stearmans to Hamilton, Montana. A few weeks before Baxter was going to arrive in a town, he would call farmers and timber growers in the area. Once he had enough work lined up to keep his pilots busy, he would send a small fleet of planes to the town. Normally, he would catch a ride to the new town in the jump seat of Mira's Stearman. No matter how tiny the town was, if it was big enough to have a landing strip, it usually had a café nearby. Once Mira and the pilots had landed, Baxter would head to the café and meet with the farmers, who had been told to bring their checkbooks or cash. Once the farmers paid, he would dispatch the planes to spray their fields. When the planes were done, he told them to circle the coffee shop and then land. Baxter would come out and give the pilots directions to their next field. The pilots took a lunch break at the coffee shop, and one attractive young waitress began to flirt with Mira, asking him about flying and whether or not he could do any "tricks" with his plane.

At the end of the day, when Mira was done with his flying, he returned to the coffee shop, and instead of just circling it once, he decided that he would show the pretty girl a few of the acrobatic maneuvers he had been perfecting. First, he buzzed the coffee shop with a fast, low pass to get everyone's attention. Then, as he looked over his shoulder to see a dozen patrons rushing out of the coffee shop door, he turned and flew a low pass doing a four-point hesitation roll. Then he did a loop. He ended with what would eventually become his signature move known across the country—a very low, inverted pass, steering with his knees while both hands hung over his head out of the cockpit.

Mira landed, feeling rather proud of the quality of his impromptu little air show. He taxied off the field to join the other Central pilots as they were tying down their planes for the night. He saw that there was a small group of men waiting for him. The moment he pulled the mixture control back to kill the engine, he could hear someone near the plane shouting. As he climbed out of the cockpit, a man in a dark green uniform with a Smokey Bear hat and carrying a revolver came up to him and yelled, "You! You could have killed me! You can't do that. I'm going to arrest you!"

Mira could see Baxter hustling across the apron to try to catch up with the group huddled around Mira's plane before things got out of hand. The angry man continued to yell, "This is U.S. Forest Service land. I'm the U.S. Ranger for this area and I'm going to arrest you for reckless endangerment! If you had crashed into the building, you would have KILLED ME!"[5]

At first, Mira thought it was a joke, but when Al arrived and he was not laughing, Mira realized that he was in serious trouble. There was a small brick courthouse in Hamilton but no judge on duty. The Forest Ranger had a key to the courthouse, and he took Mira into the dark building. He turned on a couple of lights and unlocked the cell door made of metal bars and told Mira to get inside. He slammed the door closed with anger and picked up the handset of an old-fashioned black telephone, called the local sheriff, and told him to get down to the courthouse because he had a prisoner. Next, he called the judge, who said that he was getting ready for bed, but he would be at the courthouse by 9 a.m. the next morning to handle the arraignment.

The sheriff showed up carrying a plate of fried chicken that he had obviously been eating and was clearly not amused to have had his dinner interrupted. The ranger stormed out and the sheriff looked at Mira and said, "So what did you do to get him so wound up?"

Mira shrugged his shoulders and then he said, "I flew upside down and scared him."

"What are you talking about?" the sheriff asked with a look of confusion on his face.

"Mr. Forest Ranger was eating at the café and I flew too close, upside down, and ruined his meal."

The sheriff shook his head and said, "That's it? And now that glorified Boy Scout has gone and ruined my son's birthday dinner just because he's scared of your flying."

"Yes, that is how it seems."

"You know, you talk funny. Are you a Russian?"

"No sir, I am from Czechoslovakia."

"That's in Europe right? Near Germany?"

"Yes sir."

"Did Dick Tracy give you a blanket before he locked you in there?"

"No sir."

"How about food? Did he get you anything to eat?"

"No sir."

"So he expects you to sit here all night with no food, no water, and no blanket? Well, we're not Russia." He took a heavy khaki military-issue blanket and handed it through the bars to Mira. "Now I'm going to run across to the café and I'll pick you up a burger. Don't try to escape before I get back." With that, he walked out the door. Twenty minutes later, he was back with a cheeseburger and French fries on a paper plate, and a cold Pepsi in a paper cup. He handed them to Mira and said, "I think that this whole thing is crazy, but you're going to have to wait until the judge gets here in the morning."

Mira thanked him and ate his meal in silence. He knew that he was in trouble, but he also wanted to laugh. He had lived through the Nazi occupation and hidden Jews in his basement, he survived the Russian occupation and the communist takeover of Czechoslovakia, he had hijacked an airliner, but the only time he had spent in jail was because a U.S. Forest Ranger did not like the air show he had put on for a cute waitress.

After dinner, Mira wrapped the blanket around his shoulders and fell asleep. At 9 a.m., the sheriff escorted Mira out of his cell across the hall to a small courtroom that was divided by a waist-high wooden bar. On Mira's side of the bar, there were several rows of benches that looked like church pews. On the other side of the bar, the judge was sitting behind a desk on a small raised dais, flanked by an American flag and a Montana flag. Mira was relieved to see Baxter waiting for him at the rail. As Mira approached, the court clerk read the charges, "Miroslav Slovak, you are charged with one count of reckless endangerment."

The judge said, "Mr. Slovak, how do you plead?"

Mira was nervous and worried and as soon as he opened his mouth, his memory of the English words he had been practicing failed him. He could not think of what to say. In a moment of instant improvisation, he said, "Your honor, I plead un-guilty."

There were very few people in the court room, but everyone there, including the judge, burst out laughing. "Un-guilty? Well that is a new one for me, Mr. Slovak." The judge leaned across his desk and asked, "Are you ever going to do this again?"

"No, your honor."

The judge looked at Baxter. "Al, if I fine Mr. Slovak, will you be able to pay the fine?"

"Yes, your honor."

"Mira Slovak, I fine you $100 for reckless endangerment. Al, pay the clerk on the way out." He then banged the gavel down hard.

Mira and Baxter walked back to the airstrip. "Thank you, Mr. Baxter. I'll never do that again."

Baxter stopped and watched as the forest ranger, wearing his big broad-brimmed ranger hat, walked smugly across the highway toward the café. He called his pilots together and said, "I think I'm done doing business here in Hamilton and I don't care if we ever come back, so if any or you boys want to buzz the coffee shop on the way out of town, and if that damn ranger is dumb enough to come outside, I'll give $100 to anyone who can blow that silly hat off his pompous little pinhead!"

When the planes left the airstrip, they formed up like a fighter attack group at about 2,000 feet and then, led by Mira, they peeled off and dove at the restaurant like dive bombers, each pulling up just in time to avoid crashing into the ancient-looking log building, and then roared off. After the first plane passed, the ranger came storming out, shaking his fist. The second plane blew his hat off, and the last anyone from Central Airways saw of the ranger, he was running through the dusty parking lot chasing his hat as the propeller blasts from plane after plane blew it around the yard.

There is a long aviation tradition of naming your plane. The day after the pilots had returned from the Hamilton job, Mira walked out to the flight line and saw that overnight someone had painted the name "Unguilty" on the nose of his Stearman.

Richardson came back in March 1956, and he was smiling. He met Mira in the tiny apartment over the garage. "I have a job for you, Mira!" Richardson announced excitedly.

"But I have a job," Mira replied.

Richardson's grin widened and he shook his head slowly, "Oh you might have a job, but not like this one. We are still working around the FAA rules on citizenship, so we can't get you a commercial pilot's job yet, but there is nothing that says you can't be a private pilot, so we've lined you up a job as a private pilot for one of the richest men in America."

"Really?" Mira exclaimed. "That is great. What type of plane would I be flying?"

Richardson laughed, "Mira, you're unbelievable. I just told you that you'll be flying for one of the richest men in America, and your first question isn't 'what's his name?' but it's 'what type of plane would I be flying?'"

"I don't know any rich people but I do know a lot about airplanes, so I just asked about what I know."

"Well you're going to know this name. Boeing! Bill Boeing."

Mira was stunned for a moment. Then he pointed towards the sky and said, "Boeing? Like Mr. B-17?"

"Yes, well actually the company was founded by his father, but it's the same family. And don't worry, I think he has pretty much any plane you'd ever want to fly."

Richardson used the drive back to Seattle to fill Mira in on the history of Bill Boeing and the Boeing family.

> The company was founded by Bill Boeing, Sr., in 1916. Back then, they did everything; they built planes, flew air mail, and even flew passengers. By the early 1930s, Bill Sr. was really rolling. He bought up a number of other airplane manufacturers and was at the head of a huge conglomerate called United Aircraft and Transport Company, which included Boeing Airplane Company, Pratt & Whitney, Sikorsky, Hamilton Standard Propeller, Chance Vought, Stearman Aircraft, United Airlines, and a slew of other smaller companies. In 1934, the Roosevelt Administration used an anti-trust suit to break up the company into three big pieces. The manufacturing capabilities west of the Mississippi kept the name Boeing. The manufacturing east of the Mississippi was renamed United Technologies Corporation, and the airmail and passenger operations became United Airlines. The old man was furious and he sold his stock and retired to raise race horses and go fly fishing.
>
> Bill Jr. is about 33 years old, married with four young kids, and he's one of the nicest guys you'll ever meet. He has stayed connected to some of his father's old companies, but he also runs his own business, called Aero Copter Inc., from Boeing Field in Seattle. They run a fleet of helicopters serving the timber and commercial fishing industries along the west coast from California to Alaska. You'll be Bill Jr.'s personal pilot, taking him to business meetings and site inspections and anything else that he needs. Bill has a number of different planes. I don't know what they all are, but I know for sure that he has a B-25 and a big Grumman Mallard flying boat. Most of the time

> you'll be flying his Aero Commander or a Piper Twin Apache. I think he even has an F7F Tigercat and God knows what else.[6]

Mira was still in a bit of shock. "This is amazing," he stammered.

"Oh and the best part: Bill's wife, Marci. Her family is from Czechoslovakia and they speak Czech."

"Really?" Mira asked.

"Yes, Marci was born in the small Midwestern town of Wahoo, Nebraska. She got a job working as a stewardess for United Airlines. One day Bill Jr. was on her flight, and they began to talk. Before you know it, they fell in love. When they got married, her parents (Blanche and Frank Cech) moved to Seattle. They are wonderful people. Both are fluent in Czech. You're going to feel right at home. One more thing: Marci's brother Frank Jr., everyone just calls him 'Junie' for short." He flew F-86s in Korea and he just got home. He'll be flying with you at Aero Copter." Mira's head was spinning from all the new names he had just heard. He knew that once he began to meet these people, he would get to know them and somehow remember their names and what they did. In the meantime, there was nothing to do about it. So he just watched out the window of Richardson's car as it climbed out of the dry, arid Eastern Washington desert into the lush green mountains and headed west toward Seattle and a new chapter in his life.

The next day, Richardson drove Mira to an 8,000-square-foot mansion on Lake Washington Boulevard in Seattle's Denny Blaine neighborhood. The elegant house had been built in 1906 and sat on 1.25 acres of prime waterfront on Lake Washington.

Richardson rang the doorbell and a tall, thin young man with oval glasses and a receding hairline answered the door and said, "Hello, I'm Bill Boeing. You must be Mira Slovak."

Mira shook hands respectfully and said, "I am very pleased to meet you, Mr. Boeing."

"Oh the pleasure is all mine, and please, call me Bill."

"Yes, Mr. Boeing."

Mr. Boeing led Richardson and Mira to a sitting room at the back of the house that had sweeping views of a manicured lawn that led down to a boathouse and beach. As Mira followed Mr. Boeing through the house, he noticed that Boeing was quite a bit taller than himself, and at 6 feet 3 inches, Mira did not often meet people who were taller.

The meeting seemed to be an opportunity for Boeing to get to know Mira. There was not much business discussed, and mostly Boeing just asked about Mira's life in Czechoslovakia. After a pleasant hour or so, Boeing announced, "I have another appointment Mira. It was wonderful talking with you. I'm sure we will be great friends. Take the rest of this week to find an apartment and get settled in. Be at Aero Copter at 9 a.m. Monday and we'll get you checked out on some of the planes."

As they drove away, Richardson asked, "So what did you think?"

"He is such a gentleman. You would never know that he was one of the wealthiest men in the America." Mira spent his first weekend in Seattle in the Kennedy Hotel near Wayne's office.

On Monday morning, Mira took a taxi to Aero Copter. When he arrived, he was met by Frank Cech, Jr. (Junie) and given a tour of the facilities. Mira had grown accustomed to the shoestring budget of Central Airways, and he was amazed at how immaculately maintained the planes at Aero Copter were. Mira and Junie hit it off and quickly became friends. After the first day, Junie brought Mira home to meet Blanche and Frank Sr. They lived a few blocks up the hill from the Boeings on Madrona Drive.

Blanche figured that Mira was homesick for some Czech cooking, so she fixed a huge dinner with roast pork, dumplings, and cabbage. When Mira was still walking up the sidewalk he caught a whiff of the food and told Junie, "My gosh, it smells just like home!"

When the young men came through the door, Blanche hurried over, wiping her hands on her apron, and said, "*Vítejte doma moji chlapci.*" (Welcome home, my boys.) The sound of his own native language being spoken brought a lump to Mira's throat.

Blanche was well into her fifties and a powerful dynamo of a woman with a twinkle in her eye and a hug for anyone who needed one. First, she hugged Junie, and then she turned to Mira, wrapped him in her arms, and said, "You must be Mira. Bill and Junie haven't talked about anything but you for the last week. I'm so glad to finally meet you." She broke the hug and announced, "*Vecere pripravena.*" (Dinner's ready.) Then she clapped her hands and said, "Go wash up and come to the table."

Mira smiled and thought, "This woman was definitely made from the same mold that my mother was."

Dinner was perfect and the conversation drifted between English and Czech as Mira retold the story of his life in Czechoslovakia and his escape to the West. After the meal, Junie asked Mira how he liked his hotel. Blanche was shocked! "You don't mean to tell me that Wayne put you up in a hotel! We have a spare bedroom down stairs. You can stay here until Wayne can find you a decent apartment."

Mira protested, "That is too much trouble for you, I couldn't think of it."

Junie interrupted, "Mira, once Mom has made up her mind it's no use fighting. She is going to get her way. It's so much easier to just give in. Let me drive you back to the hotel to get your things."

Mira spent his first few months in Seattle living in the Cechs' basement. Blanche treated him like a second son and Mira felt more at home than he had at any time since he had left Leopoldov for Prague in 1945. Mira tried to "earn his keep" helping out around the house wherever he could. He was in the driveway helping Frank wash the family car one Saturday afternoon when two neighbor kids on bicycles stopped by and said hello. After they rode away, Mira asked Frank who they were. Frank replied, "Oh those are the Lyford kids, Chuck and Ginny. They live a couple houses down on the left." Mira had no way of knowing, but Chuck Lyford would grow up to be an important person in his life.

Wayne Richardson lived in West Seattle. Since Mira did not have a car yet, Richardson knew he would have to do a bit of chauffeuring, so he suggested that Mira consider getting an apartment near him.

Of course, Richardson "knew a guy" who could get Mira a great deal, and before long Mira was moving into an apartment on Beach Drive, near Alki Point in West Seattle. The cozy one-bedroom apartment was across the street from the beach and had a great view of Puget Sound and the Olympic Mountains. Back at work, Mira finished all his check flights and was approved to fly any of Aero Copter's planes. He began to fly Mr. Boeing on business trips. Most of the flights were fairly short hops in the Aero Commander 500, a twin-engine, high-wing monoplane with a tricycle landing gear. The plane could carry six people: two crew members and four passengers. Mira was surprised on his first trip that there was no co-pilot assigned to fly with him, but when he got to the plane, Mr. Boeing was sitting in the right seat. "Mira, I know that you don't have your radio operator's permit yet. Let me sit over here so I can be your co-pilot and radio operator." Boeing was an accomplished pilot and had no trouble handling the co-pilot's job, and Mira enjoyed having someone to talk with while he flew.

16

Miss Wahoo: Seattle, 1956

In 1956, Seattle was infatuated with the sport of unlimited hydroplane racing. During the racing season, Seattle's two daily newspapers—the *Seattle Times* and the *Seattle Post-Intelligencer*—devoted more column inches to hydroplane racing than to professional football, baseball, and basketball combined. The two network television stations—KING and KOMO—broadcast the races live, even when accidents or bad weather delayed racing and the event stretched to nine or ten hours. The intense media exposure made celebrities out of the bold and daring drivers.

As the name "unlimited" implies, there were no limits on engine size or hull design and most of the boats were powered with 2,000-hp World War II surplus fighter-plane engines. These were the world's biggest, fastest, and loudest race boats. A typical unlimited hydroplane was 30 feet long and 12 feet wide and would fly across the water at 160 to 170 miles per hour, throwing a spray called a "roostertail" 60 feet into the air and 250 feet long.

The sport was born at New York City's Columbia Yacht Club in 1904, and its premier race was the Gold Cup. Many of the original racing rules came from sailboat racing, including a complicated starting process that involved clocks, cannons, and flags. Another rule borrowed from sail boating allowed the winning boat to defend the Gold Cup on its home water.

During the first forty-five years of Gold Cup racing, an intense rivalry developed between the sophisticated old-money yachtsmen from upstate New York and the brash *nouveau riche* of the tough and gritty motor city, Detroit. The Gold Cup shuttled between these two hotbeds of powerboat racing for thirty years. During this period, the design of the boats had stayed true to typical maritime principles. The boats were long and narrow and built out of wooden planks. If an owner wanted to go faster, he went looking for more horsepower putting two, three, or even four engines into a boat.

Some 2,500 miles west of New York, Seattle businessman Stanley S. Sayres put together an unlimited race boat for the 1950 season with the unlikely name of "*Slo-mo-shun IV*." Sayres' revolutionary new machine had more in common with an airplane than a boat. Built with thin aircraft-grade plywood and capitalizing on a distinctive airfoil shape for the deck, and two aluminum-skinned runners (called sponsons) that protruded under the boat, the *Slo-mo-shun* flew across the water faster than anything seen before. The *Slo-mo-shun* was the brainchild of veteran boat racer and Boeing Company employee Ted Jones. Respected Seattle boat builder Anchor Jensen handled the construction, and a team of Jones' friends, most of whom were mechanics at United Airlines, worked on the engine.

The *Slo-mo-shun* was powered by a twelve-cylinder Allison V-1710 out of a P-38 Lightning. In June 1950, the *Slo-mo-shun* astounded the boating world by raising the U.S. water speed record from 124.860 to 160.323 mph. The *Slo-mo-shun* followed up its speed record run with a sweep at the Gold Cup in Detroit, lapping every other boat in the race. When Sayres and his team returned to Seattle, they brought back the Gold Cup and the rights to hold the 1951 race on Lake Washington.

Nestled between Puget Sound and Lake Washington, Seattle was a city surrounded by water and boats. Thanks to the Boeing Company, it was also a city that had a deep love for airplanes and flying. There was something about hydroplanes - half boat, half airplane- that appealed to the people of Seattle like nothing before. When the 1951 Gold Cup race took place, hundreds of thousands of fans showed up on the shores of Lake Washington to line the racecourse and cheer as "their" *Slo-mo-shuns* took on the fleet from Detroit. By now Sayres had built a second boat, named the *Slo-mo-shun V.* Fueled by intense civic pride and some genuine hard feelings, a fierce rivalry sprung up between Seattle and Detroit.

By the summer of 1955, Sayres had won the cup five times in a row, and hundreds of thousands of Seattleites showed up at the lake to watch him try for his sixth Gold Cup. Unbelievably, while leading the race with just a few laps to go, one of the *Slo-mo-shun IV*'s exhaust stacks broke and the hot exhaust caught the thin plywood deck on fire. When the *Slo-mo-shun IV's* driver, Joe Taggart, stopped to fight the fire, a Detroit boat named *Gale V* slipped past and claimed the victory. Seattle was shocked. Not only had its string of victories been broken, but the Gold Cup was going back to Detroit.

In a rush of civic pride and enthusiasm for racing, three wealthy businessmen announced that they would each build new boats and represent the city of Seattle for the 1956 racing season. One of those men was Bill Boeing, Jr. The other two were Edgar Kaiser and William T. Waggoner.[1]

In late April 1956, Mira flew Mr. Boeing on a business trip to Canada. During lunch, one of the Canadians asked Boeing about his racing plans. The conversation wound through several topics and Mira learned that Mr. Boeing was serious about racing and that the boat would be powered by a G-6 Allison engine that Boeing had bought from Stan Sayres. Mira also learned that the new boat's name was going to be "*Miss Wahoo*," in honor of Marci Boeing's home town. Eventually, the Canadian asked Boeing if he had hired a driver. Boeing responded that he had not made a decision yet.

That afternoon, as Mira and Boeing flew the Aero Commander back to Seattle, Boeing looked across the cockpit at Mira and keyed the intercom in his headset to ask, "Have you ever driven a boat?"

Mira replied, "Sure, I can drive a boat."

"Would you like to drive my boat?"

"Yes I would!"

Mr. Boeing never followed up and asked Mira what type of boating experience he had, but if he had been asked, Mira would have said that the only boat he had ever been in was a kayak, and the fastest he had ever gone was 7 miles per hour.[2]

On the morning of May 9, 1956, a caravan of three trucks crept slowly up the steep grade of westbound U.S. Highway 10 from Ellensburg, Washington, toward Snoqualmie Pass in the Cascade Mountains. They were nearing the end of a 2,000-mile journey from Michigan to Seattle.

Shortly after the *Slo-mo-shun V* had won the 1951 Gold Cup, Ted Jones and Anchor Jensen had a falling out. Jones went looking for a new builder to bring his designs to life. He had to travel halfway across the country, to Bay City, Michigan, to find a builder who could match Jensen's quality and skill. Jones entered into an agreement with master craftsman Les Staudacher to build his boats. From 1954 to 1956, Staudacher built seven boats from Jones designs, including the *Miss Wahoo* for Bill Boeing Jr. and an identical hull called the *Shanty-I* for William T. Waggoner.

The caravan of trucks pulled three new Jones/Staudacher hydroplanes. They were Bill Boeing's *Miss Wahoo*, a second "spare" hull for Boeing "just in case they needed it," and Waggoner's *Shanty-I*. The boats' arrival in town was enough of a story that newspaper photographers climbed up on the arches of the Mercer Island Bridge to get photos of the caravan as it made its way across Lake Washington.[3] After the trucks crossed the bridge, the *Miss Wahoo* went to Aero Copter, on the east side of Boeing Field.

Bill Boeing, Mira, and Junie were waiting at Boeing Field as the sun slipped behind the Olympic Mountains, creating what painters call "the golden hour." It is the moment before sunset when the sun seems to burn brightest and the air is filled with a rich golden light that exposes the beauty in everything. The hull was parked next to Aero Copter's hangar. The golden light of the setting sun reflected off the newly varnished wood, and the boat seemed to glow.

With the constant noise of planes taking off and landing, Bill, Junie, and Mira had to shout to be heard as they walked around the exotic new arrival. On the runway, a big new Boeing 377 Stratocruiser was running up its engines in preparation for takeoff. Bill cupped his hands to his mouth and leaned close to Mira to shout over the howl of the Stratocruiser. "What do you think?"

Mira looked at the flawless dark-stained mahogany that curved across the long sleek deck of the new racer. "It's the most beautiful machine I've ever seen," Mira shouted back.

Boeing smiled and asked, "Do you still want to try driving it?"

"More than I've ever wanted to do anything!"

"Okay, let's do it!" Boeing said and he held out his hand for Mira to shake. Bill Boeing was a multimillionaire with teams of lawyers working on contracts and agreements, but he was also a man of honor, so once he shook hands on a deal, it was done. Mira was now officially the driver of the *Miss Wahoo*, but the hydro was a long way from being ready. It was a bare hull with no engine or hardware. It was going to be Junie's job to get the *Miss Wahoo* finished.

The following day, May 10, was an important one in Mira Slovak's life. As he was waking up and fixing his morning coffee in Seattle, U.S. Senator Warren G. Magnuson, chairman of the powerful Interstate and Foreign Commerce Committee, banged his gavel down to bring a special meeting of the committee to order. The one item of business was whether or not to make an exception for Mira Slovak to the FCC rule that prohibited the granting of a radio operator's license to non-citizens.

Magnuson spoke on behalf of Slovak, saying that "Slovak has given the U.S. Air Force incalculable assistance since arriving in the United States." He went on to say that "Mr. Slovak has been denied the ability to make a living in his chosen profession of airline captain, because of the FCC rule barring non-citizens from getting radio licenses." The committee voted with Magnuson, and Mira was granted his license. The *Associated Press* picked up the story, which appeared in papers across the country the next day.[4]

Later that same day, Bill Boeing Jr. issued a press release of his own, announcing that Mira Slovak would drive the *Miss Wahoo* in the 1956 Seafair Trophy Race, Seattle's replacement for the Gold Cup. The *Associated Press* picked up this story as well, proving that even though Mira had escaped from communist Czechoslovakia over three years earlier, he was still a hot topic for the American newspapers.[5]

Mira continued to fly for Mr. Boeing during the day, but in the evenings he and Junie would stay late at Aero Copter and work on the boat. Junie invited a number of his friends to help, and before long, there was a crew of eight to ten young men in crisp white coveralls swarming over the boat every night, installing fuel lines, oil filters, water pickups, and the hundreds of other components necessary to make an unlimited hydroplane work. The crew was entirely volunteer and worked day jobs until 5 p.m. Then they would leave their offices, stores, or repair shops and head to Aero Copter to hang up their suits and ties, switch into coveralls, and begin working on the boat. There was a radio in the shop that was tuned during the day to an easy-listening station, with the volume kept low as the Aero Copter mechanics serviced Mr. Boeing's planes. Once the *Wahoo* crew took over, the station got switched away from Pat Boone and Perry Como, and the shop rocked and rolled to Elvis Presley singing 'Heartbreak Hotel' while tools clanked and rattled. The young men working on the boat laughed easily and joked as they talked about cars, girls, and more often than not, hydroplane racing. It was during one of these evening work party conversations, with Fats Domino singing Blueberry Hill in the background and the scent of fresh varnish wafting through the night, that Mira first heard the name Bill Muncey. A young man from Detroit who drove a Seattle boat named "*Miss Thriftway*," Muncey had come within a whisker of winning the 1955 Gold Cup. In fact, for a thrilling thirty minutes, Muncey and all of Seattle thought that he and the *Miss Thriftway* had won the big race, but midway into the team's victory celebration, a race official announced that Detroit's *Gale V*, was being awarded 400 bonus points for having a faster elapsed time than Muncey's, so the Cup would be going back to Detroit. The consensus in the *Wahoo* shop was that Muncey and the *Miss Thriftway* would provide Mira and the *Miss Wahoo* with some of their stiffest competition on the racecourse.

There was a tremendous sense of teamwork in the shop, similar to the esprit de corps Mira felt in his early days with the Czech Air Force before the communists took over. At about 7.30 p.m. each evening, Blanche would show up with food to feed the entire crew. Sometimes, she brought sandwiches and chips. Other nights, it was fried chicken and potato salad.

If the weather was cold and rainy, she brought big steaming kettles of soup or spaghetti and meatballs. Mira was not as mechanically inclined as many of the crew members, so when Blanche arrived he would break away and help her set up the meals. They would often have quiet, personal conversations speaking in Czech while they worked side-by-side preparing the food. Mira looked forward to the nightly conversations in his native language, and he also appreciated the gentle mothering advice that he received from Blanche.

One afternoon in early June 1956, Mira arrived at Aero Copter after flying back from Salem, Oregon, and saw a light blue panel van with large yellow letters on the side saying "KING TV" parked in front of Aero Copter's big sliding doors. As he entered the shop he saw technicians setting up lights around the *Miss Wahoo* and stringing microphone cables. A tall, thin man with shiny black hair and sunken cheeks, wearing a blue blazer that looked at least a size too big, approached Mira and held out his hand. "I'm Bill O'Mara. I'm here from KING-TV and we would like to do an interview with you."

Mira was embarrassed by his poor English. He wanted to avoid talking in front of the cameras. "Wouldn't you rather talk to Mr. Boeing?"

"Heck Mira, we've been talking to Mr. Boeing since he first announced this boat back in November. Now it's time for action. We want to hear from the driver!"

"I don't know if my English is good enough for television."

"Don't worry, I'll ask easy questions, and if you're really unhappy with the way something comes out, we can always go back and reshoot it."

Mira reluctantly agreed and O'Mara said, "Great! This is going to be huge. I hope you're ready."

Mira was not quite sure what O'Mara meant. "What will be huge?"

"Everything," O'Mara laughed. "To start with, at least 100,000 people will see this interview when it airs tomorrow night. When race day comes, there will be hundreds of thousands more people on the beach in person and another million sitting at home watching on TV. Heck, you're going to be famous. I don't mean famous like the mayor of some small town, I mean famous like Mickey Mantle!"

Mira shook his head. "I don't want to be famous. I just want to drive Mr. Boeing's boat."

O'Mara chuckled, "Well you can't do one without doing the other." Just then a KING-TV technician plugged in a thick black extension cord and a bank of powerful TV lights flashed on, bathing the *Miss Wahoo* in bright blue white light. O'Mara nodded toward the boat and said, "It looks like they're ready for us. I'd like you to sit in the cockpit and I'll kneel next to you on the deck."

The interview went well. O'Mara asked broad, easy questions about Mira's escape. At one point, he asked, "How were you able to fly so close to the ground in the dark?"

Mira answered confidently, "It was easy because there was plenty of moonshine."

O'Mara choked back a hearty laugh, and then said, "Do you mean moonlight?"

"Yes, I was able to fly very low in the dark because there was plenty of moonlight so I could see trees and buildings." The interview continued, and Mira enjoyed being able to talk about his experiences under communism and explain what an awful system of government he thought it was.

After the interview was finished and O'Mara and the KING-TV crew had left, Junie crossed the floor to Mira and said, "So you used a lot of moonshine when you escaped?"

"Oh yes quite a lot of moonshine."

"Mira, moonshine and moonlight are very different things. Moonlight is the light we see from the moon in the night. Moonshine is homemade whiskey. So when you tell people you used a lot of moonshine to escape, they may think that you drank a lot of whiskey."

Mira laughed and said, "There were times during the escape when I wished I had some whiskey."

The next night, Mira went home to his small apartment and watched the broadcast of the interview by himself. He was embarrassed by how awkward his English was and that thousands of people were hearing him stumble trying to express simple ideas about freedom and communism. He decided to enroll in night classes at the University of Washington to improve his English.

Junie's goal was to have the *Miss Wahoo* ready for her first test by July 16. The young volunteer crew worked long hours for several weeks, arriving shortly after 5 p.m. and staying until well after 2 a.m. They got used to the uncanny silence that descended on Boeing Field after midnight, when the airplane traffic dropped to almost nothing. The small group of friends would work to the point of exhaustion and then, when Junie felt that they were too tired to be productive, he would announce, "Quitting time. Let's head for home." He would turn the radio back to its easy-listening station and switch out the lights, and the close-knit team would slip out of the shop. For a moment, the sound of car doors slamming would echo from the deserted hangars as the *Wahoo* crew left to drive through the empty streets of Seattle to their homes. Soon, they were tiptoeing to bed, next to sleeping wives with their hands and hair smelling of sawdust, fiberglass, and motor oil.

There are two equally important parts that make up a race boat: the hull and the engine. The hull is sleek and polished with an almost feminine beauty, but without an engine, it is just a collection of wood and fiberglass. The engine by itself is hard steel and cold aluminum, simmering with masculine power and potential, but capable of nothing on its own. There is a magical moment when the two are brought together and joined in a marriage of speed and grace where the whole becomes so much greater than the sum of the parts. Yet the marriage is not complete until the engine is started at least once. This consummation takes place when the boat is pulled outside on its trailer and the engine is fired for the first time. In the specialized jargon of boat racing, this activity has come to be called "trailer firing."

Before a first trailer fire, there is so much checking and rechecking of each nut, bolt, hose, and wire that they never seem to take place on time and almost always happen late at night long after sensible people would be home asleep. The *Miss Wahoo* was no different, and it was two in the morning when the big sliding doors at Aero Copter were pushed back and a yellow fork lift pulled the *Miss Wahoo* out of the shop for the first time.

The sky was clear with a bright moon, but the air was damp and chilly. Mira buttoned the top button of his shirt to stay warm. Two crewmen in stained *Wahoo* coveralls took positions on either side of the boat, holding fire extinguishers in case something went wrong. Mira and Junie climbed onto the boat. Mira sat in the cockpit and Junie stood behind him, his legs straddling the tail fin. The big 1,710-cubic-inch supercharged V-12 Allison engine they had shoehorned into the engine compartment was similar to the engine that powered the Avia S-199s Mira had flown in Czechoslovakia, so the complicated starting process was familiar to him.

Junie tapped Mira on the shoulder and said, "Okay, let's do this."

"Master power on," Mira called out, as he flipped a switch on the dashboard. An oil pressure light came on, bathing the cockpit with its red glow. Mira's left hand moved to a toggle switch on the dash marked "Boost" and switched it on. In the silence of the airport, Mira had no trouble hearing a soft metallic whirring as the fuel boost pump sprang to life. In a moment, the high-pitched sound dropped to a low growl as the pump filled with fuel. Mira watched the fuel pressure gauge as its needle climbed to 15 pounds. With his right hand, he reached out and moved the lever on the face of the magneto switch two clicks to the right and announced loudly to the crew, "Mags are hot!" He then rested his right hand on the mixture control beside his seat while moving his left hand towards two silver switches on the dashboard.

Mira felt like Dr. Frankenstein in an old horror movie, about to throw a switch and see if his creation would come to life. He cast a glance over his should toward Junie, who nodded, "Yes."

Mira nodded back and then used the index finger of his left hand to press the starter switch. The starter began to spin and engaged the engine with a solid-sounding "clunk." The huge engine began to turn over slowly. Mira could almost hear each one of the twelve pistons as they moved up and down in the massive seven-foot-long engine. After a few seconds, still holding the starter switch down with his index finger, Mira gave a tap to the primer switch with his middle finger. Deep inside the engine, the primer shot a fine mist of high-octane racing fuel into the cylinders. There was a loud boom as the fuel in one of the cylinders ignited with an explosion. Mira tapped the primer again, more fuel was fed to the engine, and there were more booms as the fuel in four more cylinders exploded. Mira held the primer down now and the single booms of each cylinder firing blended together into an awesome roar as all twelve cylinders started to thunder. Thick black smoke billowed from the exhaust stacks on either side of the cockpit and the engine sprang to life. Still holding the primer switch down with the middle finger on his left hand, Mira used his right hand to ease the mixture control forward to "Full Rich," and the roar intensified.

Junie left his position and walked past Mira to the engine, pulling a flashlight from his pocket to check for leaking hoses or other problems. There were none. He turned to Mira and gave him a "thumbs up" sign accompanied by a big smile.

After letting the engine run for a few more moments, Junie drew his hand across his throat in the universal gesture telling Mira to "kill it." He pulled the fuel mix back to "cut-off" and the engine died.

As the last barking rumbles of the engine echoed across the empty airport, Mira heard the crew began to clap and cheer. Somewhere in the darkness, a joyous voice called out "It's alive!" and everybody laughed. With the first trailer fire completed, the *Miss Wahoo* was put back into the hanger. The crew closed up and headed toward home with the roar of the engine still ringing in their ears.

Mira forgot his wallet and had to run back into the shop after the lights were off. Moonlight though the window showed him the massive airplane motor sitting in the sleek hydroplane. He was struck by how similar to airplanes these boats were. They used the same type of engine, and the same fuel. They were probably just as exciting to drive. Mira walked across the dark shop. He placed his hands on the sleek bow of the powerful boat. He felt a lump in his throat. He knew he was a good pilot, but he was not sure he would ever get a chance to fly airliners again. He hoped he would, but until then, he was going to put everything he had into becoming the world's best boat racer. He spoke to the boat like a jockey talking to his mount, "Okay girl, we're going to be a team you and me. We are going to go amazing places and do amazing things. But we're going to take care of each other too. I won't let anything bad happen to you, and you better not let anything bad happen to me."

In spite of the monumental hours the volunteers put in, they missed their target date by three days, and the launch was delayed until July 19. The night before their first run, Junie stopped Mira as he was leaving the shop and handed him a large white gift box tied up with a red satin ribbon. Mira untied the ribbon and pulled the top off the box. It contained a khaki flight suit. "That's my lucky flight suit." Junie said.

"This is yours?" Mira asked.

"Well it was mine, now it's yours. I wore it in Korea. I want you to wear it when you drive the boat." Mira held up the suit and saw the blue and gold U.S. 5th Air Force patch on the left shoulder.

"Why are you giving this to me?" he asked.

"Because if it can give you half as much luck as it gave me, we ought to win a bunch of races."

"How was this suit lucky for you?"

Junie laughed. "Well, I was flying reconnaissance in an F-86 Saber. All of its weapons systems had been removed and replaced with three big cameras. I had been sent up above the 38th parallel to look for evidence of a North Korean troop buildup. I had a couple normal F-86s flying cover on top of me. We got jumped by about six MiG-15s and they took out my cover pretty quick. I was a sitting duck without any weapons, and I didn't think that pointing my cameras at the MiGs was going to slow them down. To top it off, I was carrying a couple of external fuel tanks. As soon as the MiGs headed for me, I dropped 'em, jammed the throttle forward, and scooted for home at 600 knots. I was too darn frightened to even turn my cameras off. Well, the cameras kept rolling as these big ol' tanks of fuel dropped right into the center of a communist ammunition dump. They were full of Jet-A, so of course they blew up when they hit the ground and that caught the whole ammunition dump on fire and in a second it all blows sky high. I didn't know that anything had happened until I got back to base and they developed the film. I even ended up getting a citation for bravery!"

Mira smiled. "Yes, let's hope it is equally lucky for me."

On Thursday, July 19, Junie and his right-hand man, Les Eide, trucked the *Miss Wahoo* 4.5 miles from Aero Copter to Lloyd Jett's Marina at the south end of Seattle's Lake Washington. Most of the crew, including Mira, met up at Jett's after work, while a few crewmembers drove to Bill Boeing's home to prepare the waterfront boathouse where the *Miss Wahoo* would be stored.

The plan was to put the *Miss Wahoo* in the lake at Jett's, and then Mira and Junie would drive her eight miles up the lake to the Boeing boathouse, where the finishing touches would be put on the boat. At 28 feet long, 12 feet wide, and weighing 5,500 pounds, it took a crane to pick up the sleek mahogany and red racer and place her in the water. Just before the crane lifted the boat from its cradle, Mira climbed onto the deck and sat with his feet in the engine well, holding onto the spreader bar for the lifting slings. From his spot on the deck, he rode the *Miss Wahoo* all the way from the flatbed trailer into the water.

The crew had been working so hard to get the mechanical aspects of the boat finished that they had not had time to paint the name on the boat. The only markings on the boat were the small Coast Guard registration numbers 30 V1994, stenciled in white on either side of the bow.

When the boat was in the water, Junie and several crew members leapt from the dock to the deck and began to unhook the lifting slings and make final preparations for the first test run. It was well past 8 p.m., and the crystal-blue summer sky was beginning to deepen towards purple as the sun was slipping behind the Olympic Mountains. At last, Junie announced that the boat was ready, slipped on his own life jacket, and tossed a second one to Mira as the rest of the crew gingerly stepped back to the dock.

Mira strapped on his life jacket and crash helmet, and then took his place in the cockpit. Junie knelt to his left with one hand holding onto the tailfin behind Mira's head and the other hand grasping the side of the fiberglass cowling. "Are you ready?" Junie asked. Mira nodded. "Okay," Junie said, pointing towards the tachometer. "Let's keep it under 1,500 rpm."

The boat rocked gently as Mira looked around the cockpit. Everything was ready. Just as in the trailer-fire practices, Mira's hands glided across the dashboard to turn on the switches: master power, fuel boost, and magneto. Then he held down the starter and tapped the primer. The boat roared to life. There is no clutch or gearshift in an unlimited hydroplane. The engine connects directly to the propeller shaft, so as soon as the engine fires up, the boat is moving forward. An Allison engine idles at about 1,000 rpm, which will push a 5,500-pound unlimited hydroplane at a speed of 45 mph.

The smooth, curved sponsons under the boat lifted it up, allowing it to skim across the surface of the lake. Mira moved his hands to the steering wheel. He pressed his throttle foot down and watched as the needle on the tachometer swung up to 1,500 rpm. The boat was now moving almost 70 miles an hour and the noise and vibration were terrific. For a moment, Mira watched straight ahead as the small fleet of pleasure boats that had gathered around Jett's Marina to witness the launching moved out of the way. Mira knew he had to head north, up Lake Washington to Boeing's property, so he turned the steering wheel gently to the left. Nothing happened. The boat kept plowing forward at 70 miles per hour. Mira turned the wheel a bit more—still nothing. Mira felt a moment of panic and turned the wheel hard to the left. Suddenly the boat took a hop and turned violently to the left. "Too much!" Mira thought, as he swung the wheel back to the right. Now the boat swung wildly to the right as the spectator fleet scattered. Mira turned the wheel back to the left again and eventually got the boat moving in a straight line. "This is going to be a lot harder than I thought," Mira said to himself.

Once the *Miss Wahoo* was free of the spectator fleet and safely headed up lake, Mira and Junie turned their attention to the dashboard and the gauges that would tell them about the health of their boat. The engine noise drowned out any effort to speak. They resorted to hand gestures, pointing at a gauge and then giving thumbs up to each other if it read correctly. The tachometer held steady at 1,500 rpm and the speedometer reported 70 miles per hour. Fuel pressure was 15 pounds. Oil pressure was 70 pounds and manifold pressure was 27 pounds. Everything looked good, and Mira and Junie traded thumbs up. As they passed Seward Park, they veered gently to the left and paralleled the shore. It was still difficult for Mira to get the boat to travel in a straight line. She seemed to want to pull hard to the left, but when Mira tried turning the wheel to the right, either he did not turn if far enough and nothing happened or he turned it too far and she swung wildly to the right. Mira was frustrated and embarrassed and kept thinking, "How can I race this boat if I can't even get her to go in a straight line?"

Junie held two fingers in front of Mira's face and then made a palm down motion with his hand, indicating that he wanted Mira to press his foot on the throttle and bring the engine up to 2,000 rpm. The *Miss Wahoo* responded instantly, speeding up to 100 mph and throwing a long, tall spray of water behind her. Mira noticed that as the speed increased, the boat became much easier to steer. Junie and Mira scanned the gauges again and everything continued to look shipshape. While they were looking at the dashboard, they failed to see a long, low rolling wave that had been left by one of boats from the spectator fleet. The *Miss Wahoo* hit it at 100 miles per hour, bounced clear of the water, and sailed along for almost 60 feet with just the tip of the rudder touching the lake. The landing jolted Mira and Junie, but they both held on and there was no damage to the boat. Unlike the airplanes that Mira and Junie flew, hydroplanes did not use seatbelts. If there was an accident, racing officials did not want unconscious drivers to be trapped and drown in a sinking boat. They felt that it was safer for drivers to be thrown clear, so seatbelts were prohibited.

They sped north toward the Mercer Island Floating Bridge. Mira eased off the throttle and slowed down to 45 miles an hour as they shot beneath the western high-rise of the bridge. Moments later, as they approached Boeing's home, Mira took his foot all the way off the throttle and pulled the mixture control back to idle cut off. The engine went silent, and the boat slid to a stop. Junie was ecstatic, whooping and hollering and slapping Mira on the back. "That was fantastic," Junie yelled.

Bill Boeing, Jr., at the wheel of a 20-foot tender boat named *the Wahoo II,* cheered and clapped as he motored slowly up to the stationary *Miss Wahoo*. One of the crew members on the tender boat tossed a line to Junie, who tied it to the bow so they could tow the sleek hydro to the dock.

Mira sat quietly in the cockpit. He was stunned. This was louder, faster, and much more violent than he had expected. The boat was difficult to steer, the rocking and bouncing seemed horribly dangerous, and he could not imagine what it would be like to race side-by-side with six of these monstrous machines. It was going to be difficult to let Bill and Junie down, but he did not want anything to do with racing this boat. Mira sat in the cockpit feeling shame and disappointment as the jubilant crew towed the boat to Boeing's boathouse.

When they reached the dock, Mira put on a good face and joined in the joyous celebration, but he felt like a fraud. He decided that he did not want to ruin the celebration, but in a day or two, he would take Junie aside and tell him to get someone else to drive the boat. Mira consoled himself with the thought that Junie might want to drive the boat himself.

The sun was setting and a photographer from the *Seattle Times* asked to get a shot of Mira and the boat before it was too dark. Mira called the crew over and the photographer arranged Junie, Les, Mira, and Bill Jr. kneeling on the deck of the boat while the rest of the crew stood behind them on the dock. Everyone smiled and flash bulbs popped, and Mira felt like even more of a fake.

The Boeing boathouse consisted of a long building built half onshore and half sitting on pilings over the lake. The shore side of the boathouse could be used as a guesthouse, with a bathroom, carpeted floors, a bed, and wicker furniture. The shop side was nestled between two long docks. It had skylights, wood paneling, and a concrete floor that was painted white. A large door opened up to the lake and an overhead bridge crane that ran on rails from inside the boathouse out to the docks. As the crew used ropes to pull the *Miss Wahoo* into position for the crane to pick her up, Bill Jr. approached Mira, shook his hand, and said, "You look exhausted. Why don't you go in to the boathouse and get a drink of water?"

Mira let himself into the boathouse and drank a glass of tap water in one gulp. He sat down dejectedly on the floor and leaned against the bed. His back was sore from the unexpected hop the boat had taken when it hit the roller. Mira arched his back to stretch the sore muscle and felt a relief in tension as his back popped. He could hear the muffled sounds of the crew's celebration coming through the wall. He crossed his arms and propped them on his knees, and then he laid his head on his arms and thought, "How am I going to tell Mr. Boeing and Junie that I don't want anything to do with driving that frightening boat?"

Suddenly, all the long hours working on the boat, and the stress and worry about driving, caught up with him. He was so sleepy he could hardly keep his eyes open. He grabbed a blue velvet pillow from one of the wicker chairs and placed it on the floor, stretched out face down with his head buried in the pillow, and fell into a deep, cleansing sleep. While Mira drifted into exhausted sleep, his mind kept wrestling with his fear of the boat, and when he awoke an hour later, he was in a much better frame of mind.

"The noise was awful," he thought, "But that's easy to solve. All I need to do is wear some ear plugs. The boat's ride was horrible and it seemed to react to every wave we hit. Well that's probably because I was going too slow. The boat is designed to run at 160 mph and we were going between 45 and 100 the whole time. At 160 mph, the boat will really get up out of the water and fly across the surface, and I bet it isn't nearly as rough. The same thing is probably true about the steering, too. I never felt like I had much control of the boat, but that has got to be because the rudder is designed to control the boat at 160 mph, when the boat is free of the water and there is very little drag. At 100 mph, the rudder is just too darn small to do much good." Mira decided that he would drive the boat a couple more times and see if running her faster helped him feel better about it.

The next day, when he showed up at Aero Copter, all the other employees applauded when he came in. Junie came up to him and handed him a copy of the *Seattle Post-Intelligencer* opened to the sports page, showing a large story about the boat's launch, with a big photo of Mira and the boat. Mira wondered if this was the start of the fame Bill O'Mara had predicted.[6]

The next test session was set for Wednesday, July 26. When the shop doors were opened shortly after 9 a.m. on the 26th and the bridge crane carried the *Miss Wahoo* out into the sunlit summer morning, she looked much different than she had at the shakedown cruise a few days earlier. Large white script, outlined in yellow, said "*Miss Wahoo*" on both sides of the boat, and even larger characters on the deck said "U-77." Unlimited hydroplanes were required to have their racing number, preceded by a large "U," for unlimited, painted on their hulls to help race officials tell one boat from another. Behind the cockpit, there was the familiar white circle and red star of a Texaco logo. Above the logo in yellow lettering, it said, "Driver: Mira Slovak" and right in front of Mira's name was a small red, white, and blue Czechoslovakian flag.

The crew, some wearing clean white uniforms and others in brand new red coveralls, chatted nervously as they waited for the christening ceremony to begin. Mr. Boeing, his wife Marci, Junie, and Junie's wife Alice approached the bow of the boat where the crane held it suspended over the edge of the dock. Alice was wearing a knee-length white A-Line dress with intricate lace cutouts across the shoulders. She carried a bottle of champagne with a gold-foiled neck tied up with a red ribbon. She giggled nervously and asked Junie, "What am I supposed to do?"

"Just say, I christen thee *Miss Wahoo*, and then give her a good whack with champagne."

"I can do that." She said. "Is everybody ready?" She raised her voice to make sure that everyone could hear: "I christen thee *Miss Wahoo.*" She swung the bottle hard against the bow and it shattered in a shower of broken glass and white foaming champagne. Bill and Junie clapped as the crew cheered. A couple of pleasure boats waiting to watch the test session blew their horns.

Junie hugged Alice and then turned to the crew and said, "Okay, let's get her in the water."

As the crew used hand-operated chain falls to lower the boat, Junie and Mira went over their plans. Mira was to idle the boat 8 miles north, up the lake to the Sand Point Naval Air Station, which was on a large peninsula jutting out into Lake Washington. When he got there, he would shut it off and wait for Junie, Bill, and the rest of the crew, who would be following in the *Wahoo II*. When they arrived, Mira would make several high-speed runs on the north side of the peninsula.

The boat started easily, and with the ear plugs Mira was now wearing under his helmet, the painful roar from the previous test was reduced to an exciting but acceptable rumble. Even at an idle, Mira reached Sand Point in less than ten minutes. He shut off the engine and had to wait a while for the crew to catch up. He was surprised to see that there were a few hundred fans lining the shore and at least a dozen spectator boats waiting to watch him run. The water was calm, with just a few small swells, and the boat rocked gently from side to side. Mira could hear the rhythmic slap of the waves lapping against the underside of the boat. It was a calming sound.

When the *Wahoo II* carrying the crew arrived, it idled straight up to Mira. Junie shouted across the water, "I'm going to head about a mile to the northwest. I'll try to wave the spectators back out of your way. Then I'm going to sit down there, and I want you to make a few high speed runs towards me. Use us as a turn buoy. I want to see how she corners. Come as close to us as you can."

As Mira watched the tender boat pull away and head up the lake, he gave himself a bit of a pep talk. "You can do this," he thought, as Junie and the *Wahoo II* shrank into the distance. He was nervous, but excited to see if the boat would handle better at higher speeds. When Mira was sure that Junie had taken up his position, he reached out with his left hand and toggled the starter switch that fired up the engine. The *Miss Wahoo* got up on top of the water quickly. Mira took a brief scan of the dash to make sure that all the gauges were reading normal. Then he eased open the throttle and wound the engine up past 2,000 rpm, past 3,000 rpm all the way to 3,500 rpm. The bouncing and rocking that Mira had felt at slow speed disappeared. The *Miss Wahoo* seemed to float along on a cushion of air. The disturbing left pull that he had felt was gone too. He loosened his grip on the wheel and the boat continued to track straight and true. For a second Mira let go of the wheel completely, and the *Wahoo* still kept charging straight ahead like she was on rails. He looked at the dashboard and saw the needle on the speedometer bouncing between 140 and 150 mph. At that speed, the *Miss Wahoo* came to life. She was no longer a collection of wood, fiberglass, nuts, and bolts. She was now almost a living, breathing being; a magical cross between a dragon, a thoroughbred racehorse, and a beautiful woman. Mira looked up from the dash in time to see Junie flash past on his left as he overshot the turn. He eased up on the throttle and turned the wheel to the left. The boat did not turn immediately, but she did start to slide a bit. The sensation was similar to turning a fast car on ice. It was not impossible, but it would take a very precise touch. The slide continued a second longer and then the boat took a hop and settled into a wide arcing turn. About a quarter of the way through the turn, the boat began to slow dramatically, and as soon as the speed dropped below 100 mph, the boat began to rock and bounce again just like it had on the first day. Mira smiled to himself, and thought, "Oh, I see. She doesn't like to go slow, and there is a real art to this, trying to get her to go in the direction you want while keeping her speed as high as possible." Mira pulled out of the turn and started his return run back towards his starting point. He made another quick glance at the dash and flew back down the lake. His mind was working on the problem of getting through the turn faster and smoother. "Maybe if I don't back off quite so much and carry more speed into the turn?" Mira thought. So when he started his next turn, he did not lift his foot off the throttle nearly so much. That was a big mistake. As soon as he turned the wheel, the *Wahoo* rocked precariously onto her right side and for a moment, Mira worried that he might get pitched out. "Whoa, girl!" Mira shouted. "I guess you really didn't like that, did you?"

He came out of the turn and sped back up the lake toward Junie and the crew. Mira was still working out how to get through the turn more smoothly. "Maybe I'm waiting too long to get back on the throttle. This time I'll lift my foot, but only for a couple seconds." He started aiming just a bit to the left of Junie. When he was still about 50 yards away, he turned the wheel and eased up on the throttle. The boat started into the turn, flashing by Junie and the crew. As soon as Mira felt that the boat was sliding, he gave her full power again. To his complete surprise, it suddenly felt like the boat was going to swap ends. The rear of the boat seemed to be moving faster than the front of the boat. Mira quickly turned the wheel to the right, like you would when a car starts to spin. Amazingly, with the wheel turned right the boat continued its smooth left-hand turn. The boat got much deeper into the turn, with a lot more speed, and it was almost halfway through before her speed dropped below 100 mph and the bouncing and hobby-horsing began. Mira continued to experiment with different turning techniques. By the end of the day, he had figured out that if he approached the turn at full throttle, then backed down to three-quarters when he was 30 yards out and gave the wheel a hard jab to the left to send the boat into a skid, then once the skid was established gave her full power again and fed in a bit of right rudder, he could slide the *Wahoo* almost completely through the turn before she lost too much speed. It was a good test that went on for over an hour. Later, as Mira drove back to Boeing's boathouse, he found himself thinking, "This is something that I might be pretty good at."

The next morning, July 27, there was a big article in the *Seattle Post-Intelligencer* under a headline that said, "*Miss Wahoo* Shows Class." Reporter Cliff Harrison said, "That was Bill Boeing's *Miss Wahoo* you saw churning up Lake Washington Wednesday—and did she look good!"[7]

17

Seafair: Seattle, 1956

For more than five years, the Gold Cup had been the centerpiece of a month-long Seattle festival called Seafair, which included parades, sailing regattas, and beauty contests. Losing the Gold Cup put a huge hole in the festival, so the Seattle Yacht Club, along with Greater Seattle, Inc. (a non-profit civic organization devoted to promoting Seattle), sponsored the Seafair Trophy Race to replace the Gold Cup. The race would divide $25,000 in prize money between the top three finishers and was set for Sunday, August 5.

The designated pit area was in Mount Baker Park on Lake Washington, but with seventeen entries, there was not enough room to fit all the boats and trailers into the park. So Bill Boeing, Jr. was allowed to base the *Miss Wahoo* directly from his own boathouse.

Tuesday morning the skies were gray and overcast, with a chilly drizzle that left the racing crews looking for shelter while rain dripped from their boats. Even though it was a weekday and the weather was cold, thousands of hydro fans braved the chilly winds to be on hand at 11 a.m., when the course opened for qualifying. During a brief break in the rain, two boats—the *Miss Seattle* and the *Slo-mo-shun IV*—were able to qualify before the wind picked up and made the course unsafe for high-speed runs.

There were clearly two types of drivers in the pits. There were old racing veterans who had cut their teeth on years of experience in smaller "limited" class hydroplanes, who had worked their way into the upper echelons of the sport to drive the big unlimiteds. The Detroit owners liked these experienced veterans, and all five of the Detroit boats, as well as two of the Seattle boats, were driven by old veterans. Ted Jones, who had designed almost half of the seventeen boats in the race, felt that his new hydroplanes were so light and aerodynamic that they had very little in common with the old boats of the 1930s and 1940s, and he recommended that his boats be driven by airplane pilots. So three of the Seattle drivers—Russ Schleeh in the *Shanty-I,* Bill Stead in the *Maverick*, and Mira Slovak in the *Miss Wahoo*—were virtual rookies with almost no racing experience, but years flying airplanes.

Wednesday, another wet day, was a bust. Several boats made it on to the course, but not a single one was able to qualify. Mira and the *Miss Wahoo* tried to take to the course but broke a propeller and had to be towed back to Boeing's boathouse by a Coast Guard patrol boat.

Thursday saw more rain and high winds and not a single successful qualification. Friday, August 3, saw a brief break in the weather, and spectators streamed to the lake to watch three boats qualify, including the *Miss Wahoo*, but when the course closed at sunset, there were still twelve boats left unqualified.

On Saturday morning, the weather finally cooperated and the sun dawned on crystal clear skies and calm winds. Lake Washington was smooth with just a few slight wind ripples that sailors call "cat's paws." The majestic snow-capped Mount Rainier was visible towering over the south end of the racecourse.

The unqualified teams were anxious to get out on the lake but they had to wait. The course could not be opened until 2 p.m. Seafair included many different community events, and the Seafair Grand Parade, made up of floats, marching bands, and clowns, was scheduled to wind through downtown Seattle at noon. The overworked Seattle Police Department did not have enough manpower to cover the parade route and the racecourse, so it had decreed that the course could not be opened until the parade was finished and officers had a chance to reposition themselves to the lakeshore.

Taking advantage of this break in the action, the race promoters arranged for an 8 a.m. "drivers meeting and breakfast" at Seattle's posh Olympic Hotel, in the heart of downtown Seattle. The official purpose of the meeting was to get all the owners and drivers into one room at one time and go over the racing rules. The unofficial reason was to create an opportunity for the race sponsors and press to spend some time hobnobbing with the drivers. Most of the unqualified drivers saw the meeting as a nuisance, but for Mira, who was already safely in the race and had been isolated from the rest of the drivers at Boeing's boathouse, it was an opportunity to meet many of his competitors for the first time.

Mr. Boeing accompanied Mira to the breakfast and introduced him to several other team owners. The first people they met were the father-and-son team of Henry and Edgar Kaiser, who raced the *Scooter Too* and the *Hawaii Kai III*. Henry Kaiser was a heavy-set bulldog of a man with thick glasses, a receding hairline, and a Churchillian scowl. He was also the founder of the Kaiser empire that included seven shipyards, three aluminum mills, a half dozen steel mills, some iron mines, several hospitals, and the Kaiser-Jeep automobile company. The Kaisers had a vacation home on Lake Tahoe, where they were introduced to hydroplane racing by a neighbor named Stan Dollar, the heir to a shipping fortune. Dollar had been racing for years and drove the *Slo-mo-shun IV* when it won the 1953 Gold Cup.

After the Kaisers, Bill introduced Mira to Jay and Roger Murphy, who were young brothers with military-short hair and broad, bright smiles. The brothers took turns driving their father's boat, the *Breathless*, a robin's-egg blue boat owned by J. Phillip Murphy. J. Phillip also owned the Judson Pacific-Murphy Corporation, one of the west coast's largest steel mills.

Jerry Bryant, president of Greater Seattle Inc., stepped to a podium at the front of the room, leaned over a bulky silver microphone, and said, "May I have your attention? There are still a bunch of boats that need to qualify, so let's get started so we can head back to the lake and get out there on the water."

Mr. Boeing and Mira sat at an empty table and were quickly joined by William Waggoner, his wife Shanty, and their drivers, Russ Schleeh and Bill Stead. Waggoner's family had at onetime owned the largest cattle ranch in Texas, but when oil was discovered, they leased over 300,000 acres to Texaco and entered the oil business.

Uniformed waitresses in black dresses and white aprons began to set plates of steaming food in front of the guests, while Bryant continued to talk. Mira's mind was racing. Less than three years ago, he had been living in Soviet-controlled Czechoslovakia, and now he was sitting down to breakfast with the wealthiest capitalists in the world. He watched in awe as Mr. Boeing leaned over to the Kaiser table and told a joke to Edgar Kaiser. Kaiser chuckled and repeated the joke to the Murphy brothers, and they all laughed.

A tall, broad-shouldered man with a football physique and military short hair seated next to Mira tapped his shoulder and said, "I don't believe we've met. You must be Mira Slovak, I'm Russ Schleeh. I drive the *Shanty* for Mr. Waggoner." He held out his right hand and Mira shook it enthusiastically.[1]

A smaller man seated next to Russ leaned over, saying, "I'm Bill Stead. I drive the *Maverick*." As Mira shook Bill Stead's hand, Stead continued to talk. "We're pilots too." Stead seemed eager to establish their flying credentials, "Russ is a test pilot for the Air Force. He was commander of the XB-49 project. You know, the Flying Wing."

Mira, turned to Bill and asked, "What type of flying do you do?"

Stead replied, "Well I've got two planes of my own; a Howard DGA and an F8F Bearcat, but I'm also the Air Advisor to the Atomic Energy Commission for bomb tests at Frenchman's Flat in Nevada."

Mira was amazed—not only was he sitting with some of the wealthiest tycoons in the nation, he was also sitting with two of the nation's premier pilots. His poor English kept him from saying anything more eloquent than, "I am honored to meet you. You are both such amazing pilots."

At the podium, Bryant turned the meeting over to chief referee Mel Crook, to review the racing rules. Crook tapped the microphone to get everyone's attention and said, "Okay, let's start with the basics. This will be a 90-mile race. We will break the 90 miles into three 30-mile heats. The race course is three and 0.75 miles long, so each 30-mile heat is going to be eight laps. Is that clear to everybody? Eight laps equal 30 miles, and three 30-mile heats equals a 90-mile race. We're going to be awarding points based on your order of finish in your heats; 400 for first, 300 for second, 225 for third, and so on, down to 95 for sixth. At the end of the day, we're going to add up the points from all three of your heats, and the boat with the most points wins." Crook paused to take a drink of water, and then continued, "The course only has room for six boats at a time. Right now we only have five boats qualified, so that isn't a problem. But if we get a couple more boats qualified we will have to break each heat into two sections and divide the qualified boats equally between each section. The sections in the first heat will be called 1A and 1B and the sections in the second heat will be 2A and 2B. We're only going to run the twelve fastest qualifiers. To qualify, you'll need to run a lap of 85 mph or faster. There are seventeen boats in the pits, so some of the slower boats will miss the race. Any questions?"

Nobody raised a hand.

"Good. Moving on to the start. I need everyone's attention because this is kind of complicated. We're going to be using a clock start, so there will be a 12-foot diameter clock on the official barge at the starting line."

A reporter's hand shot into the air. "Will the clock turn from orange to black, or from black to orange?"

Crook nodded his head. "The clock will count down the last sixty seconds to the start. The clock is orange, but turns black as the time ticks down. It you look at the clock and it is half orange and half black, that means you're thirty seconds from the start. If it is three-quarters black that means you've got fifteen seconds. Does everyone get that?" There were nods from the drivers.

"Five minutes before the start of the heat we will fire a canon and put up a green flag. That will be your signal that the course is open and you can leave the pits. I want everyone to run past the starting line at least once during the five-minute period so the scorers can get a good look at your boat and confirm that you are on the course and running. You'll need to round the buoys in a counter clockwise direction and the infield is open in case you need to cut across the course. At one minute, we will fire another cannon and replace the green flag with a white flag. That will be your signal that the clock is starting to count down. You'll need to head up to the north end of the course and go around all of the buoys in the north turn. Once you come out of the north turn you've got to stay in whatever lane you are in and head to the start. When the clock turns completely black, the white flag gets replaced by a green flag and we fire the cannon again. That's the start. If you cross the line before the cannon fires, you've jumped the gun and have to run an extra lap."

Mira must have looked bewildered because Russ leaned over and whispered, "It sounds a lot more complicated than it really is. Once you do it a few times it's easy. Just be as close as you can to the starting line when the clock hits zero, but make sure you don't cross early."

As the meeting broke up, Mira and his newfound friends headed toward the exit. They were joined by a short, stocky young man with wavy hair and an infectious, gap-toothed grin on a head that looked just a little too big for his body. "Hey, fellas. Wait up." Sticking out his hand toward Mira, he said, "Hello. I'm Bill Muncey. You must be Mira Slovak."

In response, Mira held out his hand and said, "Mr. Munsley, I'm very pleased to meet you."

For just an instant, fire flashed in Muncey's eyes. "The name is Muncey." He said sternly, "Mun-see." Then he softened, "Or if you would rather, you can just call me Bill." Muncey turned toward Schleeh and said, "You know I'm a pilot too. I mean, I've got a pilot's license. I don't get to fly much anymore. Too darn busy with the boats, but when I get time I love to go flying."

Schleeh smiled politely and nodded. "It's a great hobby."

"Muncey lowered his voice to whisper to Stead and Schleeh, "Aren't you guys worried about qualifying? I mean, they've only given us a few hours to get the rest of the field into the race." Schleeh continued to smile, but there was a hint of irritation beginning to appear at the corners of his mouth. He knew that Muncey was famous for playing mind games with his competitors and getting them worked up on the beach so that they would make mistakes on the racecourse.

"Well, I guess we will just have to wait and see what happens this afternoon." Schleeh answered.

"I hope that you don't wait too long, otherwise you might miss out on that $25,000!" Muncey turned to Mira and said, "I know that you've got a reputation for having nerves of steel after your escape from the communists and all, but you aren't going to believe what that first turn is like when six screaming hydros roar in there at 160 mph. Don't try to be a hero, at least not for your first couple of heats. Just try to stay out of my way." Muncey flashed his brilliant smile again and Mira was not sure if Muncey was teasing him or being serious.

"Yes, Mr. Munsley." Mira said humbly.

Mira saw anger flash in Muncey's eyes again. "It's pronounced Mun-see!"[2]

After the meeting broke up, there were still several hours before the course would open, so rather than return to Boeing's boathouse, Mira and Mr. Boeing drove to the Mount Baker pits. Boeing wanted to let Mira get an idea of what the crowds on race day would be like. They jumped into Boeing's white convertible Porsche 356, and headed to the racecourse. A few miles from the lake, they began to run into heavy traffic. It seemed like every car in Seattle was headed toward Lake Washington. As they got closer to the course, they began to pass long lines of happy families on foot, carrying blankets and picnic baskets. The crowds grew with each block as Boeing's car inched closer to the lake. There was a carnival atmosphere complete with food vendors pushing carts selling ice cream, hot dogs, or soda pop. Interspersed with the food vendors were newsboys holding copies of the *Seattle Times* or *P-I* over their heads and calling out, "Great photos of the boats and drivers. Get your paper here!" Walking through the throng were pretty young girls wearing white skipper hats selling plastic pins bearing the shape of a white ship's wheel topped with a blue plastic hydro, to raise money to support the race.

Mr. Boeing had attended all the Gold Cups in Seattle, so he was expecting the huge crowd, but for Mira it was another shock in a long string of shocks he had experienced since agreeing to drive the *Wahoo*. Several times on their drive in, Bill looked over to see an incredulous look on Mira's face.

They parked in a special lot for competitors. As they walked towards the pit entrance, they passed a girl selling red, white, and blue Seafair programs for 50 cents each. Boeing stopped, dug into his pocket, pulled out a dollar, and bought two copies, giving one to Mira and keeping the other himself. As they got into line to enter the pits, Mira opened the magazine. His head was down reading, so he did not notice the crowd of young people quickly forming around him and was caught off guard when a copy of the Seafair program, folded back to a reveal a photo of Mira, was thrust in front of his face. Mira looked up to see a fourteen-year-old boy holding a pen and program.

"Autograph?" the freckle-faced boy asked. Mira passed the pen and program over to Mr. Boeing, convinced that the young boy must surely be asking the world-famous millionaire for his autograph. Bill chuckled and handed them back, "Oh I don't think he wants my autograph." He said, "I think you're the one they're after."[3]

Mira gave Mr. Boeing an astounded look and signed his name to the page. Instantly there were a dozen more programs thrust at him. After signing his name a few times, he began to think that maybe he should add something to the signature. He wanted to say, "Good luck," but could not remember how to spell the English words, so in a moment of frustration he wrote the Czech words "*Hodne šťastia*" (lots of luck). "Look!" One young boy exclaimed, "He wrote something in Russian!"

"No!" Mira exclaimed, "It's Czech. Czech for lots of luck." The crowd continued to build around Mira, mostly young boys with butch cuts and blue jeans, but here and there in the good-natured crowd would be a shy, pretty girl in a sun dress politely waiting her turn. After Mira signed his name for almost thirty minutes, a couple of Seattle police officers came up to escort him into the pits.

The weather stayed nice all day, and when the course finally opened for qualifying at 2 p.m., drivers were looking at some of the best water they had seen all week. There was almost a traffic jam as a dozen teams with unqualified boats tried to get a shot on the lake. Officials kept the course open until sunset, almost 8 p.m. The last boat on the water was the *Shanty-I*. Russ Schleeh left the dock just a few ticks of the clock before the sun slipped behind the Olympic Mountains, and he quickly laid down the three fastest laps of the weekend, hitting well over 170 mph on the straightaway and sliding wide through the corners to keep his boat speed up. He averaged 115.488 mph for his three laps, coming in two miles an hour faster than the next-best boat, the *Slo-mo-shun IV*, and almost setting a new qualifying record.

Sunday, August 5 was another glorious Seattle day with a cloudless blue sky and just a slight breath of wind keeping the temperature around 70 degrees Fahrenheit.[4]

Thousands of people had camped out on the shore the night before the race, and by 8 a.m., all roads leading to the lake were jammed with fans. The Seattle Police Department estimated that 500,000 people attended the race. Special buses were put on duty to move the huge crowd. The 45,000 programs that Greater Seattle had printed sold out by midmorning. Vendors ran short of food. On the lake, there were 1,080 luxury yachts tied up to the log boom that lined the backstretch of the racecourse. At the north end of the course, fans were standing at least six rows deep on both sides of the Mercer Island Floating Bridge.

Mira sat quietly in Boeing's boathouse, waiting for the race to start. He watched all the pre-race pageantry being broadcast live on KING-TV and tried to concentrate on the tasks that were ahead of him while Junie and the crew made last-minute preparations to the *Miss Wahoo.*

With twelve boats qualified for the race, the first heat of racing would be divided into two six-boat sections. Section A, consisting of the *Miss Wahoo*, the *Shanty-I*, the *Miss Thriftway*, the *Gale V*, the *Tempest,* and the *Such Crust III,* was scheduled to start at 12.45 p.m. Section B, with the *Slo-mo-shun IV*, the *Miss U.S. II*, the *Miss Seattle*, the *Gale VI*, the *Hawaii Kai III,* and the *Scooter Too,* was set to go at 1.30 p.m.

Mira and Junie had spent the night before the race drinking coffee and talking late into the evening about their racing strategy. Mira knew that the inside lanes were shorter than the outside lanes. On the Seafair course, each lane grew about 60 feet in length as you moved away from lane one. So, if two boats were equal in speed, and one boat was in lane one and another was in lane six, the boat in lane six would have to travel 360 extra feet on each lap. In an eight-lap race, that would equal more than half a mile. Mira thought he knew what he had to do to grab the inside lane, but he had never even witnessed a race, so he was still a bit unsure how it was all going to work.

At about 12.15 p.m., Junie and the crew went over their final checklist and lowered the *Miss Wahoo* into the water. Mira stood by himself, watching from the dock as the crew removed the lifting slings and wiped the windshield clean. He started to buckle up his life jacket and was surprised to find that his hands were shaking. Bill Boeing came up behind him, placed his hand comfortingly on his shoulder, and said, "Don't feel any pressure today. We all know this is your first race, so just take it easy and get used to the way the boat feels."

Junie was behind the cockpit, straddling the tailfin and called out, "Mira, we're ready for you."

Mira carefully made the short leap from the dock to the shiny curved deck and stepped into the cockpit. He pulled a cotton ball out of his pocket, tore off two chunks, and stuffed them into his ears. He slipped on his helmet and pulled on a pair of leather driving gloves. Then, he sat down in the gray upholstered driver's seat. With his ear plugs in, all the chatter on the dock sounded muffled, far off, and almost surreal. The only sound he could hear clearly was the gentle lapping of the waves against the underside of the *Wahoo*. His stomach began to settle down, but suddenly, he could hear Bill Muncey's voice in the back of his mind saying, "You aren't going to believe what that first turn is like when six screaming hydros roar in there at 160 mph. Don't try to be a hero." Instantly, Mira's stomach began to turn and churn again. Then he realized that this was exactly what Muncey wanted him to do. Muncey wanted him to be nervous and worried and doubting his abilities; that way, he would be prone to make a mistake and easier to beat. This was why people thought Muncey was such a formidable competitor—everything he did was calculated to give him an edge on the racecourse. His thoughts were interrupted by Junie shouting from the dock, "Okay, time to go!"

Mira gave Junie a thumbs up, pulled his goggles into place, and fired up the engine. As the *Wahoo* pulled away with a roar, Mira took his right hand briefly off the wheel and affectionately patted the deck, saying, "That's a good girl."

Once the *Wahoo* was clear of the dock, Mira made a gradual right turn and headed for the racecourse. It was only 2 miles from Boeing's boathouse to the Floating Bridge, so at 90 mph, he covered the distance in ninety seconds. He had been watching the TV coverage, and knew there were a half million people surrounding the course, but the TV had been black and white. He was not prepared for the dizzying array of colors lining the bridge and the shore. As he flashed under the bridge, he felt a brief flicker of darkness when the bridge's shadow raced across his face.

He darted out from under the bridge and cut his throttle back as he headed down the front straightway. Checking the stopwatch that Junie had mounted on his dashboard, he saw that he had two-and-a-half minutes until the race started. His nerves calmed down, and he began to swing his head from side to side, looking for the rest of his competition. The movement reminded him of the way his air force instructors had taught him to "keep his head on a swivel," looking for enemy fighters. Directly ahead were two roostertails moving away from him. He couldn't tell who they were. At the far end of the course, the *Thriftway* and the *Shanty* were running close together at the apex of the south turn, doing about 100 mph. They were silhouetted against Mt. Rainier, and for just a second, Mira allowed himself to appreciate the beauty of his new sport. Directly across the course, he saw the *Gale V* moving slowly. He passed the official barge and began to smell the unmistakable bitter scent of burning oil. He had a momentary flash of panic and quickly scanned his gauges. All his temperatures and pressures looked good. The smoke must be coming from one of his competitors. He swept through the south turn with about ninety seconds left before the start. Looking at his stopwatch, he saw that he was just about where Junie had wanted him to be, but when he looked up from the dashboard he saw that the entire fleet was halfway down the backstretch already. He figured that Junie must have miscalculated the start, so he put his foot into the throttle to catch the rest of the field. As he closed in on the boats ahead, the smell of burning oil got stronger and stronger. Halfway down the back chute he passed the twin-engine *Such Crust III* belching blue smoke and slowing down.

As he barreled up the backstretch, he saw a puff of gray smoke from the official barge and knew that the one-minute gun had been fired. Approaching the turn, he flashed past the *Tempest* and the *Gale V.* It was time to pick a lane, and he had to wait to see what Muncey and Schleeh, 200 yards ahead, decided to do. Muncey went wide, sliding out to lane three to kill some time, and Schleeh, who was on Muncey's right hip, was forced out to lane four. Slovak could not believe his luck. Lanes one and two were wide open to him. He slid the *Miss Wahoo* right on the buoy line in lane one and began to accelerate past Muncey and Schleeh. As he came off the turn, he saw the 12-foot-tall official clock on the barge and he suddenly realized why Muncey and Schleeh had swung so wide. They were early and in danger of jumping the gun, so they both went wide to kill time without having to slow down. Mira backed off on his throttle for a few seconds, trying to lose some speed. In his head, he cursed himself for doubting Junie's timing marks. If he had stuck with Junie's plan, he still would have gotten lane one, but he would not have had to back off so he would have been carrying a lot more boat speed when he reached the starting line. When he was sure he had bled off enough speed so that he would not jump the gun, he accelerated hard again. The engine responded with an angry growl and the tachometer began to wind up. The boat was dancing from sponson to sponson as the speedometer needle climbed from 100 mph to 110, then to 120. Mira was in lane one and was going to be the first boat to the line. He was grinning from ear to ear. "This isn't so difficult," he thought. Just then, he looked to his right to watch for the cannon on the barge that would tell him if he was a legal starter. At the exact instant the cannon fired to signal the start, Muncey flew past Mira at least 30 mph faster. He must have been going 150 mph or 160 mph. Mira accelerated to 160 mph to chase the leader, but Muncey already had a six-boat length lead on him. Muncey was out in lane three and Mira was in lane one as they rocketed down the front chute, Muncey began to move over into lane two. The *Miss Thriftway*'s roostertail made a thick, white wall of water to Mira's right. Mira knew that Muncey could move over all the way to lane one if he wanted and his roostertail would wash Slovak down and put him out of the race. Mira began to shout against the roar of the engine, "Don't do it! Don't do it!"

Surprisingly, Muncey held his position in lane two, leaving Slovak with a very narrow but drivable lane. They both barreled towards turn one. Against Mira's will, Muncey's words from Saturday came back again, "You aren't going to believe what that first turn is like when six screaming hydros roar in there at 160 mph. Don't try to be a hero." As they hurtled toward the turn, every nerve in Mira's body told him to slow down, but he kept his foot to the floor.

Mira saw the *Miss Thriftway* slow to negotiate the turn. In an instant, the *Shanty* shot into the lead from Muncey's right side and began to slide into a graceful turn out in lane four. Mira thought, "If Schleeh didn't have to slow down, neither do I." Slovak turned hard, but the *Miss Wahoo's* momentum was too great and he couldn't hold his lane. He slid out into the vicious white wall of Muncey's roostertail. Instantly, Mira was hit in the face by a fire-hose blast of water that temporarily blinded him. The right sponson bounced up; the *Wahoo* slid sideways and slammed down hard. For a moment Mira thought the boat was going to roll over or, at the very least, toss him out. He tightened his grip on the steering wheel. The *Wahoo* continued to bounce and slide sideways through the corner, coming out of Muncey's roostertail only to keep skidding into the *Shanty's*. Again, Mira was blinded and again the boat bounced precariously, almost tipping over. Somehow Mira kept the power to the *Wahoo*'s engine and it hadn't swallowed too much water. He came out of the turn in third place, a roostertail behind Muncey, who was now a roostertail behind Schleeh and the *Shanty.*

The three boats battled for the next seven laps; the *Miss Thriftway* closed in on *Shanty-I* but did not have the speed to pass her. Meanwhile, the *Wahoo* was catching the *Miss Thriftway.* On lap seven, the *Thriftway* began to slow. Slovak sensed that he had a chance to pass, so he pulled outside and rode on Muncey's right hip. Coming out of the south turn on the final lap, the *Miss Thriftway* coughed, the engine died, and the boat coasted to a stop. Mira powered around the dying *Miss Thriftway* and took second place.

Back at the boathouse, the crew, listening to the radio, began to cheer wildly. Heat 1A ended with the *Shanty-I* first, the *Miss Wahoo* second, the *Gale V* third, and the *Tempest* fourth. Muncey was able to get the *Miss Thriftway* restarted to take fifth. The *Such Crust III* had broken a gear box and never completed a lap.

Mira acknowledged the checkered flag with a wave of his hand. He reduced speed and headed back to Boeing's, exhausted. Driving in competition with a lot of traffic and churned up the water made for a much more demanding experience than running qualifying laps alone on the course.

Mira slowed under the bridge, waving to the fans, and returned to the boathouse. He shut off the engine and glided into the dock. Bill, Junie, and the whole *Wahoo* crew were going wild, cheering and clapping as if he had won. Mira had a tremendous feeling of accomplishment. He had done a good job, not perfect by a long shot, but pretty good for the first time in a race. He climbed out of the boat to a flurry of hugs, handshakes, and slaps on the back. As the crew got the *Miss Wahoo* ready to lift out of the water to prepare for the next heat, Mira and Junie walked to the shade by the boathouse to talk.

Junie handed Mira a chilled bottle of Coca-Cola and asked, "So what do you think?" Mira took a long drink from the bottle and said, "I loved it! It's a lot more physical than I expected. All that bucking and bouncing. It's not really like flying at all, but there is something about it that connects to flying. You know how a good pilot has a sixth sense about what his plane is going to do? Well it's the same thing in a hydro. You've got to understand in your gut what the boat is going to do next."

Junie said, "And do you understand what the *Wahoo is* going to do?"

Mira moved the bottle from his lips, wiped the sweat from his forehead with the back of his hand, and said, "I'm learning. After a couple more heats I think I will."

In the distance, they could hear the rumble of boats leaving the pits for heat 1B. They listened on the radio as the *Slo-mo-shun IV* led wire-to-wire to win over the *Miss U.S. II,* with the *Gale VI* finishing third, and the *Miss Seattle* taking fourth. The two Kaiser boats—the *Scooter Too* and the *Hawaii Kai III*—failed to finish.

As the teams tended to their boats and race officials drew names for the second heat, the fans on the beach were kept entertained by the red, white, and blue U.S. Air Force Thunderbirds performing aerobatics above the course. Mira stood at the end of Boeing's dock, craning his neck to watch as the F-100 Super Sabers painted intricate patterns in the sky with their colorful smoke trails. He was enjoying driving the *Wahoo*, but the powerful supersonic jet fighters were impressive. He found himself wishing he could drive the *Wahoo* and fly aerobatics between races.

When the assignments for the second section were announced, Mira was again paired against Bill Muncey. The section also included Donnie Wilson in the *Miss U.S. II* (Wilson and Muncey had been college roommates) and the *Tempest* and the *Hawaii Kai III.*

At 2.40 p.m. the five-minute gun sounded for the *Wahoo*'s second heat, and Mira, feeling a lot more confident, fired up and pulled away from the dock. In his mind, there was something symbolic about driving under the bridge to get to the course. As he came out of the shadow of the bridge into the bright sunshine on the course, he felt almost like a gladiator entering the arena. His pulse started to quicken, but this was different. At the start of the first heat, his heart raced because he was nervous. For this second heat, his heart was pounding because he was looking forward to the excitement of competition.

He used the same strategy and timing marks from the first heat. He motored past the start line at 100 mph looking for his competition, and then eased the *Wahoo* through the south turn while his competitors bunched up near the north end of the course. This time, he resisted the temptation to try to catch up. He knew that he was right where he wanted to be. As he powered up the back chute, he saw the bright pink *Hawaii Kai III* coast to a stop, dead in the water, while the *Miss U.S. II*, the *Miss Thriftway*, and the *Tempes*t were swinging wide into the north turn. With twenty seconds to go, Mira accelerated hard through the turn, moving into lane one and heading toward the start. With ten seconds to go Mira realized that he had been too eager and was going to be early again. He pulled his foot completely off of the throttle and the speedometer began to slip back from 110 mph, to 100, 80, 70, and then 60 mph.

Mira hit the starting line in lane one at the exact instant that the gun fired, but he was crawling along at only 60 miles per hour. To his left, the *Miss U.S. II*, the *Miss Thriftway*, and the *Tempest* blasted past at close to 150 mph. Mira slammed his fist against the steering wheel in anger and pressed down hard on the throttle. The *Miss Wahoo* jumped to life, accelerated quickly, and began to catch the field. The *Tempest*, out in lane four, reached the turn first but was quickly passed by the *Miss U.S. II*. The *Miss Thriftway* lost power and coasted to a stop. Mira, charging toward the turn at well over 150 mph, remembered how wildly the *Miss Wahoo* had bounced when he had tried to run into the turn at full speed, so he slowed down considerably, and the *Wahoo* slid through the corner smooth and fast. To his surprise, he came out of the turn in third place, only a roostertail's length behind the *Tempest*, which was just a roostertail behind the *Miss U.S. II*. Heading up the back stretch, the *Tempest* began to catch the *Miss U.S. II*, and by the time they got to the north turn, the *Tempest* was only a hundred feet behind. Wilson let the *Miss U.S. II* slide out to lane three to force the *Tempest* to go even wider. Mira stayed tight on the buoy line and was catching the leaders. At the end on lap one Wilson and the *Miss U.S. II* had a scant three-second lead over the *Tempest*, which held onto a two-second advantage over the *Wahoo*. The three boats continued to keep up their fierce battle through lap two. Midway into lap three, the *Tempest*'s engine let out a loud pop, and the boat coasted to a stop. Mira moved into second place and held it to the end of the race, finishing fifteen seconds behind Wilson and the *Miss U.S. II*.

After the heat was over, Mira headed back to the boathouse. He had mixed emotions. He was happy with his second-place finish and knew that he had secured a spot in the final, but he also knew that he had made a mistake for the second time in a row by starting his run to the start too soon. Mira was confident that had he been able to hit the line at full speed, he could have won the heat.

Back at the dock, Junie and the crew were celebrating as Mira came back to the dock. Mira wanted to apologize to Junie and explain why he had not won the heat, but the crew seemed so happy to have qualified for the final that Mira decided to keep his doubts to himself.

At 3.30 p.m., the fourth and final qualification section was run, and again Joe Taggart in the *Slo-mo-shun IV* led wire-to-wire, picking up another first place.

The U.S. Navy Blue Angels, flying their new blue and yellow F9F swept-wing Cougars, put on a dramatic show for the fans as race officials tallied the points for the final heat. Again, Mira longingly watched the aerobatic performance, wishing that there was a way to be in two places at the same time.

The field for the final heat was the *Slo-mo-shun IV,* the *Shanty-I,* the *Miss U.S. II,* the *Miss Wahoo,* the *Miss Seattle*, and the *Gale VI.* As Mira settled into the cockpit for the final heat, he told himself to be more patient and do everything like he had in the first two heats, but just not begin his run to the start too soon. He thought of the $25,000 prize money and told himself, "When you get to the north turn and want to start your run, count to five before you hit the accelerator, and you just might be able to win some of that money."

Junie knelt next to the cockpit. He could tell that Mira was troubled by something, so he said, "Listen, this is just our first race. We don't expect you to win today; we just want you to get a feel for the boat." Mira nodded. In the distance, the five-minute gun sounded. Junie said, "Be safe and have fun." He jumped from the boat to the dock. Mira fired up the big Allison and roared off toward the course.

For the third time that day, Mira rushed under the bridge, bursting out onto the course. He made the same half-throttle warm-up lap, following the field into the north turn. Up ahead, he saw that Joe Taggart in the *Slo-mo-shun IV* was swinging very wide into what must have been lane six or seven. Russ Schleeh and the *Shanty* took lane five. Donnie Wilson in the *Miss U.S. II* was in lane four, with Norm Evans and the bright red and yellow *Miss Seattle* in lane three. Mira could not believe his luck. For the third time that day, lanes one and two were wide open to him. He wanted to hit the gas, but he exercised self-control and counted to five before he pressed the throttle down. This was going to be a perfect start.

As the *Miss Wahoo* started to accelerate, Norm Evans in the *Miss Seattle* started to move in from lane three towards lane one. Mira was accelerating past 110 mph, approaching 120 mph. Evans was also going about 120 mph and was only a few boat lengths ahead. Evans came right across Slovak's bow, into lane one, and slammed the door closed with a brutal shower of water from the *Miss Seattle's* roostertail. Mira quickly ducked behind the windshield and chopped his throttle, trying to keep the engine from taking in too much water and flooding. He bounced out to lane three, almost coming to a stop, but was just barely able to keep going. Far to the outside, in lanes five and six, the *Slo-mo-shun* and the *Shanty* made perfect starts, hitting the line together at over 160 miles per hour. The *Miss Seattle* was a close third, and the *Miss U.S.* was fourth. Mira, soaking wet and extremely angry, was last across the line.

The *Shanty-I* came out of the south turn in first place, followed by the *Miss Seattle* and the *Slo-mo-shun IV*. The *Miss U.S. II* broke down at the apex of the turn, moving the *Wahoo* into fourth place. The *Shanty-I* averaged 116.38 miles per hour on the first lap and ran away from the field. The *Miss Seattle* and the *Slo-mo-shun IV* battled for three laps before the *Slo-mo* was able to get past the *Miss Seattle* to take second. Mira hung in fourth place for three-and-a-half laps before the *Wahoo's* water-logged engine quit running.

Schleeh finished the final heat over a minute ahead of the second place *Slo-mo-shun*. The highly partisan Seattle crowd went crazy. Along the backstretch, hundreds of yachts blew their horns and tooted their whistles. Hundreds of thousands of fans on the beach cheered and roared their approval.

Mira missed the celebration. He was sitting soaking wet on the rear cowl of the *Wahoo* as a Coast Guard patrol boat towed him back to Boeing's boathouse. He was disappointed that he had not been able to finish in the money, but he was not unhappy. It had been his first race and he had finished ahead of 13 other racers, including Bill Muncey—that was something to be proud of.

When he got to work Monday morning, August 6, the phone at Aero Copter was ringing off the hook with people calling to congratulate Mira. Eventually, he asked the receptionist to take messages; otherwise, he would never get any work done. A few minutes before noon, another call came in for Mira. In spite of his request, the receptionist called Mira to the office, covering the receiver's mouthpiece with one hand and whispering, "I think that you'll want to take this one!"

Mira picked up the phone and said, "Hello?"

A voice on the other end said, "Please hold for Senator Magnuson."

Mira looked at the receptionist with wide eyes, and she whispered, "I told you so!"

A few moments later, Senator Warren Magnuson's distinctive, gravelly voice came on the phone. "Miroslav, I hear you did real fine at Seafair yesterday. Congratulations son."

"Thank you, sir!"

"Now listen, I just talked to the President and he says that he wanted me to let you know that he signed your bill today, the one that gives you a radio license. We really appreciate all that you've done for us and we know that you want to fly airliners again, so we are going to do all we can to make sure that happens. Rest assured about that!"

"Thank you again, sir." Mira's English vocabulary was failing him.

"My secretary is signaling me that I've got another call, so I'm hanging up now. We'll talk again soon." With that, the line went dead.

When the Monday afternoon paper came out, there were several pages of photos and stories about the race. Mixed into the race coverage was a handsome photo of Mira and a story explaining that President Eisenhower had signed Magnuson's bill, officially giving Mira a U.S. Radio Operator's License.[5]

The next several unlimited races were in the eastern half of the country, and business commitments kept Bill Boeing from sending Mira and the *Miss Wahoo*, but that did not keep Mira from following the results in the newspapers and on TV.

In September, Bill Muncey and the *Miss Thriftway* went to Washington, DC and won the President's Cup. Mira was excited when he saw a press photo of President Eisenhower awarding Muncey the trophy. Mira decided that he wanted to win the President's Cup too, so he could meet Eisenhower and personally thank him for getting him his radio operator's license.

During the last week of September, Mira was approached by a somber Bill Jr. and asked to fly an important mission. Bill Boeing, Sr. was vacationing aboard his 125-foot luxury yacht the *Taconite* in Queen Charlotte Sound in Canada. The elder Boeing had suffered a heart attack, and Bill Jr. asked Mira to fly him and the family doctor to rendezvous with the yacht and offer whatever assistance they could. Bill Jr. had a four-seat Howard DGA-15 that had been fitted with floats. Bill, Mira, and the doctor loaded into the Howard and took off into a gray, overcast sky, taking about three hours to fly 420 miles across open ocean and pine-shrouded fjords to Queen Charlotte Sound. Mira landed the float plane on the calm, glassy water near the *Taconite*. The yacht dispatched a motor launch to pick up the doctor and Bill Jr., but it was too late to do anything to save Bill Sr. Mira flew home alone while Bill Jr. and the doctor stayed on board the *Taconite* as it motored back to Seattle.[6]

The *Taconite* arrived at the Seattle Yacht Club on Friday, September 28, and William E. Boeing, Sr. was officially declared dead. He was three days shy of his seventy-fifth birthday. A few weeks later, Mira flew Bill Jr. and Bill's mother Bertha back to Queen Charlotte Sound in the Howard float plane. Bertha carried an urn containing Bill Sr.'s ashes. Mira skillfully set the float plane down near the spot where the *Taconite* had been anchored when Bill Sr. suffered his fatal heart attack. Bill Jr. opened the door of the Howard and stepped down onto one of the plane's floats. His mother carefully handed him the urn. Mira slowly taxied across the picturesque sound while Bill lovingly sprinkled the ashes behind the plane and the prop wash carried them far away. Mira felt that there was something wonderfully symbolic about the ashes of the man whose name had become such an integral part of aviation being spread by the prop wash of an airplane.

Bill Jr. needed a break from the emotional blow of losing his father, and the Sahara Cup hydroplane race provided a perfect diversion. The race was held on October 13 and 14 on Lake Mead, 30 miles outside Las Vegas, Nevada. The stark beauty of the rugged Nevada desert offered a stunning contrast to the sleek and colorful hydros.

Guy Lombardo was one of the biggest names in music. His mellow big-band sound helped him sell over 100 million records. Lombardo was also a hydroplane racer who had won a number of important races including the Gold Cup, two national championships, and the President's Cup. Lombardo was headlining at the Desert Inn in Las Vegas as well as running his *Tempo VII* in the Sahara Cup.

The Sahara Cup gave the *Wahoo* team a new perspective on racing. This was the first time they would be pitting alongside other teams instead of being off by themselves in Boeing's boathouse. On Saturday morning, as Mira was walking into the pits, he passed Bill Muncey leaning casually up against the side of the *Thriftway's* equipment truck, smoking a cigarette. "Hey, Slim," Muncey called out, "I never got a chance to tell you congratulations on the job you did at Seafair. Two second places in your first two heats. That's something you should be proud of."

Mira smiled and said, "Thank you, but I should be the one congratulating you. You've won two races since I last saw you, the Gold Cup and the President's Cup. That's very impressive."

Muncey shrugged his shoulders, "I don't know if what I did was really that special. I'm just lucky enough to be driving a real fast sled." Muncey took a long drag on his cigarette, exhaled through his nose, and said, "What did I tell you about that first turn? Pretty darn exciting, isn't it?"

Mira nodded, "I almost rolled over in that first heat. I think I'm getting the hang of it. You know what I could use help with? The start, you hit it perfectly every time. How do you do it?"

Muncey crushed out his cigarette on the sole of his shoe and then flicked the butt into the dirt. He shook his head and said, "I can't help you. You're going to have to figure that out by yourself."

A look of hurt clouded Mira's face. Muncey noticed it and said, "Look, Slim, I could walk down pit row and tell any six drivers how to make a perfect start and they would all nod and smile and say thank you and then they would all go out tomorrow and keep making the same boneheaded lousy starts that they've been making their whole careers. But if I told you, you would go out tomorrow and you'd beat me!"[7] Muncey started to walk away and turned back over his shoulder and said, "You're smarter than the rest of these guys and it's going take everything I have to stay ahead of you."

An interesting showdown was brewing in the pits. All the boats on the 1956 unlimited circuit were powered by surplus World War II fighter engines. The most popular engine was the General Motors Allison V-1710, which had powered American planes like the P-38 Lightning. A few boats, most notably the *Slo-mo-shun IV*, ran a Rolls-Royce Merlin, which had powered the Hawker Hurricanes and Spitfires for England. The Merlin was 250 pounds heavier than the Allison but produced at least 500 more horsepower. The *Slo-mo-shun IV* had been destroyed in an accident during the Gold Cup in Detroit. Her owner, Stan Sayres, retired from racing and generously offered his inventory of Merlins to the *Hawaii Kai* team, along with the entire *Slo-mo-shun* crew to install and maintain the engines. The *Kai*, which had been a second-rate boat with the Allison engine, won the very first race she ran with a Merlin. Throughout the racing community, the Sahara Cup was viewed as a Rolls-Royce *v.* Allison showdown that would determine which engine would dominate the future of racing.

Mira and the *Miss Wahoo* were drawn into the first heat with Guy Lombardo's *Tempo VII* and the *Hawaii Kai III*. A huge construction crane picked up the boats one at a time and set them into the water. As Mira was strapping on his life jacket he thought about his starts and what he could do to improve them. He realized that his problem was that he was sacrificing too much speed by trying to get the inside lane. When he thought about the boats that had beaten him to the line at Seafair, they had all been outside of him, and if they were coming up to the line too early they could swing wider to kill time. He was still mulling over this thought as he climbed into the boat. The five-minute gun fired and Mira pulled away from the pits. On the spur of the moment, he decided to try an outside start. He treated the first few minutes same way he had in Seattle, slowly cruising around the course checking his gauges, making sure that the engine was working well.

When the one-minute gun fired, Mira was just entering the backstretch. He pressed the throttle to the floor and the *Miss Wahoo* jumped to life. He powered into the last turn thirty seconds before the start and swung wide around the *Hawaii Kai.* He focused on the big clock on the official barge and realized how easy it would be to coordinate the movement of the clock and his position on the course. If he was late, he would tighten up his turn; if he was early, he would swing wider, but no matter what he did he would keep his foot flat on the floor and hit the line at full speed. Mira made a perfect start, roaring across the line in lane six at the second the clock went to zero, traveling well over 150 mph. Jack Regas, driving the *Hawaii Kai,* was in lane four and about three boat lengths behind Mira, and the *Tempo VII* was right behind Regas. Mira led the field into the first turn and set the *Wahoo* into a slide. Arcing past the buoys, he picked up a couple of boat lengths on the *Kai.* As the boats roared down the backstretch, the extra 500 hp in the *Kai's* Merlin allowed Regas to pull even with the *Wahoo.* The two boats bucked and bounced into the second turn side by side. Black smoke poured from the *Wahoo's* exhaust as Mira kept the throttle wide open. The *Wahoo* pulled away again. As they rocketed out of the turn and finished lap one, the *Wahoo* held on to a slim 30 foot lead. Regas and the bright pink *Hawaii Kai* continued to chase Mira through the whole second lap.

As the race went on, the water got churned up. Each time a boat roars through a turn at over 100 miles per hour, it creates big rollers. Experienced drivers take this into account. As Jack Regas chased Mira into the start of lap three, Regas sensed that the water was getting rougher, and he backed off just a little. Mira was still a rookie. He looked over his left shoulder and saw that he had opened up almost a roostertail lead over the *Hawaii Kai.* He did not know why Regas was slowing down, but he figured that he would keep the throttle wide open and extend his lead. As Mira roared into the first turn of lap three, he set the *Wahoo* into an arc, but suddenly, the right sponson hit a huge roller and bounced almost four feet off the water, then slammed down hard into the lake. Instantly, the *Wahoo* swapped ends, throwing up a huge spray of white water and nearly pitching Mira out of the boat. The *Wahoo* came to rest facing the wrong way in lane four. Regas was close behind but was able duck into lane three to get past the motionless *Wahoo*. He gave Mira a little wave as he blasted by at 140 miles per hour.

The instant he started to spin, Mira knew that he had made a mistake. Racing seemed to be one step forward and two steps back. He had figured out how to make a perfect start, but now he had messed up by not paying attention to the water conditions. He got the boat restarted before the *Tempo VII* could pass him, and he took off after the *Kai*. Driving hard and fast, he made up a lot of time, finishing a scant two seconds behind Regas. When he got back to the dock he expected Junie to be upset, but his good-natured crew chief was all smiles and said, "Well, I guess we learned a couple of things in that heat, didn't we?"

The water that had sloshed into the *Wahoo* when Mira spun must have caused a short circuit in the electrical system, because when it came time to for its next heat, the *Wahoo's* engine would not even turn over, and Mira watched from a floating *Miss Wahoo* as Regas and the *Kai* went on to win the second and third heats to sweep the race and demonstrate the superiority of the Rolls-Merlin engine.

When Mira returned to Seattle after the Sahara Cup, he found an interesting letter waiting for him at Aero Copter. It was from Lester Jenkins, a manager at the *Seattle Times*. Jenkins invited Mira to be the guest speaker at a banquet for the Alpha Kappa Psi Alumni Association at Seattle's posh Arctic Club on November 21. Even with his difficulties with the English language, Mira knew that this was the opportunity he had been waiting for. He was going to be able to stand up in front of a large crowd of prominent American businessmen and tell them about the evils of communism.

Mira prepared the first draft of his speech, a straightforward attack on communism and all the immoral things he had witnessed in Czechoslovakia. He practiced the speech in front of Junie and the results were disappointing. "I think you need to remember that you've been invited to give a dinner speech because people want to be entertained. They want to hear about your escape and your racing, and once they start to care about you, then they will be happy to hear about life behind the Iron Curtain. But if you hit them with too much negativity right away, they may think that you are just a complainer." After several more rewrites, Mira felt he had a speech that would tell his story in a compelling way.

On the night of the dinner, he arrived early at the unique Beaux Arts-styled Arctic Building. The elegant building was covered with snow-colored terra cotta panels and featured several sculpted walrus heads lining the third-floor façade. The main ballroom where Mira would be speaking was called the "Dome Room" and its ceiling was a huge art nouveau stained-glass dome that represented the inside of an igloo. The building had been built in 1916 by the Arctic Club, an exclusive group whose membership was limited to adventurers who had gone to the Yukon and struck it rich in the Klondike gold rush.

Wearing his best dark blue suit and a white shirt with a red tie, Mira carried his speech on cards in his breast pocket, and every few minutes, he patted his pocket to make sure they were still there. When his name was called, he headed toward the front of the room as the audience applauded. Mira squared his shoulders, straightened his back, and walked with a confidence that he certainly did not feel. He was a brave man, he flew planes, he raced boats, and he was more than willing to take risks, but standing before a large audience and giving a speech in a language that he had been speaking for less than three years terrified him. He reached the podium, pulled out his note cards and started to speak in short, simple sentences. "Hello. My name is Miroslav Slovak. You may call me Mira."

"I was born in Cífer, Czechoslovakia. Like you, I have a mother and a father. Unlike you, I will never see my parents again. You see, in my homeland, I am a criminal. I have been sentenced to death."

"What is my crime?" Here, Mira paused to move to his next card, but in the moment that he paused, he noticed that the huge auditorium was silent. No one was moving. He had the audience's complete and total attention. A waiter dropped a spoon and the room was so still that when it landed on the marble floor the clang made several people flinch as if a gun had gone off. Mira started speaking again,

"What is my crime? I wanted to be like you. I wanted to choose where I lived. I wanted to choose where I would go to church. I wanted to vote for my nation's leaders. I wanted to talk honestly with my friends. But I wasn't allowed to do any of these things. So I decided to leave."

There was something about the honesty of Mira's slow, deliberate delivery and his slightly mispronounced halting English that captivated the audience. Mira slipped easily into the story of his escape. He talked about smuggling the guns onboard and the fight with the crew. He talked about the MiGs that chased him across the sky and the communists that pounded on the door. He carefully left out details that Wayne Richardson had advised him were still classified, but the story poured out of Mira like wine from a bottle. He finished by saying, "You may ask me if it was worth it to give up my friends, my family, and my career. I answer you, yes! To breathe for just one second the pure fresh air of freedom makes every bit of it worthwhile!"[8]

When Mira finished, there was silence. For an instant, Mira thought that he had failed. "Maybe they couldn't understand my English." Suddenly,

Mira's negative ruminations were interrupted by the sound of hundreds of people simultaneously pushing their chairs back and springing to their feet, applauding.

Mira was overwhelmed. He felt tears welling up in his eyes. As he left the podium, he was surrounded by men in expensive suits and women in elegant dresses. Some were reaching out to shake his hand, but many more wanted his autograph. These were not star-struck teenagers from the hydro pits. This was the cream of Seattle society, and they all wanted his autograph. Mira was reminded of a conversation that he had with Nicky Morris back in Germany just a few days after his escape. Mira had told Morris that he wanted to go to Korea and fly an F-86 against the communists. Morris had told Mira that the U.S. Air Force would never allow it and he should try to find a different way to fight the communists. Mira smiled broadly to himself. He was confident that he had just found a way to do that.

18

He Who Dares, Wins: Seattle, 1957

In April 1957, Blanche, Frank Sr., Junie, and Marci threw a party to celebrate the first anniversary of Mira's arrival in Seattle. Blanche cooked a huge meal of Mira's favorite Czech dishes. They invited all the *Wahoo* crew over. The Cechs had moved into a new house, perched on a hill above Lake Washington, with sweeping views of the lake and the Cascade Mountains. At one point during the party, Mira found himself standing alone on the deck behind the house enjoying the view. He took a moment to marvel at all the amazing things that had happened since he arrived in the US. He wondered what Honza would say if he could see him now, sipping fine whiskey on the deck of a million-dollar home and rubbing shoulders with some of the wealthiest capitalists in America. Mira knew that the "new" Honza who came back after his arrest would spout the party line, saying that Mira was a "traitor to the revolution and his fellow workers." Yet Mira felt that the "old" Honza, the "real" Honza, would be proud of Mira, the amazing friends he had made, and the exciting things he was accomplishing. Mira decided that he agreed with the old Honza; he was not going to let communist guilt deprive him of his own sense of accomplishment. He thought of a Latin phrase he had learned in grammar school. "*Qui audit adipiscitur*" meaning "He who dares, wins!" Mira felt content. He had risked a lot and he deserved the rewards that his risks had won him.

Frank and Junie joined Mira on the deck. Frank pointed at the lake and the snow-capped mountains and said, "When you left Czechoslovakia, did you ever imagine it could turn out like this?"

"Never in a million years could I have dreamed a fairytale like this."

"Was it worth it? Would you do it again?"

"I miss my mother more than I know how to say."

"But are you happy here?"

"I don't know if happiness really is the question. In America, freedom is like the air you breathe. It is everywhere, and it keeps you alive. If someone took away all of your air, you would start to choke and die, and you would do anything to find more air. You wouldn't think, 'I'd be happier with more air.' You would just go anywhere and do anything to get a breath. That is how it was for me when the communists took over. They sucked the air of freedom out of my country, and one day, I woke up choking and knew that I had to leave. No, it really was never about wanting to be happier."

Frank and Junie stood in silence. After a moment, Mira spoke again. "You know that I love to fly and I've always dreamed of owning my own airplane. Of course, the communists would never let a private citizen own something as extravagant as an airplane, but now I make good money with Mr. Boeing and I'd like to buy a plane, but I have no idea how to do it."

"What type of plane do you want?" Frank asked.

Mira pulled a folded-up magazine page out of his pocket, smoothed it against his leg, and held up a black-and-white photograph of a little open-cockpit, two-seat aluminum trainer with sporty wheel spats and a streamlined engine cowling. "It's a 1935 Ryan STA. It needs to be restored, and I was thinking that I could buy it and do the work at Aero Copter," Mira said proudly.

Frank, who handled most of the aircraft purchases for Aero Copter, said, "We might run into some difficulties getting the plane into your name because you haven't been in the country very long, but I'm sure that I could buy the plane in my name and let you operate it like it was your own." Within the month, Mira was the proud owner of a Ryan STA that he named "*Moonshine.*"

The idyllic town of Chelan, Washington, nestled on the eastern shore of Lake Chelan, in the mountains of Central Washington, was chosen to host the kickoff race for the 1957 unlimited season. The new race was called the Apple Cup, to pay tribute to the many orchards surrounding the lake. The winner's trophy was a large golden apple mounted on a heavy mahogany base.

There was still snow along Highway 10 during the first week of May as the trucks hauling the unlimited fleet wound through Snoqualmie Pass on their way to the race. As the teams got closer to Chelan, they were treated to the sight of acres of rolling orchards covered with fragile white apple blossoms.

Nine boats and a couple of construction cranes were shoe-horned into a dusty, primitive pit area on the south shore of the lake. The quaint town of Chelan, with a population of just over 2,500, was overrun by tens of thousands of fans, filling all the restaurants, bars, hotels, and campgrounds.

The race turned into something of a demolition derby with the *Maverick* and the *Wahoo* the only boats finishing the final heat. Bill Stead and the *Maverick* won the race and Mira got second.

A few weeks after the Apple Cup, Edgar Kaiser announced that he was retiring from racing but would allow the *Hawaii Kai* crew to continue to run the boat for the rest of the 1957 season. He also announced that Bill Boeing, Jr. had the first right of refusal to buy the entire *Hawaii Kai* team, including the boat and all its Rolls-Royce engines.

In June and July, there were two races in Michigan but none of the West Coast teams made the trip east. The next race in the west was the Mapes Mile-High Gold Cup Race on Lake Tahoe July 20 and 21, sponsored by Charles Mapes, Jr. and his elegant Mapes Hotel in Reno. The racecourse was nestled along the California side of Lake Tahoe's south shore, between Dollar Point and the old Tahoe Tavern Pier, with the pits and start-finish line at the massive Tahoe Boat Company complex.

Straddling the California-Nevada border, Lake Tahoe, 6,200 feet high in the Sierra Nevada Mountains, is famous for its crystal-clear water and Ponderosa Pine forests that reach out of the mountains to the water's edge. When gambling was legalized in Nevada in 1931, the Nevada side of the lake attracted a number of high-roller resorts that offered casino gaming, world class entertainment, and great food, all on the shore of one of the most pristine lakes in the world.

Junie and Les Eide had driven the truck that pulled the *Miss Wahoo* from Seattle while Mira, Bill Jr., and Marci flew down in Bill's Grumman Mallard float plane. When they arrived over the lake, Mira brought the big blue and yellow plane right down to the surface of the lake and flew a tight lap around the racecourse, skimming the water and banking through the corners.

It was a warm July afternoon when Mira and Mr. Boeing arrived at the Tahoe pits for the first time. The air smelled of pine resin and dry grass. There was a group of drivers standing near the credentials table, where they had to pick up their pit passes and sign their entry forms. Mira watched Bill Muncey, Bill Cantrell, and Jack Regas talk about their boats, and he found himself thinking that when a group of hydro drivers talked about racing, they used their hands to illustrate how their boats moved and bounced and passed each other in the same way that pilots used their hands when talking about planes.

Mira walked over to join the group. They were talking about the difference between Rolls-Royce Merlins and Allisons. Bill Muncey's *Miss*

Thriftway team had used the time between the Apple Cup in Chelan and this race in Tahoe to convert from the tried-and-true Allison to a Merlin. Jack Regas, who had been driving the Merlin-powered *Hawaii Kai* for almost a year, said, "Well, Bill, I think that you'll like it when you get used to it. But a Merlin is a lot more fragile than an Allison. It has a bunch more horsepower, but it's easy to blow up too. If you give her too much throttle too quickly you can blow the whole front end off."

Cantrell laughed, "Yeah, I seen ya getting towed in a bunch. I was gonna ask you what was going on."

Regas continued, "It's the blower drive that keeps breaking. It's a weak link and we haven't figured out how to beef it up yet, but I know the boys are working on it."

Mira was not very mechanically inclined, so he stayed out of the conversation and listened politely while the drivers talked, Mira noticed a pretty girl with blonde hair pulled back in a ponytail, holding a race program and pen, waiting patiently for the drivers to notice her. Mira made eye contact and smiled. The young woman, who was probably about nineteen or twenty, responded with a smile of her own and approached Mira holding out her program, and said, "May I have your autograph, Mr. Slovak?"

Mira took the black and gold program in his hands and noticed that the woman had the most amazing blue eyes. He flipped to the center page where there were pictures of all the boats. He noticed that Muncey and Cantrell had already signed their names. "What's your name?" Mira asked.

"It's Shelly," she replied shyly.

Mira took the pen and wrote, "To Shelly, *Hodne šťastia*. Mira Slovak." Shelly took the program back and read it, then looked at Mira and said, "I don't know what that says."

Mira answered, "It's Czech for 'Lots of luck.' I'm from Czechoslovakia."

"Oh," the girl nodded. "I didn't think that you sounded like you were from California."

Mira laughed. "I've been working on my English, but it doesn't seem to be helping. Maybe you can teach me."

The girl, realizing that Mira was flirting, said, "Oh really? What would you like me to teach you?"

"For starters, maybe you could tell me where to get a good lunch. So far all I've seen are hot dogs and popcorn, and I'd like something a bit tastier than that."

"Well, you're in luck, because I happen to be a waitress over at Conger's Café, and we make a great club sandwich."

She was interrupted by Bill Muncey stepping between her and Mira and with a perfectly frightening scowl on his face. Muncey said, "Young lady, you don't want to spend time with this man. He's a criminal in his home country."

The girl didn't know what to do, "Criminal? What type of criminal?"

Still with a deadpan delivery Muncey said, "He's a thief. He stole an airplane!"

"That's awful!" Shelly exclaimed.

Slovak stood quietly trying to figure out why Muncey was being so rude. Muncey turned so that his back was to Mira and said, "He's a kidnapper too. Twenty-three counts! You know he's been sentenced to death if he ever goes home."

Shelly held up the program, looked at Mira's autograph, slammed it closed, and hurried away without looking back. Once she was out of earshot Muncey and Cantrell burst out laughing. Muncey turned to Slovak and said, "Come on Slim, don't get mad. It was all true. Every word of it!"

Muncey and Cantrell walked off to their own boats, leaving Mira standing alone in stunned silence. A moment later Kit Muncey, Bill's wife, who had been watching the entire exchange, walked up to Mira. She was an attractive woman in her late twenties. She had short dark hair and was wearing black pedal pushers and a white blouse with "Kit" embroidered in orange over the left pocket and "*Miss Thriftway*" in three-inch tall chain stitching on the back.

"You know he likes you," she said.

Mira was a bit baffled by everything that had just happened. "Well, he doesn't act like it."

"This is just the way he treats his brother Raymond, and he loves Raymond to death."

"Really?"

"Yes, really. His father was always pitting the boys against each other in a battle of the fittest. He thought it would make the boys stronger and it's worked. I mean, look at how successful Bill is."

"So how do I deal with it?"

"It he teases you, tease him back. If he pushes you, push him back. He'll love it. I guarantee it."

"Thank you, Mrs. Munsley."

Kit cringed a little and said, "Actually it's pronounced Muncey."

Mira smiled mischievously and said, "I know it is."[1]

Fourteen boats qualified and they were divided into heats A and B. Mira sat patiently in the cockpit of the *Miss Wahoo* while the rest of the boats for heat 1A were placed in the water by the two large construction cranes. With his earplugs in and his helmet on, the typical noise and hubbub from the pits took on an almost otherworldly quality. He could still hear the scratchy voice from the portable public-address system, but he could not understand what the garbled voice was saying. The growl of the diesel-powered cranes as they strained to pick up the 6,000-pound hydroplanes came through the helmet as nothing more than a far-off rumble. The boom of the five-minute gun was something that he felt almost as a thump against his chest more than he actually heard.

The water in front of the pit area was crowded with the seven boats. Mira turned on the magneto, switched on his fuel boost pump, and was just about to hit the starter when something out of the corner of his right eye caught his attention. Roger Murphy in the *Breathless* was leaving the pits at the same time and was cutting in front of the *Wahoo*. Mira waited for the *Breathless* to pass, but just as the bright blue boat pulled in front of him, there was a backfire from its carburetor and the *Breathless* coasted to a stop directly in Mira's way. The clock was winding down, but Mira couldn't start his engine without running over Murphy's boat. Mira sat patiently as Roger Murphy struggled to bring the *Breathless* back to life. Bright orange flames came from the exhaust, and Mira knew that Murphy had flooded the engine. In his mind, Mira was coaching Murphy to clear the excess fuel. "Pull your mix control all the way back, shut off your boost pump, press down your accelerator, stay off the primer, and turn the engine over until the cylinders dry!"

Eventually, the *Breathless* coughed and sputtered, moved a few yards, and died again, but at least she had moved enough to clear a path for the *Miss Wahoo*. Mira hit the starter and roared away from the pits. He was much later than he had planned and was going to be several seconds behind at the start. He took his right hand off the wheel and reached out of the cockpit, gently patted the deck of the boat with his hand, and said. "We can do this, girl."

As he powered up the backstretch the rest of the field was already making their run toward the starting line, led by the gold and red *Shanty-I*, followed by the *Maverick*, the *Bardahl*, the *Thriftway*, and the *Miss Seattle*. The *Miss Wahoo* was in sixth. In the past, a poor start like this would have made Mira furious, but today, he felt a calm settle over him. He stayed focused on the task at hand, saying to himself, "Well, I have my work cut out for me. I can't pass them all at once, but if I go after one boat per lap, I can still win this."

Mira crossed the starting line at 150 mph. He could tell he was catching the *Miss Seattle* very quickly. He told himself, "Remember the basics. We can catch them if we keep running." He took a quick glance at the dashboard and saw that his pressures and temperatures were all good. Then he looked ahead and saw an opening in lane one. He slipped inside of the *Miss Seattle* and took over fifth place. On lap four, the *Maverick* pulled into the infield with a broken supercharger, moving the *Wahoo* up to fourth. On the next lap Mira was able to get past the *Miss Bardahl* and set his sights on Muncey and the *Thriftway*. They battled side-by-side for two laps, with Slovak taking over second place on the seventh lap. At the start of lap eight, there was a loud pop from the *Shanty*, which drifted to a stop, and Mira charged into the lead. He kept his foot on the floor and continued to put plenty of water between himself and the *Thriftway*, taking the checkered flag at the end of lap ten with a forty-three-second lead over Muncey.[2]

From far out on the course, Mira could see Junie and the rest of the *Wahoo* crew jumping up and down, waving their arms in celebration. Mira knew that he had driven a great race, but he also felt that something important inside him had changed. In the racing world, there are drivers and there are racers. Drivers can operate the boat and get it to do what they want it to do, but racers are that special breed that can make something magic happen when they get behind the wheel. Up until today, Mira had felt like a driver, but something had happened out on the course. When that calm determination settled over him at the start of the heat, Mira felt a oneness with the boat and knew that he had transformed into a racer, and he knew once that transformation took place, there was no going back. When he got to the dock, Mira was greeted with hugs and handshakes from his elated crew. After a few moments of celebration, Junie said, "All right, this was just one heat. There is a lot more racing ahead of us. Let's put her back on the trailer and get ready for the next one." Mira took off his helmet and began to unbuckle his life jacket as he walked to the end of the dock. He walked slowly, catching his breath while he savored the accomplishment. As he stepped onto the beach, he was approached by a group of reporters holding note pads and cameras.

"What was it like out there?" One of the reporters asked.

"It was nice and smooth for the first few laps, but towards the end the water was getting really lumpy."

"How did you get past Muncey so easily?"

Mira gave his head a slight shake, "I don't know. He seemed to slow down there on lap seven. Maybe he had a mechanical problem. You'll have to ask him."

A different reporter asked, "Do you think you can win it all today?"

"We wouldn't be here if we didn't think we could win it all!" Mira said with a smile.

Jack Regas in the *Hawaii Kai* won both his preliminary heats and was in the final with 800 points.

Mira and the *Miss Wahoo* were drawn in heat 2B with the *Thriftway,* the *Maverick,* the *Gale V,* and the *Thriftway Too.* The *Wahoo* led all ten laps, easily taking first place over the *Thriftway* by almost a minute and heading into the final tied with the *Hawaii Kai* with 800 points.

As Mira was buckling up his life jacket for the final heat, the same calm, focused determination that he had been feeling all weekend settled over him. He knew what it was going to take to win. Sitting in the cockpit waiting for the five-minute gun, Mira watched the wind begin to blow the branches of the trees near the pits. He could see rollers starting to build out on the course, and he knew that the water would be rough for the final heat. As the waves began to rock the boat he reviewed his strategy, "There are six boats in the final and with the points I've already accumulated there are only two boats that can beat me. They are the *Hawaii Kai* and *Miss Thriftway*. My first job is to make sure I finish the heat." There was an old cliché among racers, "If you want to finish first, you first have to finish." He couldn't afford to jump the gun or hit a buoy either, so he decided to start outside and a little behind. "That way I can stay clear of any bumping and banging going on in the first turn. Once I get safely through the first turn I'll look for Muncey and Regas and decide what to do then."

The five-minute gun sounded. Before Mira was able to hit the starter, Lee Schoenith fired up the *Gale VI* and drove right in front of the stationary *Wahoo,* sending a huge roller of blue water sliding up the *Wahoo's* curved deck and into the engine well. At 8.3 pounds per gallon, the roller had just added several hundred pounds of weight. Mira shook his head in disbelief. He waited until the *Gale* was out of his way and hit the starter. The *Wahoo* roared to life. As Mira pulled out of the pits, he gently patted the deck of the *Miss Wahoo,* like a jockey calming his mount on the way to the starting gate. Mira made a slow lap, letting his oil warm up and watching where Muncey and Regas were. When the one-minute gun sounded, he let the *Wahoo* slide far to the outside of the course. The *Miss Seattle* took lane one, the *Hawaii Kai III* was in lane two, the *Gale VI* was in three, the *Miss Thriftway* was in four, and the *Wahoo* was in about lane seven. The *Miss Bardahl* and the *Gale VI* lagged well behind the rest of the field. As Mira made his run to the start, he began to get pelted in the face by fierce splashes of water. He looked between his legs and saw that his feet were covered by several inches of water. His heart sank. Then he remembered the dousing he had taken from the *Gale VI* and realized that there was not a hole in the boat, and he could keep racing.

From his position outside, Mira got a good view of the clock and hit the line exactly when the cannon sounded. He looked to his left and saw that the *Miss Thriftway* was already a roostertail ahead of him. Mira knew that if his own start was perfect, and Muncey was way ahead, Muncey must have jumped the gun. The fleet barreled into the first turn, and all Mira could see to his left was white water and roostertails. Coming off the turn Mira passed everyone but the *Thriftway.* As Mira flew up the backstretch, he looked over his left shoulder and saw the pink *Hawaii Kai* belching smoke and struggling to get restarted at the entrance to turn one. She must have been pinched between the *Miss Seattle* and the *Gale VI* at the start, swallowed a lot of water, and lost power.

With Muncey jumping the gun and Regas dead in the water, there was no one left that had enough points to beat the *Wahoo.* All Mira had to do was finish and he would win his first race. With that sudden realization, Slovak's job changed. His one and only task was to keep the boat running. He looked at his dashboard to make sure that all his gauges were reading normal. They were. Then he backed off the throttle just a bit, slowing from 150 mph to about 130 mph. The water was getting rough so he needed to make sure the *Wahoo* did not get damaged, but he also knew that if he slowed down too much, the boat would stop flying over the surface of the lake and would start pounding through the waves, which actually presented more of a risk of damaging the boat.

He finished lap one eight seconds behind Muncey. He had to keep the *Wahoo* running for nine more laps. Normally, in the heat of competition, there was so much happening, and so many things to draw the driver's attention, that nine laps would pass in the blink of an eye, but this situation was different. He had nothing to do but focus on the engine, to will it to keep going. He was reminded of flying the burning Siebel back to base long ago in Czechoslovakia. The way his eyes kept being drawn to the gauges every few seconds felt very much the same. At the start of lap three he began to smell burning oil. He scanned his gauges yet again and everything was still good. He looked outside the cockpit and saw the *Gale VI* floating dead in the infield with wisps of smoke wafting from her engine.

By lap four, the water was rough. Just after the start line, the *Wahoo* took a leap and landed with a huge splash. At the same instant there was a searing burst of pain as something hit the back of Mira's right leg, knocking his foot off the throttle. Mira quickly put his foot back onto the pedal to keep the boat running and bent at the waist to try to look into the bilge. He did not see anything but angry water splashing back and forth. Going into the next turn, the boat took another jump and again something slammed into his legs. Clearly something had broken lose and was causing who knows how much damage. Running up the backstretch, the *Wahoo* jumped again as she plowed through three big rollers and the heavy object hit Mira's left knee and then slammed into the steering wheel, knocking his left hand from the wheel, and landed like a punch to the gut in his lap. Mira looked down and saw the red hand-held fire extinguisher that was normally strapped under his seat. Without missing a beat, Mira grabbed the extinguisher and threw it out of the cockpit.

There was a bright red oil pressure warning light on dashboard. It would turn on if the pressure dropped below 30 pounds. Midway through the south turn on lap eight, Mira thought he saw the light flicker for a second. He could not be sure. Maybe the red lenses had just caught the sunlight as he bounced through the turn. He checked the oil gauge and it had dropped from 70 pounds to 55 pounds, but this was normal. As the race went on, the oil heated up and the pressure would drop. In the north turn, he thought he saw the light flash again but still it could have been the sunlight. As he bounced through the turn, he took his right hand off the wheel and cupped it over the light to block the sun. Sure enough, it blinked again when the *Wahoo* took a vicious hop off a wave. This did not necessarily mean there was any immediate danger to the engine. It could just mean that the oil was warm and thin, and as the boat bounced and jarred through the turn, the oil splashed away from the pickup for a second, but it could also mean that there was a serious problem and the engine was about to die. Mira finished lap eight and started lap nine, still holding second. Yet if Muncey had really jumped the gun and was forced to run an extra lap, Mira would move up to first place. He drove the last two laps with his gaze sweeping back and forth between the oil pressure gauge and the red light. He saw the light blink a few more times in the turns, but it stayed off on the straightaway, which was a good sign. Mira still worried; coming off the last turn, he took his eyes off of the dashboard to watch the flag man on the official barge. Which flag would they give to Muncey? If it was a white flag, it would confirm Mira's suspicion that Muncey had jumped. A checkered flag would mean Muncey had won the heat. Mira could see the flag man holding up both flags. Yet which one would Muncey get? As Muncey approached the line, Mira was elated to see the white flag unfurled and waved for Muncey. A moment later, the checkered flag waved for him as he flashed past the barge. "We won!" Mira shouted as he pumped his fist in the air. Then, patting the deck of the *Miss Wahoo*, he said, "We did it, girl!"

There was pandemonium in the *Wahoo's* pit. Junie, Marci, Les Eide, and the rest of the crew cheered, hugged, and jumped up and down in celebration. Mira shut the *Wahoo* down early and coasted into the dock. As soon as he stepped off the boat, he was mobbed by reporters with cameras and microphones. The crew picked him up and carried him on their shoulders to the end of the dock and tossed him into the lake in a victory celebration. As everyone was cheering and laughing, the rest of the crew rushed up behind Junie and Marci and pushed them into the water, where they hugged and splashed. Everything was being broadcast back to Seattle by KING-TV, and Mira's popularity swelled.

That evening, after the *Wahoo* was back on her trailer and buttoned up for the night, Bill Boeing got a telegram that there was a business matter needing immediate attention. Victory or not, he needed Mira to fly him home in the Grumman right away. So while Mira and Boeing flew home to Seattle, Junie and Marci, acting as hosts in Bill's absence, took everyone to dinner at the Biltmore Hotel in Crystal Bay, a small resort town just across the state line in Nevada.

Crystal Bay was home to a number of posh casinos and their high-rolling customers. Robert Kennedy, Marilyn Monroe, Frank Sinatra, and many other celebrities escaped to Crystal Bay when they wanted to cut loose and relax. The four-story Biltmore was built to look like a rustic stone lodge, with a wooden shake roof and plenty of porches that offered views of the lake. Behind the lodge were quaint guest cabins and a patio that offered elegant outdoor dining. The patio was surrounded by a low stone wall and decorated in a Roman theme with grape arbors, two-handled terracotta amphorae, and nude sculptures of voluptuous garden nymphs.

The maître-d' showed Marci and Junie to a large table near the stone wall while Les and several of the other crew members went to the men's room to try to wash some of the 70-weight motor oil from their hands and scrub the grease out from underneath their fingernails.

While Marci and Junie waited for the rest of the crew to show up, the sommelier, in a black jacket and white gloves, approached the table and handed Junie a thick wine list with an image of a Roman peasant girl carrying a basket of grapes printed on the cover. Junie passed the wine list to Marci and said, "We have something to celebrate so I say, 'Let's celebrate!'" She turned to the steward and said, "There are ten of us, and I'd like to get Champagne for us all, so let's start with three bottles of Moet and Chandon Imperial Brut." When the crew came back from the restroom, they found chilled glasses of Champagne waiting at everyone's plate. After they were all seated, Junie stood, raised his glass and said, "I'd like to make a toast to the best crew, the best driver, and the best darn boat in this sport!" The crew raised their glasses and clinked them as they cheered Junie.

Eventually, a uniformed waiter came to take their orders, standing politely behind each guest. Les Eide was sitting across from Marci with his back to the stone wall and did not realize that perched on the wall, almost directly behind him, was a sensuous sculpture of a naked garden nymph. When he turned towards the waiter to place his order, he found himself facing directly into the naked crotch of the sexy young statue. "Wow!" Les exclaimed, "I was not expecting that."

The statue was only about 4 feet tall, and Les was just a bit over five feet tall himself. Marci teased, "I think she's just your size, Les. I could set you up on a date"

Les raised his glass of Champagne and toasted the statue, saying "Wahoo!" There was more laughter as the rest of the crew followed Les's lead and raised their glasses to toast the statue with calls of "Wahoo!"

The celebration wound into the night with laughter, stories, and many more bottles of Champagne. Several times during the party, particularly if there was a lull in the conversation, Les would turn towards the nymph, raise his glass, and exclaim, "Wahoo!" Each time he did, he was greeted with gales of laughter from the now tipsy race team.

Marci, having had her share of champagne, stood up and removed a large gold and white scarf from around her neck. "That poor girl is going to catch her death of cold." She walked to the nymph and tied her scarf around the naked statue's waist, arranging it like a Tahitian pareo, saying, "There! I hope she stops bothering Les and lets the poor fellow eat his dinner." As she turned to head back to her seat, she stepped on a loose stone on the patio and momentarily lost her balance. She reached out to steady herself on the statue, and to her surprise, the statue started to fall too. Les quickly stood up and caught Marci with one arm and the nymph in the other. The crew howled their approval of his heroics.

After Marci regained her balance, Les placed the statue back on the wall. "That's a lot lighter than I thought it would be. It must be just cast plaster."

Marci smiled mischievously. Across the table, Junie saw his sister smile and knew something was up. She pointed to the nymph and said, "Do you know who this is?"

Junie shrugged his shoulders and said, "I have no idea."

"That," Marci said, "is Miss Wahoo!"

"What are you talking about, Marci?" Junie asked.

"I'm so tired of seeing the disappointed look in people's eyes when I tell them that there is no 'Miss Wahoo' but the boat is just named after my home town. I want a story to tell that will excite people, and I think Les's little girlfriend here is just the story we need."

Junie shook his head and said, "I have no idea what you're talking about."

"That's okay, Junie. Maybe the less you know about this the better. I'm going to go pay our tab. Would you bring the rental car around so we don't have to walk too far in the dark?"

It took Junie a few minutes to get the car and drive between the cabins to the patio. As soon as he parked, he saw Marci and Les running toward the car carrying the naked Miss Wahoo and calling out, "Open the trunk! Open the trunk." As they ran, the scarf came unwrapped and fluttered to the ground. Marci's father, Frank Sr., was hurrying just a few steps behind the art thieves, laughing as hard as he could. Marci stopped and nodded toward the scarf and said, "Dad, pick that up. We don't want to leave any evidence!" They placed the nymph in the trunk, padded her with their coats so she would not roll, and drove off into the night like fleeing bank robbers.[3]

The next race was the Gold Cup in Seattle, on August 11. When the *Miss Wahoo's* bright red GMC equipment truck arrived in the pits on Monday morning, August 5, there was a suspicious object about 4 feet tall, wrapped in a khaki-colored canvas tarp, lashed in the corner of the truck.

Twenty boats showed up to attempt to qualify for the 1957 Gold Cup in Seattle. They fit with ease into the brand-new Stanley S. Sayres Memorial pit area. In September 1956, the City set aside a parcel of land on the shore of Lake Washington known as the Wetmore Slough and appropriated $50,000 to build a permanent pit facility. Hydro fans, with help from the Seattle Yacht Club, raised and donated an additional $35,000 toward the new park. The park featured an asphalt-paved pit area with water and electricity for each boat, as well as ten finger piers, restrooms, a pit office with phones, and a permanent monorail so boats could be launched without having to rent a construction crane. The park was dedicated on August 5, 1957.

One afternoon, Russ Schleeh approached Mira and asked, "Have you met Keith Jackson yet?

Mira said, "I know that he is a reporter for KOMO-TV and I think we've talked a few times, but I can't say that I've really met him."

"Come on," Schleeh said, "He's more than a reporter, he's their news director and he's going places in the television business so you should get to know him."

Schleeh led Mira across the pits toward a tall, broad-shouldered reporter in a blue sport coat with a military buzz cut, who was engaged in an animated conversation with Mike Welsch, crew chief for the *Hawaii Kai*. As Mira approached close enough to overhear some of the conversation, he was surprised to hear that it was a deeply technical discussion about engines. Jackson was asking Welsch, "If you are getting that much boost from the blower, do you have to do something different with the cam timing?"

Mira never heard Welsch's answer. Schleeh interrupted and said, "Excuse me Keith, but you mentioned that you'd like to meet Mira Slovak, so I figured I'd bring him over."

Keith Jackson had studied broadcast journalism at Washington State College, in Pullman, where Russ Schleeh had played football and graduated just a few years before Jackson. The two met at the 1955 Gold Cup when Jackson was covering the race for KOMO TV and they became good friends.

Keith held out his hand, "Mira Slovak! I've heard a lot about you. You've led an interesting life."

"Thank you, Mr. Jackson, I'm very pleased to meet you."

"Heck Mira, please call me Keith. Mr. Jackson was my father." Jackson and Mira enjoyed a pleasant but brief conversation before Jackson's producer called him to come interview one of the race officials.

When Mira returned to the *Wahoo* pits, he noticed a young boy, about twelve years old, standing in front of the boat. He was wearing blue jeans, rolled up at the cuffs, black Keds sneakers, and a red and white striped T-shirt. Mira knew that there was not any reason for a young boy to be in the pits. In fact, there were security guards whose only job was to keep people from sneaking in. Yet Mira also remembered what it was like to be a twelve-year-old boy. At that age, fences exist only to be climbed. Circus tents, movie theaters, and sports arenas were created just so boys could sneak in. As Mira approached, the young boy held out a Gold Cup program and a ball point pen and asked, "Mr. Slovak, may I please have your autograph?"

Mira said. "Of course." He knelt down to be at eye level and asked, "What's your name?"

"David Knowlen," the boy answered.

Mira signed the program, "*Hodne šťastia* David" and handed it back.

The young man beamed. Mira asked, "So David, what do you want to do when you grow up?"

Without missing a beat, David answered, "I want to design and build hydroplanes." After a moment, he said, "I'm going to go find Bill Muncey to get his signature too."

About twenty minutes later, Mira saw that a security guard had grabbed young David by the shoulder and was rushing him toward the exit. Mira crossed to the frightened boy and said, "David! There you are. I told you not to wander off. Would you like to come sit in the boat now?" Mira turned to the guard and said, "Thank you very much for finding my friend. His parents asked me to look after him and I got distracted, and I guess he wandered off looking for more autographs. I can take care of him now." Mira placed his arm around Dave's shoulder and walked him to the boat. When the guard left, Mira asked, "Did you ever get Mr. Munsley's signature?"

Dave almost had tears in his eyes, "No. I saw him but he wouldn't even stop to talk to me."

"Well, let's get you up in the cockpit of the *Wahoo* for now, and we'll worry about Munsley later." Mira led David up onto the deck and helped him into the seat, "Now don't touch anything on the dashboard, because she's full of fuel and ready to go for my next run, and I wouldn't want you to accidently start her." After Dave had climbed out of the boat, Mira saw Bill Boeing walk by and asked, "Bill, would you mind giving one of our young fans an autograph?" Boeing stopped and agreed, pulling a pen out of his shirt pocket.

David spent all day hanging around the *Wahoo* pit. Junie found him a terrycloth towel and asked him to wipe down the boat, which he was happy to do. Toward the end of the day, Mira said:

> You never did get Munsley's signature. Do you want to walk down to the *Thriftway* with me? I bet we could get him to sign your program now. David shook his head and said, "Nah, I don't think I want it anymore. When I came down this morning, I thought I was a *Miss Thriftway* fan, but not anymore. Now I'm a *Wahoo* fan for life![4]

The heat drew on Saturday afternoon put Mira in heat 1A with the *Gale V*, the *Miss Bardahl*, the *Miss Seattle*, and the *Miss Rocket*. On the morning of the race, Mira felt his personality taken over by the same calm, focused sense of purpose that had helped him be so successful in Tahoe. He was confident he could get the job done. Now it was up to Junie and the crew to give him the fastest boat possible. When the five-minute gun sounded, Mira hit the switch to fire up the *Wahoo's* engine. The starter turned over, the engine roared to life, and the boat pulled away from the dock, but as soon as Mira moved the mix handle to full rich, the engine died and the boat coasted to a stop. Mira tried again, the boat fired up, but again when he moved the mix handle to full rich, the engine stopped. The clock was winding down. Mira tried once more, but this time he just moved the mix control halfway, from cutoff to auto rich, and the engine kept running. "There must be something wrong with the carburetor," Mira thought.

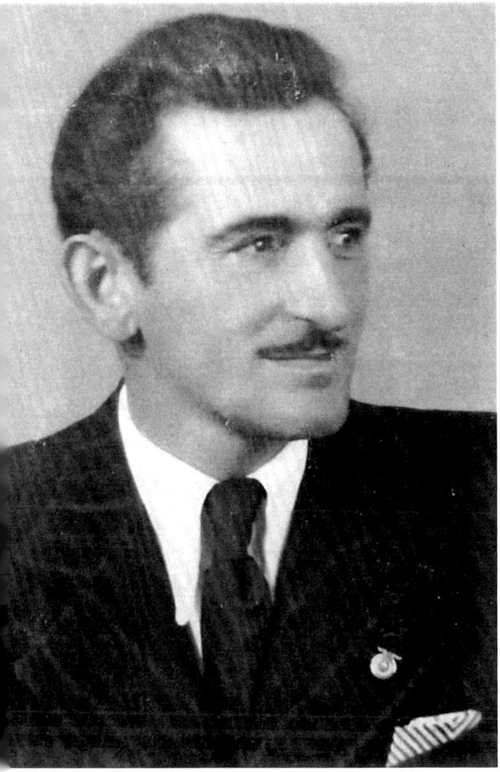

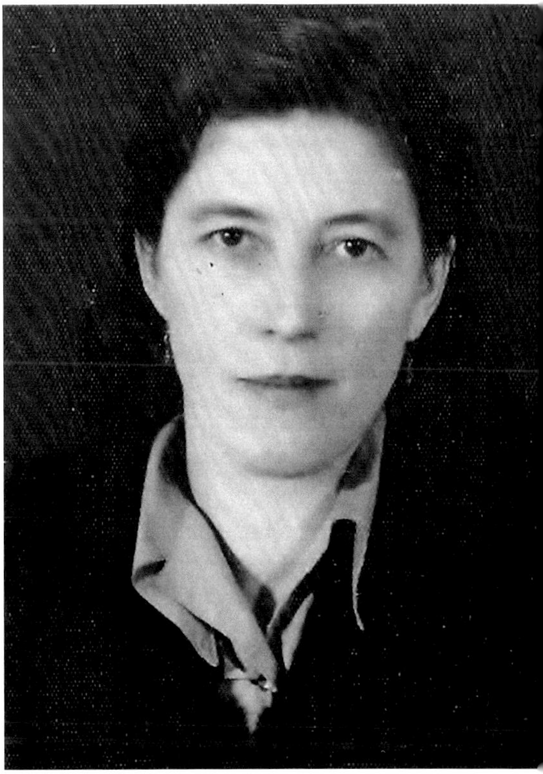

Above left: Mira's father, Jan Slovak. (*The Mira Slovak Collection of the Hydroplane Museum*)

Above right: Mira's mother, Irma Maria Kramarova, who was known to her friends and family as Maria. (*The Mira Slovak Collection of the Hydroplane Museum*)

Right: Miroslav "Mira" Slovak's photo ID as a child. (*The Mira Slovak Collection of the Hydroplane Museum*)

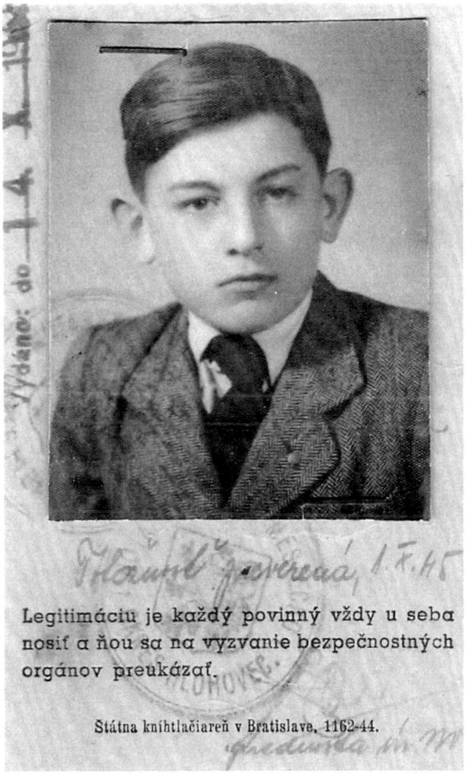

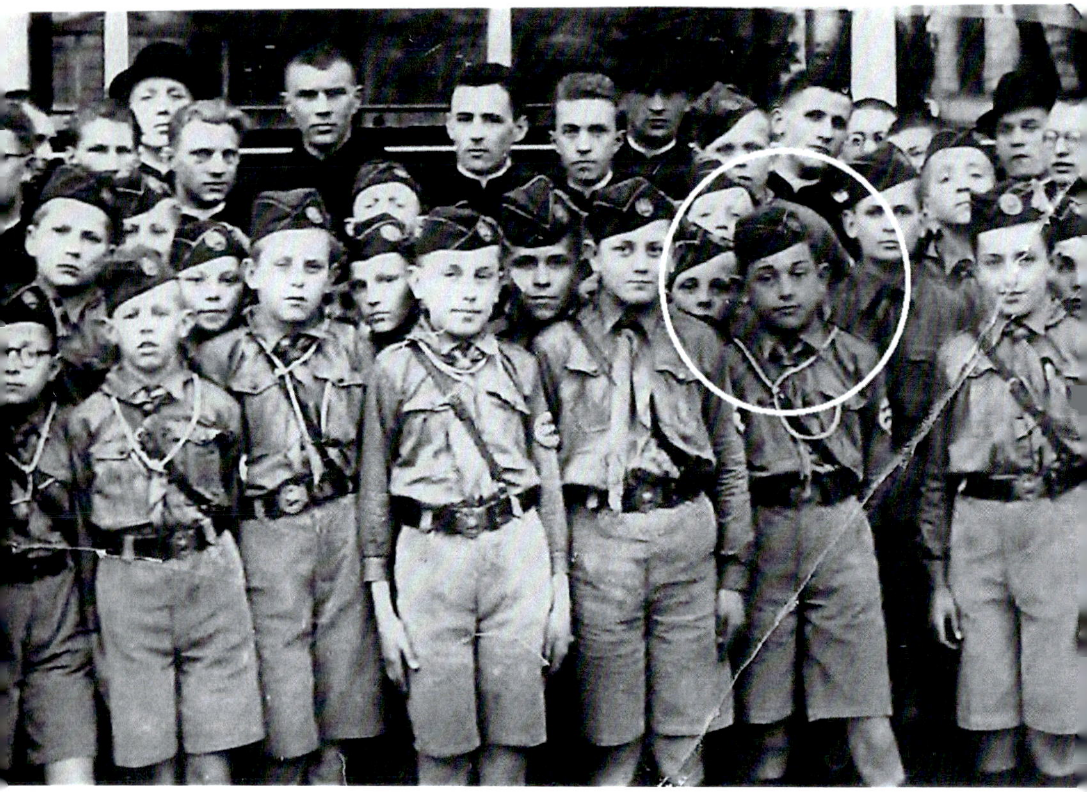

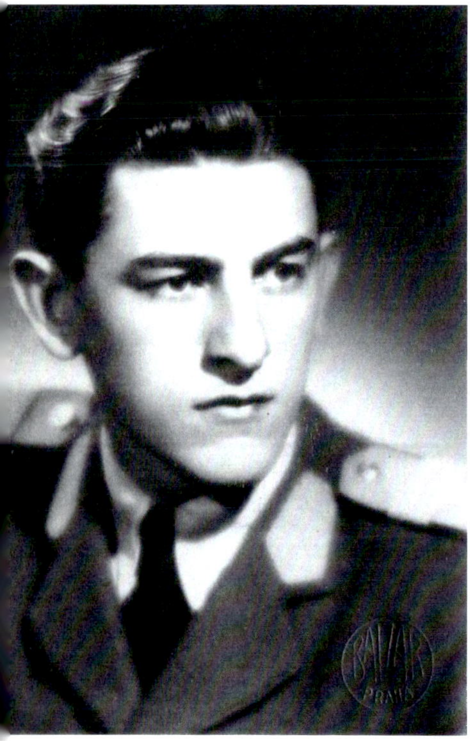

Above: A school photo showing Mira Slovak (circled) in his *Hlinkova Mladez* (Hlinka Youth) uniform. (*The Mira Slovak Collection of the Hydroplane Museum*)

Left: Eighteen-year-old Air Cadet Mira Slovak in 1948. (*The Mira Slovak Collection of the Hydroplane Museum.*)

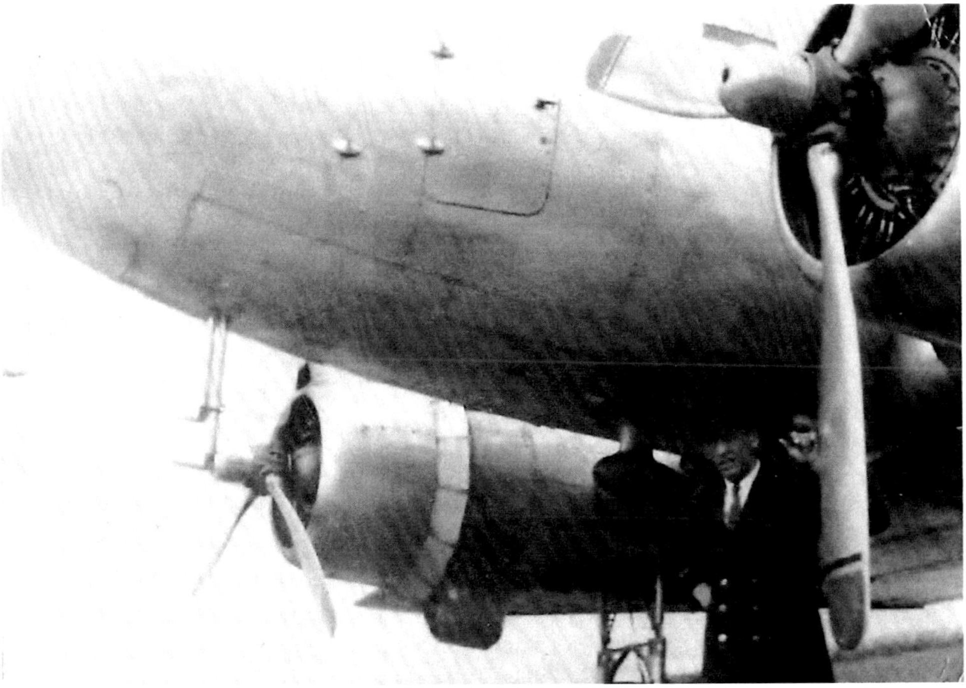

Above: Captain Mira Slovak standing under the wing of a Czechoslovakian Airlines DC-3 in 1953.
(*The Mira Slovak Collection of the Hydroplane Museum*)

Below: The first photograph taken of "The Freedom Six" on the morning of March 24. This photo appeared around the world later that day. Mira Slovak, standing second from the right, was the only person identified when the photograph was originally published.
(*The Mira Slovak Collection of the Hydroplane Museum*)

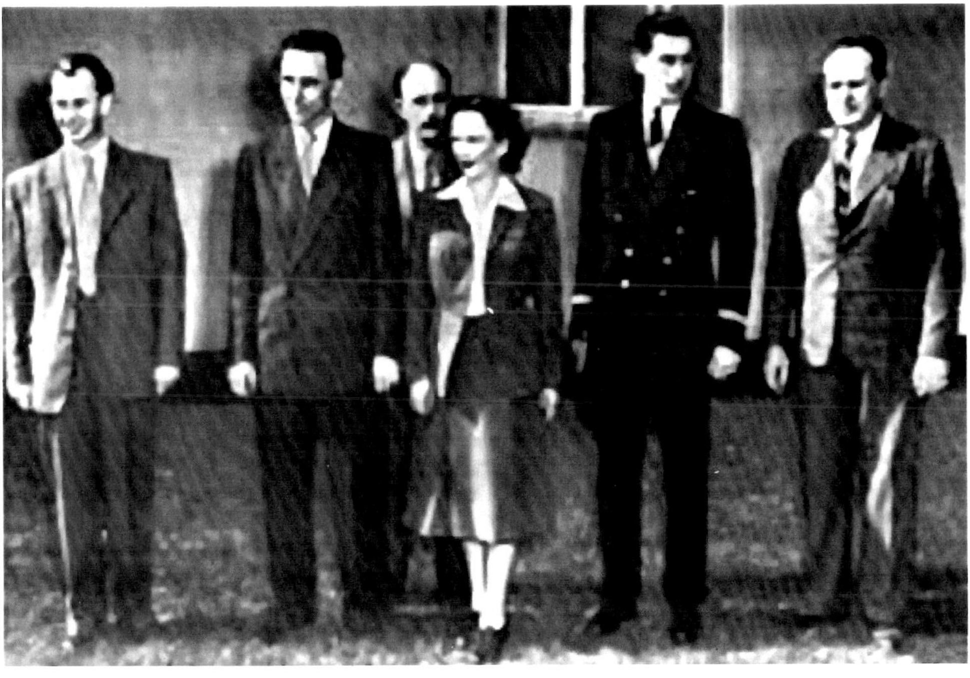

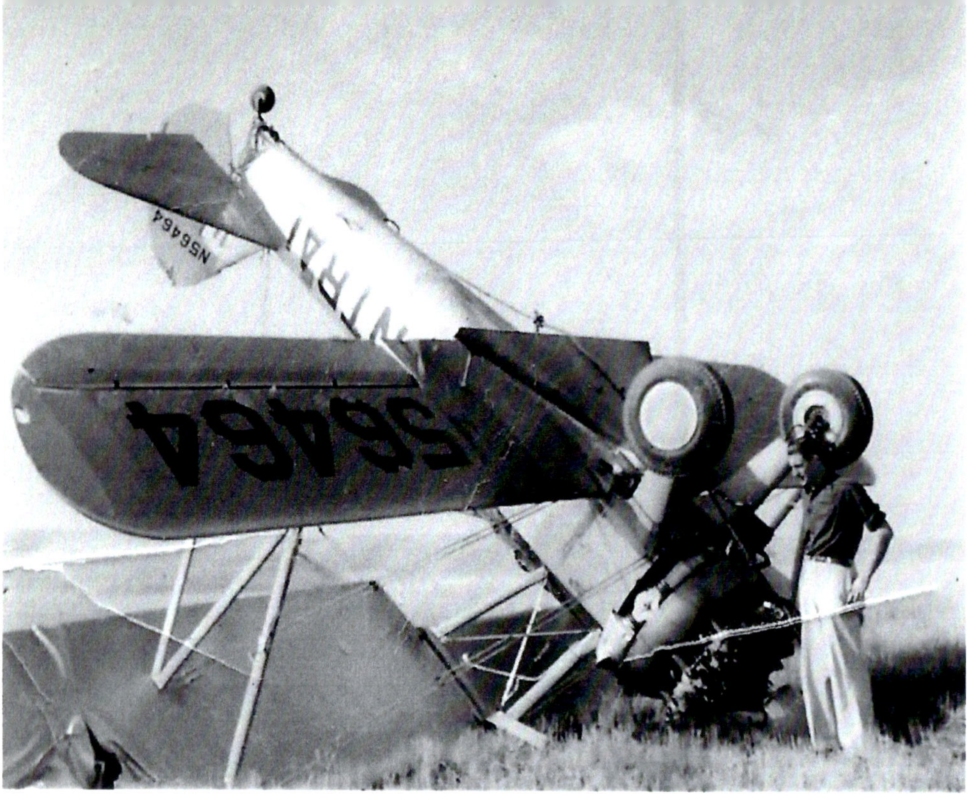

Above: A bad day at Central Airways. The brakes locked on Mira's Stearman 75 Kadet, causing it to "nose over" while landing. This is the photo that appeared in *Life* magazine.
(*The Mira Slovak Collection of the Hydroplane Museum*)

Below: The *Miss Wahoo* bounces clear of the water during the 1957 Apple Cup on Lake Chelan.
(*Bob Carver*)

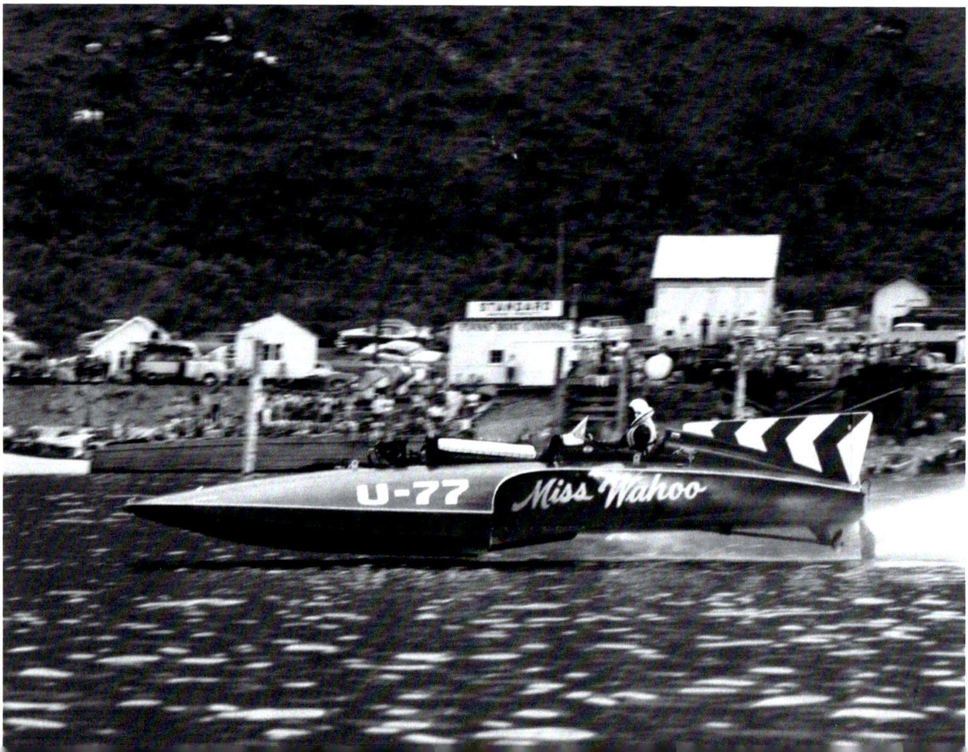

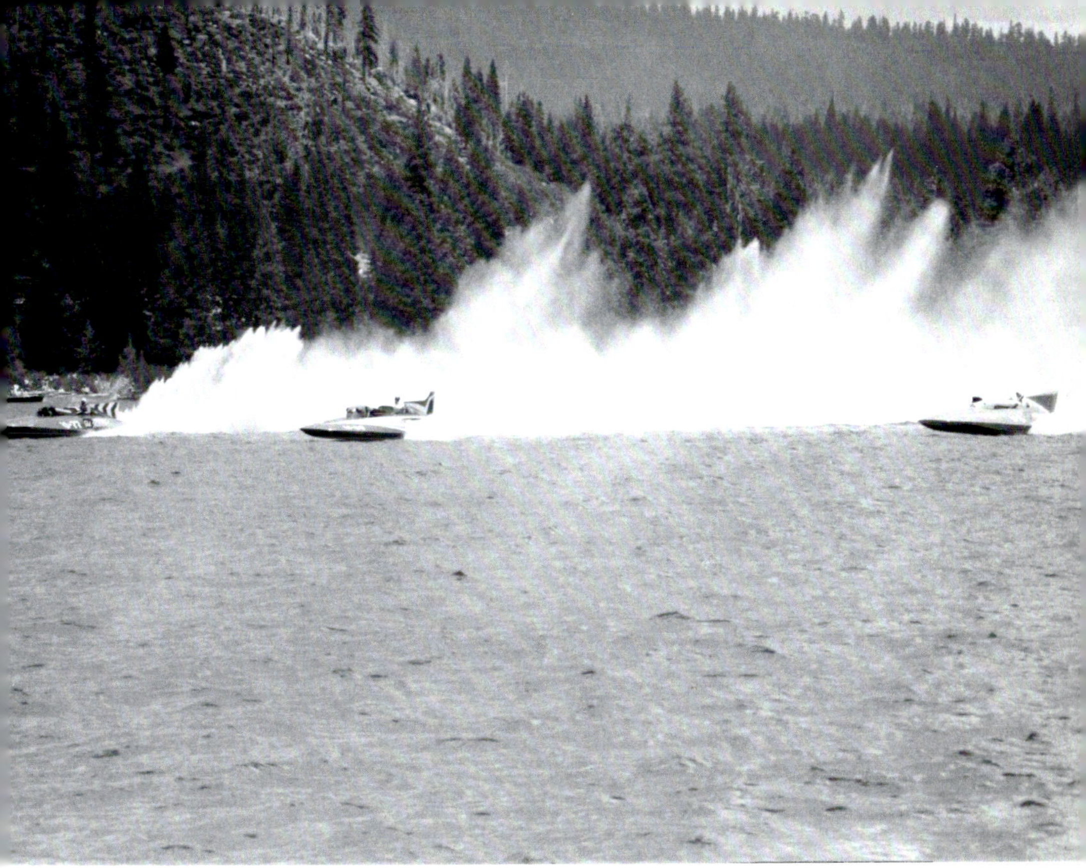

Above: Mira Slovak in the *Miss Wahoo* (left) leads Bill Muncey in the *Miss Thriftway* (center) and Jack Regas in the *Hawaii Kai III* (right) during the 1957 Mapes Mile-High Gold Cup Race on Lake Tahoe. (*Bob Carver*)

Below: Mira is about to be tossed into the water by his crew, after winning the Mapes Mile-High Gold Cup Race on Lake Tahoe. (*Bob Carver*)

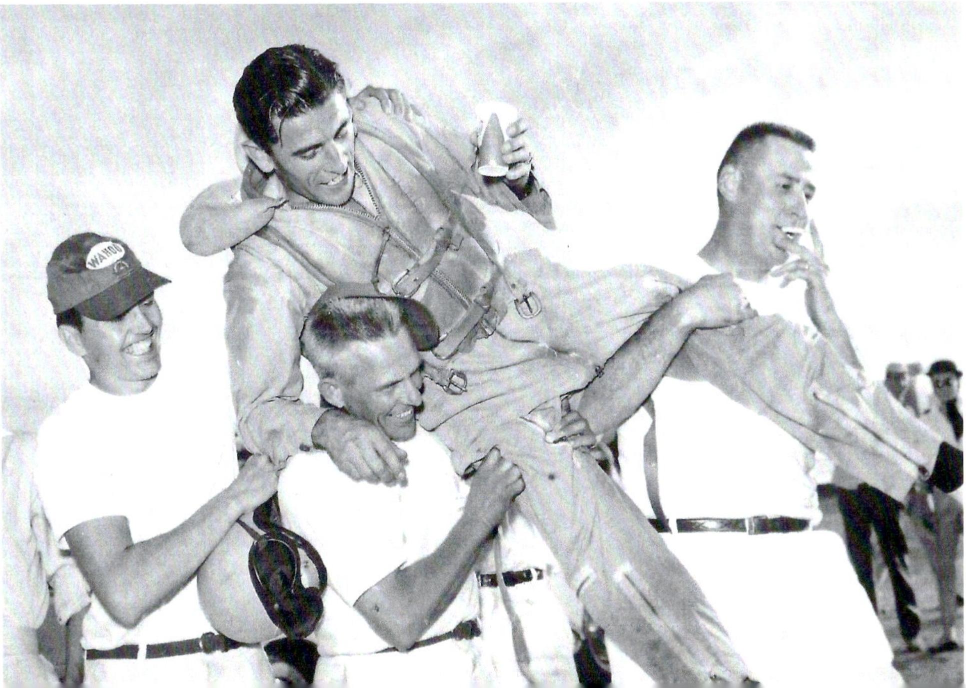

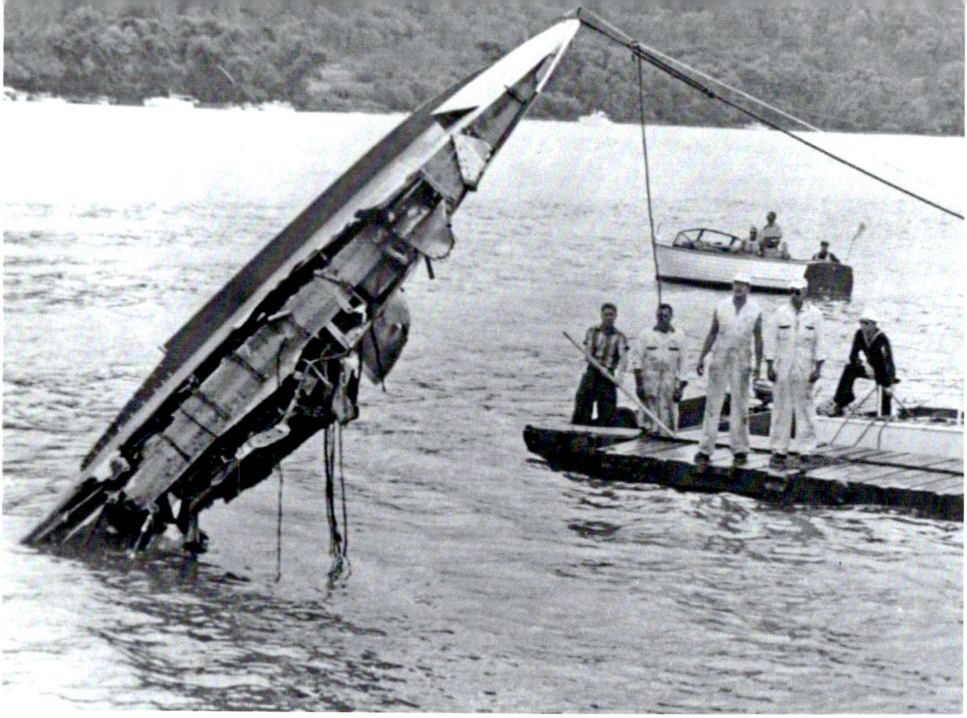

Above: The wreckage of the *Miss Thriftway* is pulled from the Ohio River after crashing during the 1957 Governor's Cup in Madison Indiana. (*The Mira Slovak Collection of the Hydroplane Museum*)

Below: Mira (center) helps transport the injured Bill Muncey from King's Daughters' Hospital in Madison, Indiana to the ambulance plane he will use to fly Muncey to Chicago. The boat's designer, Ted Jones, is on the left. (*The Mira Slovak Collection of the Hydroplane Museum*)

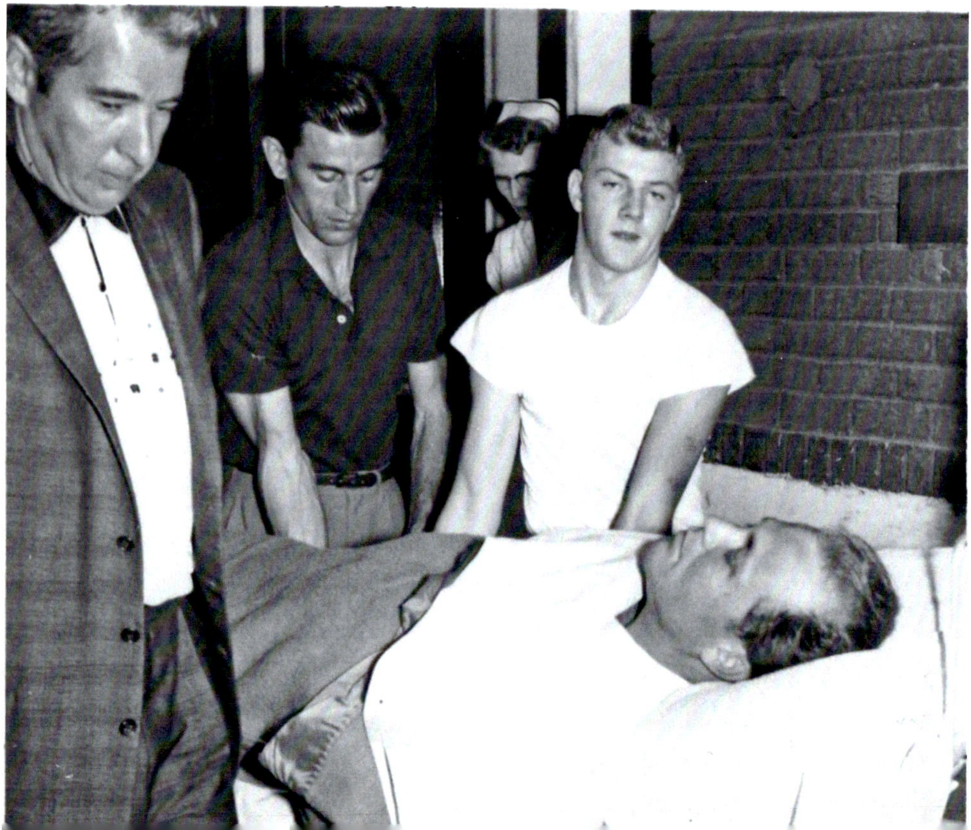

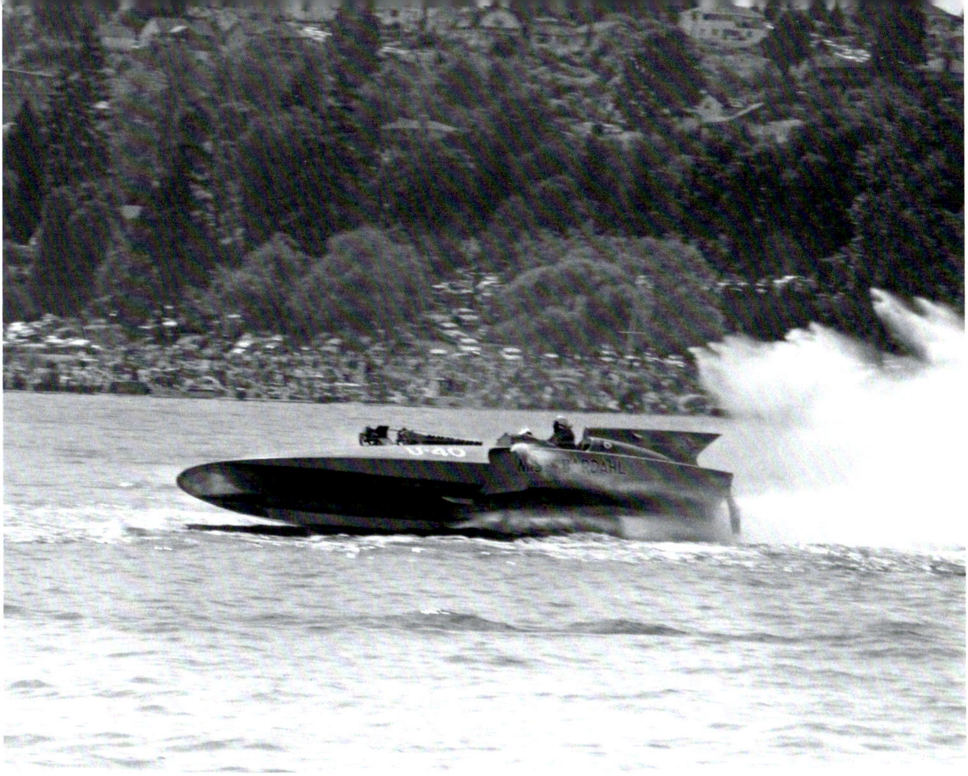

Above: Mira bounces the ill-handling 1958 *Miss Bardahl* around the Gold Cup race course in Seattle. (*Bob Carver*)

Below: Mira (left) celebrates his 1958 National Championship with a kiss from actress Jill St. John. (center) Don Wilson (right) looks on. (*The Mira Slovak Collection of the Hydroplane Museum*)

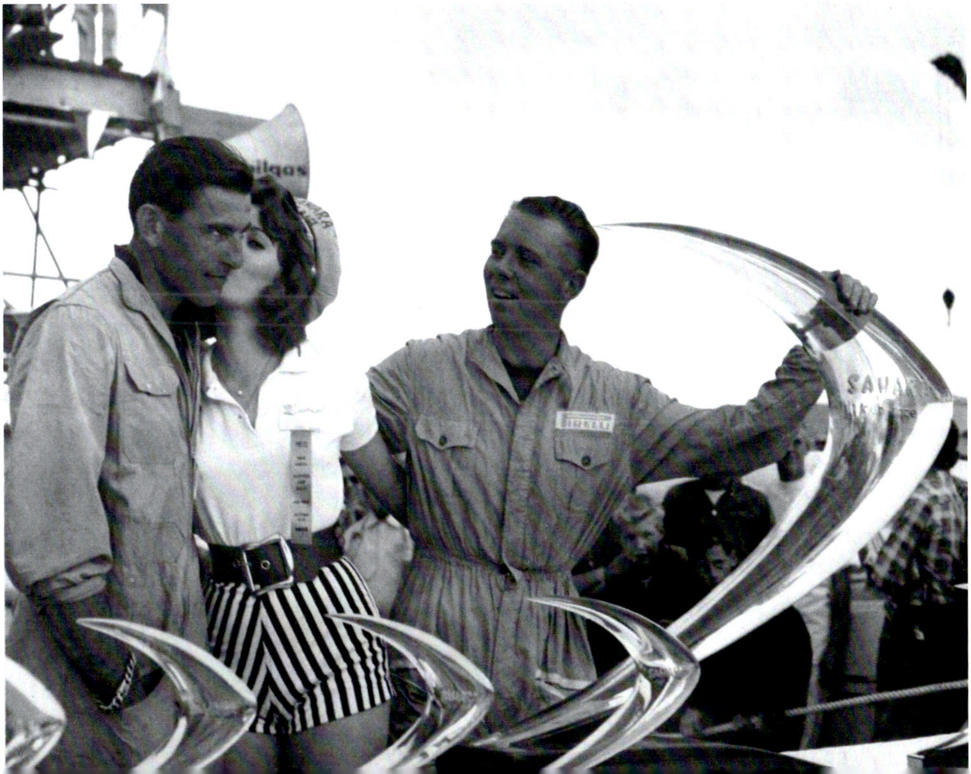

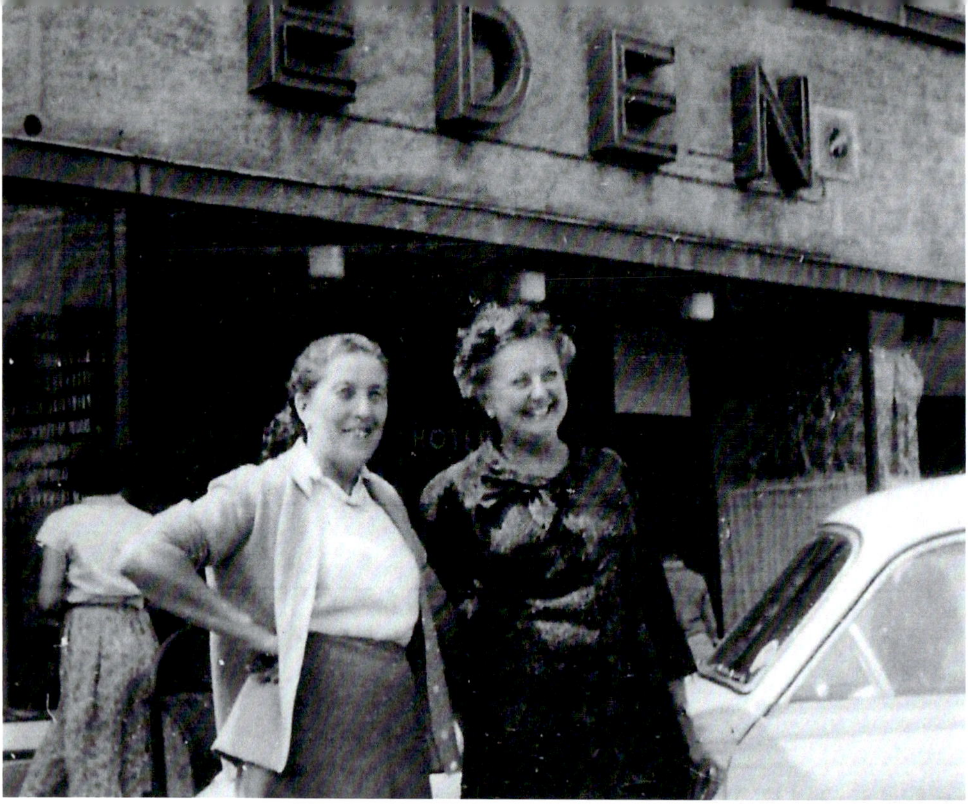

Above: In 1958, at the height of the Cold War, Bill Boeing's mother-in-law, Blanche Cech (right), snuck behind the Iron Curtain to visit Mira's mother Maria Slovak (left) at the Eden Hotel in Piestany, Czechoslovakia. (*The Mira Slovak Collection of the Hydroplane Museum*)

Below: Mira was so proud of his newly restored Ryan STA *Moonshine* that he used a photo of it for his Christmas card. (*The Mira Slovak Collection of the Hydroplane Museum*)

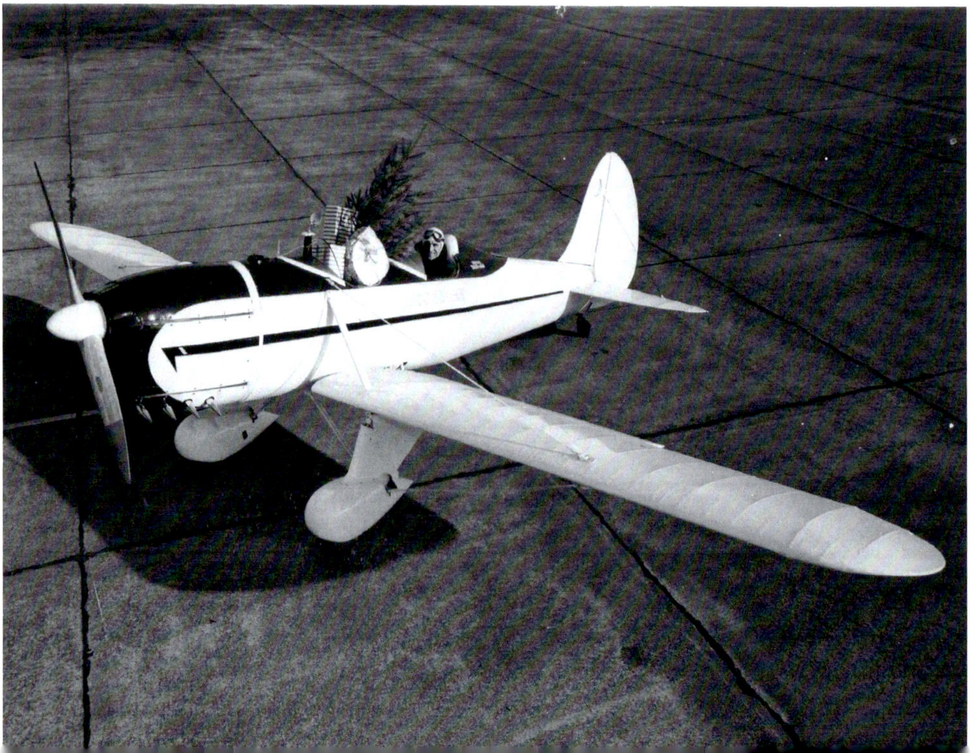

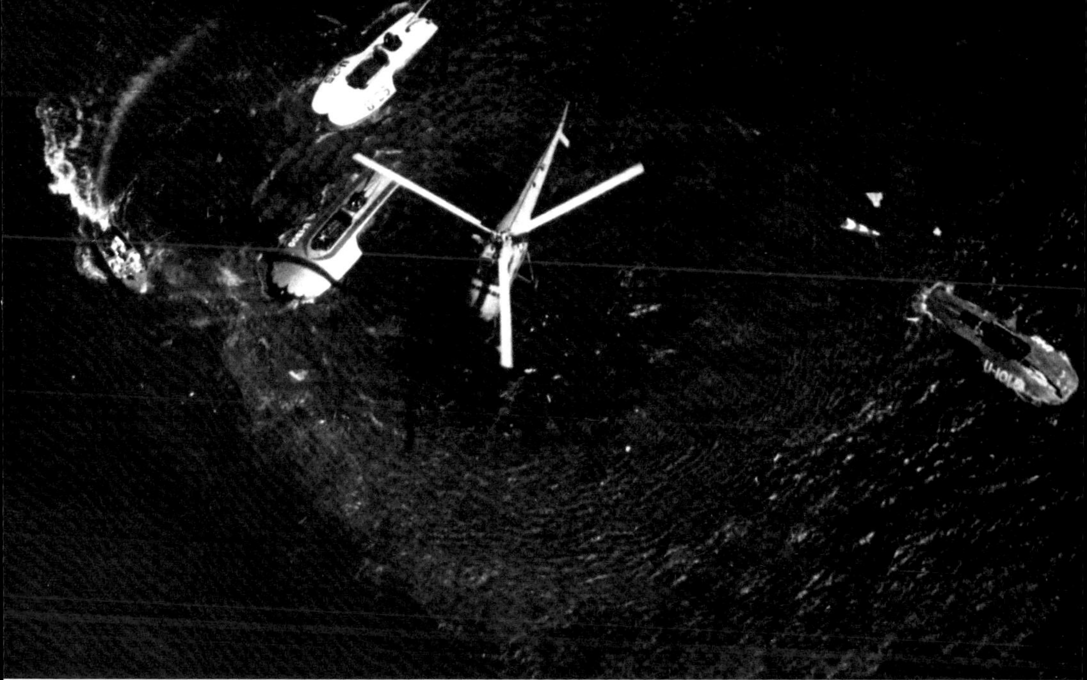

Above: The aftermath of the *Wahoo* flip during the 1960 Seafair Trophy Race. (*The Mira Slovak Collection of the Hydroplane Museum*)

Right: Ingrid Bondi on her first day as a Continental stewardess in 1960. (*The Mira Slovak Collection of the Hydroplane Museum*)

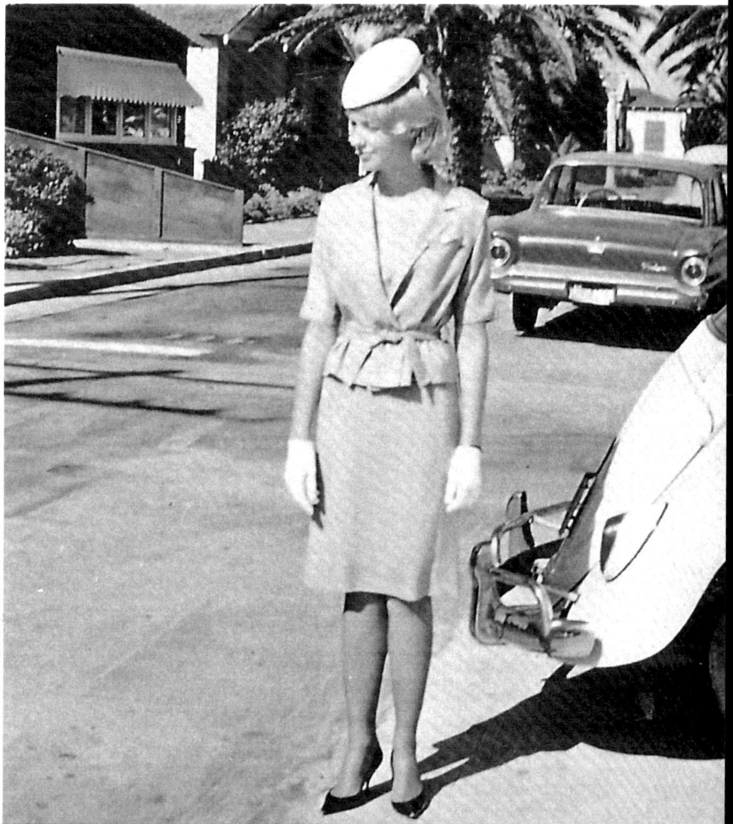

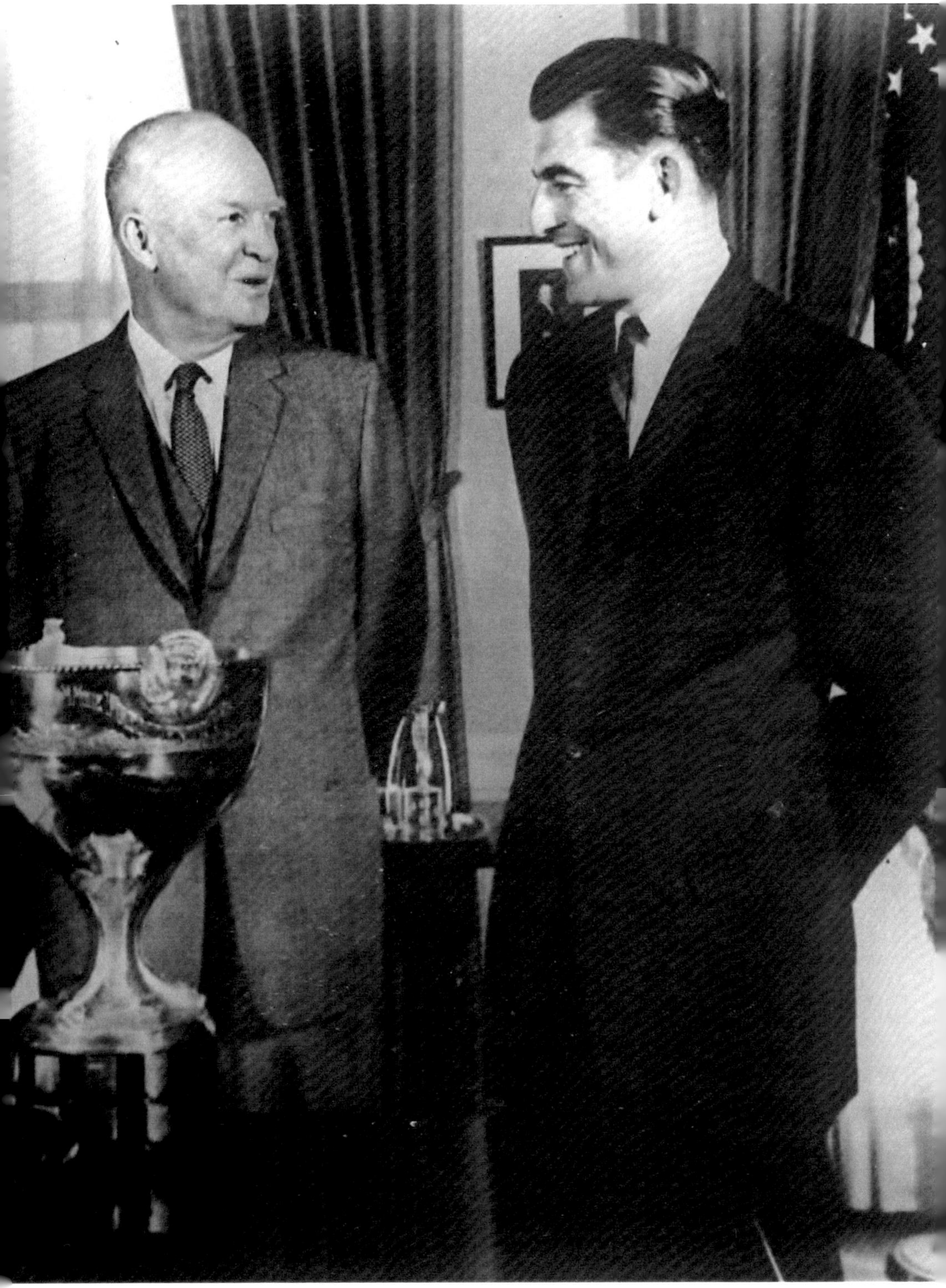

On March 17, 1960, Mira met President Dwight David Eisenhower in the Oval Office to receive the President's Cup. (*The Mira Slovak Collection of the Hydroplane Museum*)

Right: In 1962, Mira was promoted to captain on Continental Airlines' 707s. (*The Mira Slovak Collection of the Hydroplane Museum*)

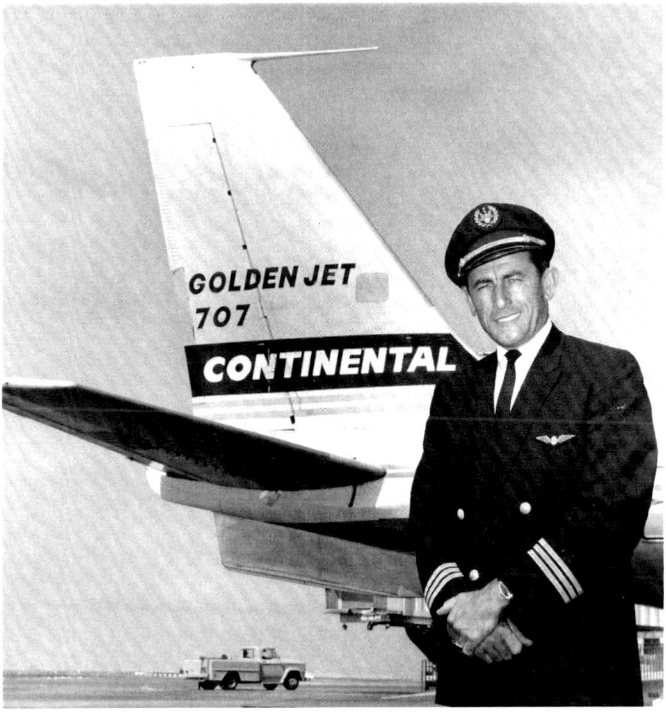

Below: Mira Slovak in the *Miss Exide* (right) battles with Bill Muncey in the *Miss Thriftway* (left) moments before the *Exide* crashes during the 1963 Diamond Cup on Lake Coeur d'Alene, Idaho. (*Bob Carver*)

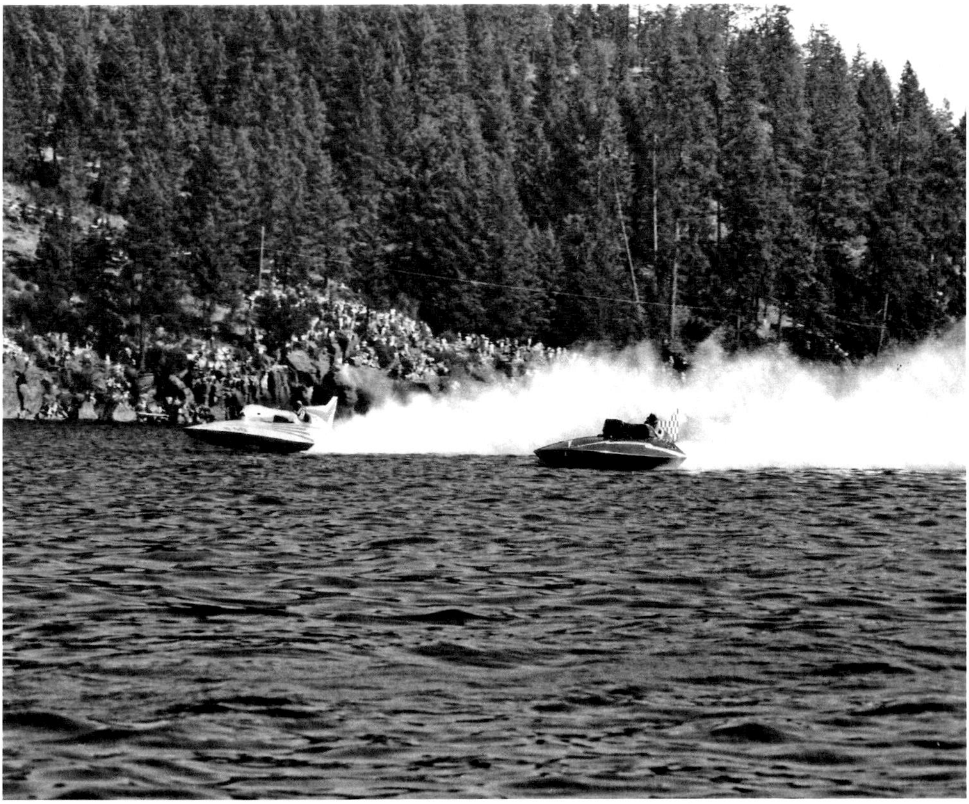

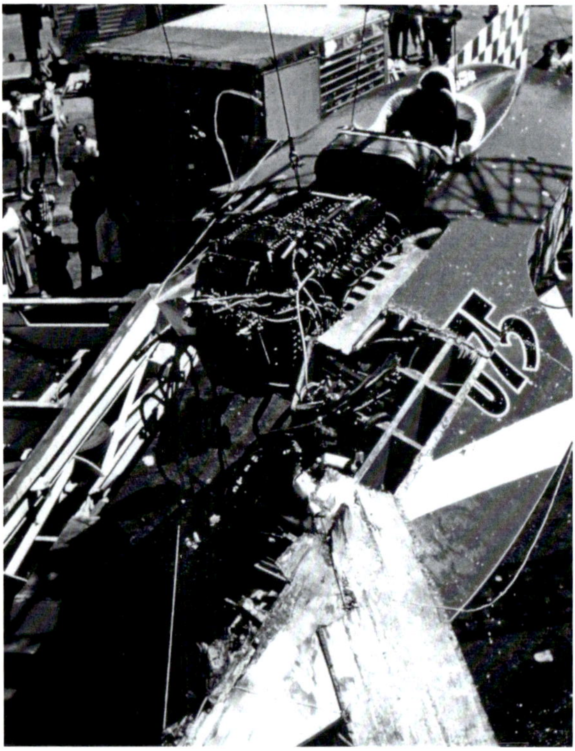

The shattered hull of the *Miss Exide* is pulled from the water of Lake Coeur d'Alene. (*The Mira Slovak Collection of the Hydroplane Museum*)

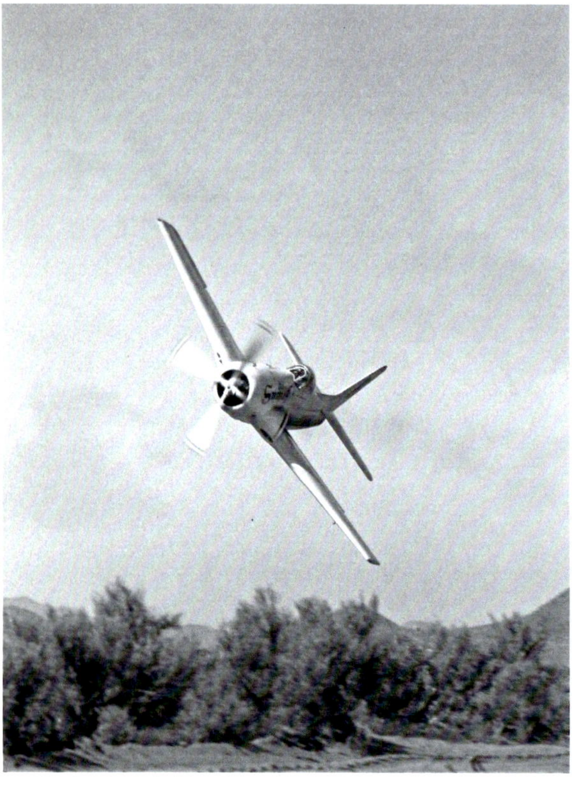

Mira Slovak flies close to the ground in Bill Stead's F8F Bearcat *Smirnoff* at the Reno Air Races. (*Jim Larsen*)

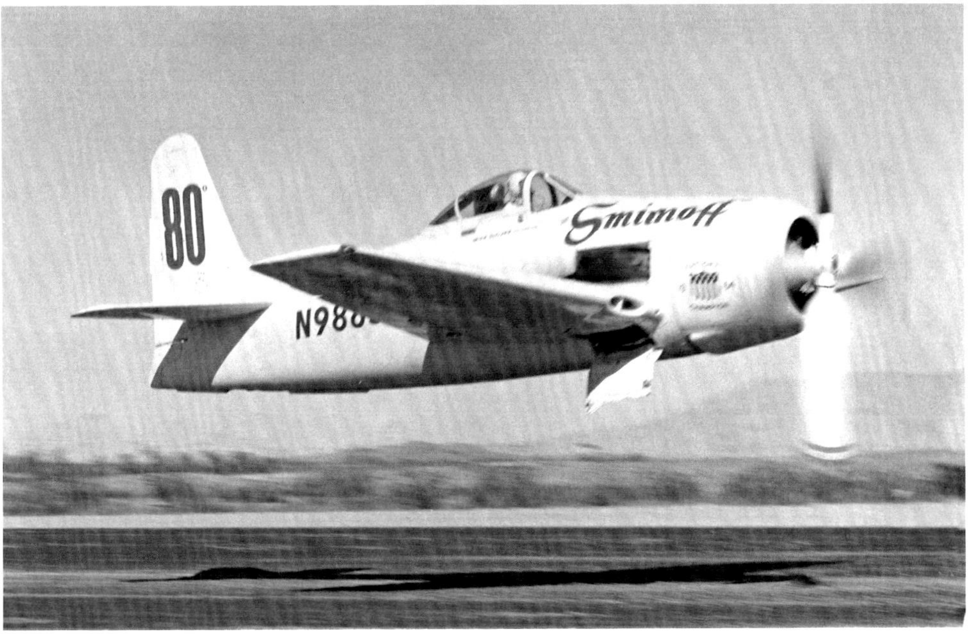

Above: After winning the National Championship in 1964 (note the Championship shield on the engine cowl), Mira returned to Reno in Stead's Bearcat in 1965. (*Jim Larsen*)

Below: Chuck Thompson was killed when the *Miss Smirnoff* hydroplane crashed during the 1966 Gold Cup. Mira Slovak in the *Tahoe Miss* (center) went on to win the race.
(*The Mira Slovak Collection of the Hydroplane Museum*)

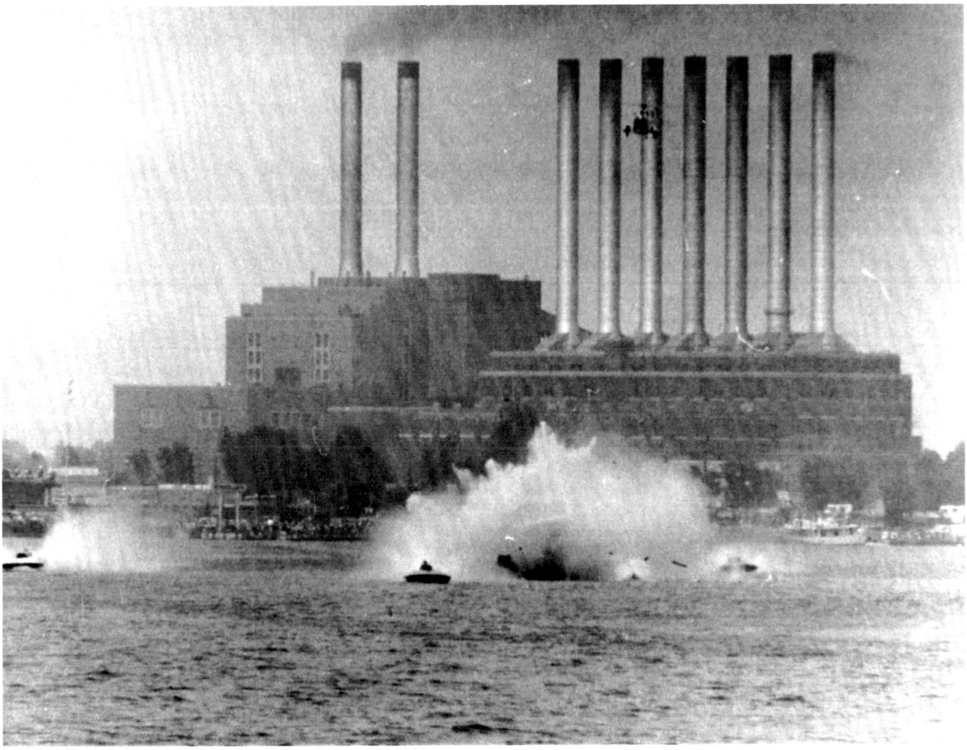

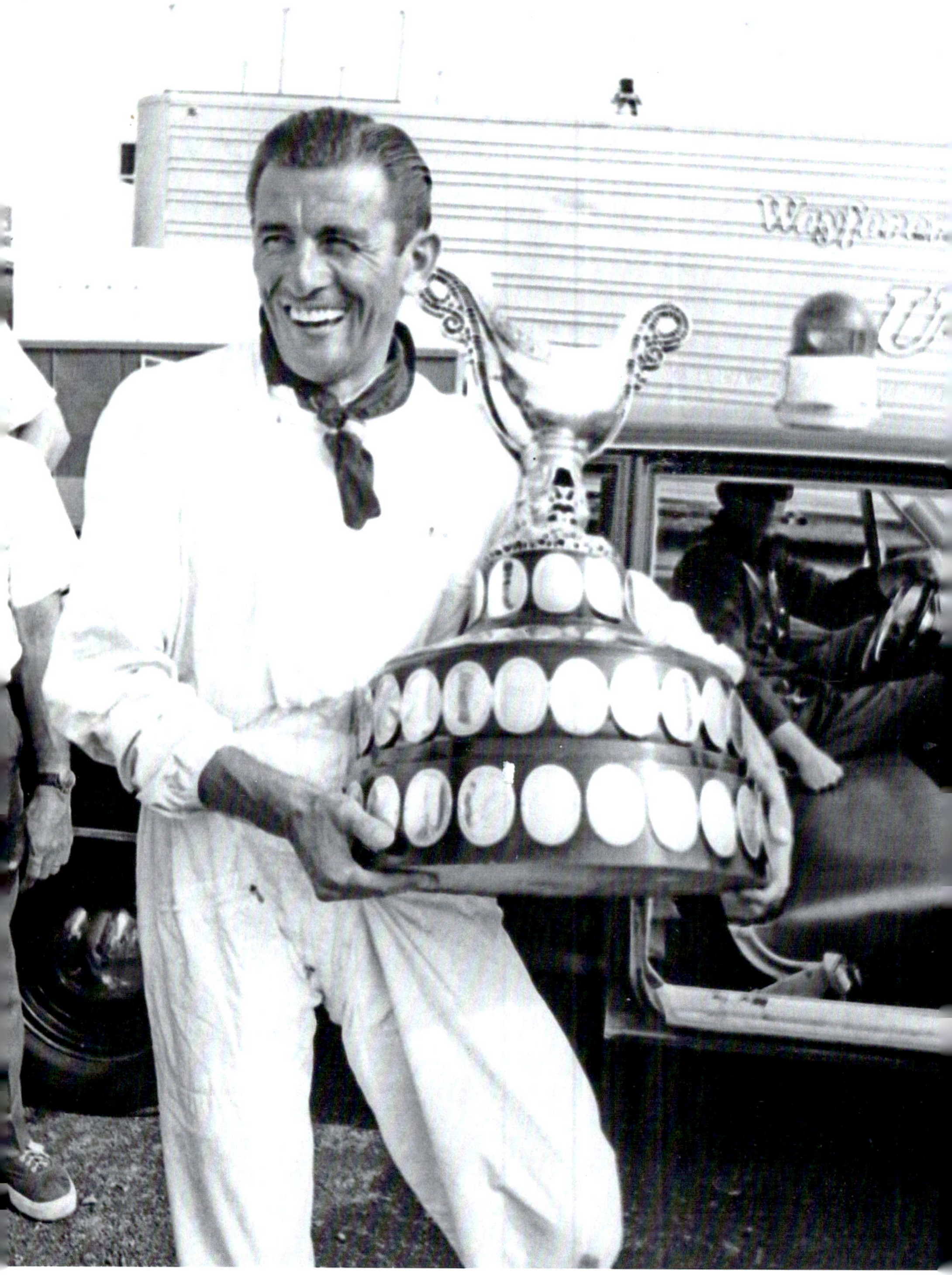

Mira Slovak celebrates after winning the 1966 Gold Cup trophy.
(*The Mira Slovak Collection of the Hydroplane Museum*)

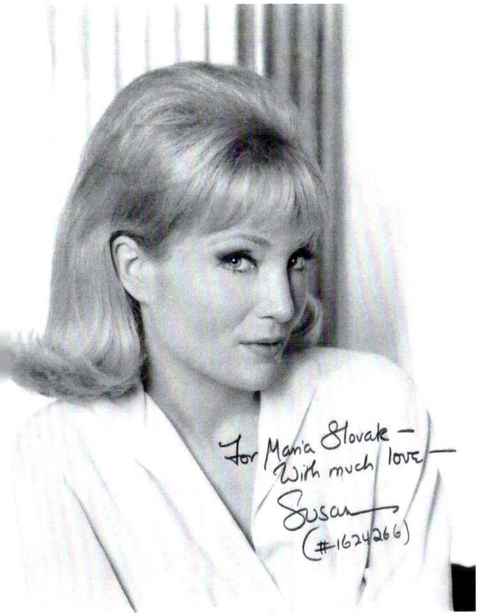

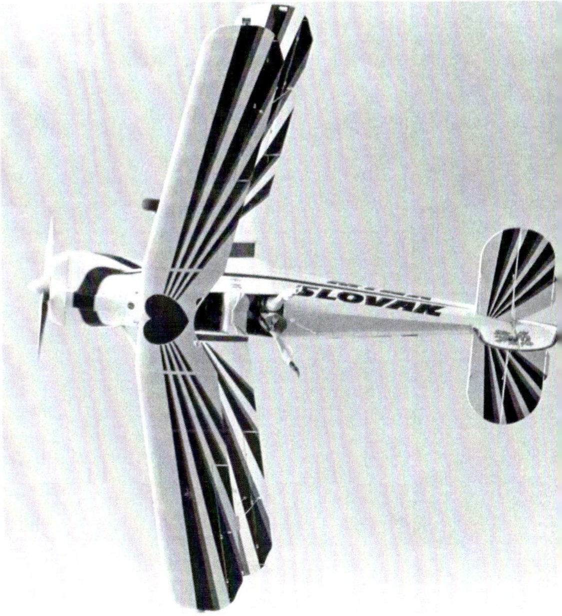

Above left: Actress and pilot, Susan Oliver. (*The Mira Slovak Collection of the Hydroplane Museum*)

Above right: Upside down with no hands on the controls, Mira performs his signature move in his Bücker 131. Note that the name "Mira Slovak" on the side of the plane is written upside down so that it will only read correctly when the plane is inverted. (*Jim Larsen*)

Below: Mira crossed the Atlantic Ocean twice in a tiny Fournier RF-4 powered glider built by Sportavia. (*The Mira Slovak Collection of the Hydroplane Museum*)

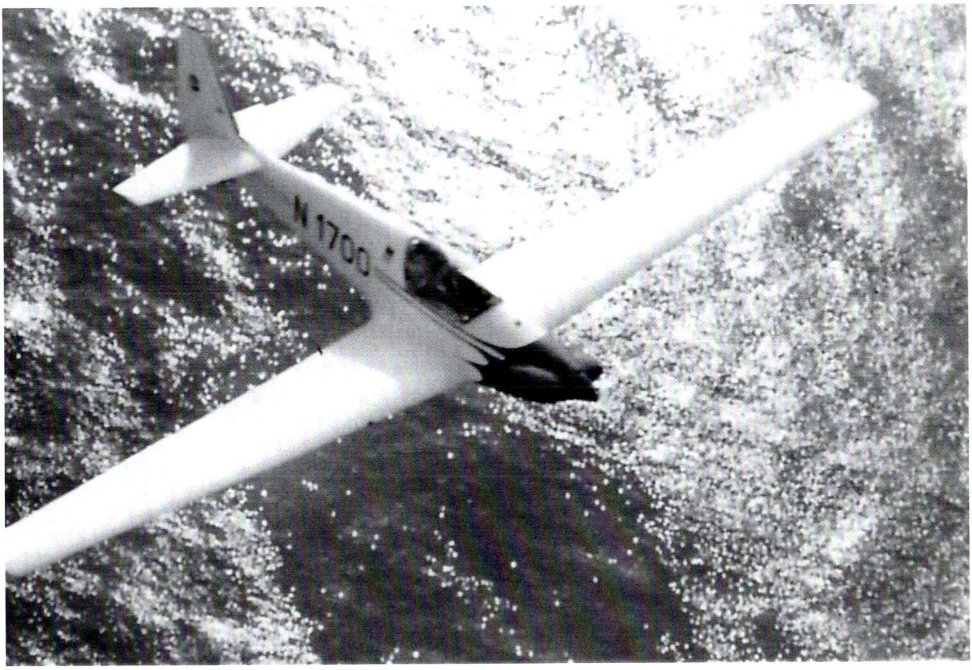

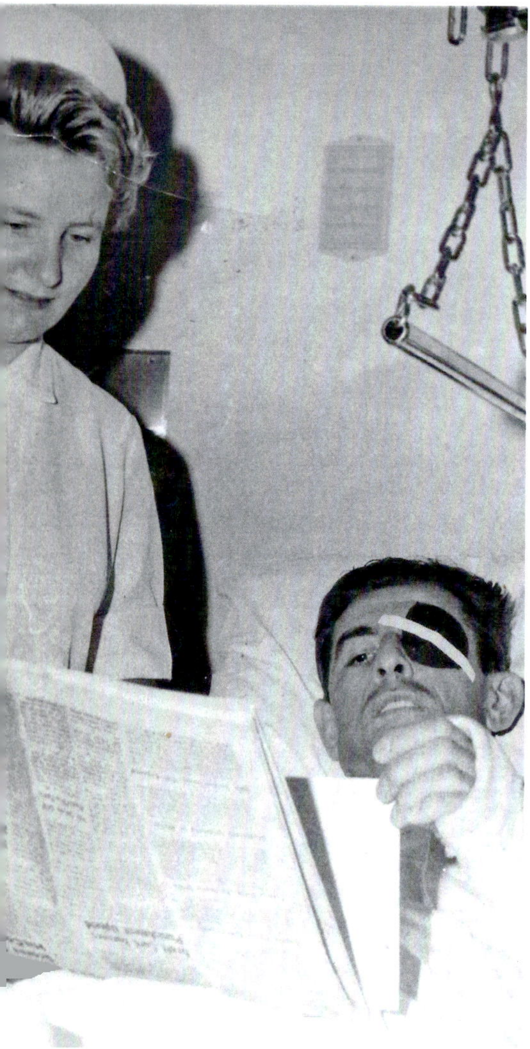

Left: Mira reading newspaper coverage about his glider crash while he recovers in the hospital in June 1968. (*The Mira Slovak Collection of the Hydroplane Museum*)

Below left: Mira Slovak and the P-38 *Mister Mennen* await takeoff at Reno in 1972. (*Jim Larsen*)

Below right: The *Mister Mennen* at speed at Reno in 1972. (*Jim Larsen*)

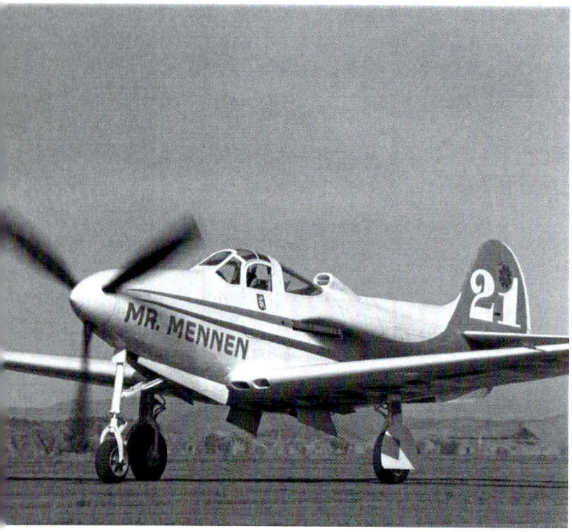

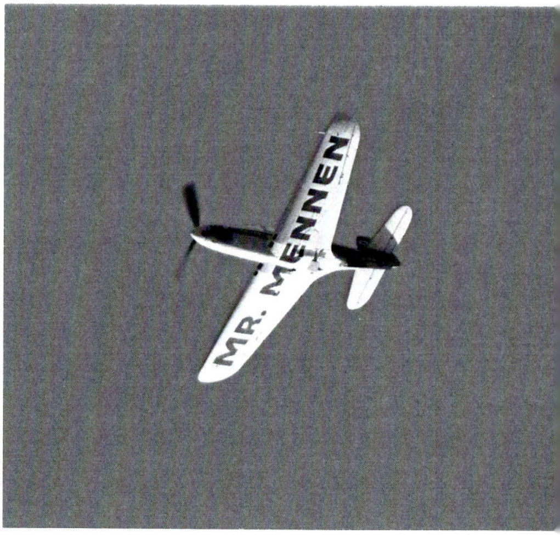

Leaving the pits as late as he did threw Mira's whole starting strategy into disarray. When he entered the north turn for the run to the start, he found that the *Miss Seattle* had already claimed the outside lane, with the *Miss Bardahl* in lane four, and the only open spot was lane one. Just as in 1956, Mira came out of the north turn and headed for the start in lane one, slightly ahead of the field. He knew he would be early so he backed down on the throttle, but he was still first across the line, followed by the *Bardahl* in lane four, and the *Miss Seattle,* the *Gale V,* and the *Miss Rocket* trailing the field. Coming out of the first turn, the *Miss Bardahl* had a slight lead. Mira was still worried about the carburetor, so he ran the first two laps at about three-quarters throttle, to make sure everything was working all right. Even at three-quarters throttle, the *Wahoo* was turning in lap averages of about 102 mph and holding on to second place, just two seconds behind the *Miss Bardahl.*

On lap three, Mira felt confident that everything was working fine and opened up the throttle. He blasted past the *Bardahl*, turning in a lap of 113.804 mph, which was a new record for the Seattle course, bettering the *Slo-mo-shun V's* old record by more than five miles per hour. Mira continued to reel off impressively fast laps until he was forty-five seconds ahead of the second place *Miss Bardahl* and beginning to lap the back markers. "Let's save some of this speed for the next heat," Mira thought as he throttled back and ran his last couple of laps at about 105 mph. He took the checkered flag, affectionately patted the deck of the *Wahoo*, and headed back to his jubilant pit crew.

As he stepped to the dock, he was met by KOMO-TV's Keith Jackson, who started the interview by saying, "I'm standing here with Mira Slovak, the Bouncing Czech who just bounced, rattled, and rolled his way to a heat 1A victory. So Mira, how did the *Miss Wahoo* handle out there?"

"Well, Keith," Mira replied, slightly out of breath, "I'm very happy with the way my boat is running."

Jackson continued the interview, "Did you realize that you set a new heat record of 108.717?"

"Gosh, Keith, I knew I was running fast but I had no idea we were that fast."

"So when it comes to the final, do you think that you'll have a dog in the hunt?"

"I think that we have a good chance of winning today."

Jackson turned to face the camera and said, "So there you have it, Mira Slovak thinks that he has a good chance to win all the marbles today." Mira was still learning English and he was often confused by Jackson's folksy colloquialisms. Sometimes he just guessed at what Jackson was asking, but so far he seemed to be getting it right.

Once the interview was over, Mira approached Junie and said, "She's running fast but I had a devil of a time getting her started. Every time I put it into full rich she died."

Junie nodded his head and said, "I noticed that. There might be a ruptured diaphragm in the carburetor, so I'm going to put a new one on and see if that fixes it.

For heat 2B, Mira saw that he was matched up with the *Shanty,* the *Maverick,* the *Breathless II,* the *Miss Bardahl,* the *Miss Rocket,* and the *Thriftway Too*. When the five-minute gun sounded, Mira went through the start sequence, turning on the master power, magnetos, fuel boost pump, and rolling the engine over with the starter. When he hit the primer, nothing happened. He waited and tried the primer again. Now he could hear other boats firing up and pulling away. The *Shanty* went by close and her wake caused the *Wahoo* to rock from side to side; still the primer did nothing. The boost pump continued to whine, and the engine continued to turn over. The gauges showed that he had plenty of fuel pressure, but nothing Mira did could make the engine start. One by one, the other boats pulled away from the pits and the *Wahoo* sat silently next to her finger pier. Mira felt a tremendous sense of frustration. Eventually, he heard the one-minute gun sound and he knew he had missed the heat. He stood up in the cockpit and turned toward Junie and the crew on the dock and said, "I'm sorry, I don't know what I did wrong, but she just wouldn't start."

Mira stepped up onto the dock and watched the boats from his heat battle on the water. Bill Stead in the *Maverick* led the first six laps of the heat but was passed by Russ Schleeh and the *Shanty-I,* who led the final four laps and won. Mira knew that he was running faster than anyone else today and he felt like the Gold Cup had been his for the taking. Unfortunately, he had just seen it slip away.

Junie got the *Wahoo* back on the trailer and discovered that there was a vacuum lock in the new carburetor that he had just installed and it had prevented fuel from entering the part of the carburetor that fed the primer circuit, so the engine was literally starved for fuel.

By the time Junie corrected the problem, the eliminations heats were over and all that was left was the final. With only 400 points, the *Wahoo* was out of the race. Mira, Junie, and Bill Boeing stood on the deck of the boat and watched as Bill Muncey won the race. The *Shanty* finished second, and the *Maverick* was third. The highest-finishing Detroit boat was Chuck Thompson's *Short Circuit* in fifth.

There was still plenty of racing left in the season, and after a day of rest, the unlimited teams packed up to hit the road for a 5,000-mile cross-country trip, running five races in just six weeks. The fleet's first stop was Detroit, for the Silver Cup. The Seattle boats dominated, with the *Hawaii Kai* qualifying fastest and winning easily, the *Wahoo* coming in second, and the *Miss Thriftway* taking third.

The next race was the President's Cup in Washington, D.C., where the *Hawaii Kai* was the fastest qualifier and won the race. The *Thriftway Too* was second and Bill Muncey in the *Miss Thriftway* was third. Prior to the final heat, the *Shanty-I* went out onto the Potomac River to do some testing. Midway through the test, the *Shanty* hit a roller and bounced hard, landing awkwardly on the right sponson, which collapsed. The impact ripped the right side of the boat to pieces, sending a plume of water and broken wood into the air and blowing Russ Schleeh out of the cockpit. He was pulled from the water and rushed to the hospital with cuts and bruises but no serious injuries. The boat was a total loss. After the President's Cup final heat, there was a second race on the Potomac, for the Rogers Memorial Trophy. The *Hawaii Kai* won again, and Mira took second in the *Wahoo.*

During the final heat of the President's Cup, the *Miss Thriftway's* left sponson had begun to come apart. Along the beach, fans watched in fear as Muncey continued to race while the gaping hole in the left sponson kept getting bigger. The *Thriftway* held together long enough to finish and return safely to the dock. The talented *Thriftway* crew had its work cut out to get from Washington, D.C. to the next race in Indiana and get the damaged sponson repaired in time for qualifying, which started in just forty-eight hours.

Junie and Mira were well aware that the *Miss Wahoo* and the *Shanty-I* were built side-by-side from the same plans as the *Miss Thriftway*. Seeing their two "sister" boats both suffer sponson failures on the same day put the *Wahoo* crew on edge. Before they left Washington, Junie promised to do a complete inspection of the *Wahoo's* sponsons and make any repairs he felt were necessary.

The next race was the Indiana Governor's Cup, on the weekend of September 28 and 29 in picturesque Madison, Indiana. Madison is a time capsule of a town, nestled in the oak and hickory forests that line the Ohio River as it rolls between Indiana and Kentucky towards its eventual rendezvous with the Mississippi. Madison, with its broad tree-lined streets and red brick buildings, had been a booming river port for paddlewheel steamboats prior to the Civil War. Commercial traffic dried up during the war, and when the war ended, much of the nation's shipping was diverted to the railroads and Madison was left behind, sitting virtually unchanged as the rest of the nation marched on into the twentieth century.

Madison had been holding powerboat races on the river since 1911. By 1957, the Regatta had become a major tourist attraction, bringing in 50,000 to 70,000 fans from Kentucky, Ohio, Illinois, and Indiana. In late September, the trees that lined the river were turning to red and yellow. The roads outside of town were lined with drying sheds full of pungent-smelling tobacco. Orange pumpkins were stacked in piles outside the local grocery store, and the air was full of the rich, tangy scent of burning leaves.

Nine boats showed up for the Governor's Cup, and for the fourth time in as many races, Jack Regas in the *Hawaii Kai III* was the fastest qualifier. River racing has some subtle yet important differences from the lake racing that Mira had grown accustomed to. First, because rivers were generally narrower than lakes, river courses had longer straightaways and tighter turns. Second, flowing water tends to follow the contour of the river bottom, so if there is a trench in the bottom of the river, there will be a dip in the water as it flows over the trench. Likewise, if there is a boulder on the bottom of the river, there will be a hump in the water as it passes over the boulder. These changes in the surface of the water may only be a few inches and not even noticeable to a canoe or rowboat. But to an unlimited hydroplane hurtling across the water at 160 mph, hitting a 5- or 6-inch swell in the water would be like an Indianapolis 500 race car hitting a speed bump on the straightway.

Saturday morning dawned cold and crisp, with a blanket of fog shrouding the river. As the day wore on, the sun burned through the fog and the thermometer hit almost seventy degrees. Heat 1A matched Mira in the *Wahoo* and Muncey in the *Thriftway.* The two drivers put on a spectacular battle, running side by side. Muncey had to turn in a blistering 115.342 mph lap to stay just a few feet ahead. The two boats were still neck and neck heading into the last turn of the last lap when Slovak hit a patch of bad water and bounced wildly, letting Muncey pull away to claim the heat by five seconds.

Sunday was hazy and muggy with a high gray overcast. Once more, the *Thriftway* and the *Wahoo* were drawn into the same heat. At the five-minute gun, all the boats pulled onto the course together. When the starter's flag dropped, Fred Alter in the *Miss U.S.* led the boats across the line in lane one, followed closely by Mira in lane two. Muncey in the *Miss Thriftway* was a couple of boat lengths behind out in lane three, but running at least 20 miles an hour faster. He quickly took the lead as he blasted down the long Madison front chute. Mira ducked inside of Alter as they entered the turn and passed him to move into second. When the boats roared out of the turn, Muncey was in first but Mira was closing the gap, while the *Miss U.S.* held onto third. Up the backstretch, the *Miss Thriftway's* Rolls Royce engine out-accelerated the Allison-powered boats and Muncey moved ahead by about three lengths. Mira kept the pressure on, holding his position, waiting for a bounce or bobble by Muncey that he could exploit. Muncey knew that Mira was stalking him, ready to scoot past if he let up for an instant, so he kept the throttle wide open. As the two boats raced out of turn two, Muncey swung wide to keep up his boat speed and gained a couple more lengths. The *Thriftway* was still in the lead as the boats blasted toward the end of lap one at 170 mph. Almost right in front of the pits, the *Miss Thriftway* hit one of the treacherous holes in the water that make river racing so dangerous. The boat took a violent bounce and landed nose first with the left sponson significantly lower than the right, so all the force of the 5,800-pound boat traveling at 250 feet per second was focused onto the recently repaired front of the left sponson, which caved in. The vicious water pressure ripped the *Miss Thriftway* apart with a geyser of spray. Muncey was thrown out of the boat and landed hard on his back, knocking him unconscious. He bounced and tumbled over the water like a doll thrown by an angry child. The damaged *Thriftway* continued to shed parts as she slowed down and began to sink. Mira saw it all from just a hundred feet behind, as broken pieces of the *Miss Thriftway* rained down on the course. He flashed past the accident scene, slowed down, and circled back into the debris field, looking to help Muncey. As the *Wahoo* came to rest, Mira climbed out of the cockpit, pulled off his helmet, tossed it in the seat, and shouted, "Billy! Billy, are you okay?" There was no answer. It was eerie how suddenly the river got quiet when the big boats shut down their thundering engines. Mira saw Muncey; he was unconscious, floating face down, surrounded by splinters of broken wood.

Without a moment's hesitation, Mira ran to the bow of the *Wahoo* and leapt into the murky river. Mira was not a strong swimmer, but he reached Muncey with a few determined strokes. Muncey was still face down, bobbing in the water with his arms hanging limp. Mira quickly rolled Muncey onto his back. When his face came clear of the water, Muncey coughed and began to gasp for air.

"I've got you, Billy," Mira called, hoping he sounded reassuring.

A Coast Guard boat arrived and lowered a Stokes rescue basket over the side as two skin divers jumped into the water. In the bow of the boat, a Coast Guardsman stood holding an orange smoke flare. The billowing smoke, visible from anywhere on the course, warned the other racers that there had been a serious accident and they should shut down their boats immediately. Mira released Muncey to the divers, who skillfully loaded him into the basket. Muncey was beginning to regain consciousness and started to moan with a low guttural wail that scared Mira. "Is he going to live?" Mira asked the Coast Guardsmen. There was no answer. The moaning got louder. "Is he going to live?" Mira asked while the injured Muncey was being lifted on board.

One of the divers said, "We don't know yet."

The current carried the *Miss Wahoo* downriver, and another patrol boat towed it back to the dock. After Muncey was loaded on board, the rescue divers helped Mira climb into the boat. He slipped off his life jacket and stood dripping water in the back of the boat. They headed for a dock on the edge of the river where the Coast Guard divers handed Muncey's stretcher to several men who jogged to a waiting ambulance. The ambulance crew slid the stretcher into the back, swung the doors closed, and accelerated out of the pits with the siren wailing to head for King's Daughters' Hospital.

Mira watched the ambulance pull away from him. He was suddenly aware of how wet he was, water dripping from his hair and down his back. His shoes were full of water and squished as he walked back to the *Wahoo* pits. A woman came up and asked, "How did it happen? What did you see?"

The adrenalin from the rescue was wearing down and the horrible impact of what he had just witnessed—the total destruction of the *Miss Thriftway* and Muncey's brutal injuries—was setting in. Mira's English was beginning to fail him.

The woman asked again, "What did you see?"

Mira said the only English word he could think of that described the scene on the water: "Pieces! Everywhere pieces!" He began to wonder if he had just witnessed Muncey's death. Tears welled up in his eyes; he tried to use the sleeves of his flight suit to dry his tears, but they were still soaking wet.

"Are you okay, Mr. Slovak? Can I get you something?"

Mira's English was completely gone now, swept away by the shock of the accident. He wanted a handkerchief to dry his eyes and blow his nose. All he could think of was the Czech word for handkerchief. He turned to the lady and said, "*Kapesnik*."

She looked at him like he was babbling gibberish. "What?"

"*Kapesnik*!"

"I'll go find you some help." She said and scurried away from Mira as fast as she could.

Mira walked down the beach mumbling "*Kapesnik*" under his breath. He stopped to watch the patrol boats bringing broken pieces of plywood and oak back to the dock. He began to regain his composure. By the time he reached the *Miss Wahoo's* pit area, the big crane had picked the *Wahoo* out of the water, and Junie and the crew were directing the crane to set her gently back on the trailer.

After two hours of course cleanup, the boats were refueled and ready to race again. With the *Miss Thriftway* out, there were only six boats left in heat two. There was no need to divide the boats into sections A and B, so they all raced together. Mira climbed into the *Wahoo's* cockpit and put all thoughts of Muncey out of his mind. He had learned from his time in the military that you had to be able to compartmentalize your mind. If something was bothering you, you had to put if off into an isolated part of your mind, and not allow yourself the luxury of thinking about it until you were finished with your mission. If you allowed yourself to worry about something outside the plane (or race boat), you would be distracted, and distracted pilots or racers crashed.

The five-minute gun fired and Mira hit the starter. His biggest competition in the heat would come from Jack Regas and the *Hawaii Kai*. Shortly after the start, the *Kai* and the *Wahoo* pulled away from the rest of the field and put on a side-by-side duel, with Regas winning by one second.

In the final heat, Mira made a perfect start, and pulled ahead of the *Kai*. He was leading three quarters of the way through the first lap when the *Wahoo* lost her propeller and coasted to a stop. Regas and the *Kai* cruised home to win their fourth straight race and clinch the 1957 National High Points Championship. It took a while for the *Wahoo* to get towed in, and when Mira got back to the dock, Willard Rhodes, the balding, heavy-set owner of the *Miss Thriftway* was waiting for him.

"How's Bill?" Mira asked.

"I think he's doing pretty well. The doctors think he's going to pull through. There aren't any broken bones, but his insides are pretty beaten up, his kidneys are crushed, his spleen is ruptured, and his stomach has torn loose from his diaphragm. He's got a hell of a black eye and there are bruises on top of his bruises, but he's tough and he'll probably recover."

"That's good to hear. I couldn't stop thinking about him; he has a wife and kids."

"I have a favor to ask. Well actually Bill has a favor to ask. "

"I'll do it. Whatever it is I'll do it."

"Good, but let me tell you what he wants. The doctors up at King's Daughters' don't think that they have the right kind of equipment to give him the care he needs. They are suggesting that we fly him by ambulance plane up to Chicago. Muncey says that if we are moving him to Chicago we might as well take him all of the way home. So I've lined up an ambulance plane for tomorrow morning to fly from here to Chicago, and then we can get him on a Northwest flight from Chicago to Seattle. But here's where you come in. Muncey says that he doesn't want anyone else to fly the Ambulance plane to Chicago but you. He says he knows you and trusts you and he won't trust anyone else."

"I will do anything that I can for Billy, but I can't fly someone else's plane without their permission."

"If I can get the owner of the ambulance plane's permission, you'll do it?"

"Of course, I will."

"Okay, well I guess that I have to make a few phone calls tonight, but plan on being at King's Daughters' tomorrow morning about 10. Oh, when I was listing his injuries I forgot to say that he almost bit his tongue in half."

"So, with his tongue hurt, he can't talk so much now?"

"No he can hardly talk at all."

"Well, if he can't talk so much, I'll fly the plane for sure."

The next morning, Mira was at King's Daughter's Hospital to help load Bill into the back of the ambulance that would take them both to the tiny Lee Bottom Flying Field in Hanover, Indiana.

Somehow, Willard Rhodes (or perhaps it was Mr. Boeing) had convinced the Air Ambulance Company to fly a twin-engine Piper Apache to Hanover, and allow Mira to fly it to Chicago. Of course, the regular pilot would sit in the co-pilot's seat and accompany Mira and Muncey to Chicago.

When the ambulance got to Lee Bottom Field, they transferred Muncey to the plane and strapped his stretcher into an empty spot on the floor where the back row of seats would normally be. As they loaded the stretcher into the plane, Muncey reached out and grabbed Mira's hand, holding on tight for a few moments. Once Muncey was secure on board, Mira, the pilot, and a flying nurse took their seats in the plane. Mira apologized for the extraordinary intrusion of taking the left seat in someone else's plane. The pilot replied that he had heard about Mira's escape from Czechoslovakia, and figured that if Bill Boeing, who could clearly hire any pilot in the world, thought Mira was good enough to fly for him, then he was darn sure good enough to fly this little Apache from Hanover to Chicago.

The flight was uneventful. As they approached O'Hare Airport, one of the busiest airports in the nation, Mira was surprised that Air Traffic Control gave him permission to land the little twin-engine Piper, taxi to the Northwest Terminal, and park literally at the base of the loading ramp for Northwest Flight 107, a Boeing Stratocruiser with nonstop service to Seattle.

Mira and the flight crew carefully carried Muncey's stretcher up the stairs, but they could not negotiate it through the tight aisle, so they helped him walk gingerly to a seat in first class. Still wearing his hospital slippers and a long bathrobe, Muncey was strapped into his seat and promptly passed out. Mira sat next to him for the five-hour flight. With Muncey in a deep medicated sleep, there was no one for Mira to talk to but the pretty young stewardesses as they hurried back and forth through the plane serving drinks and meals to their passengers. At one point, a stewardess was working her way down the aisle passing out Junior Pilot Wings to all the children on the flight. Mira sweet-talked a pair of wings from the stewardess and carefully pinned them to the bathrobe of the still-sleeping Muncey, proudly announcing to the stewardess, "See, now he is my co-pilot."

When the plane was still about ninety minutes out of Seattle, the pain medication wore off and Muncey awoke in agony. Muncey had a phenomenal pain tolerance, but every time the plane hit a bump, it jarred him and he let out an involuntary gasp. Mira saw that the frequent moans and gasps were beginning to unnerve the other passengers in first class, so he reached across and offered Muncey his hand to squeeze. For some reason, it seemed to help. Whenever the plane jolted or lurched in the rough air over the Cascade Mountains, Muncey squeezed Mira's hand and was able to stay silent.

Northwest Flight 107 touched down at Seattle's Sea-Tac Airport at 7.25 p.m., and there was a large crowd on hand, waiting behind a waist-high metal fence to greet the flight. It was decided to let all the other passengers deplane first, and then allow Kit Muncey, who had stayed home from the Madison race because she had been hospitalized with pneumonia, come on board to help Mira walk Muncey down the stairs. As soon as Kit and Bill, with his right arm hanging limp and his left arm around Mira's shoulder, appeared at the door of the plane, the crowd erupted into cheers. The noise soon died out as the fans got a good look at his sunken eyes, and the obvious pain he was in. Kit led them down the stairs as he leaned heavily on Mira's shoulder. As they began their descent, flashbulbs popped as press cameras recorded the scene. The next day, the *Seattle Times* carried a large photo of Muncey in his hospital robe leaning on Mira as they made their way down the stairs. Clearly visible on the left breast of Muncey's robe are the Junior Pilot Wings that Mira had placed there during the flight. At the bottom of the stairs, Muncey was loaded into a waiting ambulance that took him to Doctors Hospital. Muncey was confined to the hospital for a full week, while the Seattle newspapers reported on every detail of his recovery.

On October 2, the *Times* ran a headline that announced "Muncey on the Mend, Finally Able to Eat." The story told how he had eaten scrambled eggs, his first food since the accident.[5]

Mira was at work on Wednesday when he got a call. The receptionist whispered, "I think it's Muncey!"

Mira picked up the phone saying "How are you Billy?"

Muncey's badly swollen tongue made it hard to talk. "Oh Mirw, evewting hrts so baa."

"Billy, you sound just like me! Your English is terrible. Maybe we can take classes together now!"

"Don't be an asth hol."

"Well, it sounds like you're feeling better."

"I am, an I jess wann tank you fur evewting you id to hep me."

"Billy, it was nothing. You would have done it for me."

"Na I woodn't. I canna fly an airpain!" Muncey laughed, and his laughter turned into a howl of pain. "Gaw Darnn dat hrts."

"Billy, I don't think you should be on the phone yet. You need to rest."

"Na, I have anover favor. Ouwld ew please drive my limmed hydooplane at a race on Ake Tsamamish dis eekend?"

Mira was stumped. He was not sure what Muncey was asking him. He worked through each word until he got it. "You want me to drive your limited hydroplane at Lake Sammamish this weekend?"

"Yes! Yes dats it!"

"Sure, I'd be honored to do that for you."

The *Miss Wahoo* and the *Miss Thriftway* were unlimited hydroplanes that used huge airplane engines and were the biggest, fastest boats in APBA racing. There were other classes of racing that used smaller boats and automotive engines. The classes in limited racing were designated by the maximum engine size. Back in Detroit, Muncey had driven a 266 limited hydro named the *Mi-Son,* but that boat stayed in Detroit when he moved to Seattle. Muncey had run into the Cechs' young neighbor, Chuck Lyford, and his father, Al, on a skiing trip to the Cascade Mountains. The Lyfords, like most of Seattle, were crazy about hydros. Chuck was beginning to make a name for himself racing outboard hydros. Muncey talked Al Lyford into bankrolling two new limited hydros—one called the *Thrifty Chevrolier,* for Muncey to drive, and *Swifty Chevrolier* for Chuck Lyford. The last limited race of the season was October 6 on Lake Sammamish, east of Seattle. Muncey's boat was in contention to win the Region High Points, and he wanted Mira to drive for him. The only boat Mira had ever raced was the *Wahoo*, and he had no idea what limited racing would be like, but since they used the same rules as unlimited races, he could at least practice his starts. To everyone's surprise, Mira and the *Thrifty Chevrolier* won.

Mira did not think that his dive into the river to help Muncey was anything but an act of friendship, but *Life*'s October 4 issue devoted two full pages of photos to Mira and his rescue of Muncey.

The final unlimited race of the 1957 season was the Sahara Cup, on Lake Mead, near Las Vegas. The Rolls Royce-powered *Hawaii Kai III* was top qualifier and won her fifth race in a row. As promised, Edgar Kaiser retired from the sport. The *Wahoo* had mechanical problems and took a disappointing seventh, but Mira still amassed enough points to take second place in the drivers' National High Point Standings. As the *Wahoo* team was packing up, Junie reminded Mira that Bill Boeing had first right of refusal to buy the *Hawaii Kai* equipment. Junie was suggesting that Boeing buy Kaiser's engines and install them in the *Wahoo,* but he did not see any point in having two hulls. Junie also pointed out that the *Shanty* had competed in twelve races when she wrecked. The *Miss Thriftway* was in her thirteenth race when she crashed, and the *Miss Wahoo* now had nine races under her belt. He was planning on taking the 1958 season off to convert the *Wahoo* to Rolls-Royce Merlin power and go through the hull to make sure she was strong enough to survive the extra weight and power that came with the mighty Merlin engine.

19

Champion: Las Vegas, 1958

Mira had improved as a driver during the 1957 season, but Bill Boeing was worried that if Mira missed the entire 1958 season while the *Wahoo* was being retooled, he might lose some of the skills that he had developed. So he ordered a brand-new 280 cubic inch limited hydroplane from Ted Jones's son Ron and offered it to Mira and his friend Randy Pillow to race in limited races around Seattle for the 1958 season. The boat would be called the *Wee Wahoo* and was identical in design to Bill Muncey's *Thrifty Chevrolie*r and Chuck Lyford's *Swifty Chevrolier*. The three boats traveled across the northwest together and raced as a team.

There was a building boom in the unlimiteds heading into the 1958 season, with seven new hydros under construction. The Thriftway and Shanty teams were building boats to replace the ones that had been destroyed at the end of the 1957 season. Ole Bardahl, owner of Bardahl Oil Company, ordered a new *Miss Bardahl* from Ted Jones. Bob Gilliam was building a boat that would be sponsored by Sunnee Brand Meats. In Michigan, Les Staudacher was busy building three new boats—one to replace the outdated *Gale V*, another to be sponsored by a Seattle drugstore chain and called the *Miss Pay 'N' Save,* and a third for industrialist Samuel DuPont that would be called the *Nitrogen*. Bill Boeing had sold his backup hull to a group in Spokane, Washington who planned to race her under the name *Miss Spokane*.

When spring came in March 1958, the trees around Mira's West Seattle apartment began to bloom with pink and white blossoms. The Seattle newspapers were full of stories about the new unlimited teams, with speculation about when the boats would be launched and who would drive them. Mira began to feel a longing to go racing again. Somehow, the speed, glamour, and excitement had worked their magic on Mira, and he could not bear the thought of sitting on the beach for a full season. Mira asked Mr. Boeing's permission to approach other teams for a driving position. Boeing agreed, as long as Mira promised to return to the Wahoo camp when their refit to Merlin power was completed.

One of the first conversations took place with a representative of the Michigan-based Kellogg cereal company, which was giving serious consideration to buying the *Hawaii Kai III* and hiring Mira to drive her. Another call came from the Minute Maid juice company. Washington native Bing Crosby owned 20,000 shares in Minute Maid, and they were also looking at buying the *Kai*. The other teams Mira talked with were the *Miss U.S.*, the *Miss Burien*, and the new *Miss Spokane*. He felt that he had the inside track on the *Miss Spokane* job because the Spokane was identical to the *Miss Wahoo*, and Bill Boeing had sold the boat to the Spokane syndicate on favorable terms and was recommending Mira for the job.

Both the Spokane and Burien teams asked Slovak to take their boats out for test runs. Burien was a small suburb south of Seattle, and a group of merchants banded together to sponsor the former *Tempest* in an effort to promote their town.

The Burien test ride came first. Saturday, April 12 was a sparkling jewel of a day that felt like a gift from Mother Nature after more than week of gray Seattle rain. The brand-new *Miss Thriftway* was launched from Ted Jones's boathouse at the south end of Lake Washington. The Burien team took part in the festivities and sent Mira out to act as a stalking horse for Muncey's new *Miss Thriftway*. The two boats ran side by side, making long, sweeping laps at the south end of the lake. Muncey came off the lake with a big smile. As the new white and persimmon hydro glided into the dock, he stood up in the cockpit and announced to the world, "I like her!" In public, Slovak was equally as enthusiastic about the *Miss Burien*, but in private, he expressed concerns that the *Burien* was running on a shoestring budget and might not have the money to keep up with some of the better-funded teams.

Early the next morning, Sunday, April 13, Mira met Mr. Boeing at Aero Copter, where they climbed into the Howard DGA float plane and took off for a trip to Idaho. The *Miss Spokane* was scheduled to make her public debut on Hayden Lake in Idaho, just across the border from Spokane, at 2 p.m. on the 13th. Mira had been invited to take her out for a few test laps. Bing Crosby was a friend of Bill Boeing and happened to have a vacation home on Hayden Lake; he had asked Bill and Mira to join him for lunch. Mira was excited as they took off from Boeing Field and climbed into the cloudless blue sky above Seattle. As Mira and Boeing sailed over the Cascade Mountains, they chatted comfortably. Mira suspected that Crosby would want to talk about the *Miss Minute Maid* and even if the juice company did not offer him a chance to drive, he still thought he had a great shot at getting the *Miss Spokane* job.

Mira set the DGA (which stands for "Damn Good Airplane") down on the smooth surface of pine-shrouded Hayden Lake in northern Idaho, about 40 miles east of Spokane. He taxied across the lake and shut the engine off, gliding slowly to Crosby's dock. Mira stepped down to the aluminum float and tossed a nylon mooring line to a slender man on the dock. He was surprised to see that the man in khaki pants and a red pullover sweater who caught the line was Bing Crosby himself.

Boeing climbed down from the plane and made a quick introduction. Crosby shook Mira's hand and guided them to a flagstone path that cut across the lawn to a single-story 3,000-square-foot rambler. Inside, Mira saw hardwood floors, picture windows looking out to the lake, and a stone fireplace that dominated the living room. Crosby settled into a chair on one side of the stone fireplace, while Boeing and Mira sat on a matching couch on the other side. Crosby's vivacious wife, Kathryn, thirty years his junior and clearly several months pregnant, came in carrying a tray of lemonade and sandwiches. She set it on the coffee table between the men, said a brief hello, and then went back to the kitchen.

Crosby, part owner of the Pittsburgh Pirates, talked with Boeing about baseball, golf, and fishing. The *Miss Minute Maid* never came up, and Mira sensed that Crosby had never been seriously interested in the boat. After a pleasant hour Mira reminded Boeing that they needed to get to the *Miss Spokane* test. They said their goodbyes and headed back to the lake.

The *Miss Spokane* launch turned out to be disappointing too. The *Spokane* crew had decided that they wanted to let Air Force Captain Dallas Sartz, a jet fighter pilot who was native to Spokane, drive the boat. Mira put on a good face and offered Sartz advice on how to start the boat, but he was clearly disappointed not to get a chance to take her out. To add insult to injury, Mira overhead two *Miss Spokane* crewmen talking and one said "Ya' know, only a jet pilot can make a good hydro driver." Mira felt that he had been disrespected, both as a pilot and a hydro driver. It was a very long and quiet flight back to Seattle.

The following Tuesday, *Seattle Times* sports writer Hy Zimmerman ran a story on Slovak's search for a ride for the 1958 season. He wrote, "Slovak said today he will drive wherever he is welcome but admitted he was stung by the reference to jet pilots. 'I want to burst that myth,' Mira said. 'Anyone with driving instinct—jet pilot, shoe salesman, or grocery clerk—can be a good hydro driver.'"[1] The following week, Mira announced that he was going to drive the *Miss Burien* for the Lake Chelan Apple Cup but it was only a one-race agreement, and he would continue to look for a top-class boat to drive.

The Apple Cup was disappointing for Mira. The *Miss Burien* just was not in the same league as the *Wahoo.* Bill Stead and the *Maverick* qualified at 118.670 miles an hour, and the best that Mira could manage in the *Miss Burien* was 99.448 mph.

While Mira languished at the back of the field, taking a fourth and a third in his preliminary heats, Muncey's new *Miss Thriftway* was turning heads, winning both of her early heats easily. The new *Miss Bardahl* was also attracting lots of attention, with Chelan native Norm Evans behind the wheel, claiming two second-place finishes and heading into the final with a chance to take home the trophy.

In the final heat, the *Thriftway Too* crossed the starting line first and raced neck and neck with the *Maverick* through the first turn. The *Thriftway* was in third with the *Miss Burien* in fourth. Norm Evans and the *Miss Bardahl* started last but began moving through the field, bouncing past the *Miss U.S.* and pinching the *Miss Burien* tight against the exit buoy as they came off the first turn together. The *Maverick* and the *Thriftway Too* both ran into engine difficulties, and the lead passed to Bill Muncey in the *Thriftway.* The *Miss Bardahl* climbed to second. Mira and the *Burien* struggled in fourth place. Heading into the first turn of the fourth lap, the right sponson of the *Miss Burien* began to collapse, sending a shower of wood and water into the air as Mira shut off the engine and headed for the infield. On the eighth lap, with victory in sight, the *Miss Thriftway* suffered a broken blower drive gear (also known as the quill shaft), and Muncey's boat slowed to a stop. Norm Evans, in his first race in a brand-new boat, found himself in first place and coasted home to take the victory in his home town.

The raucous victory celebration, punctuated by shouts of "How about them apples!" lasted long into the night, echoing through the streets of tiny Chelan. The next morning, as the *Bardahl* team was preparing to leave town, Evans approached Ole Bardahl and said, "There is a little bit of leftover fuel in the drums we used for the boat during the race. Would you mind if I kept it and used it at my marina?"

Bardahl, still on top of the world from winning his first race, said with a heavy Norwegian accent, "Yah, sure, you can do dat."

What Bardahl did not know, and Evans had not bothered to explain, was that there had been a mistake in the fuel order and that while Bardahl had ordered ten barrels of fuel, the delivery company had somehow added an extra zero to the order and delivered 100 barrels. So when Evans was asking for the "leftover fuel," he was actually asking for ninety 55-gallon drums of fuel. When the bill from the fuel company arrived on Ole's desk on June 11, he was furious. On June 13, Bardahl issued a one-line press release: "We have relieved Norm Evans as driver for the good of the Miss Bardahl organization." Bill Simpson, Bardahl's team manager, called Mira and offered him the driving job. Mira was excited but replied, "First I must check with Mr. Boeing and make sure it is okay, and then I want to talk to Norm and see if it will make hard feelings with him."

Bill Boeing had already agreed to let Mira drive for other teams, so the call was just a formality. Boeing reminded him, "You're still my driver, and when the *Wahoo* is back, I expect you to drive for me."

Mira replied, "Of course, but since you're not racing I want to keep my hand in the game."

The call with Evans went well. Norm was honest and said, "Mira, I screwed up. I got what I deserved. There's no reason that you shouldn't take over. It's a good boat and a good team. She's all yours." On June 17, Bardahl Oil issued a one-page press release with the headline "Mira Slovak is Named Driver of *Bardahl* Hydro." Mira's first race was the Diamond Cup, on Lake Coeur d'Alene, Idaho.

Mira got his chance to test drive the *Miss Bardahl* on Lake Washington on the afternoon of June 21. It was a blustery Saturday, with black storm clouds that whirled across the sky threatening rain but never unleashing their pent-up moisture. Late in the day, the sun burst through the clouds with dramatic shafts of golden light that made the rough gray water sparkle. Mira taking over the *Bardahl* seat was big news in Seattle, and there was a crowd of shivering reporters on hand. Dozens of shutters clicked when Mira finally took the bright green-and-yellow speedster out for several impressive laps. When he came back to the dock, Mira had a big smile for Ole Bardahl and his proud crew. He posed for newspaper photographs and did several television interviews. From the outside nothing could look better. Inside, Mira was worried. The new boat "was bad in smooth water, and worse in rough water."

The boat was not nearly as fast as the *Wahoo* either; it probably was not even as fast as the *Miss Burien*. It had won in Chelan only because the *Maverick* and the *Thriftway* had both broken down. Something was going to have to change or it would be a very long season. Mira knew that he was in a delicate situation. Ole Bardahl had just spent $30,000 for a brand-new boat, and the crew had won their first race. They were proud and confident.

The team was leaving for Coeur d'Alene in just forty-eight hours. Mira was new to the team, an outsider, and he needed to let them know that there were problems, but if he was too vocal now, when everyone else was so confident, he would lose all his credibility. He decided he would keep quiet and try to figure out what to say once he had a few more laps in the boat.

Later, as he prepared to head to Coeur d'Alene, he got a call from Marshall Smith, a writer for *Life*. The magazine wanted to do another feature on Mira. Smith would be at the Diamond Cup and wanted to make sure they had time for an interview and some photos. The Diamond Cup was a new race. Like the Apple Cup, it had been heavily promoted by Seattle teams as an alternative to traveling across the country to take part in the eastern races.

Narrow Lake Coeur d'Alene, in the Idaho panhandle, is 25-miles long. It is surrounded by towering ponderosa pines and craggy basalt rock outcroppings. The town of Coeur d'Alene sits at the north end of the lake, with long, sweeping views. Unfortunately, the same long stretches of unobstructed water that provided such spectacular views also give the wind a long straight run down the lake and can create rolling swells that are dangerous for race boats.

The entire Diamond Cup week was a frustration for the Bardahl team. Rain kept them off the course on Monday and Tuesday. On Wednesday, Mira got in one slow warmup lap of 93 mph before an oil leak forced him back into the pits. Thursday the water was too rough to go fast. On Friday, the wind blew again. Mira and the *Bardahl* finally got a chance to open the boat up on Saturday and ran a lap of 106 mph in front of the *Life* photographer before the propeller broke, tearing up the bottom of the boat. The Bardahl crew worked all night repairing the damage, and by Sunday morning, the boat was good to go. The *Bardahl* was drawn into heat 1B with the *Thriftway Too*. The two boats crossed the line together and raced side by side for most of the first lap, until a vibration forced Mira to back off the throttle. He finished in fourth place, with a speed of just over 70 mph. When the boat was lifted out of the water, the crew could see that a large chunk of one of the propeller blades was missing. Mira thought the boat must have hit a stick or a floating can.

In heat 2B, the *Bardahl* was struck by yet another propeller failure, but this time when the propeller broke the whole drive line came apart. Mira joked with reporters, "When the propeller said 'Goodbye' I remembered to lift my feet all the way to the instrument panel. I needed to protect my family jewelry."[2]

Bill Stead and the *Maverick* won the final heat and captured the Diamond Cup trophy by less than two seconds over the *Thriftway Too*. As the boats headed out of town on Monday morning, the *Miss U.S.* held the National High Points lead, followed by the *Gale V* in second and the *Maverick* in third, with Mira and Muncey tied for fourth.

The next unlimited race for Mira and the *Miss Bardahl* was the Mapes Mile High Trophy on Lake Tahoe, July 28 and 29. The new *Life* came out earlier in the week and featured two full pages about Mira. It seemed that every girl that came to the Tahoe pits was carrying a copy to get autographed. In the three seasons Mira had been racing, he had gotten used to having people ask for his autograph, but after the *Life* feature, the girls were different. They were not the shy young hydro fans with pigtails and glasses. These girls wore makeup and their jeans were tighter. They did not turn their heads away and giggle when Mira smiled. They held his gaze longer and played with their hair too much. Something had changed, and Mira was embarrassed by the new attention he was getting. He thought that most of the girls seeking his autograph were too young to be so forward, and he had an ungentlemanly suspicion that they were looking for more than just an autograph. It was an awkward position for Mira. He had left Czechoslovakia over five years ago and he had not had a serious girlfriend since arriving in the United States. Yet all the attention he was getting now did not feel sincere—he did not think that the autograph seekers really cared about him. It was as if these girls were on a scavenger hunt and he just happened to be the next item on their list.

As the *Bardahl* made her test runs, Mira cautiously tried to offer some advice on the boat setup. "You know, it feels like we were really pounding on the nose that last time out. Do you think it would help if we moved some weight back? What if we put the batteries behind the seat? Would that help?" The crew continued to make improvements, and the boat's performance improved.

Mira also tried a new driving technique. He watched other drivers as they wrestled their boats down the straightaway, with their arms working the steering wheel back and forth, trying to keep the boat heading in a straight line. He suddenly realized that each movement of the wheel turned the rudder a bit sideways and dramatically increased the drag, slowing the boat. If he could manage to get the boat around the course without working the wheel so much, he was sure he could increase his speeds. It was going to take two things. First, he was going to have to tell the crew about any little thing that made the boat pull left or right, so they could sort it out and make sure it tracked straight; yet he was also going to have to put a lot of trust into the boat and believe that if he stopped sawing the wheel back and forth, it would really go where he aimed it.

Mira's new theory worked. At Tahoe, he was the fastest qualifier and won the first two heats, while also turning in the fastest lap of the weekend. Mira and the *Miss Bardahl* were battling the *Maverick* for the lead in the final heat until the boat took a wild hop and Mira missed a buoy on lap nine. The *Maverick* went on to win the race, and the National High Points race tightened up. Fewer than 200 points separated the top three boats. The *Maverick* was in first, the *Miss U.S.* was second, and the *Bardahl* had climbed to third.

Mira felt like the team was making good progress as it prepared for Gold Cup qualifying in Seattle. On August 1, just four days before the 1958 Gold Cup qualifying was set to begin, Edgar Kaiser announced that since no one had purchased the *Hawaii Kai,* he would run her one last time. Jack Regas would drive and the skillful *Slo-mo-shun* crew would tend to the "Pink Lady," as her fans called her. Kaiser went on to explain that a fan letter from an eleven-year-old girl, pleading with him to run the boat "one more time for the little people," had inspired him to bring the boat out of mothballs.

Qualifying opened Tuesday morning, and Mira's great expectations quickly turned sour. Every time he attempted to qualify, something went wrong. By Friday evening, the *Bardahl* had destroyed five racing engines and had still not managed to meet the mandatory 95 mph qualification speed. On Saturday morning, at Mira's urging, the crew put in a stock engine and with only an hour to go before qualifying closed, he was able sneak the boat into the race with a speed of 98 miles per hour. Of the sixteen boats that qualified, the *Miss Bardahl* was thirteenth fastest. To make matters worse, the *Miss Burien,* which Mira had left to take the *Bardahl* job, qualified at 111.570 mph. Things did not get any better on race day. The *Bardahl* struggled for a few laps in heat 1A before going dead in the water with another broken engine. Gold Cup rules prohibited engine changes, so the *Bardahl*'s day was finished without scoring a single point.

The only one to have a worse day at the 1958 Gold Cup was Bill Muncey, who won his first heat and was looking like a strong favorite to win his third Gold Cup in a row. Muncey made a perfect start in heat 2A. As the boats accelerated toward the first turn, he turned the wheel to start the *Thriftway* sliding into the corner, but nothing happened. The rudder had broken off, and Muncey was hurtling towards the turn with no steering. Acting quickly, he shut the engine off and began to wave his hands to warn the other drivers. The 6,500-pound *Thriftway* hurtled straight towards the log boom, where thousands of spectator boats were tied up. Luckily, a steel-hulled 40-foot Coast Guard boat was patrolling the boom, and somehow, the speeding *Thriftway* slammed into the side of the Coast Guard boat instead of the spectators. The violence of the crash threw Muncey into the water, knocking him unconscious. A Coast Guard helicopter quickly plucked Muncey from the lake and transferred him to a waiting ambulance that whisked him to the emergency room at Virginia Mason Hospital. Back at the racecourse, Jack Regas and the *Hawaii Kai* swept the day, winning every heat they entered and claiming the Gold Cup for Seattle again.

A few days after the Gold Cup, Mira was sitting in the office at Aero Copter updating his logbooks when Junie stuck his head around the corner and said, "Mira, Mom wants to know if you can swing by the house on your way home tonight. She says she needs to talk to you."

"What about?"

"I don't know. She wouldn't tell me. She was acting kind of smug. Maybe she has a secret."

"There is no telling what Blanche is up to," Mira chuckled.

Mira put it out of his mind and kept working on the logbooks. Heading towards the Cechs' after work Mira wondered what Blanche's secret was. "Maybe she's putting together a surprise birthday party for Junie." When he arrived, Blanche met him at the door, with a big motherly hug. "Follow me," she said, leading him to the kitchen table, which was set with coffee, and a white package that looked like a shirt box, tied up with a red ribbon. Mira took a seat and Blanche filled his coffee cup. "You might have heard that I took a trip out of town last month."

"Yes, Junie told me that you had gone back to Nebraska to visit some old Czech friends in Wahoo."

Blanche smiled, "Yes, but that was just my cover story." She slid the package across the table to Mira.

"Cover story? Are you a spy now? I think you're spending too much time with Wayne Richardson."

Blanche just gave Mira an enigmatic smile and whispered, "Open your package."

Mira untied the red ribbon. There was something about the ribbon and the way it was tied that made him think of Christmas mornings. As he began to lift the top off the box, he swore he could smell something familiar, but he just could not place it. He set the box top to one side and saw a layer of wax paper. Slowly, he moved away the waxed paper and saw that the box was full of homemade Christmas cookies. The comforting smells of almonds, vanilla, and cinnamon engulfed him. He looked at Blanche and felt tears starting to blur his visions. "These are … these are my Mom's cookies."

Blanche slid a small black-and-white photograph across the table to Mira. It was a snapshot of two middle-aged women with happy smiles standing together in front of the Eden Hotel in the Czechoslovakian resort town of Piešťany—Blanche and Mira's mother.

"I went to visit your mother! We spent three wonderful days together," Blanche announced with pride. "And she sent that box of cookies home for you," she added with a motherly sweetness. The matter-of-fact way she announced it made it sound so simple, but the truth was that crossing into or out of the Soviet Bloc was no less dangerous in 1958 than it had been when Mira escaped in 1953.

"How did you do it?" Mira asked incredulously.

"Wayne helped me figure it out, but honestly, it wasn't that hard. Those Communists aren't nearly as smart as they think they are."

"Wayne helped? So the CIA was in on this?"

"Oh, goodness no! The CIA would plop Wayne in front of a firing squad if they knew he had sent Bill Boeing's mother-in-law across the Iron Curtain. This was strictly a private op."

The casual way Blanche used the CIA phrase "private op," meaning a private operation as opposed to a "gov op" or government operation, made Mira want to laugh again. "How did you pull it off?"

"Like I said, it was easy. I asked Wayne to get a message to your Mom to let her know I was coming. Then I flew to Vienna and applied for a tourist visa. Nobody in the Czech Embassy had any idea that the name Blanche Cech was connected to Bill Boeing or Mira Slovak, so they gave me a three-day visa and I just took a taxi from Vienna to Leopoldov. It's about 75 miles, so it was a huge fare and the taxi driver loved it, but it really was pretty simple.

"So how was Mom?"

"Take a cookie," Blanche said, pointing at several delicate white crescents dusted with powdered sugar. "Your mother said that the *vanilkové rohlíčky* were your favorites."

Mira took one of the vanilla crescents out of the box and popped it into his mouth. "Your family is fine. I spent two days in Leopoldov and then one day up in Piešťany. They all miss you and are so proud of you!"

"Did they have any problems after I left?"

Blanche paused as she wrestled with how to answer this. "Before I go on, I have a message for you from your father. He said, 'Tell Mira that he did nothing wrong and that he is not responsible for the immoral or coercive acts of the communists. The communists are responsible for their own actions.'"

"Was it bad for them when I left?"

"Well, they took the farm house away and forced your parents to live in a two-room apartment in Leopoldov. Your brother got kicked out of engineering school. When the police came by to investigate you, your father yelled at them and said, 'You've had him from the time he was fifteen years old. So if you aren't happy with the way he's turned out, it's your own damn fault.' The police didn't like that, so they sent your father to a re-education camp for six months. He said it was more like a six-month vacation." Mira dropped his head in his hands. "No, no, no!" Blanche exclaimed. "You did the right thing. You've shown that the Communists are weak and immoral. You are the biggest hero to come out of Leopoldov ever and no one thinks that you've done anything wrong."

Blanche pulled another photo out of her stack and slid it across to Mira. It was Maria and Blanche standing on either side of Mira's brother Jarda. Mira had not seen Jarda since Christmas 1952, when he was a lanky young teenager. Now he was a tall, handsome young man. The photo made Mira beam with pride but it also made him long for all the years he had missed. Mira felt a bubble of rage start to build for the communists. How many more times would their system of government come like a wedge between him and the people he loved.

Blanche slid two more photos across the table to him, both of Jarda. One showed him wearing a checkerboard crash helmet and leaning Mira's Ogar 350 motorcycle low into a corner. The other showed him at a victory celebration with a wreath of flowers around his neck, being congratulated by a communist officer in a military uniform. "See, racing runs in the family. Jarda has been racing motorcycles, and winning races too." Mira smiled to hear that his brother was doing so well. "They are so proud of you, Mira."

"Do they know what I've been doing?"

"Oh my goodness, yes! They hear about you on Radio Free Europe, and of course I smuggled in a copy of *Life* and a few newspaper stories from the race you won in Tahoe. I also brought in one of your autographed *Miss Wahoo* photographs."

"Blanche! That was dangerous. You shouldn't have done that."

"It wasn't dangerous at all. Wayne showed me how to split the lining on my suitcase and hide everything in there. Besides, the border guards weren't looking for a grandma smuggling in photos. They were only worried about young men smuggling in guns. They hardly even looked at me."

Mira and Blanche continued to talk for several more hours. When he had made the decision to escape, Mira knew there would be repercussions against his family. He was relieved to finally know what they had been, and that everyone had survived and was healthy. As the conversation went on, Mira began to realize that he owed a huge debt to his family and that he wanted to help them. If he could find a way to get them out, he would. If he could not get them out, he would try to find a way to make their lives in Czechoslovakia better.

Two weeks later, Mira traveled east for the Silver Cup. The Detroit River course was surrounded by structures from the Golden Age of Detroit, including the Mediterranean Revival Detroit Yacht Club; the long, graceful arches of the Belle Isle Bridge; the white stucco and red-tile Mediterranean-style Detroit Boat Club; and perhaps grandest of them all, the luxurious Whittier Hotel, a Renaissance Revival-style fifteen-story tower right at the entrance to turn one. The Silver Cup promoters went out of their way to make sure that the West Coast teams that made the long trek across the country were greeted with the best hospitality Detroit could offer. The Whittier was designated race headquarters, and many of the teams, including the *Bardahl* and the *Maverick*, stayed there.

After the tribulations she had suffered in Seattle, the *Bardahl* continued to operate with a stock Allison, and Mira qualified her easily. The Silver Cup would be run on Saturday, August 21. By Friday night, eight boats had qualified and were drawn into two sections of four each. There had been some concern about an important commitment for Bill Boeing that might require Mira to fly back to Seattle, so Bardahl sent a backup driver, Harley Beards.[3] Beards was a retired Air Force pilot and had flown with Russ Schleeh. He was now working for Boeing flying chase planes on the 707 test program. Schleeh was in Detroit as team manager and relief driver for Bill Stead and the *Maverick*. Schleeh and Beards met in the pits and spent a couple of hours getting reacquainted Friday afternoon.

Mira and Beards were sharing a room at the Whittier. Mira liked to get a good night's sleep before a race, so he and Beards headed to their room early. Beards began to talk about a girl he had met that day. She was in her early twenties and the daughter of one of the race officials. Beards thought she was exquisitely attractive and he went on in great detail about the color of her eyes, the shape of her lips, and the softness of her hair. He had met her early in the day, and they spent several hours talking easily about everything imaginable. He had planned on asking her to dinner, but Schleeh showed up before he had a chance, and he did not think it would have been polite to ask her out in front of Schleeh, who was just going through a difficult divorce. Yet first thing the following morning, he was going to ask her out.

After almost an hour of nonstop talk about this amazing girl, Mira said, "You know, Harley I don't think that you're ready to sleep yet. Do you want to run across the street and get a pizza?"

"I guess that I've been talking your ear off. Yeah, a pizza sounds good."

Beards said, "Maybe we should invite Russ, it sounded like his divorce was hitting him hard."

Mira said, "Sure. I think he's up on the eleventh floor. Let's just run up and see if he wants to join us." Beards and Mira rode up to Schleeh's floor and headed towards his room. The Whittier had been built in the 1920s, before it had become common for hotels to have air-conditioning. The rooms had been built with high ceilings and a narrow window above the door called a transom. The high ceiling allowed the warm air to rise and get trapped near the ceiling, and opening the transom would allow the warm air to vent into the hallway.

As Beards and Mira approached Schleeh's room, they could see that the transom was open, and when they stood in front of the door, they could hear every sound through the open window. The moans, sighs, and giggles made it obvious that Schleeh was literally in the throes of passion.

"I don't think he's alone." Beards whispered.

"He's probably not too interested in pizza right now either," Mira whispered back.

Mira and Beards were quickly racking their minds trying to think of a practical joke to play on Schleeh. The opportunity was too rare to pass up. Mira was thinking about pounding on the door and yelling, "House detective! Let me see your marriage license."

Just then, the young woman on the other side of the door reached the peak of ecstasy and began to loudly moan, "Oh Russ! Oh Russ, oh my God Russ!"

Beards' face blanched. He pointed at the door and mouthed the words to Mira, "That's her!" Mira grabbed Beards' shoulder and they quickly ran down the hall to the elevator. Once they were headed toward the ground floor, Beards let go a string of expletives, ending with, "That no-good, back-stabbing son of a bitch! I can't believe he did that to me!"

Mira said, "Come on Harley, let's go get some pizza and try to forget about her." When the elevator reached the bottom floor, they walked across the lobby and out into a clear summer evening, to a quaint little pizzeria. They ordered a Detroit-style pizza—a deep dish pie with crispy toasted edges, baked in a square cast iron pan. Beards got a beer, but since Mira was driving the next day, he just drank water. They sat in silence and waited for their food. Eventually, Beards said, "You know I don't blame her, I mean, I never asked her out. And for goodness sake, he's a famous hydro driver. He was National Champion! His picture was on the front of *Sports Illustrated*! How is any girl gonna to say 'No' to a guy like him?" Harley took a sip of his beer, "But I'm really pissed off at Russ. He knew I liked her. That crosses a line. I'm gonna make him pay. We need to teach him a lesson!"

The waiter slid the steaming hot pizza between them. "Is there anything else I can get you?"

At the question from the waiter, Mira could see the wheels start to turn in Beard's head. "Yeah, there is something. Do you know where I could buy some firecrackers?" The waiter looked confused. Beards said, "You know firecrackers, like for the Fourth of July."

The waiter said, "I'm not sure but I'll ask around in back and let you know."

Beards helped himself to a piece of pizza. "Oh that's good!" he said. "You know it isn't the end of the world. It's not like I was going to marry her or anything."

"I'm glad you are coming around," Mira replied.

The waiter came back with two huge red firecrackers. "The dish washer had them. They're called M-80s. They each equal a quarter stick of dynamite. He wants a buck a piece for 'em."

Mira pulled out his wallet and slipped out two dollar bills and gave them to the waiter. Then he pushed the firecrackers across the table to Beards. "I don't know what you want to do, but let's just make sure that we don't get arrested tonight. I have a race to drive tomorrow."

They could not finish the pizza, so they asked to get it wrapped to go, paid the bill, and left the restaurant. As they walked back to the hotel, Mira was carrying the pizza and Beards had the firecrackers. It was now almost midnight. "Do you think we should try one out side? I mean we don't want to blow up poor Russ, do we?" Mira asked as they cut across a large deserted parking lot in front of the Whittier.

Beards shrugged, "Well that's not a bad idea." They stopped in the shadow of a tree alongside the parking lot. Harley pulled a lighter out of his pocket, lit the fuse, and tossed the firecracker. Its fuse sparkled orange in the darkness and then it exploded with a loud bang.

"I was hoping for more, but I guess it will have to do." Beards said.

When they got to the hotel elevator, Mira suggested, "Let's just take the elevator to our floor. Then we can walk up from there. If we go straight to the eleventh floor and then there is a loud bang, they're going to know it was us. So let's not be that obvious."

They two conspirators got off on the fifth floor, went to their room, and dropped off the pizza. They left their shoes in their room so that they could run in stockinged feet without making too much noise. Cautiously, they climbed the stairwell to the eleventh floor and crept stealthily down the hall past all the darkened rooms. When they got to Schleeh's room, the lights were out and transom was still open. Mira could hear snoring coming from the room.

"Help me up," Beards whispered.

Mira bent over and laced his fingers together to make a step for Beards, who placed a hand on Mira's shoulder and put his stockinged foot into Mira's hands. With a gentle heave, Mira lifted Beards up to the transom. Beards pulled out his lighter, lit the M-80, and tossed it through the open window. The instant the M-80 was out of his hand Beards jumped to the floor, and the two men ran for the stairwell. They were still a good ten feet from the fire door at the top of the stairs when they heard a huge explosion. Windows shook and a bit of plaster dust fell from the ceiling. Instantly lights all up and down the corridor came on. Mira whispered to Beards, "For a second there I thought Hiroshima was coming back!"

Beards said, "Damn, I guess that first one must have been a dud." They snuck back down to their room and stood at the window watching as police cars and even a fire truck pulled up to the front of the hotel.

After a while, Mira, feigning innocence, called the front desk and asked, "What's going on?"

The night clerk said, "Nothing serious, Mr. Slovak. Just some kids playing a practical joke and lighting off firecrackers."

"Was anybody hurt?"

"No nobody's hurt. But if I find those darn kids I'm going to beat the daylights out of them."

The next morning, Mira and Beards headed to the racecourse like nothing had happened. They saw Schleeh as they walked in and said a pleasant "good morning" to him. Schleeh smiled and said "Good morning. How did you sleep?"

Beards answered, "Like a baby."

Russ lied, "Me too."

As soon as Schleeh was out of earshot, Beards said, "Shit! He knows it was us."

"What makes you say that?"

"Because if he didn't think it was us he would have told us all about it. He would have said something like, 'Some jerk tossed a grenade into my room.' But he's saying that he slept like a baby. That means he knows it was us and he's going to do something to try to get us back."

The *Bardahl* was still down on power because it was only running a stock engine, but that also meant it was reliable. Mira scored two second place finishes in the preliminary heats and a third in the final. The *Maverick* and the *Gale V* ran an exciting race, finishing the ten-lap final side-by-side, with the *Maverick* claiming the trophy by only two tenths of a second. The *Maverick's* win also gave her a big boost in the National High Points race.

With the season almost two thirds over, the *Maverick* held a 600-point lead. After the race, Mira and Beards returned to their room to check out and head to the airport. When they stepped off of the elevator, Mira sniffed at the air and said, "That's odd."

"What do you mean?" Harley asked.

"I don't know but there is a funny smell. Sort of smoky and chemical. I don't know what it is but it's vaguely familiar. I know I've smelled it before." As they walked down the hall toward their room, the smell got stronger and stronger. Mira knew he had smelled this before. For some reason, Mira began to think of Muncey and his accident in Madison.

Beards put his key in the lock and turned the handle. Mira suddenly remembered what it was he smelled. He yelled at Beards, "Don't open..." but it was too late. The second Beards opened the door a fraction of an inch, a thick opaque cloud of orange smoke billowed out of the room—it was an orange smoke flare from one of the rescue boats.

Schleeh had gotten his hands on the flare, tossed it into the room, and closed the transom to trap the smoke inside. The orange smoke, designed to be visible in the open ocean for miles and miles, billowed into the hall. Beards pulled his shirt over his mouth and dashed into the room to open all the windows. Eventually the smoke began to drift out and the room cleared enough for Mira to go in. Everything was bright orange. Beards walked around the room, picking up whatever he came across and showing it to Mira—an orange phone, an orange pillow, an orange shoe, and even their leftover pizza, now a perfect uniform orange color. Mira went into the bathroom and saw a film of orange dye floating on top of the toilet bowl. He flushed the toilet and then called excitedly to Beards, "Hey Harley! Come quick, I've found something that isn't orange." The only thing in the whole room that was not bright orange was the porcelain of the bottom half of the toilet bowl, where it had been protected by the water. They went through their luggage and could not find anything that was not ruined. They decided that they would fly home in the green Bardahl coveralls that they had worn back from the racecourse. After inspecting the room, they left all their ruined clothes and luggage, locked the door, and headed down to the front desk to check out.

At the front desk, the friendly desk clerk went through a series of questions straight out of an employee training manual: "Did you enjoy your stay, Mr. Slovak?"

"Oh yes it was fine."

"May we call you a cab?"

"Yes please do."

"Do you need help out with your luggage?"

"No thank you."

"Is there anything else we can do to assist you?"

Mira took a deep breath, "Well yes there is. We had a bit of a party last night and it seems like it might have gotten out of hand. There might be a bit of damage to the room."

"Oh, Mr. Slovak, we didn't get any complaints about your room at all. It must not have been much of a party and I'm sure that the damage, it any, is just minor. There shouldn't be any problems at all."

Mira shook his head and said, "I think it might be more than just minor."

"I'm sure you're exaggerating, Mr. Slovak. Please don't worry. We'll take care of everything. Your taxi is ready now. Are you sure you don't need help with your bags?'

Mira and Beards sheepishly walked to the taxi and rode away. "You warned them, Mira. I heard you warn them." Later that summer, Mira heard that the *Maverick* owner, William T. Waggoner, had written a $10,000-dollar check to the Whittier to cover the damages. Beards never traveled with the team again.[4]

Two weeks later, the boats were at the Buffalo Launch Club on the Niagara River, in upstate New York, running for the William J. Connors Memorial Trophy. Only five unlimited boats showed up, but there was a full slate of limited hydroplanes on the schedule.

The race was somewhat anticlimactic. In the first preliminary heat on Saturday, the *Miss Bardahl*'s main competition, the *Miss Supertest II* and the *Maverick*, both experienced engine problems, and Mira cruised to an easy victory. In the second heat, mechanical woes knocked the *Miss Detroit* out of the race too, and only the *Wildroot Charlie* was left to run against the *Bardahl*. With just two boats left in the race, Mira decided to put on a bit of a show for the fans, slowing down to let the *Charlie* catch up on the final lap, only to pull away at the last moment and win by one-tenth of a second.

The Connors Memorial was a two-day race, with the final heat set for Sunday. The rule book didn't allow for engine changes, and since three of the five boats had blown their engines on Saturday, and the *Miss Bardahl* was running almost 10 miles an hour faster than the only other surviving boat, the *Wildroot Charlie,* Mira was confident about his chances for a victory.

Referee George Trimper called the Sunday morning drivers' meeting to order at a few minutes after 9 a.m. A large group of limited drivers gathered in front of Trimper. Mira stood in the back of the room, talking quietly and cracking jokes with Bill Stead. Stead's *Maverick*, out of the race with a blown engine, was headed back to the West Coast for repairs. Trimper was reading from a clipboard and announced, "Okay, let's go over the schedule for today. We have an unlimited test session scheduled from 10 a.m. to ..."

Before Trimper could finish what he was saying, someone in the front row interrupted him and said, "You know, I've raced here a bunch of years, and it always seems like there's a wind that comes up every day at about noon and it makes the water really rough for us. Is there any way we can run earlier in the day?"

Mira leaned over to Stead, whispering, "Who's that talking? I can't see him."

Stead answered, "That's Ron Musson. He's supposed to be a real hotshot."

Mira raised his voice in the back of the room and said, "We don't need to test, so if the little guys want to go first, that is fine with me, and we can run later in the day when the water is rougher, because our big boats can eat the rough water better than the little boats."[5]

Something in the way Mira expressed himself did not sit well with Musson. He glared at Slovak and growled, "What do you mean little guys first? Why do you call us little guys?"

Mira, who was unaware that he had inadvertently offended Musson (who was 5 feet 7 inches tall and sensitive about his height), continued on cheerfully, "I called you little guys because you drive a little boat."

Musson, muttered something under his breath that Mira could not hear. When the meeting broke up, Slovak made his way up to talk to Musson, hoping he could smooth over the hurt feelings, "You know, I have a little boat too and when I drive my little boat, I'm a little guy too, just like you."

Musson turned to Slovak and snarled, "It doesn't matter if you drive a big boat or a little boat, you're still nothing but a fucking refugee."

When it was time for the final heat, Mira knew that all he had to do was finish to win, so he ran a comfortable second place behind the *Wildroot Charlie* and collected enough points to take the victory. With the *Maverick* failing to score any points in Buffalo, the *Bardahl* picked up a lot of ground in the National High Points race, and headed to Washington, D.C., 383 points out of first place.

When the *Bardahl* team arrived in Washington, Mira called a meeting with crew chief Del Gould and owner Ole Bardahl. "Look, fellas," Mira said. "We're a few hundred points behind the *Maverick*, but they are skipping the next two races. I want to know what you want me to do. I can take it easy, just try to make the finals and collect points and see if we can take the High Points lead, or I can run hard and try to win races but run the risk that I might blow up an engine and not get any points."

There was a long pause, and then Ole spoke with his thick Norwegian accent, "Vell, Mira, I tink dat you should play it safe and go for da points, but I still vant you to win da darn race too."

Mira found a way to do both. The race in Washington actually consisted of two races. The first was the President's Cup, with two preliminary heats on Saturday and the final heat on Sunday. When the President's Cup was over, there was a second race called the Rogers Memorial, for any boats still able to run. There were not any National High Points awarded for the Rogers Memorial. Mira ran conservatively in the President's Cup, capturing third place and picking up 225 points on the Maverick. As there were no points awarded in the Rogers, it would not set the team back if he broke down, so he was able to run harder and ended up winning.

Two weeks later, in Madison, Mira ran a conservative race again and captured another third place. The 225 points he earned gave the *Bardahl* a sixty-nine-point lead in High Points as they headed to Las Vegas and the last race of the season.

The rules that covered the National High Points Championship were quite simple. Boats were awarded points only for their overall position at the end of the race, but in order to receive their points, a boat had to be running at the end of the final heat. The points were awarded based on 400 for a first-place finish, 300 for second, 225 for third place, and so on. Points that were earned in the preliminary heats were used to determine the overall race winner but did not count towards National High Points.

The Las Vegas race was sponsored by the Sahara Hotel, which went out of its way to show the drivers a great time with free shows, cocktail parties, and a hundred other distractions. Mira took the race seriously. In only his third season as a driver, he was in contention for the National Championship. The night before the race, Mira caught up with Ole Bardahl and Del Gould in the bar of the Sahara. He joined them at their table and said, "We have a sixty-nine-point lead on the *Maverick* and 106-point lead on the *Miss U.S.*. Tomorrow I can drive all out and try to win the race, or I can run conservatively and try to win the championship. I drive for you so I want you to tell me what you want."

Ole took a long drag on his cigarette and said, "I still tink we should aim for the championship."

Mira stood up from the table and said, "Okay, I'll go for the Championship, even if it means giving up on the Sahara Cup." Before Ole and Del had a chance to change their minds, Mira headed to his room.

The race took place on Thursday, October 23, just two days before Mira's twenty-ninth birthday. The Lake Mead racecourse has one of the most dramatic backdrops of any on the circuit. The races in Chelan, Tahoe, Coeur d'Alene, and Seattle were all run on blue lakes surrounded by evergreen forests. The Detroit, Buffalo, and Washington, D.C. races took place on rivers in the heart of urban centers. The Madison race was on a river surrounded by gently rolling farmland. Lake Mead was in the center of a stark desert surrounded by tall, craggy mountains. The mountains close to the racecourse were nothing but raw stone. Further back in the Black Mountain range, the peaks were covered by snow, giving the mountains a depth that somehow made the lake feel more isolated. The wind blew constantly, covering boats, engines, and spectators with a coarse dust. Whenever the wind dropped and the water settled down, the race officials launched another heat of racing.

Twelve boats qualified for the race and the *Maverick,* back from a month of repairs, was clearly the fastest in the pits. She won her first heat with an average speed of 107.665 miles an hour, while the *Miss Bardahl* only averaged 97.693 miles per hour. The *Miss U.S.,* with Donnie Wilson driving, won her first heat. In the second heat, the *Bardahl* won, the *Maverick* broke a supercharger and did not finish, and the *U.S.* took third. All three boats that were in contention for National High Points qualified for the final. There were three possible outcomes. If either the *Maverick* or the *Bardahl* won the final heat, it would win the National Championship. The *Miss U.S.* was a bit of a long shot, and the only way it could win would be if she finished two or more places ahead of both the *Maverick* and the *Bardahl.*

The *Maverick* and the *Miss U.S.* had significant mechanical damage they needed to repair. The *Maverick* team was trying to change a supercharger and the *Miss U.S.* team, which was running a Merlin engine it had borrowed from Edgar Kaiser, was trying to swap out a damaged quill shaft. As the five-minute gun fired, both the *U.S.* and the *Maverick* crews scrambled off the decks of their boats so the cranes could swing them in to the lake. As the seven finalists made their way on to the course, the wind began to stiffen and the flags on the official barge snapped and cracked.

As Mira made his warm-up laps, he kept his eye out for his competition. He needed to beat the *Maverick* and stay within one position of the *U.S.* He knew that he could run with the *U.S.*, but he was worried about the *Maverick.* He kept his head on a swivel, looking back and forth across the course, trying to spot the gold-and-red *Maverick.* He pulled up alongside the mahogany, red, white, and blue *Miss U.S.* and ran next to her for a while. He still could not find the *Maverick.* The one-minute gun fired and he checked his timing marks. As he began his run up the backstretch, he saw the *Maverick* wallowing in the center of the course, struggling to get up on a plane. As he drove by the floundering *Maverick*, he did not feel any sense of joy or relief, but he was able to put a mental check mark next to the name *Maverick*, and concentrate on going after the *Miss U.S.* As the boats lined up for the start, Mira took the inside lane, the *Miss U.S.* was next to him, and the *Thriftway Too* was outside. Donnie Wilson and the *Miss U.S.* were first across, with the *Bardahl* a couple lengths behind and the *Thriftway Too* coming up hard on the outside. Mira did not want to run the risk of overshooting the corner and bouncing through the *Miss U.S.'s* roostertail, so he slowed down. Coming out of the first turn, it was the *Miss U.S.* in first, the *Thriftway Too* in second, and the *Bardahl* a very close third. The *Bardahl* played cat and mouse with the *Thriftway Too* for about two laps before pulling away to catch the *Miss U.S.* On lap three, the *Bardahl* pulled up next to the *US* and the two boats ran side by side. At the end of the fourth lap, Mira took a gamble and dove inside, trying to pass the *Miss U.S.*. Wilson fought off the challenge. Mira relaxed back into second place, content to let the *U.S.* win the battle, knowing that he would win the war. The two boats finished one-two, with Wilson claiming the Sahara Cup and Slovak winning the National Championship.

Mira could not believe his good fortune. Starting the season without a ride and worried that he would not get a chance to race, he finished as National Champion.[6] He came back to the dock to a huge celebration. As soon as he stepped out of the boat, the crew picked him up and threw him into the lake. Quickly, they all jumped in after him, hollering and splashing. He was proud of his accomplishments, but he did feel a slight pang of guilt. He wished Bill, Junie, Les, and the whole *Wahoo* team were here. He wished that he could have won the Championship for them. "Well," he thought, "I've done it once, now I just need to go out and do it again with the *Wahoo*."

A few boats away, there was another victory celebration going on. Donnie Wilson and the *U.S.* crew were splashing in the lake too, celebrating their victory. Mira waded over to Don. The two drivers embraced in a jubilant hug as Mira shouted over the roar of the fans. "We did it Donnie, we did it!"

Once Wilson and Mira were dried off, they made their ways to the trophy stand, where the sculpted Lexan trophies were handed out by an attractive young actress named Jill St. John.

The National Championship was a big deal in Seattle, and when he returned to town, Mira was interviewed by both Seattle newspapers and all three TV stations, but he did not have much time to contemplate his success. Aero Copter was as busy as ever, and Mira had a job to do. A few days after getting back from Las Vegas, Mira was sent on a flight to Sitka, Alaska to deliver engine parts for a disabled helicopter. Since much of the

850-mile trip would take place over water, Mira took the Howard DGA float plane. With a cruising speed of 200 miles per hour, Mira figured that he could make the trip in five hours, spend the night, and fly back the next morning. The trip north went without a hitch. The November skies were threatening rain when Mira took off for the return flight. He broke through into clear sky at about 9,000 feet and headed south.

The trip home was going smoothly when suddenly, about two-and-a-half hours into the flight, the engine just stopped. It gave no warning, no bark or backfire, just sudden silence. Mira scanned the instrument panel and saw that the fuel-pressure gauge read zero. He knew he was carrying plenty of fuel, so the problem had to be with the fuel selector or the fuel pump. The selector could be used to choose which tank he was drawing fuel from. Mira hoped that he had just bumped the selector into the shutoff position. "Nope! It's right where it should be. Maybe I forgot to switch tanks after takeoff?" Mira flipped the switch to all its possible positions. Nothing helped. If it was not the selector, it had to be the fuel pump. The pump was driven by a small splined driveshaft from the engine. Once in a blue moon, a driveshaft could snap, and if that happened, there was not a lot left to troubleshoot. If the pump drive was broken, the engine was not going to get any fuel, and the plane was not going to fly. He knew that the plane was going down, and he began to prepare for an emergency landing.

Based on his air speed, total time in the air, and last known position, Mira figured that he was about 40 miles off the north end of Vancouver Island, over open ocean without any way to reach land. The first thing he did was key his radio and say, "Mayday, Mayday, Mayday, this is Howard N-52947. At latitude: N 52° 44' 58" and longitude: W 129° 48' 52" I have lost power and will be ditching in the Pacific with one soul on board." There was no response.

"Damn it," Mira said to himself. "It would be nice if someone knew where I was going down." He broke out of the clouds at 2,000 feet. The rain was holding off and the water looked flat. He was quickly able to identify the direction of the primary swells and he lined up to land parallel to them. At 2,000 feet, he was too low to be able to identify any secondary swell. Primary swells are the surface waves that are often a few feet tall. Secondary swells are the long sloping rollers from deep in the ocean. Often the primary and secondary swells move in the same direction, but sometimes local weather conditions will make the primary swells move in one direction while some faraway typhoon or hurricane while send secondary swells in a different direction, making landing a seaplane very dangerous. Without the altitude needed to see the secondary swells, Mira had no choice but to line up with the primary swells and try to land on the trough of the swell. While he still had a little altitude left, he banked the Howard into a gentle circle. He wanted to inspect his emergency landing zone and make sure there were not any big floating logs or fishing boats he was about to crash into. For its size, the Howard had a big wing and was easy to fly or land without power; however, the problem was, without power, there were no second chances. Once you bled off all your airspeed, you were committed to landing, no matter what. There could not be any "go arounds" today. As Mira got closer to the water, he was surprised to see how smooth it looked. "This should be a piece of cake," he thought to himself.

As he neared the water, he checked to make sure his water rudders were in the up position. Extending his flaps all the way out, he pitched the nose up just a bit so the floats would touch the water at the perfect angle, and then brought the DGA down gently. The plane made contact with the water and for a few deceptive seconds, everything seemed perfect. What Mira did not know was that a few days earlier, there had been a fierce storm off the coast of Japan. The huge waves that had tossed ships around in the Western Pacific had rolled east and were just reaching the Canadian Coast. When Mira set the DGA down, the water looked calm, but the placid surface of the ocean camouflaged long, sloping secondary rollers that were 8–10 feet tall, waiting for Mira.

When the pontoons of the powerless DGA hit the water, she slowed to 60 mph. The plane skimmed along the ocean, climbed up the backside of the first roller it came to, and launched itself from the top in an unfortunate attempt to regain the sky. Without any power, the poor plane could not fly, so it slammed down into the next roller, where it repeated its pitiful performance. Yet this time, it was another 10 miles an hour slower, so its leap into the air from the crest of the second roller was even less successful. On the third leap, the Howard hardly left the water at all, but it did succeed in impaling its pontoons into the top of the fourth wave and tipping forward onto its nose far enough that Mira saw green water splash against his windscreen. In the cockpit, there was little that Mira could do but hold on and pray that when it was all over the plane would be in one piece and still afloat. As soon as the spray cleared and Mira realized that the plane was not going to break up, he keyed his microphone and repeated the Mayday call. Again, there was no response.

He checked his watch. It was just a few minutes past noon. It was late in the year, and he was pretty far north. Sunset would be at about 5 p.m. The Howard DGA was, in the words of designer Ben Howard, "a Darn Good Airplane," but it was an awful boat. Mira was not sure how long the fragile plane would survive exposed to the wind and waves. He grabbed a rifle from behind the pilot's seat, opened the door, and climbed up on to the wing, where he could get a 360-degree view around him and try to wave down help. Occasionally, he saw a ship pass in the distance, but none was close enough to see him. After two hours, he crawled back into the cockpit and tried another Mayday call.

He waited all day, but no one came. After sundown, the open ocean is a cold, dark place to be sitting alone in a fragile airplane, bobbing up and down on the ocean swells like some forgotten toy. Morning came, and with it heavy fog that cut visibility to a few dozen yards. Around noon, the fog burned off. At 3.15 p.m., he saw a fishing boat about a mile away. He climbed back on the wing and waved his arms. The boat was now closer, but he was not sure if they saw him, so he aimed the rifle up into the air and fired off three quick shots, and then began to wave again. There was a slight change of course on the boat; now it was heading straight toward him. He waved again. Someone on the bridge waved back. He was going to be rescued. The fishing boat belched black smoke as the captain maneuvered close. Mira yelled across the water, "I need a tow to the closest land."

"We're headed to Namu to drop off a load of salmon. We'll take you there"

It was not until well after dark that Mira arrived in Namu, a small First Nations village on the east shore of Queen Charlotte Sound with a population of a few hundred that operated a fish cannery. There were a few bright work lights on the cannery docks, and a couple of cannery workers helped Mira tie up the plane. The cannery superintendent had a radio and was able to get a message to Seattle to let Aero Copter know that Mira was safe. The cannery operated a bunk house that the locals called "the Old Hotel." They put Mira up in one of the private rooms set aside for visiting executives.

Mira woke the next morning to the sound of ravens screaming "Cacaww" right outside his window. He dressed and went outside to see several of the big black birds fighting over a fish carcass. Namu seemed to be perched right on the water's edge, with its back pressed against steep mist-shrouded hills, while much of the town was built on stilts over the water. The only colors in Namu were green and gray. The wooded hills that surrounded the tiny town were dark green, but the slick, still waters of the bay were gray, the sky was gray, and the weathered wood siding on all of the buildings was gray. With hundreds of tons of fish being processed in the cannery each year, the town reeked of fish. The only way to get from the Old Hotel to the cannery office was along a slick wooden boardwalk that sat on pilings over the bay. At the office, Mira was directed back along the boardwalk to the cannery mess hall, where he could get a breakfast of scrambled eggs, fish hash, and toast. After eating a breakfast that did not sit well, Mira headed to his plane to see what he could find out.

It was a damp, chilly morning, and rivulets of moisture dripped off the engine cowl as Mira removed it and set it carefully on the dock. He pulled a small pouch of tools from behind the pilot's seat and dug into the engine. It did not take him long to find the fuel pump and remove the four nuts that held it in place. When he pulled it out, he could see that the shaft was broken. He hated being stranded in the wilds of British Columbia, but he was proud that he had quickly been able to diagnose the problem. He returned to the cannery office, was able to reach Aero Copter by radio, and ordered a new fuel pump. The good news was that they actually had a spare on the shelf; the bad news was that it would take almost a week to get to Namu. When the part was eventually delivered by mail boat four days later, it was only a matter of a few minutes' work to install the new pump and get back on the way to Seattle.

Growing up in the farmland of Czechoslovakia, Mira had never developed much of a taste for seafood. After spending five days in Namu eating fish hash for breakfast, fish burgers for lunch, and fish steaks for dinner, he swore that he would never eat salmon again.[7]

20

Continental: Seattle, 1959

In March 1959, Mira was invited to speak at a 4-H luncheon in Moses Lake, a small farming town 180 miles east of Seattle. The lunch was hosted by a wealthy potato farmer, whose large farm included a pasture that would work as a runway. Mira decided to fly his Ryan STA "*Moonshine*" to the luncheon and treat the 4-H kids to an air show, then land on the grass field, give his speech, and fly home. Mira asked Bill Muncey to come along. The *Moonshine* was a 1930s-vintage two-seat, low-wing monoplane with an aluminum fuselage and a fabric-covered wing. The morning sky was streaked with pink and orange when Mira and Muncey met at Boeing Field. It was a clear brisk day, and flying over the Cascade Mountains would be cold, so Mira provided Muncey with a heavy fur-lined flight jacket and an old-fashioned leather helmet with big black goggles. Mira talked Muncey through the tricky starting procedures for the vintage Ryan. The plane used a hand-cranked inertial starter, so Muncey had to crouch on the wing and turn a long metal crank while Mira sat in the cockpit using the hand-operated wobble pump to get enough fuel pressure to prime the engine. After a couple of tries, the old engine coughed to life with a cloud of blue smoke. With the engine running, Muncey stepped down from the wing, pulled the wheel chocks, and bounded back onto the wing and into the front cockpit.

There was not much traffic, and the tower quickly cleared Mira for takeoff. As they climbed out of Boeing Field towards 7,500 feet, Puget Sound sparkled, with toy-sized green-and-white ferry boats gliding toward Vashon and Bainbridge Islands. Mt. Rainier, pure and white in its winter snow, glowed in the distance. Mira followed Highway 10 east as it cut through the green pine-shrouded mountains. Muncey was like an excited child, pointing out dramatic sights on either side of the plane—jagged cliffs on the left, plunging waterfalls frozen into exotic ice sculptures on the right.

In no time, they were through the mountains and over the flat desert of Eastern Washington. Visibility was unlimited, and Mira let Muncey take over the plane and fly toward Moses Lake. They picked up the Columbia River and flew east above the sheer rock walls of the gorge. Muncey tried a couple of gentle turns and was impressed by how easily the powerful little stunt plane responded to his commands. As they approached the farm, Mira took back control and brought the plane down to 500 feet. He circled the farm right on time at noon. Mira could see a group of about fifty kids and their parents, standing in an open field, looking up at him. He began his air show with a low fast pass from east to west, making sure to waggle his wings directly over the kids. The kids waved back enthusiastically. He pulled into a loop, then a stall turn followed by a hammerhead dive, pulling out less than 100 feet above ground. He climbed away from the spectators with a half loop maneuver called an Immelmann, which led to a Cuban Eight, and a couple of Split S's. Muncey was cheering and waving like a kid on a rollercoaster. Mira ended the show with another low-level, high-speed pass, but this time, he was inverted, taking his hands off the controls, hanging them upside down out of the cockpit waving at the kids. Muncey was hanging upside down with his hands out too, clapping wildly while the spectators waved back and cheered with excitement.

Mira rolled back into level flight and prepare to land. He noticed a dark line of clouds building on the northern horizon. The clouds' position indicated that this was probably a quick-moving cold front. Mira had not seen anything on the weather charts that morning, so he was going to have to keep a sharp eye on this development, but since the clouds were still a long way off, he thought there should be plenty of time for lunch and their speech. Mira made a neat landing on the grass strip and taxied toward the spectators. He shut the engine down, and the propeller spun to a stop while he and Muncey removed their leather helmets, goggles, and jackets. As they climbed from the plane, Muncey told Mira, "Gosh that was swinging! I can't believe how much fun that was!"

"Glad you liked it." Mira handed Muncey one end of a leather cockpit cover and said, "Help me snap this in place. If the weather changes you won't want to fly home in a wet seat."

The farm owner came over and thanked Mira for the show. They were quickly surrounded by a large group of excited kids in flannel shirts and cowboy boots. The farm owner led Muncey and Mira towards the barn where lunch was being set up. Many of the kids began asking Mira for autographs. At boat races, Muncey and Mira were equal, and they often stood side-by-side to sign autographs. Here in Moses Lake, after the air show, Muncey could have been invisible. None of the kids swarming around Mira asked Muncey for anything. Muncey forced himself to smile, but Mira could see the hurt look in his eyes each time a young fan brushed past him to get to Mira.

"Hey, that's Billy Muncey over there. Don't forget to get his autograph. Billy's won the Gold Cup twice!" A second crowd began to form around Muncey, who Mira continued to promote. "Did you see the film of the boat that sank the Coast Guard cutter? Well, that was Billy driving."

Eventually, all the kids and parents had their autographs and Mira and Muncey walked into the cavernous barn, which smelled of hay and diesel fuel. "Thanks, Slim," Muncey whispered. "That was a nice thing you did there."

"Don't worry about it," Slovak whispered back. "I had to do something. My hand was starting to cramp up from all of the autographs I was signing."

Inside the barn were tables loaded with platters of fried chicken, Tupperware bowls of potato salad, and trays overflowing with chocolate chip cookies. Over lunch, Muncey and Mira talked with the parents. When they finished their meal, the farmer stood up and introduced Mira, who started talking about his escape from communism. He had just finished with the hijack story when there was a childish squeal from the back of the barn and a little girl shouted, "Look! It's snowing!"

The kids ran to watch as thick flakes slipped out of a low gray sky and began to cover the ground. Mira watched the snow swirl down. The cold front he had seen earlier must have barreled in, pushing away the clear dry air that had given them such a beautiful morning. Mira thought of something his first flight instructor back in Czechoslovakia used to say. "When it comes to the weather, there are only two types of pilots—patient pilots and dead pilots." There was no way Mira was going to try to fly back over the mountains in a snowstorm.

He called Muncey over and said, "Billy, I think we are going to be here for a while. Would you mind coming up front with me and we can talk about hydros?"

Muncey laughed, "You're asking if I would mind standing up in front of a group of kids and talk about boat racing? I can't think of anything I'd enjoy more."

Mira called the kids back into the barn and announced, "We know that the speech was supposed to end at four o'clock, but the snow has caught us by surprise, and we aren't going to be able to fly out until it clears up, so if it's okay with you, we're just going to keep telling stories until it stops snowing."

Mira finished talking about the escape, and then he and Muncey took turns telling stories about their wins and near wins. Mira talked about diving into the Ohio River after Muncey's Madison accident. Muncey talked about meeting Eisenhower and Mira talked about winning the National High Points Championship. Time flew by, and soon it was time for the kids to go home. When the barn doors were slid open again, yellow electric light spilled out into the night to reveal a world that was covered in white. Mira looked into the night sky and saw stars twinkling above. The fast-moving cold front had passed through Moses Lake, dumping 4 inches of snow, but was now long gone. Mira figured that it was safe to head home. He approached the farmer and said, "I think we can fly out now, but it's going to be tough to see the runway in the dark. Do you think you could get a few of your buddies to drive their trucks out onto the field and use their headlights to give me some runway lights?"

"Heck, yeah," the farmer answered, "We'd be happy to! Hey fellas! We got a job to do."

The quiet of the snowy evening was shattered as a dozen farm trucks rumbled to life and moved into position along the makeshift runway. Meanwhile, Muncey and Mira carefully brushed all the snow off the *Moonshine,* making sure that the control surfaces were free of ice and snow.

With Muncey's help cranking the inertial starter, Mira got the *Moonshine* running and they taxied into position to take off. Half a dozen trucks lined the runway, with their headlights illuminating cone-shaped patches of snow. Beyond the headlights, there was total darkness. Mira ran the engine up, released the brake, and sailed down the runway toward the headlights. In an instant the plane was airborne and climbing into the night. From the air, even with the snow, it was fairly easy to pick out Highway 10 and head west toward Seattle. The flight home was bone-chillingly cold but otherwise uneventful. The lights of Seattle seen from a small plane at night were spectacular, and both Bill and Mira felt pride looking down at their adopted home.

A few weeks later, on Saturday, April 4, a windy overcast day that threatened rain, Muncey's new *Miss Thriftway,* a replacement for the boat that sank the Coast Guard cutter, was launched. The ceremony took place at Ted Jones's waterfront boat shop in Kennydale, on the southeast side of Lake Washington. A horde of reporters crowded around the boat. With a Dixieland jazz band playing in the background, Jane Ramsey, the wife of crew chief Jack Ramsey, splashed champagne on the bow of the boat before it was lowered into the water. Muncey climbed aboard and the band struck up "Anchors Aweigh" as the brand-new hydro pulled away from the dock. Muncey was planning to drive ten miles up lake to the Stan Sayres Pits, where an even larger group of fans and reporters was waiting.

Muncey's attention was focused on the dashboard and the dozen or so gauges that told him about the health of his mount. His eyes scanned back and forth from oil pressure to water temperature, to manifold pressure to engine speed to boat speed, and then back again. As he rounded the south end of Mercer Island, he began to open up the throttle a little. He was running along at about 100 miles per hour and everything felt perfect. Suddenly, he had the uncanny feeling that he was being watched. He knew that there were countless spectators along the shore, but this was different; it was as if there was someone looking directly over his shoulder. He knew it was a crazy sensation, but he looked to his left to see if maybe Jack Ramsey was holding onto the tailfin to go for a ride—no one was there. He looked to his right—no one there either. He was alone in the boat but he still felt that there was someone looking over his shoulder. Then he looked straight up, and not more than 75 feet above him, hanging upside down from the belts of the cockpit of the *Moonshine*, was the smiling face of Mira Slovak. For an instant, the speeding boat and the acrobatic airplane matched speed perfectly. Then Mira slowly and clearly mouthed the words, "See you later, Billy!" He rolled the plane upright and flew west toward Boeing Field. Muncey pressed down the accelerator and powered up the lake, laughing heartily.

The first race of the 1959 season was the Lake Chelan Apple Cup, on May 10. This would be the first test for the new Rolls-Royce Merlin engine in the *Wahoo*. There were a couple of cosmetic changes on the boat as well. Bill Boeing had bought a radio station in Seattle and the frequency was 101.5, so the *Wahoo*'s U-number was changed from U-77 to U-101. The word "Miss" was dropped from the boat's name and now she was just called the *Wahoo.*

The race was a disappointment for the *Wahoo* team. They were the tenth-fastest qualifier and were almost 20 miles an hour behind Bill Stead and the *Maverick*. Mira couldn't use the power of the mighty Merlin engine; every time he tried to open her up, he felt a tremendous vibration. He ran two heats, limping around in fourth place. He didn't make the final, and the illustrious debut of the new Merlin engine only netted a seventh-place finish overall.

Junie decided that they needed new propellers to make the Merlin work. They ordered the props, but did not see any point in going to the races until the new propellers showed up, so the *Wahoo* did not race again until the

Gold Cup in Seattle, in early August. The new propellers did the trick. The vibration went away and in Gold Cup testing, Mira and the *Wahoo* were posting some very fast laps.

Mira was on the dock when Muncey and the *Miss Thriftway* returned from their Gold Cup qualifying run. As Muncey climbed out of the boat, Mira noticed that he had a pink scarf tied to the back of his helmet. Keith Jackson and a cameraman met Muncey at the end of the dock for an interview. Mira stood close enough to eavesdrop, "Hi Keith!" Muncey said into the microphone as he began to unbuckle his helmet. Let me get this off, I can't hear a thing with it on." He took off his helmet and pulled out his ear plugs, then quickly ran his fingers through his damp hair to try to get it to lay down, "That feels better! Sorry, I couldn't hear earlier. How fast did we qualify?"

"111.111 mph."

"Really? 111.111? Wow, that's amazing, I don't know if I could have planned it any better than that."

"So how is the new *Miss Thriftway* performing?"

"Oh just great, Keith! I couldn't ask for a better ride."

"Are you getting all of the 'new boat bugs' worked out?"

Muncey unzipped his life jacket and began to shrug it off of his shoulders. "Yeah, the boys are doing just a marvelous job. Before this last run, Ted Jones trimmed the air traps and shallowed up the sponsons, and I've got to say we've got all of the kinks worked out."

"So Bill, I can't help but notice the pink scarf. What is that about?"

Muncey grinned his big, friendly, gap-toothed grin and said "Well, Keith, Kit is expecting again. She's due to give birth in early September. This will be our third. We already have two boys, and I love 'em so much, but you know Kit's beginning to feel a little outnumbered around the house, so I'm wearing this pink scarf to see if it won't help us get a girl this time around."

"Well, good luck with that, Bill!"

Mira and the Wahoo were ready to qualify a few moments later. After hearing Muncey's explanation about the pink scarf, Mira quickly took off his shoes, removed the dark blue socks he was wearing, and tied them together. They were too short to wrap around his neck like a scarf so he just tied them to the elastic strap on the back of his goggles. As he slid the goggles into place over his helmet, the blue socks dangled from the back like a medieval talisman.

"Excuse me!" he said as he politely tried to push through the crowd of reporters to get to the cockpit of the *Wahoo*.

Jackson saw the socks dangling from Mira's helmet and called out, "Mira, what are the socks for?"

Mira turned to the group of waiting reporters and said, "Billy Munsley is wearing a pink scarf in hopes that his wife will have a girl. I wear these blue socks to make sure that she has a boy!" Everybody laughed and Mira stepped into the boat and roared away to qualify at 112.971 miles per hour, with one lap above 114.

On race day, Mira easily won his first heat, turning in the fastest lap of the race. The *Wahoo* was running extremely fast and Mira was feeling so confident that as he was reeling off one fast lap after another, he was beginning to rehearse his victory speech in his mind. ABC Sports was broadcasting the final heat live all across the country. Mira knew that if he won the race, his trophy acceptance speech would be seen by millions of people, and he did not want to be mixing Czech and English words.

After their heat 1A victory, Junie had the crew make a complete inspection of the boat. They found a cracked frame in the right sponson. The experienced crew sprang into action, cutting out a couple of aluminum doublers to bolt over the crack. As the time drew near for the second heat, the crane swung its lifting hook over the *Wahoo*, waiting to pick up the boat the second the crew was finished. All around the *Wahoo*, other boats were going into the water, while the crew continued to work feverishly.

Finally, Junie announced that the repair was done, and the crew scampered off the boat as the big crane gently picked her up from its trailer, swung towards the water, and began to lower her. When the boat was barely three feet above the lake, the crane suddenly stopped with a loud clunk. Something was wrong with the crane. Mira, wearing his helmet and life jacket, paced the dock as the *Wahoo* hung helplessly from her lifting slings. One by one, the *Miss Thriftway*, the *Miss Spokane*, the *Gale VI*, the *Miss Seattle*, and the *Breathless II* pulled away from the pits and headed onto the racecourse. Mechanics swarmed over the crane and finally, moments before the one-minute gun fired, the *Wahoo* was lowered the last few feet into the water. Mira scrambled into the boat and hit the primer to get her started. The engine sputtered and turned over with a belch of black smoke.

Mira was anxious to get out onto the course. He brought the mix control forward to give the engine more fuel, but he was too early and flooded the engine. The engine died and the boat drifted helplessly. The one-minute gun fired as he struggled to get the boat restarted. Eventually, Mira got the boat started, but he was so far behind that the officials waved him off the course and he didn't score any points. However, the 400 points he scored in the first heat were enough to get him into the final.

In the final, Mira hit the starting line perfectly. The *Miss Spokane* was about a dozen boat lengths ahead, so he knew that the *Spokane* would be penalized a lap for jumping the gun, and that meant he was actually in first place. Midway through the second lap, Mira decided to show everyone just how fast the *Wahoo* was, and he powered past the *Spokane* to take the lead on the racecourse. As he finished lap after lap in the lead, he began to calculate the points and knew that even if he won the heat, there was no way he could win the race, but Bill Muncey, who was now in second, could win his third Gold Cup if he were to win the final. Heading up the backstretch on lap nine of ten, Mira lifted his foot off the throttle and pulled to the right toward the log boom to let Muncey take the victory. As Muncey roared past, Mira gave a friendly wave. Unfortunately for Muncey, when the *Miss Spokane* was penalized for jumping the gun in the final, it moved the *Maverick* up one spot so it was in a points-tie with the *Thriftway.* After almost an hour of deliberation, the *Maverick* was awarded the victory based on a total elapsed time that was 13.3 seconds faster than *Miss Thriftway.*

On Wednesday, August 26, Mira was called to the phone at Aero Copter. When he picked it up, he heard Wayne Richardson on the other end of the line say, "Mira? Are you sitting down? I have some great news! We've been working a couple of projects with Robert Six at Continental Airlines. Let's just say he owes the CIA a favor, okay? Anyway he's agreed to hire you! You need to get to Continental's Headquarters in Denver right away and start training. You can come back to Seattle to finish out the racing season, but you're going to be flying for Continental!"

Robert Six was a legend in the aviation world. He had started flying sightseeing rides in a fabric-covered biplane back in 1929 and had worked his way up to become president and CEO of one of the world's biggest airlines. Six was famous for his blunt management style, but he was a genius when it came to running his airline. Mira asked, "What type of plane will I be flying?"

Wayne laughed out loud. "Damn it, Mira, you are consistent! That's exactly the same thing you asked me when I told you about the Boeing job."

"Well, it is still the thing that matters most to me. So do you know what I'll be flying?"

"As a matter of fact, I do. I figured you were going to ask me, so I asked Six. He said they're going to start you out as a copilot on one of their DC-3s, but they have ordered a slew of brand-new 707s from Boeing, and as soon as they start to take delivery, they'll train you to be a captain on a 707."

For the time being, Mira decided that he would keep the waterfront apartment on Beach Drive, and just rent something near the airport in Denver. Seattle was his home and he was not ready to give it up yet. He was still going to be driving the *Wahoo*, so he would be spending a lot of time in Seattle and did not want to have to rent a hotel room each time he came to town. Besides, there were plenty of pilots who lived in their own home towns and "deadheaded" (went along for a ride on a flight that they were not working) to get to or from their "domicile," airline slang for whatever hub the airline had assigned them to work from. The airline industry was based on seniority within the airline, so even though Mira had five years as chief pilot for Bill Boeing and three years as a captain for Czechoslovakian Airlines, he would be starting at the bottom of the totem pole at Continental, flying as a first officer (commonly called a co-pilot, second in command behind the captain) in a DC-3.

On September 8, Kit Muncey gave birth to a happy, healthy baby boy. He was named Kenton, in honor of Bill's friend, band leader Stan Kenton. Bill and Kit asked Mira to be Kenton's godfather.

21

This is Your Life: Seattle, 1959

The next race for Mira and the *Wahoo* was the President's Cup on September 19–20. The Soviet Union seemed to dominate the news that month. On September 14, the Soviet space program successfully crash-landed its Lunik 2 rocket into the Sea of Tranquility on the moon, marking the first time a man-made object had left earth and landed on another celestial body. It also confirmed to the American people that the Soviets still held a commanding lead in the race for space. The next day, Soviet Premier Nikita Khrushchev arrived at Andrews Air Force Base for an eleven-day tour of the U.S. Khrushchev made news where ever he went, but he grabbed the headlines on the 19th when he became furious after his request to visit Disneyland had been turned down for "security reasons." Khrushchev gave an angry interview where he snapped, "Why not? What do you have there? Rocket launch pads?"

Eisenhower was busy with Khrushchev and could not attend the President's Cup, but he promised to invite the winner to the White House for a trophy presentation once his schedule cleared up.

The morning of the 19th was one of those magical summer days that happen in late September when the sky is a deep, cloudless blue, the sun is warm, and the wind ruffles the leaves with just enough force to keep everything comfortable. The President's Cup pits were on Hains Point and the racecourse stretched out on the Potomac River, between the Point and National Airport. The race was a two-day event, with heats one and two on Saturday and the final heat on Sunday.

Heat 1A saw Bill Stead in the *Maverick* cross the starting line first, with Mira and the *Wahoo* several seconds behind. By the end of lap one, the

Wahoo was running side-by-side with the *Maverick*. On lap two, the *Wahoo* set a new course record of 113.445 mph and breezed past the *Maverick*. The *Wahoo* held the lead for two more laps. Stead, trying to catch up, entered the upriver turn too fast. The *Maverick* took a big hop, dug in a sponson, and rolled over. Red flags and orange smoke bombs halted the race as a soaking-wet Bill Stead climbed onto the aluminum bottom of the overturned *Maverick*. Mira was declared the winner of the first heat, while the *Maverick*, missing its tail fin, windshield, and a large piece of the deck, was hauled back to the pits and lifted out of the water.

A few moments before the start of heat 2A, Les Eide discovered that the *Wahoo* had a burned piston in the number one cylinder. Thinking quickly, he pulled the spark plugs out of the damaged cylinder so it would not get any worse and sent the *Wahoo* out with only eleven working cylinders. Even with eleven cylinders, the *Wahoo* gave Donnie Wilson and the *Miss U.S.* a great race, chasing the beautiful mahogany and red boat for all five laps, finishing only a few seconds behind, in second place,

The weather on Sunday was just as nice as Saturday had been, but the wind was a few miles an hour stronger, making the course a little lumpy. Bill Stead, checked for injuries and released from the hospital, was back in the pits doing color commentary with WAML TV. The only two boats with enough points to win the race were the *Miss U.S.* and the *Wahoo*.

For Mira, the President's Cup was more important than any other trophy on the circuit, even the Gold Cup. He wanted to win so he could meet Eisenhower and personally thank him for signing the bill that gave him his radio operator's license. Mira trailed the *U.S.* by 100 points, but he had a faster elapsed time, so the race would come down to whoever won the final heat.

Wilson and the *Miss U.S.* got across the starting line first, and inside, but Slovak was running faster on the outside, and they drew even heading into turn one. When the wind was blowing and the water started to get rough, running outside became a bit of an advantage. From his position in lane three, Mira could survey all the racing lanes and move in or out searching for smoother, faster water. He could also pin Wilson tight against the buoys, forcing him to run in rougher, slower water. Coming out of turn one, Mira scooted a couple of boat lengths ahead. When the *Miss U.S.* tried to answer the challenge, she hit a roller and bounced sideways, almost throwing Wilson into the river. Slovak extended his lead to three boat lengths. The two boats battled side by side, with the *U.S.* in lane one and the *Wahoo* slightly ahead and outside, searching back and forth between lanes two and three. Halfway through lap three, Wilson tried crossing the *Wahoo's* wake to move outside to find cleaner water. Coming out of turn one for the last time, Mira let the *Wahoo* drift wide to conserve all the speed he could. At the same time, he saw *Miss U.S.* dive inside him, tight to the buoy line, with a tremendous head of steam. The *U.S.* took a vicious bounce and turned sideways in a tower of spray. From his position of relative safety wide and outside, Mira saw a dark shape come arcing up, through the spray. It was Wilson, catapulted 30 feet into the air at 150 mph. Wilson hit head first and was enveloped in another cloud of spray. Instantly red flags waved and orange smoke bombs shut the course down. Mira returned to the pits as Wilson's unconscious body was pulled from the river and rushed to the hospital. He regained consciousness in the ambulance but spent a week in the hospital recovering from a serious concussion.[1]

Mira was awarded a small take-home trophy in a dockside ceremony after the race but was told that the President's "people" would be in touch to arrange the Oval Office visit later in the year.

Monday morning, as the *Wahoo* crew was packing up to return to Seattle, Mira put on his dark blue Continental uniform and headed to National Airport to catch a plane to Chicago with a connection to Denver. It felt almost disloyal to be leaving the team behind, but he had a new job and he was going to do everything he could to be the best pilot that Continental had ever hired.

As the plane climbed out of National, Mira caught a quick glimpse of the racecourse on the muddy Potomac River and was overwhelmed with a sense of pride in his adopted country. In the six short years since his defection, he had come to America, established himself as one of the best boat racers in the world, gotten a job with a great airline, and was going to meet President Eisenhower. None of this would have been possible under communism. As Mira got off the plane in Chicago to change flights, he saw a discarded newspaper lying across one of the seats in first class. It was folded open to the sports section and showed a large picture of a smiling Mira being kissed by the Regatta Queen, Nancy Priest, with a caption that said, "A Big Day for Mira."

When he arrived in Denver, he went straight to Continental's headquarters. He was still feeling excited and proud, thinking to himself that his new life in America was going just about perfectly. He was called into the office of the director of operations. Mira saw a copy of the paper open to his picture lying on the director's desk. He smiled broadly, expecting the director to congratulate him on the race win and maybe ask a few questions about racing.

The director had a grim look on his face and did not ask Mira to take a seat, so Mira remained standing while the director picked up a piece of paper from his desk, cleared his throat, and read out loud, "First Officer Slovak, your contract states that while employed with Continental Airlines you will do nothing to cast the airline in a negative light or bring the airline unfavorable publicity. It is the determination of this office that powerboat racing is dangerous and reckless and that having Continental's good name associated with a dangerous and reckless sport will cause passengers to assume, incorrectly, that Continental's pilots are reckless and that flying on Continental Airlines is dangerous. It is the determination of this office that you have violated the terms of your contract and you are hereby dismissed from your employment." The director put the paper down and said, "Security will now escort you off Continental's property and your final paycheck will be mailed to your home."

Mira was stunned. Thirty seconds ago, his world had been perfect and now it was crumbling. The scene reminded him of the StB officer in Kosice who threatened him after he had saved the ice-laden Li-2. Yet how could this be happening in America?

Mira returned to his apartment and paced the floor. Eventually, he called Bill Boeing at Aero Copter to ask for his old job back. Boeing was incredulous. "That's crazy! Does Six know about this?"

"I don't know. I would think so, but I'm not sure."

"Don't worry Mira, I'm going to call Robert and see what's really going on. What's your number? I'll call you right back." Mira sat dejectedly on the edge of the bed. In less than five minutes, his phone rang again. No one else had the number, so Mira said, "Hello, Mr. Boeing," as he picked up the phone.

There was a loud, course laugh on the other end of the phone, "No, this isn't Boeing. This is Robert Six. This is the most god damn foolish thing I've ever heard of, and if you don't get your ass back to work right now, I might fire you again."

"You mean I've still got a job?"

"Of course you do, but I'm not sure I can say the same for the jackass that tried to fire you this morning." Within a week, Mira was flying as first officer on flights out of Dallas.

On October 19, 1959, Mira flew back to Seattle. He had a meeting scheduled for the next afternoon with the district director of the Immigration and Naturalization Service, John Boyd. The meeting took place in room 104A of the Federal Courthouse in Seattle. It was just a few doors away from Wayne Richardson's mysterious Room 12 in the same building. The meeting went well, with everything seeming to be in order with Mira's paperwork, and he began making plans to take the citizenship examination. Once the meeting was over, Mira headed to Blanche and Frank Cech's house in hopes of enjoying a home-cooked Czech meal with his surrogate family. No sooner had he walked in the door than the Cechs' phone started to ring. It was Director Boyd saying that there was a serious issue with Mira's application and he needed to return to his office right away.

Mira got back to the courthouse a little before 7 p.m. It felt deserted, and his heels clicking on the marble floor echoed in the empty corridor as he headed for Boyd's office. Something wasn't right; it seemed unusual that he would need to meet with the director so long after normal business hours.

Director Boyd was seated behind a large desk, flanked by an American flag and a portrait of Eisenhower. As Mira came in, Boyd stood and reached across the desk to shake hands. He was a tall, distinguished gentleman with wavy silver hair and a firm handshake. "Thank you for agreeing to see me at this late hour. I know this is, ah, well I mean to say that ... well this is a bit, a bit unusual."

Boyd seemed nervous and suddenly Mira began to get worried. "Something's not right," Mira thought.

Out in the hallway, he could hear a commotion. There were voices followed by a hoarse whisper of "Be quiet or he'll hear us!" Mira had been in America for six years, but he still remembered the StB and the way the angry men in the long green coats would sweep into a room and make a sudden arrest, so the unusual noises in the hallway were causing him concern. Suddenly, the door swung open and three men came in. One was carrying a camera, another had a bank of bright electric lights on a pole, and the third man, apparently the leader of the group, had a microphone in his hand and walked directly toward Mira. He stood up, looking around the room trying to figure out what was happening. The man with the microphone was vaguely familiar, but Mira had witnessed plenty of arrests in communist Czechoslovakia, and three men suddenly bursting into a government office late at night seemed more like an arrest than any other explanation he could think of.

The man with the microphone walked right up to Mira and said, "Excuse me gentlemen, my name is Ralph Edwards, and I'd like to thank you for allowing this interruption, Mr. Boyd." Mira's eyes darted back and forth between director Boyd's face and Mr. Edwards' face. He still couldn't figure out what was happening. Edwards continued to talk: "I'd like the applicant here to know that this interruption will in no way invalidate the proceedings here tonight. Is that correct, Mr. Boyd?"

"That's right Ralph, we would be only too pleased to continue with this hearing tomorrow in view of the unusual circumstances here tonight."

Mira's mind was racing. "Who is this and what is happening to me?"

Edwards was talking again. "Which enables me to say, come on up here, boy." Edwards moved Mira up in front of the camera. "Miroslav Slovak, daredevil, sports champion, a man who is totally unwilling to settle for less than man's fundamental freedom, this is your life!"[2]

Suddenly, it all made sense. Mira realized that nothing was wrong with his application, this was no sudden arrest; this was an American television show. *This is Your Life* was a popular show on NBC on Tuesday nights. Each week, they surprised a celebrity with a short half-hour biography. Mira wanted to laugh. Years in communist Czechoslovakia had trained him to always expect the worst.

Edwards, was speaking again. "We have a car waiting outside to take you to the Moore Theater, Second and Virginia, right here in Seattle, where there is a whole crowd waiting for you and we will re-live your stirring life." Edwards turned to face the camera directly. "But meanwhile here is Bob Warren with a word about Joy Dish Soap."

As soon as Edwards said the word "soap," the TV lights were turned off and everyone rushed out of the room. Edwards grabbed Mira's arm and said, "We've got to run. We have a police motorcycle escort set up to take us to the theater." They all raced out side into a chilly wet October evening, piled into a couple of waiting Ford station wagons, and roared off towards Second Avenue. When they arrived at the theater, Mira was surprised to see that the marquee was lit up, saying "*This is Your Life* Mira Slovak with Ralph Edwards."

The production crew met the cars as they screeched to a stop under the theater marquee. Mira was blinded as the bright television lights were turned back on and cameras began to broadcast live images into the homes of millions of TV viewers across the country. Edwards bounded from the car and two ushers cleared the way as Edwards and Mira ran inside. They headed down the main aisle of the theater and Mira was stunned to see that the auditorium was packed with hundreds of people, not an empty seat anywhere, and they were all cheering and applauding for him. On the stage, Mira saw a backdrop made from a map of Czechoslovakia next to a map of Germany, with an airplane propeller separating them. To the right of the maps was a comfortable-looking couch.

As Edwards reached the stage he began to talk again, "We're certainly happy to be in Seattle tonight and bring you the story of this wonderful young man." Edwards pointed at the couch and said, "Come on over here and sit down, Mira. Oh, those Seattle police are great, aren't they Mira? That's the best ride I've ever had. Does your hydroplane go that fast?"

"I doubt it!"

"Yes, Mira Slovak, this is your life. A life with two beginnings. The first at your birth in Cífer, Czechoslovakia on October 25, 1929 and the second 23 and a half years later at Ruzyne airport, where you sat at the controls of an idling twin-engine aircraft belonging to the government-controlled Czechoslovakian airline."[3]

Edwards sat on a stool next to the couch and began to tell the story of the escape, while stock footage of a DC-3 was projected on a screen. Mira was listening to Edwards's voice, but he was still in something of a daze. Suddenly, he heard Edwards say, "And here are two of those co-planning passengers, Mira, who with you risked their lives for freedom. Then from Prague, now living in Stickney, Illinois, Hannah and Helmut Cermack!"

Mira stood to see Hannah and Helmut run out from behind the curtain at the back of the stage. Hannah reached Mira first and gave him a big hug. Helmut came a few steps behind and shook Mira's hand. Seeing two old friends from Czechoslovakia was a powerful reminder of how much he had sacrificed to come to America. Edwards interviewed Helmut and Hannah, asking them both several questions about the escape. The next guests Edwards brought on stage were the two passengers who had decided to say in the West, Bohumil Suran and Antonin Valejnicek. They too embraced Mira with tremendous enthusiasm. Edwards continued to work his way through the story. The next guest was Nicky Morris, Mira's first Counter Intelligence Corps handler in Frankfurt. Morris told a story about how limited Mira's English vocabulary was and how for several weeks the only English that Mira could pronounce was "cherry pie." So no matter where they went to eat, all Mira ever got was a slice of cherry pie.

As the program went on, Edwards brought out Al Baxter, who talked about the time Mira got arrested in Hamilton, Montana, and Bill Boeing Jr. to talk about the *Miss Wahoo*. The last guest was Blanche Cech. Edwards described Blanche as "Mira's second mother." She talked about her trip to Prague to visit Mira's mother and revealed to Mira that Maria had taken a vow to not cut her hair again until she saw him. Blanche was caught off guard with how emotional she became as she talked about Mira's mother, and she began to tear up. This of course brought a lump to Mira's throat and tears to his eyes. As the program concluded, Edwards told Mira that he was being given a number of gifts, including a movie camera, a projector, new cufflinks, and a brand new 1960 Ford Falcon. Later that night, NBC hosted a large party in Mira's honor at the Olympic Hotel, where he got an opportunity to catch up with Helmut, Hannah, Nicky Morris, and everyone else.[4]

The last race of the 1959 season was the Lake Mead Cup, outside of Las Vegas. It is hard to imagine a race going any better. The *Wahoo* was the fastest qualifier and won all three heats and the trophy, setting the mark for the fastest lap with a speed of 114.

For the rest of 1959 and on into early 1960, Mira focused on Continental Airlines and getting back into the role of airline pilot. One day, Mira arrived at Continental to hear several of the pilots talking about a new stewardess named Ingrid Bondi. She was a beautiful young blond who had just emigrated from Sweden. She was having difficulty learning English and Mira offered to give her lessons. Ingrid smiled at the dashing Slovak and said, "You have a reputation for fast cars and fast boats and fast planes and fast women. I don't want anything to do with that!"

22

Meeting Eisenhower: Washington, D.C., 1960

The winter of 1960 had been unseasonably warm in Washington, D.C. By early March, the cherry blossoms that lined the National Mall were starting to bloom. On the night of March 16, the weather turned foul and a heavy storm swirled across the city, dumping six inches of snow. By the morning of the 17th, the famous DC cherry blossoms were encased in ice and looked like sugar-coated candy treats.

As the capital began to dig out from the storm, Mira waited patiently for a cab under the protective awning of the Willard Hotel. A black and yellow Checker cab pulled up, with dirty snow clinging to the underside of its fenders, and the burly driver leaned across the front seat to the passenger window and shouted, "Where you going, Bud?"

Mira reached into the breast pocket of his expensive blue suit and pulled out a small square envelope. He carefully opened it to retrieve a thick white card with a pale-yellow image of the White House printed on it. Turned over, the card revealed elegant handwritten calligraphy that said:

Captain Miroslav Slovak,

The President requests the pleasure of your company at the White House on March 17, 1960 at 12 o'clock.

Please present this card at the West Entrance

The cabbie jumped out of his car and hurried to open Mira's door. "So you're gonna see Eisenhower? I've never had a fare going to see the Prez! Wait until I tell my wife. She ain't gonna believe it!"

The late-season snow was causing traffic to back up all across the city. Mira's cab inched slowly down Pennsylvania Avenue, turned right on 15th St NW, then left toward the White House. His pulse raced as the cab drove slowly in front of the White House. The long, sloping lawn leading uphill to 1600 Pennsylvania Avenue was a blanket of pure white. Mira had been dreaming of this day since he first saw General Eisenhower, the victor, standing in the back of an open car parading through the war-ravaged streets of Prague, Czechoslovakia, in 1945.

The cabbie slowed and turned onto West Executive Avenue. A Marine guard in dress uniform with a white cap and red piping on his dark blue jacket blocked the way. The cabbie rolled down his window and handed over the card from Mira's invitation. The guard read it, handed it back, and saluted. "Please proceed to the West Entrance. You are not cleared to park, so please drop Captain Slovak off and then exit the grounds via E Street."

At the West Entrance, another Marine guard, who could have been a twin to the first, saluted and opened Mira's door. Mira unfolded his lanky 6-foot 3-inch frame from the back of the cab and presented his invitation. The guard took it and said, "Follow me, sir," pivoted on his heel, and walked up the short concrete stairs into the West Wing of the White House.[1]

Mira sat patiently in the waiting room off of the Oval Office. Eventually he was joined by Bill Boeing, who had flown in from Seattle. At 11.55 a.m., an aide for Eisenhower ushered them into the President's office. On the corner of Eisenhower's heavy mahogany desk sat the polished gold President's Cup. As Mira and Boeing entered the room, Eisenhower stood up and walked from behind the desk to meet them in the center of the office, "Mr. Boeing, Captain Slovak, how very nice to finally meet you. I apologize for not being able to present the trophy at the race, but with Premier Khrushchev visiting, I figured I had better give him my full attention." In a lighthearted conspiratorial tone, he added, "But to tell you the truth, I'd have much rather been with you two at the race." Eisenhower pointed to some red upholstered chairs flanking a white marble fireplace at one end of the room and said, "If you have time, let's take a seat. I have some questions about this boat of yours. Are you using the Allison or the Rolls-Royce?"

Boeing and Mira never dreamed that Eisenhower would have any interest in or knowledge about hydroplane racing. As they began to answer the question, it became obvious that as Supreme Allied Commander in Europe during World War II, Eisenhower was familiar with both Rolls-Royce Merlins and Allisons because they had powered the fighters in the Allied air forces. Eisenhower seemed to be enjoying talking about something other than politics. Eventually, the conversation moved away from boats to airplanes. Eisenhower turned to Boeing and said, "I'm embarrassed to say this, and I'd never admit it to any of my Air Force generals, but I don't really understand what the big deal was about getting airplanes to fly through the speed of sound. Why was that so difficult?"

Bill Boeing felt like a schoolboy who had just been called up in front of the class to read an essay that he had forgotten to write. Boeing was a bright man, but he was not an engineer, and he had never been involved with the day-to-day operations at Boeing. His father had sold it off when he was still only twelve years old. Boeing understood aerodynamics, but he wasn't comfortable briefing the President of the United States on control surface flutter and transonic shock waves. Before Boeing was able to answer, Eisenhower's aide came in and said, "Mr. President, General Goodpaster is here to see you." Boeing relaxed, thinking he had been "saved by the bell." Eisenhower waved away the aide and said, "I've spent most of the morning with him. He can wait a few more minutes, I want to hear the answer to this." He turned back to Boeing and said, "Go ahead please."

Mira, recognizing Boeing's discomfort, jumped in. "Do you mind if I try to explain?"

"Go ahead, Mira," Boeing said casually, while his eyes betrayed a thousand "thank yous."

"Well, Mr. President, it's not that going faster than the speed of sound is all that difficult. Bullets, cannon balls, and artillery shells do it all of the time, but it is difficult for a winged vehicle to do it and maintain control. A plane flies because of lift, and lift only exists because there is a difference of pressure between the top and the bottom of the wing, with more pressure being on the bottom. So as the plane is flying along, it is pushing all this air in front of it, creating a dense wall of air right in front of the plane. As the plane approaches the speed of sound, the plane is moving too fast for this dense wall of air to stay ahead of the plane, so that wall starts to move over the plane, and as it does, it seriously disrupts the pressures on the wing and forces the center of lift back. Airplanes can only fly level because of the relationship between the center of lift and the center of gravity, so if you suddenly move the center of lift back by quite a bit, the plane becomes nose-heavy and dives into the ground. At the same time this is going on, the wall of dense air, which we are going to call a shock wave, is making all the control surfaces flutter back and forth too, so the pilot can't regain control of the plane and pull it out of its dive."

"So how did we solve that?"

"It was really a pretty simple but ingenious idea. We just began to angle the wings back so that the shock wave only hit one small section of the wing at a time. And the plane never went into the nosedive. We also beefed up the control surfaces to keep them from fluttering."

Eisenhower turned to Boeing and said, "This young man is quite impressive." Then he turned to Mira and said, "Where did you learn about aerodynamics?"

"When I was in the air force back in Czechoslovakia."

"Czechoslovakia? What a beautiful place. I went there. I was in Prague right after the war."

"I know. I was there too. I saw you and waved."

"Did I wave back?"

"No, I don't think so."

"Well, you should have come over and said 'Hello.'"

"I think that General Patton's Third Army Corps was standing between you and me so I didn't try it." Now it was Eisenhower's turn to laugh.

The harried aide came in again and repeated the message that General Goodpaster was waiting. Eisenhower waved him away. "Are you ready for your trophy?"

"Yes, Mr. President. But first, I would like to thank you personally for signing the bill that allowed me to get a radio operator's license and eventually a job flying for Continental Airlines."

"Oh, that's right. You defected from communist Czechoslovakia, didn't you? What was that like?" Mira launched into his well-rehearsed speech about the hijacking. The aide came back with a White House photographer and stood silently behind Eisenhower until Mira finished the story.

The actual presentation went quickly. Mira and Boeing stood next to the President's desk as he handed the trophy to Mira.[2] The photographer took several photos with his big 4 × 5-inch press camera. When they were all done posing, Eisenhower shook hands with Boeing and Mira and they were ushered out of the room. Mira looked at his watch. It was 12.40 p.m. The meeting was supposed to take fifteen minutes, but they had ended up spending forty-five minutes with the President.

23

Leaving: Seattle, 1960

The first race of the 1960 season was the Apple Cup, on May 8. Most race fans and sports reporters felt that the boat to beat would be the *Miss Thriftway*, because earlier in the year, on February 16, Bill Muncey had driven the *Thriftway* to a new world water-speed record of 192.001 miles per hour on a measured mile course on Lake Washington, making the *Thriftway* the fastest propeller-driven boat in the world.

Slovak got time off from Continental Airlines to race in Chelan. He clearly was not intimidated by Muncey's record. It was one thing to be able to go fast in a straight line, but to win races, you had to be able to get through the turns fast. Slovak in the *Wahoo* outperformed Muncey and the *Miss Thriftway* to become the fastest qualifier. Third on the qualifying ladder behind Slovak and Muncey was Ron Musson, who had been hired to drive the *Hawaii Kai III,* which had been purchased by Joe Mascari.

Race morning was chilly and clear. The drivers were wearing coats as they gathered for the pre-race drivers' meeting. Mira walked into the pits with rookie driver Rex Manchester, a tall and good-looking ex-Marine from Spokane who was a successful limited driver. Muncey and Musson were standing together at the pit entrance, smoking cigarettes. Mira said a pleasant "Good morning."

Muncey answered with, "Morning, Slim."

Musson blew a stream of smoke out of the side of his mouth and said, "Stand back boys, we 'little guys' don't want to get in the way of the hotshot refugee."

Muncey gave Mira a confused look and said, "What's that all about?" Mira shook his head and walked away.

Musson turned to Manchester and said, "See, he's running away. It's what Slovak does best. He ran away from the commies, and now he's running away from me." While Manchester laughed, Mira just kept walking.

Heat 1A was made up of the *Wahoo,* the *Thriftway,* the *Hawaii Kai*, and Sam DuPont's *Nitrogen*, which was driven by Norm Evans. It was the first race of the year and the start was pretty ragged. All the boats were late. As they moved around the west turn, getting ready for the run to the start, the *Nitrogen* was in lane one, the *Wahoo* was way outside in lane four or five, and the *Thriftway* and the *Hawaii Kai* trailed the field. The *Nitrogen* was first across the line, seven seconds late. The *Wahoo* was running fast on the outside and pulled up alongside the *Nitrogen*. Meanwhile, Muncey and Musson were catching the field. Musson ducked into lane one and Evans slid out to lane two. Muncey was flying up from behind Mira in lane three. As he entered the first turn, Slovak, thinking that Muncey was still way behind and outside, moved in to take lane three next to the *Nitrogen*. Muncey, just a few boat lengths back, and running 160 mph, got a fire hose to the face as the *Wahoo's* roostertail drenched him. The *Thriftway* coasted to a stop while the *Wahoo* sprinted away to an uncontested victory. The rule book said you needed a three boat-length lead to change lanes, so Mira was not penalized, but from Muncey's perspective, it looked like a dirty move. Mira ran the first lap at 113.684 miles per hour, which was the fastest lap of the day. Muncey got the waterlogged *Miss Thriftway* restarted and finished third.

Mira returned to the pits, shut off the boat, and coasted in to the dock. He leapt from the boat to celebrate the victory with his crew. He was surprised by how somber everyone on the dock was. "What's wrong?" he asked.

"You need to go apologize to Muncey. You got him really good!" Boeing said.

"How? He was way outside, wasn't he?"

"Nope he was in lane three and you hosed him down going into the first turn."

"Oh no!" Still wearing his life jacket, he headed toward the *Thriftway* pit calling out, "Billy! Billy!"

Muncey was surrounded by reporters and was being interviewed live by KOMO-TV. As Mira approached, Muncey turned and pointed at him, "You bastard!"

"What the hell are you talking about?"

Muncey turned to the reporters and said, "That son of a bitch hosed me down. He didn't think he could beat me fair and square, so he tried to put me out of the race with his roostertail before it even started!"

"I didn't see you, Billy! God help me I didn't see you!" Muncey ignored his apologies.

They were both drawn into the next heat. When the five-minute gun sounded, the two boats pulled away from the pits together. While the boats were still getting up to speed, Muncey stepped on the accelerator hard and jumped ahead of the *Wahoo*. Then, with a sudden jerk, he swung the wheel to the left so that the *Miss Thriftway* cut right across the *Wahoo's* bow, and the *Thriftway's* roostertail showered Mira, drowning out the *Wahoo's* engine.

Mira was furious—what he had done was a simple accident; what Muncey did was intentional. He restarted the *Wahoo* and took off after Muncey. He flew the *Wahoo* up the backstretch and caught the *Thriftway* in the west turn. They made a perfect start, hitting the line side by side at 160 mph. Muncey was inside and Mira was outside as they roared into the first turn together and were still side by side when they came bouncing out onto the backstretch. The two boats continued to run neck and neck for a full lap. Midway through lap two, the *Wahoo* seemed to slow on the backstretch and the *Thriftway* pulled about five boat lengths ahead. It was a feint. Mira dove through Muncey's roostertail and stole the inside lane, then accelerated hard and barreled past the *Thriftway* into turn two. Muncey was looking over his right shoulder trying to find Mira while Mira blew past him on the left. Mira hugged the buoy line while Muncey swung to the outside to make the turn as wide as possible and preserve as much speed as he could. From outside in lane five, Muncey was running at least 20 miles an hour faster. He tightened up the turn, dove towards the exit buoy, and mashed the accelerator to the floor, hoping to time it perfectly and reach the exit a fraction of a second before Mira and douse him with his roostertail again. Mira saw what Muncey was up to and came up with a countermove. Three quarters of the way through the turn, while Muncey and Mira were still on converging paths that would bring them together at the exit buoy, Mira turned hard to the right so that the speeding *Wahoo* flashed across the bow of the *Thriftway* at 90 degrees, almost like he was crossing a "T." The *Wahoo's* roostertail soaked Muncey and the *Thriftway* coasted to a stop. The *Wahoo* pulled into the lead all by herself while Muncey struggled to restart the *Thriftway*.[1]

After a few moments, Muncey was able to get going again and began to chase down the *Wahoo*. On the fifth and final lap, the Thriftway pulled even with the *Wahoo*, and then with a loud bang, the *Wahoo's* waterlogged engine broke and Mira coasted to a stop in the infield. Muncey roared by to win the heat.

Back at the dock, during the post-race interviews, Muncey had some choice words for Mira. "Today is Mother's Day, and he wanted to kill me in front of my wife on Mother's Day! I'd have run him down if I hadn't backed off! I have a wife and children. Slovak's a bachelor. Maybe he doesn't care."

Mira sat out the next heat, saying, "We're in racing for fun. When the fun goes, I want to get out. I was wrong and I knew it. It was dirty, but he was dirty with me, so when that happens, I say 'Okay, smell it yourself.' I'm not proud about it, but I did it. I could say it was an accident, I could say I couldn't keep the boat tight on the turn. But no, I did it on purpose."[2] Mira went on to say that he was "disgusted and sick" about the whole incident and quickly left town to return to Denver and flying airliners.

Muncey won the final heat and the race. When he came back to the pits, he was all smiles for the reporters. "Well, that was superb! I won this race as a Mother's Day gift for my wife Kit and our three sons."

A reporter asked, "Do you have any hard feelings for Slovak?"

Muncey responded with, "It's hard to have hard feelings when you win!" Yet there were hard feelings, and it was three years before Muncey and Mira exchanged friendly words again.

The first week of August 1960 looked to be big one for Mira. On Thursday, August 4, *Sports Illustrated* published a big story about Mira, calling him "One of the top two drivers on the unlimited hydroplane circuit."[3] On August 7, Mira would compete for $10,000 in Seattle's Seafair Trophy Race, and the next day he was scheduled to take his citizenship test and finally become a U.S. citizen.

The media in Seattle were fascinated by the Slovak-Muncey fight. One radio station ran a call-in poll so listeners could vote about whose side they were on. The poll ran seventeen to one in Mira's favor, and to no one's surprise, most of Mira's supporters were young women.

Race day morning was warm and sunny. Crowds were huge and enthusiastic. Seventeen boats had qualified, and the field was divided into three sections for the first heat. Mira was in heat 1B and Muncey was in 1C, so the anticipated rematch between the two would have to wait. On paper, heat 1B looked pretty easy for Mira, with his stiffest competition coming from the *Miss Spokane* and the *Miss Seattle Too,* both boats he had beaten several times before.

At the start of the heat, Mira grabbed lane one and was first across the line but was moving slowly. The *Seattle Too* was in lane two and the *Miss Spokane* in lane three. They both flew past Mira on the run to the first turn. Mira knew that he had blown the start, so he accelerated hard toward the turn. He caught the *Miss Spokane*, but the *Seattle Too* was far enough ahead that Mira had to run in water that was churned up and lumpy. He could not reach anywhere near full speed, and he lost more ground. Coming out of the turn, he was over ten boat lengths behind and falling back. The *Too* crossed into lane one, and then Mira had to deal with even worse water. Heading up the backstretch, Mira moved outside, looking for smoother water. He found it in lane two and put the accelerator down hard, rocketing up the back stretch and gaining on the *Seattle Too.* While the *Too* slowed to enter turn two, Mira kept the throttle wide open, thinking, "I'm going to catch him now."

As the *Wahoo* started to slide into the turn, she hit the *Miss Seattle Too's* wake and took a big hop, landing sideways, with the right sponson digging into the water and throwing up a tower of spray. The boat tipped violently to the right. Mira tried to hold onto the steering wheel but felt it pulled from his hands, and suddenly he was flying through the air. His first thought was, "I'm out of the boat!" He landed hard on his back at over 150 miles per hour. The air was punched out of his lungs. Like a diver from a high dive, he penetrated deep into the water. He was equally aware of three sensations at once. First was the sudden silence of going under water. The noise of the boats and their roaring engines all disappeared. Second was the violence of the water trying to force itself into his nose, mouth, and ears. Third, he desperately needed to breathe and he could not. Nearby, the *Wahoo* continued to tumble across the surface of the lake, shedding parts. The tailfin broke off, the cockpit flew high into the air, and pieces of broken deck littered the water.

After what seemed like an eternity, but was actually only a second or two, Mira surfaced. He spit water from his mouth and tried to take a deep breath, but he could not. For an instant, his mind filled with fear. "Am I going to die?" He tried again and still could not breathe. "You've just had the wind knocked out of you," he told himself, "You'll get your breath back soon." He tried to breathe a third time. This time, he made a rasping, gasping sound and felt a small bit of wet air fill his lungs. He gasped again and finally felt his lungs fill, but he swallowed water too and began to cough. Each cough sent waves of pain through his body. He was floating on his back. His lifejacket was keeping his face just barely out of the water. He opened his eyes and saw blue sky above him. Then, the bright yellow bottom of a Coast Guard rescue helicopter slowly moved into view. It hovered over him, not more than 30 feet in the air. The rotor wash was powerful and whipped the water into tiny darts that stung his exposed face.

A door on the side of the copter was open and a man wearing a black rubber wetsuit and swim fins was sitting on the door sill of the copter. He was Tom Regan, a King County Sheriff's Deputy who volunteered with the Coast Guard Auxiliary. He slid feet first out of the door and landed with a splash a few feet away. With only a couple of strokes, Regan reached him. "How do you feel?" he asked. Mira could not think of any English words and continued to gasp for air. The helicopter used an electric winch to lower a rescue basket, which sank into the water next to Mira. Regan maneuvered Mira into the basket. The copter started to winch the basket up. The rotor wash was intense, and Mira was aware of how cold he was. It was a warm summer day, but he felt himself start to shiver as if it were well below freezing. As he reached the helicopter, his teeth were chattering. The basket was pulled inside and the copter flew back to the Stan Sayres Pits, landing on a barge anchored at the eastern tip. An ambulance crew was waiting, and as soon as the copter landed, Mira was transferred to a gurney and wheeled past a sea of worried faces. Mira recognized Bill Boeing, Junie, Bill Stead, and Donnie Wilson. The uniformed ambulance drivers loaded Mira into the back of the ambulance and swung the door closed. One of the ambulance attendants pulled out a pair of shears and quickly cut the straps on Mira's helmet and life jacket, tossing them to one side. He checked Mira's pulse and began prodding his arms, chest, and legs, looking for broken bones. Mira continued to shiver. The attendant said, "He's going into shock." Mira was wrapped in a heavy, coarse khaki-colored army blanket. With its siren blaring, the ambulance raced away, making it to Seattle's Virginia Mason Hospital in a few minutes.

During the ambulance ride, Mira's head began to clear, and he could tell that aside from a whole bunch of sore muscles and bruises, he was not really hurt. He was embarrassed and angry with himself. The *Wahoo* was a much better boat than the *Miss Seattle Too*, and if he had just been patient he would have had plenty of time to catch her. He made a lousy start and then compounded the error by trying to make up too much ground too quickly. "Well, I won't make that mistake again," he thought.

At the hospital, he was helped out of his wet driver's suit and given a complete examination. The emergency room doctors confirmed that there were not any broken bones, but considering the violence of the accident, they were worried about a concussion and internal injuries, so they wanted to keep him for forty-eight hours' observation. They admitted Mira to the hospital and wheeled him to a private room. A short while later, Bill Jr. and Junie showed up. They were worried about Mira, and Mira was worried about the *Wahoo*. "How bad is it? Can she be repaired?" Mira asked.

"Shhh," Bill said. "Don't worry about the boat. We want to know about you. How are you?"

"It was my fault. I blew the start, and then I drove too hard into the turn. It was entirely my fault. Did the *Wahoo* sink?"

"I don't care about the boat. I want to know how you are doing."

Junie chuckled and said, "Bill, I think he's fine. If he wasn't asking about the boat I'd be worried, but he's more worried about the boat than he is about himself. That's typical Mira."

"Are you okay?" Bill asked again.

"Yes, I'm fine, but how is the boat? Can we repair her?"

"I'm glad that you're fine, because there's something I need to say to you. The *Wahoo* can be repaired, but I'm not going to do it. If we rebuild, and have another accident, the odds are going to stack up against us. You know I only got into this sport for fun, and today, watching the *Wahoo* crash and thinking that maybe you were dead, I realized that I'm not having fun. I don't want to do this again. I'm retiring. There is always a right time to get out and this is the time. The *Wahoo* is finished!"

The room was silent. Mira spoke first. "I've always said that we'll finish together. We've done our share. So if you are done, Mr. Boeing, I'm done too. It's up to the other guys now."[4]

"Okay," Junie said, "I guess we need to call a press conference."

That was when it hit Mira. Not only was the *Wahoo* finished and he was finished as a driver, but if he was being held at the hospital for forty-eight hours, he was going to miss his citizenship examination too.

24

Citizen Slovak: Seattle, 1961

Mira stayed in the hospital a few more days, and then moved into the Cechs' house to recuperate. He was able to reschedule his citizenship test for August 18. The test consisted of a list of 100 questions. The examiner can ask any ten questions from the list, and the applicant must answer at least six correctly. Mira answered all his questions correctly, including: Who was the first President of the United States, how many years is a senator's term, and how many Supreme Court Justices are there?

Mira would need to return to Seattle for an oath-taking ceremony, but the flight back to Denver was not quite so gloomy for him, knowing that he had finally cleared the last hurdle to becoming a U.S. citizen.

Before the Seafair Race, Continental had assigned Mira to fly with forty-year-old veteran captain William Albert "Bill" Hart, who had served in World War II, flying for the Army Air Corps in North Africa. He began flying DC-3s for Continental in 1946. Hart's father, Jess, had been a captain for Continental since before the war, and together they had made up Continental's first father-and-son flight crew when they flew a DC-3 together on December 4, 1946. Even though Hart was only eight years older than Mira, they quickly developed a "mentor-student" relationship, based on Hart's fourteen years of seniority at Continental.

Pilots joke about their jobs as "hours of boredom punctuated by moments of sheer terror." During the time Mira and Hart flew together, there were never any moments of sheer terror, but they passed the many hours of boredom by telling each other stories from their past. Mira talked about Czechoslovakia and Hart related stories about growing up in the Southern California town of Santa Paula.

When Mira returned to flying after the *Wahoo* accident, Hart could tell that something was different. Mira wasn't able to express it, but Hart thought he knew what was going on. He had been through it himself at the end of the World War II, when he and thousands of other young men had returned from combat. Some men thrived under the intense pressure of combat. The split-second life-or-death decisions, the respect of their fellow men, and the sense of purpose were an intoxicating mix. Many veterans had a hard time giving it up and returning to the normal day-to-day life of commuting to work, buying groceries, and mowing the lawn. Hart imagined that Mira's life in racing, his escape from communism, and his work with the CIA had held the same attractions to him that combat had for so many World War II veterans. Giving it all up suddenly was causing him the same type of problems that returning pilots faced at the end of the war. Hart had been able to battle through it and he thought he knew how to help Mira too. The answer was in building a new life that provided reason and purpose. Hart figured that he knew of a perfect place for Mira to find that purpose.

Mira and Hart often flew Continental flights into Los Angeles. One September afternoon when the autumn winds blew the smog away and the warm air that rushed past their car windows smelled like sagebrush and cypress, they drove out of Los Angeles on U.S. 101 and headed north through the Santa Monica hills to the Santa Clara River valley. There, nestled between citrus orchards and oil wells, was Hart's home town of Santa Paula. Sitting beside the Santa Clara River, with a population of 13,000, Santa Paula boasted a gem of an airport with runways of crushed gravel and aprons of green buffalo grass. It was a Mecca for sport flyers. Hart gave Mira a first-rate tour of the town and airport and ended up introducing him to his cousins, Mildred and Rex Wells. Mildred was well known in the aviation community for her extraordinary ability to repair and replace fabric on older planes.

To people who do not fly, an airport is a collection inanimate structures—hangars, ramps, taxiways, fuel trucks, an FBO (Fixed Base of Operation), and of course the runway. To a flyer, an airport is a living thing made up of a collection of familiar but unique personalities. Every airport has a mechanical wizard who can fix anything. No matter what your problem is, he can walk into the back room of his cluttered shop and find the one part you need to get your plane flying again. There will often be a couple of airline pilots who are frustrated by the big, stable, multi-engine planes they fly for a living. They are bored with planes that reduce flying to riding from point "A" to point "B" in an air-conditioned room full of gauges and needles, so they keep a bright, sexy little stunt plane on the side, and like a cheating husband, the minute they can slip away from their safe stable airliner they are down at the airport tending to their shiny new stunt plane. You will also find a veteran or two who flew in the last war, and they always seem to know everything and are happy to tell you exactly what you did wrong, just a few moments after you did it, but no one can remember seeing them actually fly a plane in years. There will usually be two or three maintenance shops or charter operations or crop dusters that are teetering on the verge of bankruptcy, but somehow survive from day to day. Mira felt at home and he recognized every skilled, quirky personality at the Santa Paula Airport as a kindred soul who loved flying as much as he did. He began making plans to bring *Moonshine* down for some work. In the back of his mind, he felt a connection to Santa Paula that he knew would pull him back again and again.

Mira returned to Denver, and his mood improved when he found that the beautiful Ingrid Bondi was assigned to his flight. He asked her out again, and again she said no, but at least she still smiled when she was saying no.

In the middle of October, he got a long-distance phone call that caused him to clap his hands together and exclaim "yes!" Junie called to tell him that Bill Boeing had turned the damaged *Wahoo* over to the crew and told them to "do whatever they wanted" with the boat. They had worked day and night, and the boat was repaired; if Mira could get the time off, they were going to race for the 1960 Gold Cup on Lake Mead, outside Las Vegas, on November 14.

Sixteen boats showed up for the race, and Mira qualified at 113.250 mph, coming within half a second of being the fastest qualifier, losing out only to Donnie Wilson's 114.697 in *Miss U.S.* Unfortunately, race day was windy and the race was canceled. Flying back to Denver, Mira felt as if a weight had been lifted from his shoulders. The *Wahoo* was back in one piece, like an old friend resurrected from the dead, and he had been able to go back out in the boat and turn in some impressive lap times. The sense of embarrassment and guilt after the Seafair accident was wiped away.

On January 4, 1961, Mira returned to Seattle and took a cab from the airport to the Federal Courthouse. He had come for his oath-taking ceremony for U.S. citizenship. Wearing a dark suit, a white shirt, and a thin dark tie, he entered the courthouse, walking past Wayne Richardson's door with the unobtrusive number twelve painted on it. When he got to the elevator bay, he checked the directory for Judge John Bowen's courtroom. He pushed the button and waited along with several other nervous applicants and their families. When the elevator dinged and the doors slid open, they all crowded into the tiny car. Moments later they reached their floor and with another ding, the metal doors opened and the anxious group of passengers headed into U.S. District Court for the Western District of Washington. Mira was surprised to see that the large courtroom was packed. Including Mira, there were 104 applicants on hand in Judge Bowen's courtroom to take their oaths. The applicants represented the far reaches of the globe. The tangle of voices and accents in the courtroom sounded like the lobby of the United Nations.

Mira was nervous. He knew he did not have anything to worry about, but this was still a big step and it was only natural to be anxious. He looked around the crowded room, hoping to see a friendly face. He made eye contact with Ernest Ayers, the naturalization examiner who had administered his citizenship test. Ayers gave Mira a thumbs-up, and Mira smiled and returned the gesture.

The bailiff entered the court and announced, "All rise for the Honorable Judge John C. Bowen." The babble of voices was replaced by the scraping of feet and rustling of clothes as more than 100 people stood at once.

Judge Bowen, in a long black robe, entered the courtroom and took his seat at the bench. "You may be seated," he said, as he picked up a single piece of papers from his desk and said, "Is applicant Miroslav Slovak in the courtroom?"

Mira stood and raised his hand. "Here, your honor. I'm here."

"Please approach the bench."

Mira felt a tightening in his stomach as he walked past all the other applicants. His earlier anxiety was now giving way to genuine concern. He wondered, "Is there something wrong or is this some new unexpected accolade like the *This is Your Life* program from the previous year?" He stopped in front of the bench and looked up at Judge Bowen. "Your honor?"

Bowen looked at paper and said, "Mr. Slovak, have you ever been a member of the Communist Party?"

Mira was stunned. He felt his heart begin to pound and was short of breath. What was happening? It took a few moments to gather his wits, but then he said, "Yes your honor ... In 1948, I was forced."

The Judge held up a hand to stop Mira and pointed at the paper. "It says here that you formally renounced your membership in the Communist Party on June 16, 1955. Is that correct?"

"Yes your honor."

Judge Bowen said, "Mr. Slovak, U.S. law prohibits granting citizenship to anyone who has been a member of the Communist Party until at least ten years after they have renounced their membership. That means that the earliest that you will be eligible to apply for citizenship will be June of 1965."

Mira was in shock. He tried to think of something to say, but the only words that came to him were Czech, and he knew that addressing the judge in Czech wouldn't help his case. Suddenly Ernest Ayers was standing next to him saying, "Your Honor, I am Ernest Ayers, the naturalization examiner who approved Mr. Slovak's application. May I approach the bench?"

"You may."

"Your honor, the statute you reference does indeed bar citizenship to members of the Communist Party, but it also provides an exemption for cases such as that of Slovak. Mr. Slovak did not voluntarily join the Communist Party, but was coerced in order to obtain food and other essentials of living."

"Is this true, Mr. Slovak?"

"Yes, your honor."

A second man appeared next to Mira. "Your Honor, my name is Richard F. Broz and I am an Assistant United States Attorney, prepared to argue on behalf of applicant Slovak." It was highly unusual for a U.S. Attorney to appear suddenly at an oath-taking ceremony. Judge Bowen was taken aback.

"We have, ahh," he looked at a folder on his desk, "We have 103 other applicants who are awaiting the administration of their oaths, so let's proceed with them first, and then I'll hear your arguments in support of applicant Slovak. Mr. Broz, when you do present your arguments, please provide the court with the full text of the statute in question."

"I will, your honor." Broz turned and left the courtroom, presumably in search of a copy of the statute. Judge Bowen asked Mira and Ayers to take their seats. He then asked all the remaining applicants to stand, raise their right hands, and repeat after him as he administered the oath.

Mira felt miserable watching 103 refugees becoming U.S. citizens while he sat dejectedly in a chair at the side of the court room. Ayers whispered encouragement. "Don't worry. We can get this all sorted out." When the oath was finished, there was a rousing cheer from many of the new citizens. Husbands and wives kissed and families hugged and laughed. After a few moments of celebration, the happy families headed out of the courtroom to start their joyous new lives. Eventually, there were just a few people left in the room. Mira and Ayres sat by themselves as the court staff prepared for the next trial. The only one left in the gallery was a reporter for the *Seattle Times* waiting to see how Mira's hearing turned out. Finally, Broz returned, carrying a large beige book with a red band on the spine.

Judge Bowen signaled Broz, Ayers, and Mira to approach the bench. Broz opened the dictionary-sized book and read, "U.S. Code, Title 8, Chapter 12, Subchapter III, part II, page 1424. No person shall hereafter be naturalized as a citizen of the United States who is a member or affiliated with the Communist Party."

Mira hardly heard the words as Broz read on and on. His mind was filled with the horrible consequences of the denial of his citizenship. He would lose his job at Continental; then his apartment. Maybe he would have to move back into the Cechs' basement again. His negative train of thought was derailed when Broz finally read, "If such person establishes that such membership was involuntary or was for the purposes of obtaining employment, food rations, or other essentials of living …"

Judge Bowen interrupted Broz and said, "Applicant Slovak, do you claim that you were coerced into joining the Communist Party and that you only joined to be able to work and eat?"

"I do, your honor."

"Do you have any hesitancy in accepting citizenship?"

"No, your honor. I know how people in my country were treated and how their property was taken. I can be a strong hater of communism and loyal citizen of the United States."[1]

Judge Bowen nodded thoughtfully. "Mr. Slovak, please raise your right hand and repeat after me."

"I hereby declare, on oath, that I absolutely and entirely renounce and abjure all allegiances and fidelity to any foreign prince, potentate, state, or sovereignty of whom or which I have heretofore been a subject or citizen; that I will support and defend the Constitution and the laws of the United States of America against any and all enemies, foreign and domestic; that I will bear true faith and allegiance to the same;

"That I will bear arms on behalf of the United States when required by law; That I will perform non-combatant services in the Armed Forces of the United States when required by law; That I will perform work of national importance under civilian direction when required by the law; and that I take this obligation freely without any mental reservation or purpose of evasion: so help me God."[2]

As Mira completed the oath, he felt silent tears of pride and joy roll down his cheeks. He closed his eyes to savor the moment. He thought he was alone in the almost empty courtroom, but suddenly he felt someone giving him a fierce bear hug. He opened his eyes to see Wayne Richardson embracing him with tears in his own eyes.

"That was a close one," Richardson said.

Mira ran a finger in between his shirt and his neck and said, "Whew! That was pretty rough."

Richardson shook Broz's hand. "Thank you for coming to bat for us there at the last second."

Broz shook Richardson's hand and said, "I'm always happy to help."

Richardson put his hand on Mira's shoulder and said, "I promised you'd get here. It took a little while longer than I'd hoped, but here we are. You're a U.S. citizen and you're flying for a U.S. airline!"

The two friends took the elevator to the first floor and walked across to the Kennedy Hotel. Richardson took Mira to the big circular booth in back of the restaurant and ordered him a gigantic rib eye, well done, and a couple of cocktails. Mira sat with him all afternoon as one after another, Mira's closest friends came by to congratulate him.

25

New Beginnings: Seattle, 1962

Junie Cech tried hard to find a sponsor for the 1961 Seafair Race. For a while, he was sure that he had the backing of the Washington Athletic Club. He was so sure that Mira scheduled time off and flew to Seattle. On the day the *Wahoo* was set to move into the pits, the deal fell apart, and Mira ended up watching the race from the pits. Even without a boat, Mira still drew attention. On Saturday, August 5, the *Seattle Times* ran a photo of Mira and a headline that said, "No Boat, But Guy Is Still A Hero." The story claimed, "Mira Slovak and the *Wahoo* won't appear in the Seafair Race, but he was still the most popular guy in the pit area." Ron Musson won the race driving Mira's old *Miss Bardahl,* and the newspaper headlines said, "Musson dethrones Muncey." In an interview in Monday's paper, Mira said, "This is the last boat race I'm seeing from outside of a boat. I can't take this."

Without racing to distract him, Mira was able to devote more of his attention to flying. He was promoted from DC-3s to 707s. By early winter 1962, he was ready for a vacation. He took a skiing trip to the Swiss Alps. On his way, he changed planes in Frankfurt and picked up a German aviation magazine. Casually thumbing through the pages as he waited to board his next flight, he saw that the Czech Air Force was selling off its outdated Bücker Bü 131 trainers. Mira had learned to fly in a Bü 131, and like a young man pining for a long-lost love, he had always wanted to be reunited with one. So he cut short his skiing and began hunting Bückers. He found one in Vienna, Austria, but it was too far gone and he did not think it could be restored. He found a second plane in Zurich and shipped it back to Mildred and Rex Wells at Bassett Aviation in Santa Paula, to have it restored.

While Mira was in Switzerland buying his Bücker, Bill Stead and Chuck Lyford were hatching a plan that would stun the aviation world. Lyford and Stead were in Cincinnati for the 1962 American Power Boat Association Winter Meeting.

Chuck Lyford had grown up two doors down from Blanche and Frank Cech. He was a dozen years younger than Mira and was fascinated with boat racing. He began driving eight-foot JU (Junior Utility) outboards at eleven years old. By the early 1960s, Lyford was driving a 7-liter hydro named the *Challenger,* and won back-to-back national championships in 1960 and 1961. He was at the 1962 APBA Winter meeting to collect his trophy. Stead was at the meeting to pitch a new unlimited race to be held on Lake Tahoe and sponsored by casino magnate, Bill Harrah.

Lyford had been introduced to flying by Mira, who often took him up in the *Moonshine* to perform aerobatics over the Seattle suburb of Bellevue. Stead and Lyford became friends and began to talk about airplanes. Lyford pointed out that they were only an hour and a half drive away from the Air Force Museum at Wright-Patterson Air Force Base and that he had never seen it. Stead offered to drive up with him, and the two soon set off on a road trip. On the way, they began to talk about the National Air Races that used to take place in Cleveland. The races began in the early 1920s and were a huge deal until they were canceled in 1949 after Bill Odom's P-51 Mustang *Beguine* crashed into a house, killing a young mother and her infant son.

Lyford and Stead figured with all the people they knew who owned Allisons and Merlins, plus all the people they knew who could put on a race, it would be easy to bring back the National Air Races using World War II-era fighter planes and unlimited hydroplane rules. Stead suggested that his 250,000-acre Sky Ranch outside of Reno could host the event. Nevada had become a state in 1864 and a centennial celebration was planned for 1964; Stead felt certain that he could get the air race funded as part of the centennial festivities. Suddenly, the dream started to look very real.

In early 1963, Continental moved its headquarters from Denver to Los Angeles and Mira moved to LA, renting an apartment on the ninth floor of the elegant Barrington Plaza on Wilshire Boulevard. Ingrid Bondi continued to fly on Mira's flights. He continued to ask her out, and she continued to politely say no. It was now something of a running joke, with Mira and Ingrid's friends wondering if Mira would give up before Ingrid gave in.

Between the 1962 and 1963 racing seasons, Mira was offered a job driving Milo and Glen Stoen's brand-new *Miss Exide.* Before accepting the job, Mira wrote to Bill Harrah, offering to drive his new *Tahoe Miss.* Harrah's team manager, Harry Volpi, sent Mira a letter thanking him for his interest but concluding, "I regret to say, we have already secured the services of Chuck Thompson from Detroit."

Mira went ahead and signed with the Stoen brothers. The boat was sponsored by the Exide Batteries Division of the Electric Storage Battery Company, of Cleveland, Ohio. The name Exide was short for "Excellent Oxide" battery. Designed by Ted Jones and built by Ed Karelsen, the new boat had a thinner profile and a wider beam than most of Jones's previous designs. Mira's new job driving the *Exide* was announced in the *Seattle Post-Intelligencer* with a quarter-page story on June 4, 1963. The headline read: "Colorful Hydro Driver Returns." The *Miss Exide* was colorful, too. The company's press release said the boat was "mandarin red and aqua blue." The boat also had a red-and-white checkered tailfin and bright white lightning bolts on the deck. She was given the number U-75, to celebrate the company's seventy-fifth anniversary. The new boat was launched at Stan Sayres Pits on the afternoon of Friday, June 7. It was a cold day, with black clouds that turned the wind-ruffled waters of Lake Washington slate gray.

Launching a new unlimited hydroplane was a full-scale media event. TV lights glared as Milo Stoen's wife, Ginny, christened *Miss Exide* by shattering a bottle of Champagne across the boat's bright-red bow. Bill Muncey and Ron Musson were both on hand to witness Mira's return to racing. Seattle's news media predicted that the 1963 season would be a battle between Muncey's tried-and-true *Thriftway* and Musson's new *Miss Bardahl*. Muncey and Musson were cordial but kept out of the limelight, eventually walking to a long finger pier that would allow them a close-up view of the *Exide* at speed. A crane lowered the boat into the water and Mira walked out on the dock, helmet in hand. Just before he leapt across to the deck, Seafair Queen Gail Reid, in a sparkling tiara and white satin robe, gave Mira an enthusiastic kiss on his cheek, leaving a bright red lipstick imprint.

As he settled into the seat, camera shutters clicked and flashbulbs popped. The brand-new boat smelled of sawdust, fiberglass, and fresh paint. Mira tried to block out all the distractions. The joyous ceremony on the dock might have been light-hearted, but it was time for serious business. Fans and reporters thought of test sessions as fun and safe. In reality, they were one of the most dangerous parts of racing. The hundreds of parts to a new unlimited hydroplane were untested; any one of them could fail with catastrophic results. Adding to the stress was the fact that Mira had not been in a race boat for three years and was feeling a bit rusty. Mira concentrated on the *Exide's* dashboard. The old routine came back easily, and he began to flip the shiny silver toggle switches—master on, magnetos on, boost pump on, mix handle all the way back; hold down the starter switch, wait three seconds, and tap the primer; wait three more seconds, tap the primer again, and the engine thundered to life. The *Exide* moved away from the dock, picking up speed.

Stan Sayres Pits fronts a small lagoon in Lake Washington. To exit the lagoon, drivers have to make a fairly hard right turn. When the boat was traveling at about 50 miles per hour, Mira turned the steering wheel to the right to head toward the racecourse. Unbelievably, the boat began to point left toward the shore. Mira centered the wheel and the boat tracked straight again. "Is the steering hooked up backwards?" Running out of room in the lagoon, Mira had to act fast. He turned the wheel cautiously to the left and the nose of the boat swung to the right. He had a choice to make. He could try to drive the boat the way it was or he could shut it off and wave for a tow back to the pits to tell the crew about the problem. With all the media milling around, it would be impossible to keep the issue a secret, and it would be embarrassing to the Stoens and their brand-new sponsor.

Mira figured that he could handle a few laps with the steering backwards. He performed acrobatics and flew inverted frequently, and when you fly inverted, you have to think of the controls as being reversed because up has become down and left has become right, so by comparison, dealing with backwards steering would be easy. He continued onto the, course but just to be safe he began to chant, "Left is right, right is left. Left is right, right is left." He lined up on the straightaway and began to accelerate. The boat sped up to 120 mph and was handling nicely. He approached the first turn and it took every bit of self-control he could muster, but he swung the wheel hard to the right and the boat turned smoothly to the left. He made a wide, sweeping turn and headed back up lake. He made six fast laps, checking the instrument panel several times so he could tell crew chief George McKernan what all the gauges read. Before he came in, he caught sight of Muncey and Musson standing at the end of the dock. He could not resist a bit of showmanship and made two high-speed passes close to the dock before bringing the boat back to the pits to a standing ovation from the assembled fans and media. Climbing out of the boat, Mira declared that it was "Terrific!" Back on the dock, Mira was mobbed by reporters as he tried to take off his helmet and life jacket.

"How was it?"

"It was good to get back in a boat."

"How did the boat feel?"

"It's very responsive. Especially on the turns, but I couldn't learn much today. When we get up to 150 or 170, then we'll learn something."

One of the reporters pointed at Muncey, who was making his way through the crowd. "Are you going to take care of Muncey this year?"

"No, no, I'm only going to take care of one person—me!"

The wind began to pick up and soon the water was too rough to run again. The crowd broke up as the crew directed the crane to set the boat back on its trailer. While the team was packing away their tools, Mira called to George McKernan, "Hey Yorge, we need to talk." Mira put his arm around George's shoulder and walked with him to the end of the finger pier and said, "Yorge, we have a problem, when I turn the boat to the left, she goes to the right. When I turn to the right she goes to the left."

"Oh no! We put the steering box in backwards!" McKernan exclaimed.

The *Exide's* first race was the Gold Cup in Detroit on July 7. This was essentially a shakedown run for the new boat. Mira qualified at 107.570 mph, which placed him seventh fastest out of seventeen boats, but well behind Muncey and the *Miss Thriftway's* 116.33 mph. Mira ran a conservative race, finishing every heat he started and earning the team a fifth-place finish overall. Musson and the *Miss Bardahl* won.

The next race was the sixth annual Diamond Cup on Lake Coeur d'Alene, Idaho. The pits were crowded with thirteen boats when the course opened for qualifying Thursday morning, July 25. The temperature was over 90 degrees Fahrenheit. The air smelled of pine needles and racing fuel. Mira qualified respectably as the fourth-fastest boat at 109.312 mph but well behind Ron Musson's 118.421 mph. The *Miss Bardahl* was on a three-race winning streak, Ron Musson was the big new name in unlimited racing, with one newspaper asking, "Can Musson dethrone Muncey?"

The Diamond Cup was a two-day race, with one set of heats on Saturday, and a second and the final on Sunday. There was a drivers' meeting the Saturday before the first heat. As Mira was heading to the meeting, he heard a voice behind him saying, "Hey! Hey Slovak, wait up." Mira turned to see Musson hurrying toward him with a big grin. "Well, maybe all the hard feelings with him are behind us now," Mira thought. As he got close, Musson wagged a finger toward Mira and said, "Remember, us little guys get to go first!" and brushed past him into the meeting. Mira shook his head and thought, "Five years! This has been going on for five years now. When will it stop?"

Mira had an easy time winning heat 1A on Saturday. In heat 1B, Muncey battled deck-to-deck with Musson until the *Miss Bardahl's* Merlin engine broke a connecting rod and the green-and-yellow boat drifted to a stop while Muncey crossed the finish line to take the victory. Sunday was another perfect sunny day, and huge crowds came to the lake to watch the race. Mira won his second heat and so did Muncey. For the second time in as many days, the *Miss Bardahl* had failed to finish. All along the beach, the fans were excited. Muncey and Mira both had 800 points and the final heat was shaping up to be something they had not seen in three years—a classic Muncey/Slovak battle, with the winner of the heat winning the race.

In the pits, the crews were working hard under the blistering sun, preparing their boats for the final. One of the most important elements in the complicated equation of how to make a race boat go faster is the propeller. In the 1960s, a racing propeller for an unlimited hydroplane was only about 13.5 inches in diameter but could cost thousands of dollars. The propellers were machined out of steel and spun at about 10,000 rpm. Even the engineers who designed and built propellers did not fully understand how they worked. No two propellers acted the same way and no two boats responded the same way. Most teams had as many propellers as they could afford and tested them at the start of the season to find out which one was fastest in a given situation.

The Stoen brothers had one propeller that was faster than all their others, but they had never tried it on their new boat. Aside from being especially fast, this particular propeller had an unsettling characteristic. It lifted the rear of the boat a bit more than any of their others; since a hydroplane balances like a teeter-totter at the back of the sponsons, lifting the tail forces the nose down. The last time this propeller had been used was on the *Seattle Too*, in the 1962 Gold Cup. As the boats ran to the first turn at well over 160 mph, the *Seattle Too* took three hops, nosed in, and disintegrated.

The *Exide* had been riding poorly all through the Diamond Cup and had been prone to taking big leaps out of the water. Some crew members felt that the new boat was "too loose" and was getting too much air. Maybe bringing the nose down closer to the water was exactly what the wild-riding boat needed, so the decision was made to put the *Seattle Too* propeller on the *Exide* for the final heat.

Mira was nervous about the final. In an interview with Harry Missildine of the Spokane *Spokesman Review* he said, "I don' want to soun' cheeken but she isn't riding so good. I'd like to win, but I don theenk it's too safe to poosh her too fast right now."

A few moments later, Rex Manchester walked by, and Mira said, "Hey Rex, why don' you go out and race Munsley and I'll stand on shore and watch?"

The race was live on Spokane's KREM-TV, with cameras rolling as the boats pulled out from the pits. During the five-minute period, the two veteran drivers dueled to get on the inside of the other, and Mira won. They ran to the starting line with Mira in lane four and Muncey in lane five. Mira was first across the line, leading by a boat length, with Muncey on his hip. They roared into the first turn and Mira extended his lead. Heading up the back chute, the two boats began to pull away from the rest of the field. Coming off turn two, Muncey put on a burst of speed and pulled even with Mira as they flew past the official tower at 165 miles an hour to complete lap one. Muncey took a slight lead of no more than 50 feet as they started lap two and the *Thriftway's* roostertail blocked the *Exide* from view of most of the fans.

Suddenly, there was a tower of spray to Muncey's left, and broken parts of the *Exide* began to rain down on the course. The *Exide* had taken a couple of big hops and nosed in. The amount of energy released when a 6,500-pound boat noses into the water at 165 mph is almost the same as when 4 pounds of TNT is detonated. Mira was thrown through the windshield, gashing his face and knocking out teeth. He lost consciousness as he tumbled across the water. Behind him, the force of the water ripped the *Exide* to pieces, and splintered wood sailed into the air.

When the spray cleared, only the *Exide*'s checkerboard tailfin was still above water, and in a few brief seconds it was gone too as the boat sank 125 feet to the bottom of the lake. Red flares arced into the blue sky as the race officials warned the other drivers of the accident. The debris field was littered with wood and Styrofoam flotation. Warner Gardner, driving the *Notre Dame,* stopped and dove into the water, just like Mira had gone in after Muncey in 1957. When Gardner reached Mira, his first thought was, "He'll never survive." Mira was unconscious and bleeding from a large cut across his chin and from the space in his mouth where his front teeth should have been. Gardner rolled him onto his back and let the life jacket hold his face above water. A patrol boat arrived, carrying doctor Alexander "Bud" Barkley, who jumped into the water to tend to Mira. Gardner, Barkley, and a Coast Guard swimmer were able to load Mira into a stretcher and get him onboard the rescue boat that rushed him back to the pits, where a waiting ambulance, with its siren wailing, sped him to Lake City General Hospital. Preliminary reports from the hospital indicated that Mira had a broken right ankle, two missing front teeth, a gash on his face that required twenty-seven stitches, and was suffering from shock. In the rerun of the final heat, Muncey racked up enough points to win the race. The headline in the *Seattle Times* the next day read, "Muncey Wins, Slovak Back in the Hospital."

A few days later, Willard Rhodes announced that he and the *Miss Thriftway* were retiring at the end of the Seafair race. For the first time since 1955, Bill Muncey would be without a ride.

By Tuesday, July 30, Mira was in good spirits, flirting with the nurses, and he announced that if Milo and Glen Stoen could get a new boat put together in time, he wanted to drive it at Seafair. Working fast, the Stoen Brothers contacted Bill Boeing and purchased the *Wahoo*, along with four engines and all the gearboxes, propellers, and spare parts. If Mira was healthy enough to drive, they would be happy to have him; if not, they wanted Donnie Wilson to take over.

On August 1, the Stoens sent a plane to Coeur d'Alene to pick up Mira. When he got back to Boeing Field, he was met by Blanche, Marci, most of the *Exide* team, and a slew of reporters, who snapped photos of Mira with his leg in a cast and his face bandaged. He limped across the pavement to Aero Copter, where he held a brief press conference before getting a ride to Virginia Mason Hospital. Doctors determined that Mira had broken ribs and a couple of cracked vertebrae. He stayed at Virginia Mason until the next week. He was released in time to head to the Seafair pits and watch the replacement *Miss Exide* being launched. The *Exide* crew had only been able to change the name on the sides of the boat, but kept the *Wahoo's* mahogany deck and U-101.5 number. They had also added lightning bolts and a checkerboard tailfin. Behind the cockpit, it still said, "Driver: Mira Slovak."

Mira was publicly saying that he wanted to drive but he knew that he was not healed enough to get back into a boat. He also knew that in the last three races he had been in two serious accidents, and that Continental Airlines was thinking hard about allowing him to continue racing. The *Exide* was going to need a new driver, at least for Seafair. Donnie Wilson was not available, so Mira suggested Russ Schleeh. He was a good driver, he had been successful driving the *Shanty-I*, and he and Mira got along well. Russ signed on for a one-race deal and did well, getting the *Exide* qualified at 112.111 mph. Everyone agreed that as soon as Mira was up to it, he could have his old job back.

With no boat to drive, Mira sat with Keith Jackson in the play-by-play booth and provide color commentary for the race. Bill Harrah's *Tahoe Miss* won the race. The *Miss Bardahl* was second and the *Exide* was third.

On August 29, Continental gave Mira an ultimatum—he could race hydros or he could fly but he could no longer do both. Mira choose to fly for Continental. His retirement was announced on September 1. The *Miss Exide's* replacement driver, Bill Brow, won back-to-back races at Madison and Washington, D.C. in the former *Wahoo* hull. Mira was crushed to be giving up racing, but he did not mourn for long.

On September 20, Mira took delivery of his restored Bücker. Bassett Aviation and the Wellses had worked magic, and the old biplane sparkled like a gem. Tight new fabric stretched flawlessly over the Bücker's intricate skeleton. She was painted white, with black stripes trimmed in gold. Along the fuselage were tall black registration numbers—N121U. Behind the cockpit were the words, "Mira Slovak 'the poor refugee.'" On the vertical stabilizer was the gold lion of free Czechoslovakia, except that it was not actually the lion from the Czech coat of arms. Mira had not been able to find a photograph of the coat of arms, so, he had the painter copy the lion from the logo on a can of Coors beer.

On October 9, Mira took her up for the first time. The Bücker is a tiny plane, with an overall length of just under 22 feet and a wingspan of only 24 feet 3 inches. From inside the cockpit, the wings look almost too short to be believed. The 95-hp Walter Minor engine can push the plane to 115 mph, but flying a Bücker is not about speed; it is about the pure wind-borne joy of flying. There were a couple of features that made the Bücker especially agile in the air. First, unlike so many other biplanes, the Bücker had ailerons on both sets of wings. Additionally, where most planes connected the control stick to the control surfaces with cables, the Bücker used metal pushrods. These innovations gave the rugged little trainer highly responsive controls. Wearing a brown leather flight jacket, a matching flying cap, and black goggles, Mira taxied N121U to the head of runway 22 West, which paralleled the Santa Clara River. He ran the Walter Minor up to 2,000 rpm, did a magneto check, and released the brakes. The pretty little plane began to roll down the runway.

He watched as the air-speed indicator in the center of the instrument panel began to rise. At only 25 knots, he felt the tail of the plane come up and he was rolling level. At 40 knots, the plane began to feel light on her feet as if she wanted to spring into the air. At 60 knots, the plane lifted off. Mira flew over the end of the runway and began to climb to 500 feet. He banked to the left and circled the airport. For Mira, flying a Bücker again for the first time in a dozen years felt like coming home. Everything he loved about flying he had learned in the cramped cockpit of a Bücker biplane; it was safe and familiar, yet also exciting and rewarding. It was like reuniting with your first love and falling back into her arms for a warm, familiar kiss.

Mira climbed to 5,000 feet and headed 15 miles west toward the Pacific Ocean and the long sandy beaches that would make an emergency landing site if something went wrong. On his way, he tried an aileron roll, and the plane had a fantastic response rate, completing the roll in only six seconds without losing any altitude. Mira laughed and thought there was nothing as fun as watching the blue sky and the green earth trade places while framed by the wings and flying wires of a biplane. Next, he tried a stall. The plane climbed straight up and slowed, then stopped, without sliding off in either direction. With a quick kick of the rudder, the plane fell away in a smooth, well-mannered left turn and resumed level flying. It was time for a loop. He started with a slight dive to assure that he hit maximum airspeed and then pulled back on the stick, and the light plane responded crisply, climbing into the blue California sky. He began to lose speed at the top and ended up with more of a parabola than a smooth circle, but there would be plenty of time to practice.

After almost an hour, Mira returned to Santa Paula. Picking up the landing pattern south of town at 1,500 feet, he used visual landmarks to guide himself home. He made his cross-wind turn when he saw Peck Road and descended to 850 feet. When he was over the old junkyard, he turned onto the downwind leg. Then he turned onto the base leg when he crossed over the Santa Ana River, and onto the final when saw Highway 126. Descending toward the runway, he locked the tail wheel in place. He made a final check of the bright orange windsock at the southeast corner of the runway to see if there was a cross wind. There was not, so he reduced his air speed to 70 knots and set the Bücker down with almost no bounce. He cut the throttle, felt the tail touch down, applied the brakes, and taxied back to his hangar. It had been a perfect test, and as Mira would joke later, he "fell in love at first flight."

26

"Gentlemen, You Have a Race!": Reno, 1964

In early 1964, both Bill Stead and Chuck Lyford were making plans for the return of unlimited air racing. Stead was writing letters to line up political support for the race. Lyford headed to Bardahl Oil Company, in Seattle's Ballard neighborhood, and asked Ron Musson, who was now Bardahl's director of marketing and promotions, if Bardahl would sponsor his new P-51 for the National Championship Air Races. Not only did Musson agree, but he directed the talented *Miss Bardahl* hydroplane crew to assist Lyford's crew chief, Dwight Thorne. The *Bardahl* crew introduced Thorne to high-dome pistons, counterweighed crankshafts, and super-heavy quill shafts. When the *Bardahl Special* was finished, it had the most powerful Rolls-Royce engine that had ever been put into a Mustang. A stock Merlin at takeoff power is limited to 3,000 rpm and 60 inches of manifold pressure. The Bardahl engine turned 3,600 rpm with 110 inches of manifold pressure. The plane also received an all-white paint job, with the name and registration numbers in gold, trimmed with black.[1]

Stead was making extraordinary progress with the air races. First, Nevada Governor Grant Sawyer appointed him to the Nevada Centennial Commission, which was tasked with finding ways to celebrate the state's 100th anniversary. Then Stead persuaded the commission to allocate $40,000 towards putting on the new race. To top it all off, KOMO-TV news and sports director Keith Jackson was hired away from KOMO by ABC. Jackson, who was friends with many of the hydro drivers, including Stead, worked briefly in the news end of the network, but he really hit his stride when he was assigned to ABC Sports and began working for ABC's eclectic program *Wide World of Sports*, an innovative show that "spanned the globe to bring you the constant variety of sport; the thrill of victory and the agony of defeat." With his position at ABC Sports, Jackson was able to promise Stead that he could give the new National Championship Air Races a large, nationwide audience. As soon as Bardahl learned that *Wide World of Sports* was covering the air races, it agreed to sponsor the TV broadcast, too. Like a jigsaw puzzle, all the pieces were falling into place. Stead now had everything he needed to put on his race—money, a location, and the promise of national media.

As bulldozers started plowing into the barren scrub land of Sky Ranch to carve out runways, parking lots, and taxiways, Stead began to prepare his own racer. His powerful Grumman F8F-2 Bearcat was produced at the end of World War II and was the last piston fighter manufactured by Grumman before it switched to jets. With a 35-foot wingspan and a 2,300-hp radial engine, the Bearcat could reach speeds in excess of 420 miles per hour. Stead had all the protective armor and weapon hard points removed. He also had the empty gun ports covered to streamline his plane for racing.

Stead knew that he would be too busy managing the race to fly his Bearcat. Lyford suggested that Stead offer Mira Slovak the job. Stead liked the idea and told Mira about the race. Mira said yes but wanted to test the plane. Lyford flew Mira down to Reno as soon as he got a break from Continental. They left Boeing Field one morning with the 6-foot 3-inch Mira shoehorned into the tiny jump seat behind Lyford's cockpit. After he landed, Lyford taxied his sleek P-51 Mustang up to Stead's thick, stubby Bearcat. As Mira climbed down from the Mustang and walked across the apron, he was reminded of a pilot who once said, "A Bearcat looks like a bullfrog standing on its tip-toes." With the two planes parked side-by-side, it was easy to compare the design philosophies of the Army Air Corps and the U.S. Navy. The Air Corps wanted to create a graceful flying machine; the Navy simply wanted to cram as much horsepower as it could into an aluminum can, and stick wings on it so it will fly. The Mustang and the Bearcat were almost the same size and weight, but the Bearcat's Pratt & Whitney engine had 2,800 cubic inches of displacement compared to the Mustang's Rolls-Royce Merlin with only 1,650.

Lyford had already briefed Mira on the plane, so it was not long before he climbed into the Bearcat, using the spring-loaded steps built into the side of the fuselage. The Bearcat's tiny cockpit smelled of fresh paint. Mira had to crouch down to get the canopy to slide closed over his head. As he belted himself in, he looked around to familiarize himself with the cramped cockpit. Most of the levers and knobs that control the plane are on the left. Just below Mira's left arm were the trim wheels for the rudder and elevator.

Still on his left but closer to his knees were the flap controls. Higher up, almost at the level of the canopy rail, were the throttle, pitch, and mixture controls. The right side of the cockpit contained the switch panels and circuit breakers that controlled all the electrical components. Sticking up from the center of the cockpit floor was the control stick, capped with a textured black rubber grip that looked a lot like a sports car gear shifter. Straight ahead, in the very center of the instrument panel, were two large gauges—the horizon indicator and compass. Surrounding them were several smaller but still-important gauges—air speed indicator, tachometer, altimeter, climb indicator, and manifold pressure.

When Mira looked out of the windscreen, he was struck by two sensations. First, he felt like the nose of the Bearcat was impossibly short and he must be sitting almost on the accessory housing of the engine. Radial engines are so much shorter than inline engines that it was a common phenomenon for pilots switching from an inline engine to feel like the cockpit was too far forward. Second, the four-blade propeller looked huge. It was at least 18 inches longer that the P-51's propeller.

Mira taxied to the end of the runway. He double-checked that the tail wheel was locked and ran the big Pratt & Whitney up to 2,000 rpm to do his magneto check. He had to stand on the brakes with all his weight to keep the massive propeller from pulling him down the strip. Stead had warned him to make sure he lined the plane up carefully before he pushed the throttle forward because, "You don't really fly the Bearcat during takeoff; you just sort of aim it." Slovak pulled the stick back against his stomach, let off the brakes, and began to move the throttle forward. The acceleration down the runway was instantaneous and awesome. When he reached full power, he loosened his grip on the stick and let it come to neutral. The plane seemed to lift off on its own. With the plane's massive engine and huge propeller, Mira was anticipating that it would want to pull to the left, but he did not feel any torque or swerve at all. He pulled back the red lever that raised the landing gear as the plane climbed effortlessly into the pale blue high-desert sky. The Bearcat was designed to fly from aircraft carriers in the Pacific and protect the ships from Japanese kamikazes. To do that effectively, the Bearcats had a tremendous rate of climb: from takeoff to 10,000 feet in just under ninety seconds. Mira had to keep a constant eye on his altimeter, because every time he looked away he gained a couple hundred feet of altitude. He was surprised to find out that the Bearcat's ugly stumpy looks on the ground belied the most beautifully handling high-performance, high-powered fighter he had ever flown. The extra 800 hp that the Bearcat carried over the P-51 meant that he could do things in a Bearcat that P-51 pilots could only dream about. After an hour of aileron rolls, high-speed turns, and practiced stalls, Mira headed back to the airport. He reduced power to slow the plane to about 140 knots and entered the landing pattern. The plane behaved well throughout the entire pattern as he lowered the flaps and then the landing gear. He was down to 110 knots as he turned off the base leg onto his final approach. He remembered that Stead had warned him that the Bearcat did not float at all, and would literally stop flying the moment he got the nose up, so Mira was careful to make sure he was only a few feet off the runway when he pulled the stick back to raise the nose. True to Stead's warning, the plane dropped onto the runway with a sudden thump. Any other plane would have bounced a few times with such a forceful touchdown, but the Bearcat, was designed to slam onto the pitching deck of a Navy carrier and stay down. So the rugged plane stayed glued to the runway. Mira chopped the throttle and taxied back to Lyford and Stead. He pulled back the mixture control to kill the engine, slid back the canopy, and happily announced to the world, "Oh, I think I'm in love! This plane is amazing!"

There had not been an unlimited air race in the United States in fifteen years, but there were about a dozen hydroplane races each year, including one on Lake Tahoe, near Reno. To fill the countless volunteer positions needed to put on a successful race, Stead turned to the hydroplane community for his timers, scorers, and race officials. To keep things simple, they adopted the entire hydroplane rule book, including the same point system. They would also have elimination heats broken into "A" and "B," and a final heat on Sunday, with the winner determined by total points.

As race day neared, Stead reached back to his hydroplane connections once more and asked Ralph Hart, president of Heublein, Inc., if he would be interested in expanding his *Miss Smirnoff* unlimited hydroplane sponsorship to include a Smirnoff unlimited airplane too. Hart said yes, and before long Stead's sleek white plane was trimmed with red letters saying "Smirnoff Vodka." Like the boat, the plane's racing number became eighty, to advertise that Smirnoff Vodka was 80 proof.

The National Championship Air Races at Reno ran for nine days, starting on Saturday, September 12, wrapping up on Sunday, September 20. Each day was packed with events, including balloon races, vintage aircraft fly-ins, parachute demonstrations, biplane races, homebuilt midget races, National Aerobatic Championships, flyovers by the USAF Thunderbirds, and of course the National Championship Air Races for unlimited airplanes. The weather was warm and dry, with lots of wind, and if you had to pick three words to describe the event, they would be dust, dust, and dust. All the bulldozing and earth moving that Stead had done to turn Sky

Ranch from scrub land to a makeshift airport left acres and acres of loose, sandy dirt exposed to the wind, a recipe for choking dust that covered everything. Army Air Corps veterans were reminded of operating in North Africa during World War II. Competitors had to wipe down their planes several times a day.

Over the nine-day event, 50,000 fans showed up, along with dozens of airplanes, helicopters, and balloons. One of the big draws was the daily air show put on by Bob Hoover, who was the demonstration pilot for North American Aviation and flew a yellow-and-black P-51 Mustang. Hoover was a native of Arkansas and spoke with the slow, dignified accent of a southern gentleman. He had been a pilot for the Army Air Corps during World War II and had been shot down and taken prisoner by the Nazis. Near the end of the war, Hoover had escaped, stolen an FW-190, and flown to freedom. Many aviation experts felt that Hoover was one of the best pilots ever to fly a plane. He would often end his show with something that became his signature move that he called his "Tennessee Waltz." He would fly his Mustang along the show line in front of the stands, with only one wheel touching the ground and his wing tip less than a foot above the runway. Then he would rock to the other wheel, going back and forth from one wheel to the other, the whole length of the grandstands. As a representative of North American, Hoover dressed more like a businessman than a pilot, and fans were surprised when he would park his plane at the end of his routine and step out of the P-51 wearing black business slacks, a white dress shirt, a narrow black tie, and sometimes even a straw plantation hat.

Eight World War II-era fighter planes entered the unlimited race—three Bearcats and five Mustangs. When the unlimiteds began arriving, several pilots elected to land first at Reno Municipal Field and then drive to Sky Ranch to inspect the improvised landing facilities. When qualifying opened up for the unlimiteds on Monday, September 14, conditions were less than ideal. The landing strip was little more than a 2,000-foot-long stretch of dry, sandy road, with some World War II-surplus steel matting laid over it. Stead explained that he was still working to improve things. He had road rollers coming in to compact the sand, and oil sprayers to keep down the dust. Some of the pilots were skeptical and worried about their safety. Stead responded that he would continue to do all he could to improve the landing strip, but that they had all operated from worse strips in the past, especially anyone who had flown combat in World War II, and that it was critical that the unlimiteds land and take off from Sky Ranch, because they were the main attraction, the guys that fans were paying to see. Stead went on to explain that *Wide World of Sports* had not sent a large enough crew to film two separate locations. They would be at Sky Ranch to cover the race and insisted on being able to film the takeoffs and landings, as well as having access to the pilots for post-race interviews. A few of the pilots, led by Bob Love and Lockheed test pilot Darryl Greenamyer, continued to worry that the crude Sky Ranch landing strip was unsafe. Stead agreed to let the unlimiteds fly their test laps and qualification attempts from Reno Municipal while he finished working on the field at Sky Ranch, but when it came time for racing on September 18, all the planes needed to take off and land from Sky Ranch.

Bob Love qualified Lyford's highly modified *Bardahl Special* with an average speed around the 8.5 mile oval of 395.46 mph, Darryl Greenamyer was second in a modified Bearcat at 359.51, and Mira was third with the *Smirnoff Vodka* at 356.29. There were a few hair-raising moments during qualifying when Mira made a low pass and hit a 13,000-volt power line that served the tiny community of Spanish Springs. When Mira returned to the field, the crew noticed burn marks in the paint, where the high voltage power lines had arced against the plane. Efficient crews from Nevada Power Company repaired the downed line that night. It was hit again by Bob Love the next morning. NPC repaired the line once more, only to have Slovak clip it again. The power company then advised the few dozen people living in Spanish Springs that they would have to do without power until the race was over.

As with any large event, there were many small problems, but for the most part things went well, until the morning of the 18th, when the first set of unlimited heats was set to run. Much like the drivers' meetings that were held on the morning of a hydroplane race to go over rules and safety procedures, a pilots' meeting was called by Stead. The wind was blowing as the drivers gathered in a circle behind the bleachers. *Wide World of Sports* cameras rolled as Stead explained the starting procedures, and told the pilots that they were going to use Bob Hoover's yellow Mustang as a pace plane. The competitors would line up in the order of qualification on Hoover's right wing, and when Hoover felt that everyone was in position he would lead them to the line and turn them all loose. He would then climb and orbit the field, and act as a chase plane to help anyone who had an emergency get back to the ground safely. Hoover continued to discuss safety procedures with his smooth southern drawl:

> Now ya'll have plenty of speed, so if you have a problem, the first thing I want you to do is pull up and try to gain as much altitude as you can. You'll be flying almost 400 mph, so even with your engine out you still ought to be

> able to get quite a bit of altitude. I'll join you and then together we'll work out what to do next. You'll have two choices: You can bail out or you can bring the plane in. You're all wearing parachutes, so that's your first option. And if you're on fire you need to get out. Don't even think of trying to save the plane. Get out. I've bailed out five times and there's no shame in that.[2]

When Hoover was done, Stead got down on one knee and gathered the pilots like a quarterback calling a play. The *Wide World* camera crew zoomed in on his face. He looked right at Greenamyer and said, "I've heard a lot of talk from a few pilots that this field isn't safe. That's bullshit. This field is safe. Could it be better? Of course it could, and I'm working on it. But Bob (Hoover) has been flying off it several times a day every day. And any pilot who's even a half-assed pilot can land out here. So I don't want to hear any more about this not being safe."[3] Greenamyer spoke up, "Maybe the Mustangs can land in this crap, but you can't land a Bearcat on this strip. They're not set up for this type of field; it's too stiff and my wheels are too narrow. They don't absorb the rough terrain the way a Mustang can."

Stead couldn't believe what he was hearing. He looked at Greenamyer and said, "Slovak doesn't seem to have any trouble landing his Bearcat here. Maybe you should ask him how he does it."

Love said, "How about it we take off from Municipal, but land here after the race? Is that okay?'

Stead looked around at the circle of pilots. He knew that they were divided just about in half and this was going to be the best deal he could get, "Okay. You can take off from Municipal, fly your heat race, then come back here so you can get interviewed by Keith Jackson. If you don't land at Sky Ranch after your heats, you'll be disqualified. Got it?" There was some grumbling, but there was agreement between the pilots, and the race would go on.

As in a hydroplane race, the qualifiers were drawn in to two sections. Heat 1A would be Bob Love in Chuck Lyford's *Bardahl Special*, Clay Lacy in the purple P-51 *Bonzai*, Walt Olrich in a blue Bearcat, and E. D. Weiner in another P-51. Heat 1B would be Darryl Greenamyer in his modified Bearcat, Mira Slovak in Bill Stead's *Smirnoff*, and Ben Hall's *Seattle Miss.*

The planes for the first race lifted off from Municipal and headed to Sky Ranch. Hoover orbited the course at about 1,000 feet. The grandstands were packed and there were huge public-address speakers set up every few yards with the volume high enough that the fans could hear announcer Sandy Sanders describing the race over all the engine noise. Hoover had radio contact with the planes, telling one to slow down and another to speed up until they were all in line. Each plane could talk to the control tower, but the planes were not allowed radio communication to each other or their pit crews.

The wind began to pick up and the flags that lined the bleachers whipped and snapped. Bob Love lined up on Hoover's right wing tip. Outside of him were Walt Olrich, Clay Lacy, and finally E. D. Weiner. As the planes lined up over the runway, Hoover pushed the throttle forward and his Merlin spun up to 3,000 rpm, with 61 inches of boost, as he aimed for the starting line. Tens of thousands of fans were on their feet cheering as Hoover led the four racers down the course. The sound was deafening as he reached a speed of 350 miles per hour at 50 feet above the desert floor. As the planes rushed toward the starting line, Hoover banked left and pulled back hard on the stick to send his Mustang climbing inside and above the racecourse. At the same moment, he keyed his microphone and announced to the pilots and control tower, "Gentlemen, you have a race!"

The *Bardahl Special* dove toward the desert, pulling up a scant 20 feet above the sand. Love banked the plane around the pylons and blasted through the turn. His first lap was over 405 miles per hour. His closest competition was Walt Olrich at 341.76 mph. Love flew flawlessly for the first three laps, but on the fourth lap, on the east end of the course, Love, with half a lap lead on the field, inexplicably flew inside two of the pylons. He continued to run away with the race lapping two of the other planes. When he landed at Sky Ranch, he was apparently unaware that he had been disqualified. He taxied over to the *Wide World* crew, shut off the plane, and slid open the canopy for his interview. To the few pilots standing on the apron who knew Love well, it was apparent why he had missed the pylons. He was nearsighted, and without his glasses, he had trouble seeing at a distance. He was also a bit vain and did not want the ABC crew to film him wearing glasses, so he did not wear them for this heat. With Love's disqualification, Olrich moved up to first and Clay Lacy took second.

Heat 1B was anticlimactic. With only three planes in the heat and the fastest plane in the field already disqualified, Slovak saw an opportunity to earn a lot of easy points. As the only pilot with experience running a points race, he was familiar with the old boat-racers' saying, "You can't win a race in the first heat, but you sure can lose it." Mira knew that a mistake in the first couple of heats—like missing a pylon, getting disqualified, or pushing your engine too hard—could knock you out entirely. His qualifying speed was only 3 mph behind Greenamyer and there was a chance he could run with him, especially if he could steal the start and get inside, but if he tried that and blew up the engine, he would be out of the race. He was quite a bit faster than Ben Hall's *Seattle Miss*, so he elected to let Greenamyer go, and just make sure he stayed ahead of Hall. The race worked out the way Mira had anticipated—Greenamyer crossed the line first, Mira was second, and Hall was third. When the race was over, the planes grabbed a bit of altitude, backed down their throttle settings and let everything, including the pilots' emotions, cool down. As Mira circled the field, he saw Greenamyer's silver Bearcat descend toward Sky Ranch to land. The Bearcat touched down and clouds of dust came up from the main wheels, and then, to Mira's shock and surprise, Greenamyer applied power, pulled up and flew away toward Reno Municipal. Mira was not sure what he had just seen, but when he landed and taxied off the field, he was met by his old friend Keith Jackson and the ABC Sports crew telling him that he had won the heat. Greenamyer had refused to land at Sky Ranch and was disqualified.

Later, after the TV interview was finished, Mira was surrounded by fans with race programs asking for autographs. One fan, an older gentleman with a military-style haircut, said, "Last night I was in a bar and I heard someone say that Darryl Greenamyer was the best damn pilot God ever made."

Mira did not like these types of conversations and politely said, "I wouldn't disagree with that."

The race fan was thoughtful for a moment, and then said, "Well, I just saw the best damn pilot God ever made refuse to land his Bearcat on that dirt runway, but you did. Does that mean that you are a better pilot, or just more reckless?"

Slovak shrugged and said, "The answer to that question is between God and Darryl Greenamyer."

On Saturday, September 19, Love drew into heat 2A against Olrich and Lacy. Once more, Love flew away from everyone, taking the checkered flag and landing carefully on the dusty runway at Sky Ranch. Lyford was thrilled and Stead was genuinely happy to see his friend's plane perform so well. After being disqualified on Friday, Greenamyer withdrew from the race, leaving only Slovak and Ben Hall to fly in heat 2B. Knowing that the fans paid good money to watch a race, Slovak decided to put on a show. He was at least 10 mph faster than Hall's *Seattle Miss,* but Mira raced side-by-side with the *Seattle Miss* for ten laps. First Hall would have the lead, then Mira. They swapped positions until the last moment, when Mira pulled ahead, winning by under nine seconds.

Sunday the 20th was the last day of the event and the final heat for the unlimiteds. The wind began to blow and by race time there was a 40-mph crosswind that left the stands almost empty. Yet the temper tantrum that Mother Nature was putting on was nothing compared to Bob Love's tantrum. He protested his disqualification, saying that he did not miss any pylons, and even if he did, he should have been made to run an additional lap or two, which would have dropped him down to third place in his heat, but not disqualified him from the heat completely. Stead listened, and in an attempt to be fair, agreed to give Love third-place points. As the planes followed Hoover around the pylons for the start of the 1964 Reno final, the points were: Slovak with 800, Lacy with 700, Love with 625, Hall with 600, and Olrich with 525. Slovak knew that all he had to do to win was finish ahead of Clay Lacy.

Hoover led the planes down to the start, and to everyone's surprise, Mira blasted into the lead from lane one. At the first pylon, Mira flew so low that dry sage brush caught in the *Smirnoff's* prop-wash tumbled across the sand. Love slid wide and Mira extended his lead. Heading up the backstretch, Love pulled even and they flew side by side. Both planes were buffeted by the 40-mph winds. Mira's Bearcat rocked from side to side and Love's Mustang surged into the lead. Mira could not catch up. All he needed was second place, so he let Love go. He relaxed too much and Clay Lacy slipped by. Lacy held second through the end of lap three, but as the planes headed into the first turn on lap four, Mira made his move. He slipped his white and red Bearcat, now streaked with gray oil stains, under Lacy, skimming the desert 20 feet off the sand. He pushed the throttle all the way forward to find a burst of speed and blew past the "Purple People Eater" to take second and wrap up enough points to secure the overall race win. Love took the checkered flag first, Slovak coasted in second, and Lacy took third. Yet Mira was the National Air Racing champion for 1964.

He landed, shut off the engine, slid open the canopy, and was surrounded by reporters shouting questions, "Mira, you've won hydroplane races and now an airplane championship. How does it feel?"

"In the race, I was very lucky. I cannot come close in my airplane to Bardahl's. I cannot come close to Bob Love as a pilot. He is a tremendous pilot. I knew I couldn't beat the other F8F, Greenamyer, because that was a very hot airplane. And that purple son-of-a-gun from Van Nuys with Clay Lacy flying. If he had a few more laps he would get me right there. As a person, I don't think I have a chance to compete against guys like that. The thought of winning the race, to me was ridiculous."[4]

"If you didn't think you could win, where did you expect to finish?"

"I figure that if I finish around third or fourth I am doing real well. So I just climb in that Smirnoff Bearcat and every once in a while I check to make sure that the throttle and the pitch control are as far forward as they go. I hold the stick with both hands and I am pulling 7 *gs* around the buoys, I mean pylons. The right things were working for me. I think that I was the least qualified guy in the circuit. But Lady Luck turned against the other pilots and they lost."[5]

Just down the runway a few yards, Bob Love was giving a different type of interview. He claimed that the officials "were just a confused bunch of people making up rules on the spot." "We had the only racing plane here! But the way the rules were handled, you could have run this race in a Comanche and won. You won't see me here next year. We came down here to win, not fight with idiots." When asked about missing the pylons, he snapped, "We flew the course as it should have been flown." The next morning Love's home town newspaper ran a story in the sports section under the headline, "San Jose Pilot Raps Slovak's Air Victory." Love was never asked to fly for Bardahl again.

Time magazine carried a story about Mira's victory in its October 2, 1964 issue. Coincidently, this was the issue that announced the results of Supreme Court Chief Justice Earl Warren's investigation into the assassination of President John F. Kennedy. The issue carried a large portrait of Lee Harvey Oswald on the cover. At first, Mira was conflicted. While he was proud that such a prestigious magazine was still finding him newsworthy ten years after his defection, he was reluctant to show his friends a magazine that had one of the world's most hated criminals on its cover. Then, it struck him that the magazine actually offered a wonderful comparison. Mira had lived in a communist country and had defected to come to the West. Once in the West, he had used his freedom to achieve great things and was loved by thousands of people. Oswald had lived in a free country and had defected to live in the communist Soviet Union. Oswald had committed an awful crime and was hated by millions. Mira felt that comparing Slovak the defector to Oswald the defector offered insight into the morals and values of each form of government.[6]

27

The Rumble in Rockford: Illinois, 1965

In the fall of 1964, Mira did something that many Americans have done but that would have been denied to anyone living in the Soviet Bloc. He started a business called Mira Slovak Aviation and he planned to sell airplanes. The first plane he bought was a Citabria ("Airbatic" spelled backwards). Champion Aircraft introduced the Citabria in 1964 as an entry-level aerobatic plane for weekend pilots, for only $4,890. Mira thought it was an ideal way for amateur pilots to break into the exciting sport of aerobatic flying. In February 1965, *Flying Magazine*'s new associate editor, James Gilbert, an articulate Englishmen who also happened to be an accomplished aerobatic flyer, wrote a review that was critical of the Citabria. Gilbert, who had impeccable flying credentials, having just won the prestigious 1964 Esso Voltige Trophy, combined with a dry English wit, wrote a tongue-in-cheek parody of the book of Genesis that damned the Citabria with faint praise. Mira sent a letter to *Flying Magazine* not only challenging Gilbert's statements, but also offering to face off with Gilbert in a one-on-one aerobatic duel to prove who had the better understanding of aerobatics.[1]

Flying Magazine, which had run a large story about Mira after his win in Reno, recognized the draw of his name and wanted to cash in on a great marketing opportunity. It accepted the duel on behalf of Gilbert and arranged for the competition to take place at the Experimental Aviation Association meet in Rockford, Illinois, during the first week of August 1965. The EAA had been founded in 1953 by the godfather of the home-built airplane community, Paul Poberezny. He recognized early on that not everyone who wanted to own an airplane could afford an airplane, so he championed the obvious solution, which was to build your own. The EAA show quickly became the aviation Mecca for offbeat and unusual airplanes, expanding quickly beyond the tiny home-builts to embrace planes of every kind, including antiques, restored warbirds, stunt flyers, and ultralights. The EAA show soon attracted thousands of fans. To assure a fair competition, *Flying Magazine* arranged for a panel of judges that would include Poberezny to preside over the duel. Each contestant would get to fly a five-minute freestyle show with twenty-five points awarded in each of four categories—accuracy, timing and position, scope and variety, and artistic merit.

Slovak would be allowed to fly his Bücker, and Gilbert would be in a borrowed Great Lakes Special. The showdown was scheduled for August 4. Gilbert arrived at Rockford on Saturday, July 31, hoping to get in a few days of practice before his rival showed up. Gilbert spent Sunday working on stories for *Flying Magazine* and watching the sky for the arrival of his Great Lakes. On Monday, the biplane swooped in, and Gilbert was able to get in two good practice sessions. Slovak was busy flying passengers for Continental. Gilbert got a second day of practice on Tuesday and there was still no sign of Slovak.

On Wednesday, a telegram arrived saying that Mira was hemmed in by thunderstorms in the southwest and he could not get his little Bücker into the air. For a moment, Gilbert breathed a sigh of relief, believing the contest would be canceled or at least put on hold. The relief was short-lived; Bob Hoover, with his Rockwell Mustang, went to Poberezny and offered to take over for Mira. Poberezny ordered that the show must go on. Gilbert, knowing how talented Hoover was, declined the offer. Yet before Poberezny could reach Hoover, the PA announcer reported that Gilbert had accepted. With no choice but to face the music, Gilbert climbed into the sporty Great Lakes and took to the sky. The 185-hp biplane climbed smoothly to 1,000 feet while thousands of eager fans watched. Gilbert planned to start with an outside snap roll. He advanced the throttle and gave the Great Lakes full left aileron; at the same time, he pushed the stick forward and stepped hard on the left rudder pedal. To his dismay, the plane did a lazy three-quarter roll and stopped. Gilbert kicked the rudder again to finish the roll but his confidence was shot. Gymnasts, ice skaters, and aerobatic flyers agree that the first maneuver in your routine is the critical one. If you can "stick" that first one, it all goes well, but if you fumble it, the rest of the routine will be a disaster because you end up worrying so much about the mistake you just made that you do not concentrate enough to avoid the next mistake, and soon your mistakes begin to feed off each other and multiply.

One mistake led to another and another, while the knowledgeable audience on the ground cringed and moaned. Mercifully, Gilbert's five minutes ended and he landed, wishing the ground would open up and swallow him and the plane.

Hoover and his powerful Mustang flew their normal flawless routine full of loops, hammer heads, and crisp snap rolls. Hoover ended with his famous "Tennessee Waltz," skating the Mustang from one wheel to the other with his wing tips barely inches above the grass. He landed to a chorus of cheers. When the show was over, Poberezny whispered to Gilbert, "Why don't we call this an exhibition and not announce the score?" Gilbert agreed and headed back to his hotel room to replay the disastrous routine over and over in his mind. The next day, the thunderstorms in the Southwest parted, and Mira was able to get his Bücker into the air, arriving at Rockford late in the day. He had just replaced the 95-hp Walter Minor engine with a brand new 200-hp Lycoming that promised to make the Bücker's legendary aerobatic capabilities even better. Mira greeted Gilbert with a courtly bow that befitted the stylish duel they were taking part in. There was more bad news for Gilbert. The EAA schedule had gotten too tight to allow both Mira and Gilbert to fly, so Mira would get to do his show, and the judges would compare it to the show that Gilbert flew the day before.

Mira flew a solid, professional show with perfect round loops, tight Cuban Eights, and trim snap rolls. Of course, Mira ended his routine with his signature high-speed, low-level inverted pass, waving at the fans along the flight line as he hung upside down in the Bücker's cockpit. It was not even close. Mira won unanimously.[2]

The next morning, he flew out to Seattle so he could provide color commentary for the live TV broadcast of the 1965 Gold Cup. Ron Musson and the *Miss Bardahl* won for the third year in a row. Alone in the tiny cockpit of the Bücker as he flew home, Mira had plenty of time to think about the duel. He knew that the "Rumble in Rockford," as *Flying Magazine* had chosen to bill it, was not a real competition, but it was the first time that he had won any recognition for his stunt flying, and he liked the feeling. He decided to enter more competitions.

The National Championship Air Races in Reno in 1964 had lost money, but they had done enough to revive interest in air racing that Bill Stead was willing to give them another try in 1965. He cut out a few of the airshow acts and shortened the event from nine days to seven. He also changed two of the most controversial rules for the unlimited races. He did away with the requirement to take off and land at Sky Ranch, and he turned the final heat into a winner-takes-all event. From then on, the preliminary heats only counted to get a plane qualified for the final heat, and once a plane was in the final the only thing that matter would be the order of finish.

Sky Ranch was much improved in 1965. The runway was smoother, the parking lots were oiled down, and there was a lot less dust, but it was still essentially a dirt airfield in the middle of the desert. Fresh off his "win" at Rockford, Mira entered the National Aerobatic Championship that would be part of the 1965 Reno event. Mira got an interesting reception when he and his sporty little Bücker arrived at Reno in early September. There were of course many fans that were happy to see him defend his 1964 title. Yet there was a small and vocal cohort that did not think the point system was fair, and they angrily insisted that Bob Love had been the "real winner" the previous year. Some in this group even went so far as to claim that Mira and Stead had deliberately made up the rules as they went along to ensure that their plane won.

Mira was frustrated by the controversy, but tried to keep his thoughts to himself. Boat racing had been run by these same rules for almost sixty years, and from the race promoters' perspective, there were actually some advantages to the system. First of all, it allowed the racing action to be spread out over several days. The unlimiteds were clearly the big draw of the event, but running them on only one day would disappoint the fans, so three days of racing made good economic sense. Second, a three-day event offered a plane that had a mechanical problem earlier in the race the chance to get repaired and back into the race the next day. Besides, there was nothing new about the idea of accumulating points to determine a winner in the aviation world. That was how aerobatics worked. You flew three routines and were scored on each routine. At the end of the final day, the guy with the most points won. What is more, all the pilots in 1964 knew it was a "points" race before they had signed up.

Reno is a small city, and Mira could not avoid the naysayers forever. One night before the race, he was having dinner at a small steak house in Reno and was approached by a middle-aged man in a Bardahl baseball cap. Mira could tell by the unsteady gait of the man that he had probably been drinking. As soon as he opened his mouth, the strong stench of beer breath confirmed it. The drunken fan said one word. "Disgraceful!" Mira ignored the comment and continued to eat his meal. The fan said it again, louder, "Disgraceful!"

Mira put down his fork and looked up. "Do you have a problem?"

The drunk placed his hands on Mira's table to steady himself. Slurring his words, he said, "Damn right I've got a problem. Bob Love is a hero! He shot down six MiGs in Korea an' you stole his fricken race!"

Mira felt his blood begin to boil. He wanted to stand up and punch this loud mouth in the nose, but he controlled his emotions and said, "I'm sorry you feel that way."

The drunk took his hands off the table and displayed six fingers and held them in Mira's face, as if Mira could not grasp the number six. "Six damn MiGs! An' you stole his race."

The drunk swayed back and forth. Mira wanted to stand up to face the drunk eye to eye, but his airline training in how to deal with unruly passengers taught him that might escalate the situation, so he stayed seated and signaled for a waiter. When the waiter approached, Mira looked at the drunken fan and said, "I can see that you don't like the points system. That's easy to understand, considering it uses all of that complicated mathematics. But I'd like to remind you, that it is not the point system that cost Captain Love the race. It was the fact that he missed the buoys."

As soon as Mira said the word "buoys," the drunk began to laugh, "They're not buoys, they're pylons. You must not be much of an air racer if you don't even know they're called pylons."

Mira grimaced at his own mistake. "Yes of course, pylons. But if Captain Love had missed two pylons in Cleveland, he wouldn't have won there either." He then turned to the waiter and said, "This man is bothering me. Would you please ask him to leave?" The waiter grabbed the drunk by the collar and shoved him out the door.

Most of the planes from 1964 returned in 1965. Many of the teams had gone to considerable lengths to "clean up" their planes and make them more streamlined to increase speed. Lyford's *Bardahl Special* was still very fast, but Darryl Greenamyer's Bearcat was now being prepared by engineering wizards Bruce Buland, Pete Law, and Ray Poe, who had improved it tremendously. They were not going to have any trouble keeping up with the *Bardahl.* Clay Lacy's *Cal Airmotive* was also flying very fast. Greenamyer and Lyford both won preliminary heats and went into the final as the odds-on favorites.

Sunday, September 12 was a beautiful day with clear blue skies and not much wind. The six planes in the final were equally divided, with three Mustangs and three Bearcats. Bob Hoover handled the start again, and when he released the planes for the final with his now-famous call, "Gentlemen, you have a race," Greenamyer's Bearcat swooped right down on the deck in lane one. Lacy was a few feet above in lane two, Lyford was low in lane three, and Mira was outside and a bit behind. Greenamyer and Lyford broke away from the pack to battle for first and second. Mira and Lacy raced for third and fourth. The two leading planes put on a great duel for four laps until the air inlet on Lyford's Mustang collapsed and he had to settle for second. Clay Lacy took third and Mira came in fourth.

There was an unlimited air race in Los Angeles followed by one in Las Vegas. Lyford and the *Bardahl* won them both and accumulated enough points to claim the 1965 National Points Championship.[3] In the Aerobatics Championship, Harold Krier was first, and Mira finished back in the pack.

In the world of hydroplane racing, 1965 was another great year for Ron Musson and the *Miss Bardahl*. Along with winning the Gold Cup, they also claimed the National High Points Championship. Rex Manchester and *Notre Dame* were second. George "Buddy" Byers and the *Miss Madison* took third and the *Tahoe Miss* came in fourth. For most boat owners, the *Tahoe Miss's* two race wins and a fourth in National High Points would have been considered a successful season, though not for Bill Harrah, who had invested a lot of money into his unlimited team and expected better results. In 1965, the *Tahoe Miss* had set a number of fast lap and course records, but the *Tahoe* broke down and failed to finish in over 20 percent of her heats. Team manager Harry Volpi told Harrah that the problem was their driver. He felt that hard-charging Chuck Thompson was too rough on the equipment and ran harder than was necessary. Thompson felt that the problem was Volpi and his "Rube Goldberg" turbo-charged Allisons that produced tremendous horsepower but could not be depended upon to hold together for a complete race. In the end, Thompson was fired and Volpi hired the *Miss Madison's* talented driver, Buddy Byers. Yet before Byers ever got a chance to sit in the boat, he was injured in a devastating accident while driving his seven-liter hydro *Chrysler Queen* at the January 15, 1966 Orange Bowl regatta in Miami. Byers retired and Harry Volpi had to find a new driver. He remembered that back in 1963, Mira had applied for the job. After a few phone calls, Mira agreed to come out of retirement, but the new assignment would not be announced until May, once Mira had permission from Continental Airlines.

28

The Best of Times, the Worst of Times: Washington, D.C., 1966

Pilots are a superstitious lot, although few will admit it. They owe their lives and livelihood to the disciplined application of scientific principle, but there is not one who does not, on some level, believe in luck and fate. It comes from risking your life day in and day out and seeing firsthand the capricious nature of death. Every pilot who has more than 500 hours in a log book can tell you of a situation where they should have died but were rescued by some quirk that was beyond explanation. Their stories have endless variations because there are endless ways to die in an airplane—military pilots who missed a mission because a ten-cent part failed, and the guy who went in their place never came back; airline pilots who pride themselves on always staying at their assigned altitude, who just one time let the plane wander 100 feet below and end up missing a mid-air collision by exactly 100 feet; private pilots who fly 300 miles, land, and taxi to their hanger only to have a major mechanical breakdown as they park in front of their own door. Luck seems to play a big role in the fate of a pilot, but the problem with luck is that it eventually runs out.

Mira loved his white, gold, and black Bücker. He was proud of the work that Bassett Aviation had done to restore his plane. Mira became friends with Wally Bassett, who owned the company. Along with running Bassett Aviation, he also flew charters out of Santa Paula. On March 9, 1966, Bassett was flying three members of a Las Vegas-based hunting party along with two hunting guides from Santa Paula to Santa Cruz Island in the Channel Islands National Park, 50 miles off the coast of California. He became lost in the fog and crashed while attempting to turn around and fly home. A second plane from Santa Paula, with two more members of the hunting party onboard, crashed a few moments later. There were no survivors from either plane. The Santa Paula Airport community was devastated.[1]

Seven weeks later, Mira got another jolt. Bill Stead had taken his Formula One race plane (also sponsored by *Smirnoff*) to a race in Tampa, Florida. Formula One planes were home-built planes with a 190-cubic inch engine and wing span of about 12 feet, capable of speeds close to 200 mph. While coming in for a landing in Tampa on April 28, Stead's plane suddenly went out of control, crashing into the bay. Stead's chest was crushed and he died instantly. The floating wreckage was pulled ashore and accident investigators determined that a tiny part, a cotter pin that cost less than a penny, had been left off a bolt that held on one of the ailerons. Without the cotter pin to keep it from turning, the nut on the end of the bolt vibrated off, letting the bolt fall away, which caused the aileron to come loose, which put the plane into a sudden bank to the left. Stead was traveling at over 100 miles an hour, just a few feet above Tampa Bay, and did not have time to recover. He was forty-six years old.[2]

The funeral was held in Reno on May 3, and Ron Musson, Rex Manchester, Russ Schleeh, and Mira were all honorary pall bearers. For the first time since they had met, Mira and Ron were able to talk as friends without Ron making a reference to "little guys."

While Mira was in Reno, he stopped by the *Tahoe Miss* shop and Bill Harrah arranged a press conference to announce Mira's new position as the *Tahoe Miss*'s driver.

The first unlimited race of the 1966 season was the new Suncoast Cup on Tampa Bay, Florida. Mira flew into Tampa International Airport on Tuesday, June 7, and as the 707 made its final approach, he watched the blue water rush by the windows and said a silent prayer for Bill Stead.

There were eighteen boats on hand for the new race, including a brand-new, radically designed *Miss Bardahl,* featuring a forward cockpit. Bill Muncey was there driving the *Miss U.S.* Rex Manchester was in the *Notre Dame* and Bill Brow was driving Mira's old *Wahoo*, which had changed owners and names again and was now Bernie Little's *Miss Budweiser.*

Mira was excited to be back among his old friends after three years away, but there was definitely a new order. Musson was the reigning king with three Gold Cup wins in a row. Bill Brow, Rex Manchester, and Chuck Thompson were Musson's main competitors. Muncey had won only one race in the years Mira had been away. Schleeh and Regas were retired, and of course Bill Stead was dead.

The major backer for the race was Bernie Little, so when the course opened on the morning of June 8, it was only natural that the first boat out onto the water was the *Miss Budweiser*. Brow qualified her easily with a three-lap average of 106.132 mph. Next up was Rex Manchester in the *Notre Dame*. Before he could get up to speed, the wind began to blow and nervous officials put up the red flag to close the course, calling for a thirty-minute hold. At the end of the hold, the wind was blowing even stronger, causing the colorful pennants that lined the pits to snap and pop while the palm trees along the pit road swayed back and forth. A quick call to the Weather Bureau confirmed that Hurricane Alma, a rare late-spring storm with winds over 120 mph, was headed up the west coast of Florida, directly toward Tampa Bay. Race director Phil Cole ordered the pits evacuated and arranged for a police escort to help convoy the entire racing fleet to safe storage in a city warehouse.[3] In the middle of the night, Alma altered direction slightly and passed 30 miles to the west of Tampa, but it still did considerable damage to the pit area. The convoy process was reversed and the boats were back in the windblown pits by Thursday afternoon.

Qualifying was postponed until Friday to give the race committee time to make the necessary repairs to the pits and judges' stand. The winds continued to ruffle the water on Friday, so it was decided to let all boats and drivers that had raced in 1965 skip qualifying. New boats and drivers that had not raced in 1965 would still need to prove that they were up to the challenge. On Saturday the 11th, Mira took the *Tahoe Miss* out and ran three safe, comfortable laps for an average of 101.695.

The *Tahoe Miss* was three years old and very fast, faster than the *Wahoo* for sure, but the powerful auxiliary-stage Allisons she was using were fragile, plaguing the boat with reliability issues. Mira and team manager Harry Volpi along with crew chief Andy Anderson discussed strategy and decided that their main goal for the first two races was just to run consistently and get some starts and finishes under their belt. They would wait until the Gold Cup in Detroit, to unleash the boat and run hard.

The reporters, gathered in the soggy pits with no racing to write about went, looking for stories. They paid special attention to two boats—the new *Miss Bardahl* and the *Notre Dame*. The *Bardahl* drew attention because it had such a radical look. It was lower and wider than the other boats and the cockpit was well ahead of the engine. Publicly Musson claimed that the boat "was handling beautifully." Yet privately, he complained that there was a strange vibration he could not identify, and that he was seated so far forward that "things happen before I feel them, and by the time I feel them, it's too late to do anything to correct the situation." The *Notre Dame* was getting attention because she seemed to be the best-prepared boat in the pits and Manchester was the odds-on favorite to dethrone Musson, if it were possible. Rex Manchester had never won an unlimited race; he had come close several times in 1965, finishing second in the Diamond Cup and the Gold Cup, and ending the season with a second behind Musson in National High Points. Manchester was a reporter's dream. He was a tall, handsome ex-Marine who spoke passionately about his determination to break into the winner's circle in 1966.

Sunday morning was hot and clear, without a hint of clouds or a breath of wind. The water in Tampa Bay looked flat, but that was deceptive. Hurricane Alma had spawned long, sloping rollers that were impossible for the drivers to see. They angled across the course, causing the boats to bounce precariously, and the race quickly turned into a demolition derby. Before the race even started, the *Miss Bardahl* broke an oil pump in her gearbox and had to withdraw. In her first heat, the *Smirnoff* took a wild leap and jarred driver Bill Cantrell so badly that he decided to turn the boat over to his old friend Chuck Thompson. The *Miss Budweiser*, running in her first heat, spun so hard that Bill Brow broke two bones in his right shoulder. The *Tahoe Miss,* true to her reputation of being fast but unreliable, blew an engine and did not score any points. Muncey and Manchester each won their first heat.

With Bill Brow unable to drive, Bernie Little had under an hour to find a replacement. Luckily, Donnie Wilson, who lived in Florida, was watching the race from a yacht in the center of the course. Little got a message to Wilson, and forty-five minutes later, Wilson drove the *Miss Budweiser* to a convincing victory in heat 2A. Muncey and the *Miss U.S.* won heat 2B, and Chuck Thompson in the *Smirnoff* finished 2C a few seconds ahead of Manchester and the *Notre Dame.* Heading into the final heat, Muncey had 800 points, Manchester had 700, and the *Budweiser* and the *Smirnoff* were tied at 569.

The water for the final was horrible, and the boats bounced and sloshed around with lap speeds well under 100 mph. The *Notre Dame* won the heat with a 96.017 mph average and the *Miss U.S.* was second at 93.630. Muncey and Manchester were tied on points, meaning the winner would be determined by who had the fastest elapsed time. Manchester was confident that his time was better, and he returned to the dock to celebrate what he thought was his first ever unlimited victory. While Manchester and his crew celebrated, the officials huddled. After almost forty-five minutes, there was an announcement over the PA system. By a margin of two-tenths of a second, Muncey's time was faster; Manchester was crushed.[4]

As the teams packed up to head to Washington, D.C. for the next race, the *Miss U.S.* and *Smirnoff* teams announced that their boats were too badly damaged to be repaired in time and they would skip the President's Cup in order to be ready for the Gold Cup in Detroit over the July 4 weekend.

As qualifying got underway in DC, the media seemed to taunt Manchester. The *Detroit News* ran a Friday headline that read, "Unlimited Driver in a Rut as a Second-Place Finisher." The *Washington Post* had a headline that said, "Manchester Hopes to End No. 2 Stigma in Presidents Cup." Manchester responded, telling reporters, "I'm beginning to wonder whether I'll ever shake loose from that second-place jinx. It's really beginning to bug me. It's getting embarrassing."

The real surprise of the weekend was that the *Miss Bardahl* was turning faster laps than any other boat. Along the Hains Point bulkhead, crews were beginning to pay attention whenever the new green-and-yellow boat headed out on to the race course.

The President's Cup was a two-day race, with the first set of heats late in the afternoon on Saturday and the second set, along with the final, on Sunday. Manchester and Musson both won their Saturday heats and were drawn together into heat 2B on Sunday, setting up a dogfight between the tried-and-true *Notre Dame* and the radical new rear-engine *Miss Bardahl.*

Sunday morning was warm and humid with a high haze that diffused the light, erasing shadows and muting colors. There was a full card of limited races on the schedule, with the unlimiteds running only heats 2A at 3.30 p.m. and 2B at 4 p.m., with the final scheduled at 5 p.m. Mira would be flying back to Los Angeles right after the race, so he checked out of his room, picked up a newspaper from the front desk, tossed his luggage into his rental car, and walked across the parking lot to the coffee shop for some breakfast.

As the hostess led him to a booth, he passed a table where *Boating News* reporter Eileen Crimmin and photographer Bob Carver sat finishing their breakfast. Mira stopped briefly to say hello, and then took his seat at a booth a few yards away. A waitress carrying a carafe of coffee approached Mira's table, turned over a white ceramic mug, filled it with coffee, and took his order for dry wheat toast and a cup of sliced fruit. The order came quickly.

Mira unfolded the paper and began to read as he sipped his coffee and ate his food. He was distracted by loud voices and a commotion at the hostess station. He looked over the top of his paper to see Manchester and Musson trying to walk to a table. They were both clearly drunk and had the look of two revelers coming in late after an all-night bash. Musson was the worse off of the two. His eyes were mere slits and he leaned heavily on Manchester for support. Manchester had one arm wrapped around Musson's shoulders and used his free arm to stabilize himself against the nearest table or booth as they staggered across the restaurant. They stopped in front of Carver and Crimmin's table. Manchester steadied himself on the back of Carver's chair.

Crimmin asked, "Are you two just getting in?"[5]

Manchester nodded and said, "We've been celebrating. I'm going to win today!"

Musson closed his eyes and slipped towards the floor. Manchester caught him and dragged him to the nearest empty booth, where he announced, "Coffee, we need coffee!"

The waitress approached with her coffee pot and Manchester said, "Leave that here. We're going to need a lot." He began to pour Musson and himself cup after cup. Musson began to wake up. Before long, he was slumped over the table, holding his head in his hands and moaning softly.

Mira hid behind his paper to finish his breakfast. He did not get along with Musson in the best of circumstances and he had no idea what Musson would be like when he was this drunk. He slipped a few bills under his plate and headed for the exit without saying anything. As he left the coffee shop, he looked at his watch; heat 2B was almost eight hours away. He figured both Musson and Manchester would be sober enough by then.

With only two heats to run, the unlimited pits on Hains Point were fairly relaxed and quiet as the crews spent the day tinkering on their boats and watching the limiteds race. By noon, Musson and Manchester were both in the pits, looking none the worse for their late-night adventures. Manchester had brought a Yamaha 250 motorcycle to get around the pits, and as they waited to race, he, with Musson sitting behind, scooted back and forth from boat to boat, talking with drivers or crew and signing autographs for fans.

At 3 p.m., the big cranes began to lift the boats into the water for heat 2A. Mira would be running against Donnie Wilson and the *Budweiser.* It would be the first time in Mira's career that he raced against the former *Wahoo.* It was something of a melancholy experience for Mira to see "his boat" lowered into the water for someone else to drive. "This is like watching someone else kiss my girlfriend," Mira thought. He put on a good face and headed down to the *Budweiser* pit to shake Donnie's hand and wish him good luck. Wilson won the heat and Slovak, holding to the plan that he and Harry Volpi had mapped out at the start of the season, took it easy to grab second.

When Mira returned to the dock, the boats for heat 2B were already in the water. The sleek 32-foot-long *Bardahl,* with her tall tailfin that looked like the dorsal of some massive shark, rocked in the gentle waves as Musson settled into the cockpit. Down the pits, the white, blue, green, and gold *Notre Dame* glistened in the sun. Also in heat 2B were the *Miss Dixi Cola,* the *Wayfarer's Club Lady*, the *Savair's Mist,* and the *Gale's Roostertail.* When the five-minute gun fired, all the boats started and moved on to the course. After a few minutes of fighting for lanes, the boats stormed out of the west turn and headed toward the start, with the *Bardahl* in lane one, the *Notre Dame* in two, the *Dixi Cola* in three, the *Wayfarer's* in four, and the *Gale's Roostertail* trailing the field. Musson and Manchester hit the line side-by-side at full speed and roared into the first turn pulling away from the rest of the field. The *Bardahl* glided beautifully through the corner and opened up a boat-length lead on the *Notre Dame.* As they thundered up the backstretch at over 165 mph, Manchester began to chew away at Musson's lead. They were side by side again as they entered turn two, where the *Bardahl* made another smooth turn and pulled ahead by a boat length. The boats slid out of the turn and flew down the front stretch.

As they reached the start line, the *Bardahl* seemed to slow a bit and Manchester pulled ahead to lead by about a boat length. The *Notre Dame* hit some rough water and took three small hops. The *Bardahl*, inside in lane one and just about a boat-length behind, hit the same rough spot. She took two small hops and then on the third, she buried her nose in the water and exploded into a shower of spray and splinters. Manchester did not see the accident and continued to race toward the corner. The water was only 8 feet deep where the *Bardahl* crashed, and the nose of the boat struck the bottom of the river and disintegrated into countless pieces. The rear 17 feet of the boat tumbled out of the spray and then sank. Over the PA system, the announcer screamed, "It broke in two! The boat broke in two!" Around the course, red flags went up and smoke flares were lit.

Musson was floating motionlessly in the water at the start line, but inexplicably, the rescue boats did not move. Bob Fendler, driving the *Wayfarer's Club Lady,* was behind the accident. He slowed to avoid the debris, drove all the way to the first turn, turned around, and motored slowly back to the crash site, still arriving long before any rescue boats began to move. Fendler shut off his engine and ran up to the bow of the *Wayfarer's,* pointing at Musson's body and waving for the rescue boats. Finally, one of the Coast Guard patrol boats reached the scene, loaded Musson's body into a Stokes basket, and returned to the pits. The stretcher holding Musson's body was carried to shore and laid on the pavement. As stunned rescue personnel stood by in shock, Donnie Wilson pushed his way through the crowd and began to perform CPR on Musson until he was loaded into the ambulance. Eileen Crimmin estimated that it took rescue personnel ten to fifteen minutes to get Musson out of the water and to the ambulance. Afterward, Bob Fendler angrily complained to the officials about the slow rescue, shouting "They just didn't move! Why didn't they move?" The boats from 2B were craned back onto their trailers to be refueled, while course boats brought in whatever splintered remains of the Bardahl floated to the surface. The pits were hushed and solemn as everyone awaited word on Musson's condition.

The boats for 2B were put back in the water for a rerun. Manchester grabbed his helmet and headed toward the dock. The PA crackled and a somber voice announced, "Ron Musson, driver of the *Miss Bardahl*, suffered fatal injuries in the accident just witnessed." Manchester let the helmet fall from his hands. It hit the grass with a hollow thud and rolled to a stop a few feet away. He lowered his head and stood motionless. After a few seconds, he reached down, picked up the helmet, and headed to his boat.

With the boats already in the water and fans lining the course, there was not time for second-guessing or recriminations. The drivers were professionals and they had jobs to do. Most, including Manchester, were ex-military and had seen death before, but there was a numb feeling in the pits as the boats pulled onto the course for the rerun of 2B. The drivers only got halfway through the first lap when a nervous course worker accidently fired a red flare. Again, the race was stopped and the boats returned, to be lifted out of the water and refueled. The third running of 2B was finally finished after 6 p.m.

By the time the lineup for the final was announced, owners and drivers had a couple hours to think about Musson. There were two schools of thought. Some drivers and officials wanted to cancel the rest of the race out of respect for him, while others insisted that the race needed to be completed because "that's what Ron would have wanted." Eventually, it was decided to go ahead with the race. Manchester was leading with 800 points. Wilson was second with 700, and Mira was in third with 600. The battle was going to be between Manchester and Wilson, with whoever won the final heat claiming the trophy. Hydroplane drivers are warriors, and death affects warriors differently than it affects common men. A common man seeing a deadly accident will think to himself, "That was awful. I need to be careful or it might happen to me." A warrior will see the same accident and think, "I must not let fear take hold. To let that accident allow fear into my heart would be disrespectful to the dead, so I must run harder to prove that I'm not afraid."

As the boats were being put into the water for the final, Mira walked to the Budweiser pit to wish Donnie Wilson good luck. He also wanted to tell him to "Take care of my girl" (the old *Miss Wahoo*). As Mira approached the *Bud* pit, he heard raised voices and saw Wilson and Bernie Little standing between two trucks arguing. Mira heard Little say, "That's bullshit! If you want to stay on the beach, stay on the beach and I'll get someone else to drive, but if you go out there in my boat, you're going to race to win. I won't have you putt-putting around in last place!"[6] Mira quietly walked away.

The five-minute gun for the final heat fired at 7.15 p.m., two hours and fifteen minutes late. The afternoon sun reflected off the water at a low angle, making it hard for the drivers to see. Wilson and Manchester were fighting for the inside. Mira elected to stay out of the fray and start outside. As they ran to the start Wilson was in lane one, Manchester was in two, the *Chrysler Crew* in three, and Mira out in four. Mira led the boats across the line and into the first turn but was quickly passed by Wilson and Manchester. Coming out of the first turn, the *Notre Dame* had a slight lead, but then the *Budweiser* passed her. Accelerating up the backstretch, the *Budweiser* pulled ahead by two boat lengths. At the halfway point, the *Notre Dame* found some speed and was gaining. At three quarters of the way up the backstretch, the *Notre Dame* stuck her nose into the lead. Just before they reached the turn, the *Notre Dame* was half a boat length in front. She bounced off a roller and took a long low hop, landing level and bouncing again. After the third bounce, the *Notre Dame* landed on her right sponson and slid sideways, landing on top of the charging *Budweiser.* The bow of the *Budweiser* hit the underside of the *Notre Dame* and speared the right sponson, which broke away.

Meanwhile, the left sponson of the *Notre Dame* landed directly on top of the *Budweiser's* cockpit. Instantly, there was a massive explosion of water and debris. Manchester's body was flung into the air. Mira, who was only a few yards behind in lane four, watched the disaster unfold in horror. He lifted his foot from the throttle but was going too fast to stop. He flashed past the tumbling wrecks, spun the boat around and was first at the scene of the accident. He saw Wilson floating face down. Running to the bow of the *Tahoe Miss*, he dove in and swam to Wilson as the *Bud* and the *Notre Dame* sank a few yards away. When Mira reached him, he saw that there were three big cracks in the helmet. That was enough to tell him that things were bad. He knew what to expect when he rolled Wilson over, but it still broke his heart to see the grievous wounds to his friend's face. The force of the impact had ripped Wilson's visor off. He was covered in blood. Mira knew Wilson was dying and held him in his arms as the waves rocked them. Mira tried to comfort Wilson. "It's okay Donnie, I've got you. You're going to be okay. The rescue boats will be here any second." He tried to wipe the blood out of Wilson's eyes, but there was just too much.

As he treaded water holding Donnie Wilson's lifeless body in the cold Potomac, he was reminded of the 1958 Mapes Trophy Race, when Wilson had won and Mira had taken second to clinch the National Championship. Their crews had thrown them both into the water to celebrate. They had hugged and splashed and laughed. Here they were again in the water, Mira holding his friend close, but this time there was no laughter and no celebration. A Coast Guard 40-footer came up next to them, and Mira helped get Wilson's body on board. The patrol boat turned quickly and headed to the pits, leaving Mira treading water alone in the river.

When Mira was hired by Harrah, he had decided that he was going to use his old yellow Bardahl life jacket. It had great sentimental value to him. He had worn it when he won his first National Championship in 1958, and he hoped it would bring him luck in 1966. Unfortunately, the old jacket was no longer waterproof, and the kapok flotation began absorbing water. The jacket was getting heavier and heavier. Mira tried to swim back to the *Tahoe Miss*, but the current had carried the boat too far down river and he could not reach her. He had never been a strong swimmer, and now with the old life jacket soaking up water and weighing him down he was beginning to have a serious problem. He tried to wave his arms over his head to attract the attention of a patrol boat, but whenever he raised his arms up, he started to sink. He realized that he had to get help soon, and the only way to do it was with his voice, so he began yelling for help. Eventually, a patrol boat that was picking up broken pieces of wood from the two shattered race boats heard Mira, got him on board, and took him back to shore. The whole way back to the pits, Mira kept asking, "Where's Rex? Where's Rex?" No one on the patrol boat seemed to know. When they arrived at the pits, Mira finally got an answer. Manchester, like Musson and Wilson, had been transported to George Washington University Hospital and declared DOA.

The pits were in a complete shambles. Crewmen, owners, and drivers were kneeling on the ground sobbing. Patrol boats were bringing in huge chunks of floating wreckage and stacking them in piles on docks or next to empty trailers. To add to the chaos, the sun was setting. Mira's brain was reeling from everything he had been through and he needed to get away to think. He walked back to the *Tahoe* trailer, changed out of his wet uniform, dropped off his water-logged life jacket and helmet, and told Harry Volpi that he needed to catch a flight back to LA because he was supposed to fly for Continental Airlines the next day. Volpi told Mira to go. Yet as Mira walked away, Volpi asked cautiously, "Will we see you in Detroit for the Gold Cup?"

Mira paused and said, "Of course you will. I've always known that these types of accidents were a possibility; that is why I never take any unnecessary risks or drive any faster than I have to. Really, this changes nothing except that I will be more grateful for every sunrise, because you never know when the last one is coming."

Mira hurried to his rental car and drove to Washington National Airport, on the other side of the Potomac, to catch his flight back to LAX. It was dark as his plane took off, but he could see lights reflecting from Hains Point onto the Potomac and wondered if the crews were still packing up. He was in the air flying away from the death and carnage on the racecourse. For a moment, it seemed like something that had happened to someone else, then he realized that in his hurry to leave the pits, he had forgotten to change his socks, and inside his shoes, where no one could see, his feet were soaking wet with dirty, blood-stained water from the Potomac.

As Mira flew away from DC and the shattered boats lay shrouded beneath the dark waters of the Potomac, the saddest of all ironies was announced to the few fans still at the river. The brutal accident in the final heat was so devastating that there would be no rerun. The race was over and the results would be based on the points accumulated prior to the final. That meant that Rex Manchester, with 800 points, was the winner. Yet there would be no trophy presentation, no flash bulbs popping, and no kisses from the queen. Manchester's body was already in the morgue beneath George Washington Memorial Hospital, being prepared to be shipped to Seattle.

Monday morning's papers in Seattle carried banner headlines: "Musson, Manchester, Wilson—3 Hydro Drivers Killed in Race," accompanied with pages of graphic photos of the accidents and recaps of the drivers' careers. By Tuesday, the stories changed. Photos of the mangled wrecks and grieving widows dominated the papers and the headlines switched to "Why? Hydro Widows Ask" and "Hydro Widows ask Why Didn't They Halt Race?" Wednesday's papers carried details of the funeral arrangements but the shock in the media was turning to anger. *Seattle Times* sports reporter Hy Zimmerman wrote an editorial entitled, "It's Time for a Second Look at Hydroplane Racing." In it he said, "Let not a single tear be shed for the sport itself. It fed and fatted on the promise of peril and the skulk of death.... Did not tragedy, plus the civic chip on our shoulder, help elevate hydroplaning to hysterical heights? ... We do not call for abolition of hydroplaning. Some men ever will risk their lives in boats, racing cars, in trick flying. We do call for second thought on the semi-civic sponsorship and aggrandizement of entertainment wherein death may become a participant."[7]

Don Wilson's funeral was Wednesday, June 22. Manchester and Musson were buried in a joint service on Friday, June 24, at Evergreen Washelli Memorial Park in Seattle. After the service, Mira, Bill Muncey, and Russ Schleeh walked up to each casket, laid a hand on the cool polished mahogany, and said goodbye.

It was a solemn field of unlimiteds that showed up in Detroit for Gold Cup qualifying on Monday, June 27. With the *Miss U.S.* and the *Smirnoff* returning, the field included seventeen boats. Bernie Little, who had a firm contract with Anheuser Busch to have a boat at every race, bought a new hull and had Bill Brow back in the cockpit of the new *Miss Budweiser* when qualification opened at noon. Bill Muncey and *Miss U.S.* topped the qualification ladder at 115.138 mph. Chuck Thompson and the *Smirnoff* were second at 112.500 mph. The *Budweiser,* with Bill Brow, was third at 108.542 mph, and Mira and the *Tahoe Miss* were a tick of the clock behind, at 108.288 mph.

The Gold Cup was the largest sporting spectacle in the United States, with hundreds of thousands of fans coming to the banks of the Detroit River to enjoy the race. The 1966 race fell on Sunday, July 3, in the middle of the three-day weekend. It is not clear if it was the race's position in the center of the holiday weekend, or morbid curiosity sparked by the deaths in Washington, D.C., but the crowd on hand for the start of the race Sunday morning was over 300,000. The race would be carried live on Detroit's WXYZ-TV and with a tape delay to a national audience on ABC's *Wide World of Sports*. Mira and Muncey were drawn into heat 1A, and the fans were expecting a knock-down drag-out fight between the two veterans. The boats were lowered into the water a few minutes before noon. Mira strapped on his life jacket and helmet, balled his hands into fists, and punched the palms of his racing gloves to make sure they were snug. Then he took his place in the cockpit. The weather was clear and warm, with no wind. The *Tahoe Miss* rocked gently from side to side as crewmembers stepped on and off the deck to make final preparations. Mira's normal pre-race jitters were worse than usual as he remembered what happened in DC. He forced any thoughts of Donnie Wilson from his mind and began to concentrate on beating Muncey. The five-minute gun sounded at noon; Mira started the boat and moved out onto the river.

The Detroit course is a pear-shaped three-mile oval. The big turn is on the east end of the course near the Belle Isle Bridge. The small turn, on the west end just past the Detroit Yacht Club, is called the "Roostertail turn," named after the Schoenith family's Roostertail restaurant that overlooked the race course. There were a lot of rough spots on the river, but the one that had worried Mira all week was called the "Whittier bump." Directly in front of the Whittier Hotel and just before the boats enter the Belle Isle turn are some gouges on the bottom of the river. Depending on how fast the river flows, these rough spots cause three large bumps on the surface. When the water was flowing fast, the bumps were really bad; when the river was slow, the bumps were far less noticeable. Mira used the time between the five-minute gun and the one-minute gun to search out the Whittier bump and find out how bad it was going to be and which lane it was lurking in. He made a warm up lap in lane one at about 95 miles per hour. Directly in front of the hotel, the *Tahoe Miss* leapt from the water and landed precariously on its right sponson, then rocked back and forth from side to side. "Wow," Mira thought, "the water must really be flowing fast. Because that's the worst I've ever felt the bump."

Mira cruised on past the Belle Isle Bridge, headed up the backstretch toward the Detroit Yacht Club, and got ready for the start. He decided that he was going to start in lane four. He drove deep into the Roostertail turn, and then stepped down hard on the accelerator. He was focused on the big orange-and-black clock on the starting tower. He was in perfect position. He looked around for Muncey and to his surprise he saw him a half lap away, heading up the backstretch, not even past the yacht club yet. For an instant, Mira doubted himself. "How can Muncey be so far off? Maybe I'm the one that messed up?" Mira checked the clock and knew that he was right on time. Maybe Muncey had a mechanical problem? Slovak accelerated across the starting line, followed by several slower boats. The Gold Cup is a long race, and with a half lap lead on Muncey, Mira decided to take it easy and run at reduced speed unless Muncey caught up. Behind him, Muncey was driving like a bat out of hell. He was clearly upset with himself for missing the start. Muncey was running full throttle and tight on the buoy line. The bright red and white *Miss U.S.* was rocking and bouncing, but she was also making up a lot of ground. By the end of lap two, Muncey had Slovak in his sights and figured he would catch him on the next lap. Both boats headed down the front chute towards the Whittier. Mira was 200 yards ahead in lane three, traveling at about 120 mph. Muncey was in lane one and traveling at least 160 mph. Mira eased past the bump without a bobble. When Muncey hit it, the *Miss U.S.* sailed into the air. When she came down, her right sponson hit first and there was a huge explosion of water. The engine cowling, tailfin, and rear cowling all went flying into the air. Muncey was thrown out of the cockpit but miraculously landed on the deck. Somehow, he got back in the driver's seat and the boat kept going. The steering wheel was bent and Muncey had the wind knocked out of him but amazingly he was able to finish the heat. Mira came in first, the *Savair's Probe* was second, the *$ Bill* was third, and Muncey finished in fourth. As soon as Muncey returned to the pits, he collapsed in the cockpit of the boat and had to be lifted out. The *Miss U.S.* was badly damaged in the accident and had to be withdrawn from the race. Eventually, the boat was scrapped without ever being repaired.

Chuck Thompson and the *Smirnoff* won heat 1B with ease. Mira captured heat 2A and Thompson won 2B. So far, the race had not seen much competition. Slovak and Thompson were tied with 800 points and drawn into heat 3A. The fans expected a dynamite matchup. Thompson had driven for the *Tahoe Miss* team from 1963 to 1965. When he was fired, there was a lot of bad blood. More than anything, Thompson wanted to beat the *Tahoe,* win the Gold Cup, and prove that Harry Volpi, not Chuck Thompson, was the reason the boat had not lived up to its potential.

Heat 3A was set to go at 2.50 p.m. At about 2 p.m., Mira went looking for Thompson and found him getting his life jacket on. Mira offered his hand and said, "Good luck." Thompson was fifty-four years old and had a compact, stocky boxer's build. His thinning silver hair was cut into a military-style crew cut. He shook Mira's hand and said, "You know I love you like a brother." Then, pointing toward Harry Volpi, who was standing on deck of the *Tahoe Miss,* he said, "But I hate that son of a bitch and I'll do anything to beat him, so be careful and don't get in my way, because if I have to, I'll run you over."

As the boats pulled away from the pits, Thompson, who had almost twenty years' experience racing on the Detroit River, wanted lane one. Mira, remembering what had happened to Muncey in lane one earlier in the day, was content to let Thompson have it, and moved out to lane three. The *Miss Budweiser* was on Mira's right in lane four. The *Savair's Probe* was outside in lane five. The *$ Bill* and the *Chrysler Crew* trailed the field. At the starting line, Thompson had a slight lead over Mira as they flew down the straightaway. Both boats sped past the Whittier bump without incident. Heading into the big Belle Isle turn, Thompson stretched out his lead a bit. Coming off the turn, Mira opened up the throttle on the *Tahoe Miss.* It was the first time all year that he had used full power in an actual race, and the boat responded with astonishing speed. He caught the *Smirnoff* by the middle of the backstretch and pulled into the lead. A brief second after the *Tahoe* blasted ahead of the *Smirnoff,* there was a loud bang from the *Tahoe's* engine, followed by a puff of smoke, and the boat drifted to a stop. Thompson sailed past Mira and back into the lead. Half a lap later, the *Chrysler Crew,* running in last place, caught fire. Bill Sterett, the owner-driver, jumped into the river to escape the flames.

Gold Cup rules require that the race be stopped whenever a driver is in the water, so red flags and smoke flares sprang up around the course and the boats returned to the pits. It was a lucky break for Mira. His crew was able to get the *Tahoe Miss* repaired in time for the rerun of the heat, which was set to start at 4 p.m. Mira noticed the wind beginning to pick up and ruffle the water. By the time he was getting into his boat, he figured that it was blowing about 10 mph. When the wind blows against the current on the river, the course gets very lumpy and Mira thought to himself, "Oh boy, the Whittier bump is going to be even worse than before."

In the restart of the heat, Thompson went for the inside again. Slovak stayed out in lane three and the *Probe* was in lane four. The *Miss Budweiser* and the *$ Bill* were late and behind. This time, Slovak got the jump on Thompson and led going across the starting line. The two boats screamed down the straightaway at over 165 mph. As they approached the bump, Mira lifted his foot ever so lightly. It was something that racers called "feathering the throttle." It was meant to allow the engine and propeller to slow just a bit, which causes the back end of the boat to drop slightly, bringing the nose up, and giving the boat a better attitude to handle rough water. As Mira slowed and skipped uneventfully over the bump, he looked to his left and was shocked to see Thompson blast past him. Clearly, Thompson had not thought it necessary to back off. As Thompson pulled half a boat length ahead of Slovak and hit the first bump, the *Smirnoff* leapt a couple of feet into the air and came down level. She hit the second bump and landed hard on her right side. The right sponson rebounded, rocking high into the air and showing the complete underside of the boat to Mira. Then the left sponson hit and the boat spun 180 degrees and slammed into the water stern first. A cloud of spray and broken boat parts flew into the air. Mira could not believe what he had just seen. The crash reminded him so much of the Presidents Cup accident from two weeks earlier that for a moment, he thought he was having a nightmare. Mira cut the throttle on the *Tahoe* and looked over his shoulder to see if he could turn around and go back to the scene. The *Smirnoff* sank instantly. Unlike in DC, a Coast Guard helicopter was following the start and within seconds of the accident, the big Sikorsky HH-52 dropped a rescue swimmer into the water. Thompson was floating face down and by the time the swimmer had him turned over, the helicopter was settling into the water a few feet away.

Mira saw that there was nothing he could do, so he motored slowly up the back stretch towards the pits. Within forty-five seconds of the accident, the helicopter had Thompson on board and was flying toward a landing zone to transfer him to an ambulance that would speed him to Detroit Receiving Hospital.

After the boats were back on their trailers, a special owners' and drivers' meeting was called at the judges' stand for 6 p.m. The eleven remaining drivers and their team owners were loaded into several small pleasure boats to be carried up river to the official tower. Jerry Green, a sportswriter for the *Detroit News,* got into the same boat with Slovak. As they waited for the rest of the passengers, Mira perched on the port gunwale and spoke candidly about the accident he had just witnessed, "He shouldn't have been going on the inside. We were side by side. We were less than ten feet apart, maybe five—too close. There was a big hole and he dug in deeper than I did. I looked over and saw sponsons and everything flying. There were pieces in the air. It was exactly the same thing when Rex Manchester and Donnie Wilson had the same duel in Washington."[8]

The last passenger to come on board was Dr. Sinclair Finch. As soon as he was seated, the boat pulled away from the pits. The sun had slipped behind a bank of clouds and the water took on a gray cast. It was exactly 6.04 p.m. Finch had to raise his voice to be heard over the drone of the engine. "Chuck's heart stopped on the way to the hospital, but they got it going again. His chest was crushed." Finch paused to wipe tears from his eyes. "I guess I better tell you. I just received word. Chuck passed away. He never recovered consciousness. The shock was too much." On the official tower, the owners and drivers discussed what to do next. It was too late in the day to continue the race, but they voted to come back on Monday, July 4, and finish.

The following day, the beautiful summer weather gave way to gray overcast and rain showers. Racing would not get underway until noon, so salvage divers took time in the morning to raise the shattered remains of the *Smirnoff.* The jagged, splintered wreck was placed on its trailer just a few feet from the *Tahoe Miss*. Morbid fans milled around the wreck, occasionally breaking off a small piece of the blue and red deck to take home as a souvenir. Joe Falls, sports editor for the *Detroit Free Press*, spotted Slovak sitting quietly by himself next to the *Tahoe* drinking water from a paper cup. "You feel like running today?" Falls asked.

Mira looked surprised by the question, "Sure, sure I feel like running. I feel okay. If I didn't, I'd let someone else run. I wouldn't want to cause trouble for the other drivers if I wasn't ready."

Falls followed up, "I mean, I thought what happened yesterday.'

"You can't let that bother you. Chuck was my friend, but I've lost a lot of friends in the past year." Mira paused, trying to think of how to make his point. "They killed ... what? ... 350 people on the highways this weekend. Nothing is said about that. Nothing is said about all of the drinking and fooling around that leads to these accidents." Mira sipped his water. "We'll keep running. It's the only way."[9]

With the *Miss U.S.* and the *Smirnoff* out of the race, there was not any serious competition left for Mira. He easily won the rerun of heat 3A and headed into the final heat with a 300-point lead. All he needed to do was finish and he would score enough points to clinch the victory. When the final started, everyone on the beach was shocked to see Mira make a perfect start, charge across the starting line in first place, and take a couple-hundred-yard lead into the first turn. On the *Wide World of Sports* broadcast, Bill Muncey, who was helping Keith Jackson with the play-by-play said, "I'm surprised that Mira is turning it on as hard as he is." As soon as Mira reached the apex of the first turn, he felt that he had proved to everyone watching that he was far and away the fastest boat on the course, so he slowed way down to run conservatively and assure that he would finish without risk of damaging his equipment. One after another, the slower boats passed the *Tahoe Miss*, but it really did not matter. All Mira had to do was finish and the long-sought-after Gold Cup would be his. For five laps, Mira coasted along at three-quarters throttle until he saw the checkered flag wave. He patted the side of the boat with his right hand and said quietly, "Thanks, girl, for taking care of me."

He headed back to the dock, shut off the boat, and coasted in. When the crew had lines on the boat, he stood up and turned to the fans and made a courtly bow from the waist. He jumped to the dock and was met by Keith Jackson and the ABC camera crew.

"Let me take off this bucket, I cannot hear. Well, Keith, after so many years, finally." Mira smiled broadly.

"Took a long time." Jackson said.

"It was hard work of the crew, Mr. Harrah, Harry Volpi, and all the people who help us. It's a great, great achievement for all of us."

"How many times did you try for it Mira? Before you got it?" Jackson asked.

"It was a long time." Mira said humbly.

"Well let me offer you the congratulations of a personal friend. We're delighted for you."

"Yes, thank you very much, Keith."

"I know that you knew that all you had to do was finish and you had it."

"Yes, it is kind of unfair for the people to go out there and not put a good show on, but we try for the Gold Cup, which is the greatest trophy for all of us. This is the reason we play it safe. Not putting any show on, just finishing fourth or fifth and we make it." Mira said almost apologetically.

"Well you can't forget that you won three of 'em and that's where you got your edge."

"Yes, it helped."

"Well again congratulations and I know there are thousands of people around this country that are delighted for you."

"Thank you very much, Keith."

Jackson turned and faced the TV camera. "Mira Slovak, the Flying Czech, finally winning the Gold Cup. The 1966 Gold Cup, a race that has been marked by tragedy and misfortune, but great excitement as always, and that is the story from the pits. The champion has been chosen and he is Mira Slovak, driver of the *Tahoe Miss*."[10]

The victory celebration in the *Tahoe* pits was muted. The crew was quiet as they packed away the boat. Chuck had been their driver and more important their friend for three years. No one mentioned it, but everyone knew that Chuck had been pushing harder than normal because he wanted to beat the *Tahoe Miss*. He wanted to prove himself. Many of the crew members were feeling a tangle of emotions. Of course, there was sadness but for some, there was also a good bit of guilt. In spite of the stoic face that Mira put on for the reporters like Joe Falls and Keith Jackson, the accidents and the deaths did impact him deeply, and when it came time for Chuck's funeral, he felt that he just did not have the strength to face another one—his fourth in eight weeks. He hoped that Chuck would understand, but he stayed home.

Across the nation, there were mixed headlines. Some papers trumpeted Slovak's triumph but others called for an end to racing. In Seattle, Hy Zimmerman wrote a scathing editorial under the headline, "And Now, Four are Dead." The editorial opened with, "Now four men have been killed. To what purpose? The most vehement apologist for hydroplaning, no matter how hard he scrapes the statistical barrel, cannot prove the activity as safe as other sports or the cause as noble … We ask no discontinuance of the sport, if that it be, let those who will risk. We ask somber reflection on the aura with which we have surrounded the endeavor."[11]

Ten days later, the boats pulled in to a new race site in the western Canadian resort town of Kelowna, British Columbia. After the string of devastating accidents that claimed most of the top contenders, Mira had an easy time winning his first two heats and coasting to a fourth place in the final to tally enough points to win the race.

A week later, the unlimiteds were back in the U.S. at the inaugural Tri Cities Atomic Cup on the Columbia River in Kennewick, Washington, a new race site without the long heritage and big budget of Seattle's Seafair. The race organizers were looking for a way to keep the fans entertained between heats but could not afford to book the Blue Angels or the Thunderbirds. Mira saw an opportunity and offered to fly an aerobatic show with his Bücker. The promoters quickly worked out the details; after each heat of racing, Mira would get out of the *Tahoe Miss* and run up the ramp from the dock to a waiting helicopter that would fly him to the Pasco Airport. There, he would strap into his plucky little Bücker and fly back to the course and put on a twenty-five-minute one-man air show. The show was fast and exciting but was basically the same show that Mira had flown at Rockford a year before. When it came time to end the show, something caught Mira's eye. The Tri Cities racecourse was bordered on the east end by a long, tall bridge that the locals call "The Blue Bridge." There was something about the bridge that called to Mira. He spent much of his life flying large airliners several miles up in the sky, and even though he knew that while he flew a 707 from Dallas to Los Angeles at 30,000 feet, he was precisely where he was supposed to be, there was no visual point of reference to check himself against. Yet flying under a bridge meant that you had to fly the plane with pinpoint accuracy and put it exactly where you wanted to. To fly under a bridge upside down would be pretty amazing, and to fly under a bridge upside down without even having your hands on the controls meant that you had the type of skill and daring that only came along once in a generation. Mira ended his show in Tri Cities by flying over the bridge, turning around and rolling over into inverted flight, then flying under the bridge, upside down, with no hands on the controls, and then flying the length of the front straightaway upside down, waving at his fans. The race did not turn out nearly as well as the air show. The *Tahoe Miss* broke down in two of its three heats, but the one heat it did finish, it won.

Two weeks later, the unlimiteds raced in Seattle for the Seafair Trophy. Mira led the first heat for three laps before the supercharger broke, forcing him to limp through the rest of the heat in third place. Andy Anderson and the crew swapped out the damaged engine and they won their next two heats, but their point total was only good enough for second place.

The next week, they raced in Coeur d'Alene, and it is hard to imagine a better weekend. Mira was top qualifier at 116.631 mph. He won his first two heats, turning in the fastest competition lap of the weekend at 107.356 mph. Then he was loaded into the back of a Kootenai County Sheriff's cruiser and rushed to the Coeur d'Alene Air Terminal, where his Bücker was waiting. He flew an air show over the racecourse that captivated the enthusiastic crowd, landed back at the Air Terminal, and jumped back into the police cruiser, which rushed to the course with its siren blaring. He hurried to the waiting *Tahoe Miss,* strapping on his life jacket and helmet as he ran to the dock, got into the boat, and went out to win the final heat and claim the Diamond Cup with a perfect 1,200 points. He also opened up a sizable lead in the National High Points Race.

On Tuesday morning, August 16, Mira took off from Coeur d'Alene in his sturdy little Bücker for a thirteen-hour flight to Los Angeles International Airport. He flew at about 9,000 feet and quickly left the green timber of northern Idaho for the dry brush of eastern Oregon. The long time alone in the air allowed Mira time to think about all that had happened in the last few months. He was proud of what he had accomplished in Coeur d'Alene. He remembered standing on Bill Boeing's dock back in 1956, watching the Blue Angels perform over the Seafair racecourse and wishing he could fly in an air show and race a hydro at the same event. Now he had done it, and he was pretty sure that no one else had ever done that before. He watched the miniature world below him roll past and began to think about Wilson, Manchester, Musson, and Thompson. He wondered if the situation were reversed, if he had died instead of them, would any of them give up hydroplane racing to play golf or tend gardens? Of course not. To a man, they would all continue to live life the way they always had. There is a belief shared by pilots, soldiers, and race drivers: "When your time is up, your time will be up." Fate is the hunter that will track you down and find you no matter where you hide, so don't be afraid. Live life to the fullest, because when death comes for you, it will not matter if you are sitting in a rocking chair sipping tea or hurtling across the water at 200 mph—death will claim you either way.

With his mind clear that for him it was the right thing to continue to race, his thoughts turned to something else that was bothering him. There were plenty of people who were beginning to say that Mira and the *Tahoe Miss* only won the Gold Cup because "all the good boats crashed" and "all of the fast drivers were dead." The *Seattle Times* ran a story by Georg Meyers with a headline that said, "Mira Slovak's year, Victory by Default?" The bitter article ended with, "If he continues his present winning pace and emerges as the national champion of 1966 he will have a hard time persuading even himself that he did not become victor by default."

Mira, of course, knew that this whole line of thought was foolishness. He knew that he had been running in the same heats where Donnie, Rex, and Chuck had been killed. He knew that he could have taken the inside lane and he chose not to. He knew that in both cases, had he not made the decisions that he did, it would have been his boat that was smashed beyond recognition and his body floating face down in the cold water. He knew that it was madness to think that somehow, he was less of a champion because he had the skill to avoid accidents that others had not. Yet Harry Volpi had thought up a solution and had suggested it to Mira between heats at Coeur d'Alene. What if Mira drove the *Tahoe Miss* to a new world water speed record for propeller-driven boats? It would quiet all of the critics who said Mira and the *Tahoe Miss* were not fast enough. It would prove that he was the fastest driver in the sport and the *Tahoe Miss* was the fastest boat. The more Mira thought about it, the more it seemed like a perfect solution. Mira decided that as soon as he got back home, he would call Volpi and tell him that he was on board for the record run.

He landed at LAX and found a place to store his Bücker for a few days while he made some flights for Continental Airlines. On August 20, he finally returned to Santa Paula. On August 23, the *Tahoe Miss* team issued a press release announcing that they were going to try for a new speed record on Lake Tahoe between October 17 and 31.

A few days later, on August 27, Mira was back at his hangar in Santa Paula and spent all morning washing and polishing his plane. He was meticulous about keeping the plane sparkling clean. After five air shows in five weeks and a 3,000-mile round trip from Santa Paula, across the northwest and back, there was plenty of cleaning to do. It was a warm day and the big sliding doors were open to let a breeze blow through and keep the hangar cool. Mira had the cowling off and was elbow deep in the engine compartment with a red shop towel, cleaning the Lycoming. Hearing footsteps behind him, he looked over his shoulder to see a man and a woman standing side by side. The man was about Mira's own age and had sandy-colored hair. He wore round glasses that made him look a little like an owl. Next to him was a lovely blonde woman in her mid-thirties. She had stylishly short bobbed hair, a curvaceous figure, and piercing blue eyes.

The man spoke first, walking forward holding out his hand. "Mr. Slovak? Hello. I'm Hal Fishman from KTLA-TV in Los Angeles." He turned towards the woman, "This is my friend, Susan Oliver." She held out her hand and turned on a 10,000-volt smile while virtually purring, "Mr. Slovak. I'm charmed to meet you."

As Mira took her hand, he instinctively knew three things—first, Fishman and Oliver were not a romantic couple; second, Oliver radiated a powerful, feminine poise and confidence that made her one of the most exciting women he had ever met; and third, she was as attracted to him as he was to her.

"I'm very pleased to meet you." Mira said, making direct, significant eye contact with her, as he raised her fingers to his lips and lightly kissed them, "How may I help you?"

Fishman spoke first, "Well Susan is an actress. She's been on loads of TV shows: *Bonanza*, *Star Trek*, *Route 66*, and *The Twilight Zone*. You name it, she's been on it. Right now, she's doing *Peyton Place*." Oliver held up a graceful hand to stop Fishman's list. Mira noticed a look of embarrassment on her face and he understood what she was feeling. People often confused his list of accomplishments with who he was, and it bothered him. It led them to believe he was someone different. Mira could tell that she did not want him to see her as just an actress. She wanted something else.

"Mr. Slovak. May I call you Mira?" she asked with a voice as cool and sparkling as iced Prosecco. He agreed. "Mira, I am a pilot. Albeit a very new pilot, but nonetheless I am a pilot. I've been asked to take part in a celebrity airplane race at Reno this year. I read in *Flying Magazine* that you won at Reno last year."

"Actually, it was two years ago." She blushed girlishly at her mistake. It made Mira want to kiss her.

"You won at Reno. I was wondering if you could give me some pointers on how to win my race."

Mira chuckled and said, "My number one is do not crash." She laughed. "No, I am serious. Do not crash. You cannot win if you do not finish, and you must never take a risk that will keep you from finishing. Number two, you must understand that you are not racing any of the other planes and pilots. You are really only racing yourself, because if each time you race, you perform better than the last time, it means you are getting better, and that is more important than winning." Mira could tell that he was not making sense to her. "I'm sorry if my words are not helpful. English is not my first language, so maybe I'm not expressing myself correctly. Maybe words are not the best way to express what I'm trying to say. Maybe I should take you flying someday?"

"How about now?" she said with a smile that was so perfect it was almost impossible to resist.

Mira gestured toward the Bücker, with its engine cowling lying on the floor, and said, "My plane is not ready today, and tomorrow I am flying for Continental. Next weekend I have a hydroplane race in Indiana."

She was clearly disappointed, but she was not about to give up. She handed Mira a slip of paper and said, "Here is my phone number. If something changes and you have time, call me."

Mira folded the paper and put it into his wallet. "We will see."

The following weekend, Mira raced in Madison, Indiana. He won again and extended his National High Points lead even further. On the flight home from Madison, he found himself pulling Susan Oliver's phone number out and looking at it every few minutes. When he got back to LA, he called her and invited her to his apartment, where he promised to make her a home-cooked Czech meal. To Susan, the invitation sounded a little too much like a seduction setup, and knowing how strongly she was attracted to him, she did not think that she could resist, so she said no, and insisted that he take her on a proper first date to a real restaurant. Between Mira's complex schedule flying for Continental and driving the *Tahoe Miss*, and Susan's production schedule for various TV shows, it was difficult to find a day they were both free. Finally, she said that she would be attending a fundraising party for a Hollywood charity called "The Thalians," hosted by her friend Debbie Reynolds, later that week. Maybe Mira could accompany her there? Mira said he was flying that day, but agreed to meet her at the party as soon as he was finished.

The party was at the "Wolf's Lair," a famous home in the Hollywood Hills that was built to look like a French chateau. It sat on a sprawling compound above the Hollywood Reservoir, with a view of the famous Hollywood sign. It had been built in the roaring twenties by the quirky and eccentric real estate developer Milton Wolf and featured turrets, arches, and spiral staircases.

Shortly before Mira had moved to LA, he bought a bronze-colored Jaguar XK-E Roadster. When he pulled up to the valet stand at the end of a line of Bentleys and Mercedes, he was glad that he was driving something with a little status. He gave the keys to a uniformed valet and walked across the Wolf's Lair's elegant grounds, past trees strung with white lights and hanging lanterns. It was a warm summer evening and the air smelled of cedar and eucalyptus, mingled with Chanel No. 5. Most of the men were in tuxedos and the women were in evening gowns. Mira felt underdressed in his plain black suit. He stepped into the elegant home through an arched stone entryway, into a foyer with carved wooden beams and leaded-glass windows. He worked his way through massive rooms that were crowded with Hollywood's elite. He saw countless faces that looked familiar, but he had not been interested enough in American film or TV to be able to recall their names. He finally spotted Susan on the pool terrace at the back of the house overlooking the Hollywood Reservoir. She was wearing a tight sleeveless black velvet dress that must have cost more than his mother's entire wardrobe. Her hair was pinned up and she had long sparkling earrings. As she hurried across the room to greet him, Mira thought that she looked every bit the movie starlet people told him she was. She kissed him politely on the cheek and said, "Oh good! I'm so glad you made it. I have champagne, do you want some?"

"Please."

She raised a perfectly manicured hand to stop a waiter in a tail coat carrying a silver tray of champagne glasses and handed Mira a drink. "Now, let me introduce you to my friends." She grabbed Mira's free hand and pulled him toward the mass of revelers. Susan headed first toward Debbie Reynolds, but on the way passed Kirk Douglas. "Kirk, this is my friend Mira. He's the pilot I've been telling you about."

Douglas held out his hand and said, "Very pleased to meet you, Milo."

Mira started to correct him and say "It's Mira," but before the words formed in his mouth, Douglas had turned his back and was headed away. Next, they met Paul Newman, who was a big fan of motorsports of all kinds, and had actually heard of Mira. They exchanged a few brief words about racing.

As they turned away from Newman, they bumped into Natalie Wood, who gave Susan a big hug and turned to Mira saying, "So, this must be your pilot friend?" Natalie held out her hand and said, "How wonderful to meet you."

Mira took her hand in his and raised it gently to his lips and said, "Charmed, I'm sure."

Natalie giggled and said, "Oh, a real gentleman. You hold on to this one, Susan."

A few moments later, Debbie Reynolds picked up a microphone and said, "I'd like to make an announcement. We have a special treat in store for you tonight. We have busses pulling up out front right now that will take you all down to Grauman's Chinese Theater for a special sneak preview of Paramount's new film '*Is Paris Burning?*'"

Mira and Susan were much more interested in getting to know each other than in seeing the new movie. Susan whispered in Mira's ear, "Unless you're excited about the movie, why don't we sneak away and grab a quiet dinner together?"

Mira agreed, and they headed to the valet to pick up their cars. Susan was driving a 1932 Mercedes Benz convertible with a cream body and black swooping fenders. As she settled herself into the sporty roadster, the valet pulled up in Mira's Jag. She smiled at Mira and said, "Let's go to La Scala. Last one there pays!" She slipped the powerful classic into gear and it pulled away with a throaty growl. Mira's car was much newer and had great handling, so he had no trouble staying right on Susan's tail as they raced through the dark Hollywood Hills and wound down into the city. He pulled up alongside her as they sped along Santa Monica Boulevard toward La Scala in Beverly Hills. They slowed for a traffic signal, but just before the light went red, she accelerated through the intersection, leaving Mira stopped at the light. She reached the valet stand, tossed her keys to the valet and was leaning, vamp-like, against a street sign when Mira pulled up. "So you're supposed to be a hotshot racer? What will your fans say when they hear you got beat by a girl?" She laughed.

As they walked into the legendary eatery, the owner, Jean Leon, met Susan with a kiss on the cheek and said with his heavy Basque accent, "Suzan darling, who eez zhis handzome man?" Susan introduced Mira while Leon, carrying two menus, led them towards the back of the restaurant and a booth with soft red leather upholstery and dim romantic lighting. "May I get you zomting from za bar?"

"Oh yes, I'd love a bottle of cabernet and a plate of fried mozzarella."

"Excellent choices, Madame," Leon said, and left the table.

There are few things more exciting than a really good first date, and Mira and Susan were having a wonderful time. As they waited for their wine, Mira said, "There aren't a lot of women who fly airplanes. What made you want to become a pilot?"

Susan became very animated when she talked about flying. It was one of the things Mira liked about her. "Well, at first I didn't. I was in Paris, gosh, I think that it was 1959. And I was flying home with Gene Kelly. Do you know Gene? He's an amazing dancer. So we're on this fully loaded Boeing 707. First we went through a terrible storm and had to make an unscheduled landing in London. Then somewhere over the middle of the Atlantic we suddenly went 'bump in the night.'"[12]

The waiter came to the table and interrupted the story while setting a plate of warm, crunchy fried cheese smothered in fragrant marinara sauce on the table, and then poured two glasses of a rich crimson-colored cabernet.

Susan took a sip of her wine and continued her story. "With a sharp lunge, the plane started falling, tumbling hard. It was impossible to tell if we were going down or up, or around in a spin, but the g-forces became so severe that everyone was jerked downward by a force six to eight times their own weight. People began screaming just to fight back at the terrible pressure on their faces and bodies as down we hurtled, pulled by gravity's giant magnet."[13]

Susan paused to take a bit of the cheese with her fork and sipped at her wine. She made a self-deprecating little laugh and said, "I remember thinking, 'I can't go now. My billing will be lousy.' Headlines flashed briefly in front of me: AIRLINE DISASTER! GENE KELLY KILLED! Then under 'Other Victims', my name listed alphabetically as Oliver comma Susan comma actress comma New York City."[14] Susan laughed at her own foolishness and went on. "I was thinking that it would all be over quickly, that there was no way the pilot could pull us out. But that great man, Captain Waldo Lynch, did." Susan raised her glass as if to toast Captain Lynch. "About three seconds before we would have plunged into the ocean forever, Captain Lynch was able to regain control and pull the plane out of its dive and return to proper cruising altitude. After an hour and a half's more flight we managed to make a safe landing in Gander, Newfoundland.

"Needless to say, I wasn't much on flying after that. But it's hard being an actress when you can't fly. Most of the jobs are either in LA or New York and you have to be able to move quickly from one to the other. [15] Oddly enough it was a hypnotist in a night club who got me over my fear of flying. The irony is she cured me so well that I not only got back on commercial planes, but I took up flying myself!"[16]

After Susan finished her story, the waiter came to the table to take their orders. As they waited for their food, Susan asked Mira about his escape from the communists. Mira had told the story countless times and was easily able to weave a fascinating description of his adventure, which captivated Susan. Behind all the sweetness, excitement, and romance of a first date is the real mission, which is to find out if the other person is suitable and available for a relationship. Susan was very direct and at the end of Mira's story she asked, "So, are you seeing anybody?"

Mira smiled and said, "No. 100 percent single. How about you?"

Susan answered with a demure "No." She shook her head gently and her glittering ear rings swayed side to side. "I've been taking a bit of a break from dating. I was in a two-year-long romance with Sandy Koufax, but it didn't work." They sipped their wine and Susan described what her relationship with the two-time World Series MVP Los Angeles Dodgers pitcher had been like—how she had sat in the stands watching him throw two of his no hitters and the glamour of going to the World Series. She described how he hated being a celebrity, and they would try to sneak into tiny little dive restaurants on the outskirts of LA, where no one knew them so they could eat in peace. In the end, they wanted different things and had drifted apart, but they were still very good friends.

For their second date, Mira picked Susan up in his convertible Jaguar and brought her to his apartment at the elegant Barrington Plaza on Wilshire Boulevard. Susan felt as nervous as a schoolgirl as they rode the elevator up to the ninth floor. When they arrived at his apartment, she was impressed to see that Mira had placed a low glass coffee table in front of a large picture window that looked out over the LA skyline. On the table, he had set cloth placemats with matching napkins and crystal glasses, along with a bouquet of roses and tapered candles.[17]

There was a glazed duck roasting in the oven and a pot of red cabbage simmering on the stove. The apartment smelled like heaven. After they came in, the first thing Mira did was light the candles, then baste the duck, and then whip up a batch of frosty Mai Tais. In her entire life, no other man had treated Susan so special. She knew right then that she would be unable to resist his charms. They lounged against the pillows on the floor, in front of the low table, talking and flirting while the duck cooked, the sun set, and the lights of LA winked on.

Susan told Mira about her early days in acting. Her rise in her career had been almost as meteoritic as Mira's had been. In the early 1950s, she had lived in virtual poverty in Greenwich Village and attended Sandy Meisner's famous Neighborhood Playhouse School with a number of other struggling actors, including Joanne Woodward and Steve McQueen. "I lived at 717 Greenwich Street in the tiniest apartment. Steve would come by and eat gobs of corn on the cob and sweet potatoes. One day he took me on his motorcycle up to 125th Street, where we ran out of gas. I had twenty cents. Steve used fifteen to buy gas and I took the nickel and called my mother."[18]

After five years working on and off Broadway, she went to Hollywood in 1957. In less than a week, she landed the leading role in a major Warner Brothers movie called *Green Eyes*. She had blue eyes but was still able to play the title character because the film was shot in black and white. When *Green Eyes* wrapped, Jack Warner offered Susan a seven-year contract.

She talked easily about her time at Warner Brothers, working opposite famous stars like Elizabeth Taylor and Eddie Fisher in films like *Butterfield Eight*. Mira knew next to nothing about Hollywood. "Why should I know these people? They don't fly anything." She could talk openly and honestly without feeling like she was name dropping or trying to impress him.

When the timer dinged to signal that the duck was ready, Susan followed Mira into the kitchen. He opened the oven door and, using a mitt, pulled out the metal roasting rack. Somehow, the glass roasting dish with the beautiful duck and its crisp dark brown skin slid off the end of the rack and fell to the floor. The glass dish shattered into a million shards while the delicious-smelling duck rolled across the floor into a corner of the kitchen. Susan was mortified and wondered how Mira would react to the disaster. Mira looked at the ruined duck, turned towards Susan, shrugged his shoulder and said, "Well, I guess we're going out for dinner." They both began to giggle. As the giggles turned in to belly laughs, Susan wrapped her arms around Mira's neck and kissed him for the first time. Later that night, as they headed to bed, Mira made a touching ceremony of taking the 8 × 10-inch silver picture frame that sat on the nightstand next to his bed and slid out his mother's photograph to replace it with one of Susan.

Mira's next race was on Mission Bay in San Diego, the weekend of September 24 and 25. Susan could not come because she was flying in the celebrity airplane race in Reno on the 24th. She did well, leading most of the race, but took a wrong turn shortly before the finish and ended up taking second place behind actor James Francisco. Mira flew his Bücker down to Lindbergh Field in San Diego so he could perform his air show act for the crowds in between heats.

With only two races left, and the *Tahoe Miss* holding a huge lead, Mira and the *Tahoe Miss* seemed like a virtual lock for the Championship. For any other team, this would have been cause for joyous optimism and unity, but not so for the *Tahoe Miss*. The fragile balance of power between team manager Harry Volpi and crew chief Andy Anderson was falling apart. Anderson, looking at their big lead in points, knew that their goal was in sight and he just wanted to play it safe and run conservatively, grab a few seconds or thirds, and wrap up the championship. Volpi, seeing the big cushion they had, figured he could afford to take a risk and decided to put in one of his powerful, but still untested, experimental turbocharged engines, and try to stun the racing community with unexpected speed and power.

Volpi insisted that Anderson replace the dependable race engine with a new turbocharged one. When Anderson refused, Volpi threatened to fire him. Anderson complained directly to Mr. Harrah, who called Volpi on the carpet and insisted that the team run their normal race engines and do everything they could to win the championship. Harrah told Volpi he could run the big turbochargers later at the world water speed record trials in October, once the season was over and the championship was secure. Volpi gave in to Harrah's demands, but then fired Anderson for going behind his back to speak to Harrah. Anderson appealed his firing to the employment department of Harrah's Club and was reinstated, and then marched into Volpi's office and told him, "You can't fire me, I quit!" It was against this highly volatile and unhappy backdrop that Mira arrived in San Diego to try to win his second national championship.

Bill Harrah told Mira, "Run safe, collect as many points as possible, but don't risk the equipment."

It was tense in the *Tahoe Miss* pits, but Mira did as he was told, qualifying comfortably a few mph below the top speed of Bill Brow and the *Miss Budweiser*. Then he took second place finishes in heats 1C and 2B. As soon as he got back to the beach from heat 2B, he jumped into a police cruiser that rushed him to Lindbergh Field, where he got into his waiting Bücker, flew back to Mission Bay, and performed a thrilling air show. He landed at Lindbergh and got another police ride back to the pits, just in time to jump into the *Tahoe Miss* for the final heat. On the run to the start, Mira realized that the *Tahoe Miss's* engine was well down on power and just could not keep up with the rest of the fleet. He floundered around in last place until the engine died completely and the boat drifted to a stop. Brow and the *Miss Budweiser* went on to win the heat and the race, while Mira stood helplessly on the deck of the *Tahoe Miss* as she rocked quietly with the waves. When the towboat operator came to toss Mira a rope, he hollered, "Congratulations!"

"What for?" Mira shouted back.

"The guy on the radio said no one can catch you now. You've won National High Points!"

When Mira got back to the pits, a couple of crew members shook his hand. Several fans lined up to ask for his autograph, but there was no celebration. The crew did not cheer or clap or toss him in the water the way his Bardahl crew had in 1958. This was so very different.

The next weekend was the tenth and final race of the 1966 season, on Folsom Lake's Granite Bay, outside Sacramento. Susan came along, anxious to see her first unlimited race. She was impressed by the speed and power of *Tahoe Miss*, but the knowledge that four drivers had been killed earlier in the season kept her from being able to enjoy watching Mira race. He won his first two heats, and then put on another air show in his Bücker before heading out for the final heat. A second-place finish in the final would have given the *Tahoe* enough points to win the race. Mira had the *Tahoe Miss* running in second when a connecting rod broke and punched through the side of the engine block. The long, bloody 1966 unlimited season that had lasted for five months and claimed four drivers came to an end for Mira as the big red hydro coasted to a stop. The disappointed *Tahoe* crew trucked the hydroplane back to Reno to prepare for the assault on the world water speed record, while Mira flew Susan home.

The existing record was 200.419 mph, set by the *Miss U.S.* in 1960. To break the record, Mira and the *Tahoe Miss* would have to better it by 1.5 percent, to 203.497 mph. To do that, they would have to make two runs through a measured mile course, averaging less than 17.7 seconds per run. Bill Harrah spent more than $10,000 setting up a course along the picturesque Nevada side of Lake Tahoe, between Deadman Point and Cave Rock, with the pits located on the sandy beach in Zephyr Cove. There was a 5-mile run into the measured mile, and 10 miles available for the run out. The American Power Boat Association issued a twelve-day sanction, authorizing the Tahoe team to make an official record attempt between October 19 and October 30. Mira arrived at the pits on the morning of the 19th, just after sunrise. The sky was dark blue, painted with streaks of pink, as the last few stars faded away. The lake lapped softly on the sandy beach while the crew members prepared the boat. The temperature in the pits was just above freezing, and the *Tahoe Miss* was covered with droplets of condensation. As the thin 0.25-inch birch plywood skin cooled faster than the thick oak frames, the condensation was much thicker over the deck than it was over the frames. At this early hour, Mira could see the boat's entire intricate skeleton outlined in condensation droplets on the deck. He approached the boat alone. It had only been two weeks since he last drove, but somehow the boat looked alien to him, more of a stranger than a friend. He walked to the bow of the *Tahoe Miss* and laid his hands on the deck and leaned in to whisper, as if he was talking to a horse, "Where are we going, you and I? What will we find out there on the water? Whatever it is and wherever we go, let's take care of each other, shall we?"[19]

The speed run was open to all of the unlimited teams but the only other team to show up was Bernie Little's *Miss Budweiser*, driven by Bill Brow.

Volpi did not want to turn the *Tahoe Miss* over to Mira until he was confident that everything was perfect, so he took the boat out first. He could not get the boat to plane, and it just wallowed in the water with its engine straining until something broke. She was towed back to the pits to be lifted onto her trailer so her engine could be replaced. Bill Brow and the *Miss Budweiser* did not perform any better. The 19th drew to a close with neither boat making it onto the course. The next morning, the wind began to blow and Lake Tahoe was soon covered with whitecaps. The boats did not leave their trailers all day.

That night, during dinner at the Zephyr Cove Lodge, the head chef, Jimmy Hill, began to banter with Mira, claiming that he "could drive the *Tahoe Miss* a thousand times better than Mira!"

Mira joked back, "Really, you think so? Well I can damn well cook a thousand times better than you!"

The next morning, the water was still too rough to run, and while the crew worked on the boat, waiting for the wind to die down, Mira walked across the sandy beach to the Zephyr Cove Lodge and through the green painted kitchen door. He found Chef Jimmy and handed him a shopping list—four ducks, three heads of red cabbage, 2 pounds of bacon, onion, celery, vinegar, a bell pepper, and croutons. "What is this?" Jimmy asked.

"It is dinner. Take the night off, I'm cooking tonight."

"I don't know if Mr. Harrah would like me to take a night off without his permission."

"Okay, then you can stay and be my sous chef, but tonight I'm making dinner."

While the wind blew and the waves rolled up onto the beach, Mira traded his driver's suit and crash helmet for a white chef's coat and a tall *toque blanche.* He toiled in the kitchen for hours making roast duck seasoned with garlic and caraway seeds, Czech bread dumplings with croutons, sweet red cabbage with bacon, French onion soup, and a tossed green salad.

The dinner was a huge success and several diners asked for seconds and even thirds. When the table was clear, Jimmy presented Mira with a contract from Harrah, offering to hire him as a student cook, guaranteeing him eight hours of work a day and a starting salary of $2 per hour, but he was expected to report for work at 5 a.m. the next morning. Mira read the contract out loud and when he got to the part about reporting at 5 a.m., he announced, "5 a.m.! Not me. I quit and will stick with boat driving!"

The next day, Saturday, October 22, the weather was perfect, but the reluctant *Tahoe Miss* and her big turbocharged engine still refused to cooperate. Volpi's attempts to coax the boat up onto plane only resulted in another blown engine. Sunday was not any better, nor was Monday. As the crew began to pull another of Harry's broken engines from the boat, a fan called out from behind the pit fence "What number engine is this?"

Mira quipped back "We don't number them anymore; we just call them 'Next.'" It was actually their fourth engine. They started their mission with seven engines and lots of confidence. They were now down to three, and Mira had not been able to make even one high-speed pass on the mile course. While Mira waited for the engine to be repaired, he gave an interview to *Associated Press* reporter Morton L. Saltzman. Mira said that every time he drove his race boat he gave communism "a punch in the nose." He went on to explain, "Racing was a small way to remind Americans of my escape and my experience with communism." The quotes appeared in various newspapers across the country the next morning and for the first time, there was criticism. Hy Zimmerman of the *Seattle Times* wrote a story under the headline "Enough is Enough:"

> Come off it Miro. It's getting a bit thick. Miro Slovak was quoted as saying he feels he gives Communism a "punch in the nose" each time he races a boat at speeds that could end his life. How? Can't you just see Mao shudder each time Miro steps into a hydroplane?—Americans, particularly those taking punches at Red noses in the muck and ooze of Viet-Nam, hardly need

> reminder of Communism's threat. Race your boat Miro, fly your plane upside down, seek your thrills. But don't paint your pleasures patriotic![20]

Mira was shocked and hurt by the *Times*'s negative reaction. He knew that part of it was that Zimmerman had soured on hydro racing after the deaths on the Potomac, but Mira could also see that America was changing. There was a growing antiwar movement that was protesting the war in Vietnam, and patriotism was increasingly seen as old fashioned and out of touch with modern values. Mira was not about to give up on his mission to spread the word about the dangers of communism, but he knew that he was going to have to craft a subtler message.

Tuesday the 25th was Mira's thirty-seventh birthday. He kept the information to himself, thinking, "When we set the record and have something to celebrate, I'll tell the crew and then we can make it a double celebration." The *Miss Budweiser* was not fairing any better than the *Tahoe Miss*, and Tuesday ended without a successful run for either boat. The *Tahoe* crew was trying to remain optimistic, but Mira could see that the frustration was beginning to take its toll.

On Wednesday, Volpi finally gave Mira the go-ahead to take the boat out. It was a cold morning, and Mira knew that if he really got up to speed, the chilly air rushing past the cockpit would freeze him, so he put on his heavy leather flying jacket to stay warm. In previous runs, the turbocharger's exhaust swirled into the cockpit, making it difficult to breathe, so Mira wore a fighter pilot's oxygen mask. The run started promisingly. The boat popped right up on plane, and Mira made a northbound run at barely quarter throttle, but still saw 173 mph on the speedometer. "If this one holds together for a full-throttle run, we'll break the record easily." He turned around to make the southbound run, still above 160 mph. As he came out of the timing traps, he slowed to turn, planning to make a couple more runs, giving the powerful turbocharged engine a bit more throttle each time. He was doing 125 mph and was right in front of the pits when his world exploded into fire and noise. The turbocharger blew up with a massive "boom" and the boat was engulfed in a ball of flame. Mira ducked behind the windshield, cut the throttle, and shut off the fuel, but the fire continued to roar. He smelled burning leather and realized his jacket was on fire. Next, he smelled burning rubber and knew that his oxygen mask was starting to melt. He slammed his palm down on the red disc in the center of the dashboard to activate the carbon dioxide fire extinguishers, then stood up in the burning boat and jumped sideways out of the cockpit. He hit the water with his back and felt the air punched out of his lungs as he began to tumble across the lake. He tried to tuck into a ball to protect his arms and legs. When he finally stopped rolling, his first thought was how cold the water was. Next, he thought, "If I'm worried about the cold I must not be hurt."

Harry Volpi sped across the lake in a crash boat. He reached Mira, but his small boat did not carry any skin divers or a rescue basket. There was only a water ski ladder that Mira had to climb by himself to get into the boat. As he climbed on board, his left hip hurt so badly that he screamed in pain. Volpi rushed Mira back toward shore. Mira started to shake uncontrollably. Whether it was shock or cold water, Mira could not tell. At the dock, Mira was met by Dr. Cliff Wright, an old friend, who wanted to bundle Mira into a waiting ambulance and get him to the hospital. When Mira refused to go, the two had an argument on the dock, punctuated by nervous laughter from Mira and earnest pleading from Wright. Eventually, Wright did an examination on the dock. Mira had first- and second-degree burns to his face. His helmet and flight jacket were burned, his pants ripped, and he had serious bruises on his arm. During his tumble across the lake, his hip had been knocked out of joint, and then back in, but there were no major injuries, and the shock was beginning to wear off.

Mira limped across the beach to the Lodge to get a dry change of clothes. Once alone, he reflected that "If it is the type of accident that only requires a change of clothes, I'm pretty lucky." Just then, he caught sight of himself in a mirror and thought that the pale white skin around his eyes, protected by his goggles, surrounded by the angry burned red skin on the rest of his face, made him look like some strange owl. "Maybe I can tell people it's just sunburn?" That night, the crew presented him with a belated birthday cake that was decorated with a *Tahoe Miss* made out of red frosting and a small guardian angel looking down from the corner of the cake.

There were four more days left on the sanction, but everyone knew that the record run was over. All seven powerful turbocharged engines were wrecked. Volpi sent a crewman up to the shop in Reno to pick up some of the normal racing engines. Once the regular engine was installed, Mira went out and made a few passes through the timing traps at over 160 mph, well below the record. Finally, on Sunday, October 30, the sanction expired and the *Budweiser* and the *Tahoe* teams packed up to head home.

Mira was disappointed, but the disappointment did not last long. Czechoslovakia had reformed its travel policy, and Maria was allowed to visit the U.S. She flew into Seattle and Mira flew up to meet her. It was a joyous reunion as Maria, now sixty years old and graying, walked off the plane carrying two shopping bags overflowing with homemade treats. Mira ran towards his mother and swept her up in a long, tearful embrace. It had been thirteen years since they had seen each other. They both had aged, but the bond between them had done nothing but grow stronger.

Mira drove to the Cechs' house overlooking Lake Washington. As soon as his rental car pulled into the driveway, Blanche dashed out the door to embrace Maria like a long-lost sister. After a quick tour of the lovely home, the three of them sat around Blanche's kitchen table talking in Czech. As the conversation bounced back and forth, Maria unpacked a box of homemade cookies, Blanche poured coffee, and they talked long into the night.

The next day, Mira took Maria on a tour of Seattle, showing her Aero Copter, Stan Sayres Pits, and his old apartment on Alki Point. When they were done in Seattle, Mira and Maria flew to Los Angeles, where Mira again played tour guide, making sure that she saw the famous Hollywood sign, the Walk of Fame, and Grauman's Chinese Theater, where they looked for the footprints of Marilyn Monroe, Frank Sinatra, and John Wayne. That night, they met Susan for dinner. Maria gave Mira a garnet ring that she had worn when she was younger. In a touching gesture, Mira slipped it onto Susan's finger. Afterwards, Maria flew to Houston and caught a connecting flight to Paraguay to visit the Engels family. They had immigrated to South America as soon as the Nazi surrender was signed.

Shortly after Maria left, Jarda came to visit. When it was time for Jarda to return home, he decided not to get on the plane, and asked for political asylum. With Mira's assistance, Jarda was granted a work visa and given a job working for Bill Harrah. Harrah had an amazing collection of cars and was always adding more. Jarda's job was to drive a truck around the U.S., picking up Harrah's newest additions.

29

Flights Over Water: The North Atlantic, 1967

Susan's relationship with Mira was unlike anything else she had experienced. With other men, she had been strong, confident, and an equal. She knew that her strength and independence were what attracted Mira to her, but the longer she was around him, the more insecure she became. Mira's total lack of interest in Hollywood had at first been liberating and refreshing, but it was becoming a problem. If Mira sincerely thought that the whole Hollywood scene was frivolous and pointless, then it also meant that on some level Mira felt the same about her career, and that was devastating to her. Aside from an obvious physical attraction, the only thing that the two really shared was a love of aviation, but in the aviation world, Mira was a famous pilot with an international reputation and over 15,000 hours in the air in dozens of different airplanes. Susan was a new pilot with less than 400 hours, and most of that was in small trainers; she was really just a novice.

She wanted to find a way to impress Mira—to show him she was his equal. One night, she was having dinner at her favorite Beverly Hills restaurant, La Scala, with her friend Hal Fishman. They were sharing red wine and white pasta, and Hal announced, "I have a brilliant idea for you, Susan. Here you've been studying Russian for a number of years now, plus you have your instrument and commercial ratings. Why don't you combine the two and do a record flight across the North Atlantic and go on into Moscow for the Moscow Film Festival? If you can get permission from them, it'll be a big deal because no American light plane has been allowed in there for years."[1]

Susan had had enough of La Scala's cabernet that the idea sounded good, so she raised her glass and clinked it against Hal's. "Sure, why not?"

When Susan told Mira of her plan, he responded cautiously. He knew that Susan had only been flying two years and was not nearly experienced enough to make a solo transatlantic flight in a single-engine plane. Mira knew of a ferry service that would not send a single-engine plane over the north Atlantic unless the pilot had at least 3,000 hours. He also felt that she was doing this to try to impress him, and that seemed like the wrong reason. Another nagging thought was that for Susan to try such a major endeavor with such limited experience meant that she really did not understand flying the way she should. He kept his doubts to himself and told Susan that he would help her train for the flight, but if in his opinion, she was not ready to go, she must promise to pull out.

Susan began by working with her Russian instructor to write a letter to the Soviet Air Ministry seeking permission to fly to Moscow. To everyone's surprise, the Soviets agreed, but she must enter the country from Copenhagen between August 14 and 21, 1967. Armed with her approval from the Soviets, she approached her friend Al Rockwell at Rockwell International and asked for a sponsorship. Rockwell agreed that if Susan would buy a Rockwell Aero Commander 200, Rockwell would underwrite the whole expedition and work with the Federal Aviation Administration and International Civil Aviation Organization to assure that all the proper permits, flight plans, and paperwork were taken care of. Susan was thrilled and bought a brand-new blue-and-white Aero Commander 200 for $30,680, with a few thousand dollars down and a promise to make payments of $650 per month.

Susan began to attend air shows to promote her sponsor. Sometimes, Mira would be at the same show performing in his Bücker. When they were lucky enough to be together, people treated them like aviation royalty, crowding around them both, asking for autographs and interviews.

Susan missed an air show in Oregon while her plane was being refitted with better navigational aids; Mira went anyway. After he finished his performance, he was approached by a stocky man with thinning hair and a round face. The stranger held out his hand and said, "Hello, I'm Ernest Gann."

Mira did not know the Hollywood crowd that hung around Susan, but Ernest Gann was a name he recognized. Gann had started out as an airline pilot, but he began writing novels in his spare time. His books sold well. By the mid-1950s, he was America's premier aviation writer, and by the mid-1960s, he had written screenplays for eight of his bestselling books, turning them into successful movies starring some of Hollywood's strongest leading men, including John Wayne (*Island in the Sky* and *The High and the*

Mighty), Clark Gable (*Soldier of Fortune*), and Rock Hudson (*Twilight for the Gods*). Mira was impressed that someone as successful as Ernest Gann would even know his name.

"Hello, Mr. Gann, how may I help you?"

"Oh, hell, Mira, call me Ernie!"

"Yes sir, Mr. Gann, I would be happy to call you Ernie."

"So Mira, that Bücker of yours sure is a beautiful plane. Have you ever considered selling it?

Mira was caught off guard. "Mr. Gann, my Bücker is very special and I don't think I'd ever sell it."

"That's too bad. It's a wonderful plane and I'd give you darn near anything you wanted for it." Gann paused and then said, "If you're done flying for the day, why don't you join me for a beer?" Mira agreed.

Most general aviation fields have at least one small mom-and-pop restaurant that serves burgers and beer. Gann and Mira walked across the grass apron to a tiny building surrounded by a rickety wooden deck. Hanging in one of the windows was a red neon sign flashing the word "Beer!" They found an empty table on the deck that overlooked the runway and each ordered a cheeseburger and a mug of beer. While they waited for their meals, Gann said, "Tell me how you got started in aviation." Mira felt at ease with Gann and shared his personal history, including the stories of the burning Siebel, flying the iced-up Li-2 into Kosice, and finally his escape from communism. Gann had spent many years piloting DC-3s. He was impressed by Mira's understanding of the rugged twin-engine plane and amazed at how closely some of Mira's experiences mirrored Gann's own. The two became friends and spent much longer chatting over their beers than either had intended. When the mugs were empty, they parted ways, but only after Mira made Gann promise to come visit him in Santa Paula.

In the summer of 1967, Mira was working to upgrade to captain on Continental's 707s. At the end of July, he made the jump. It was a huge accomplishment. In an effort to convince Continental of his commitment to flying he resigned from the *Tahoe Miss* team to concentrate 100 percent on upgrading to Captain. When Mira had defected in 1953, he was a captain for a major airline. It had taken fourteen years, thousands of hours, and quite literally an act of Congress, but finally, Mira was back where he belonged—flying in the left seat for a major airline.

Mira was scheduled to fly his Bücker to Seattle to perform in between heats at the Gold Cup race on Lake Washington. On July 30, he got a phone call from Bill Sterett, owner of the *Miss Chrysler Crew*. The boat had already won the World Championship race in Detroit. Sterett had been running his seven-liter hydroplane *Miss Crazy Thing* at the Inboard National Championships in Guntersville, Alabama and had crashed hard, dislocating his hip. Sterett was calling from his hospital bed and wanted to know if Mira would drive at the Gold Cup for him. Mira said, "Of course, I'd be happy to as long as I can get Continental's approval!" Continental gave their okay and Mira headed to Seattle.

When he arrived in Seattle on August 2, Mira was surprised by a story in the *Seattle Times* where Chuck Hickling, who had replaced Mira as driver in the *Tahoe Miss* (now called the *Harrah's Club*), commented, "Mira won't do much in the *Chrysler Crew*. Only Bill Sterett can drive that boat." When the *Times* asked Mira to respond, he said, "He is absolutely right. Nobody can replace Bill Sterett." He then went out and turned a lap of 114.407 mph—the fastest in the boat's career

The day before the Gold Cup was the Seafair Trophy Race. Most of the top teams chose to skip the race to save their equipment. Mira and Bill Muncey, who was driving the *Miss U.S.*, decided that the fans deserved to see a race, so they elected to run. When the race started, Slovak and Muncey hit the line side by side, Muncey in lane one and Mira in lane two. They battled deck to deck for five laps in a classic Mira *v.* Muncey duel that saw the lead change hands several times, with Mira sneaking ahead to win at the last second. Mira's fastest lap was over 112 mph, and his heat average was 107.355 mph. Both were all-time bests for the *Chrysler Crew.* The second heat was every bit as close as the first, until Muncey's engine broke and the *Miss U.S.* went dead in the water. Mira coasted around at 96 mph to win the heat. Mira was declared the race winner. It was the forty-first unlimited race and his tenth career victory. As soon as the Seafair Race was over, Mira jumped into a waiting helicopter and was shuttled to Boeing Field, where his Bücker was waiting. He flew back to the racecourse to put on another of his now-famous air shows. He finished the show, landed back at Boeing Field, and then rode the helicopter back to the pits to be on hand for the draw for the first heat of the Gold Cup. The following day, the *Seattle Times* ran a story that detailed Mira's day under the headline "Mira Was Everywhere."

Sunday morning was gray, with a high overcast that blocked the sun. The local TV stations were idled by a strike of the IBEW, so there would not be any TV coverage, and the audience at the lake swelled to record levels. Heat 1A promised to be a hard-fought battle, with three of the top qualifiers meeting up. The field included a new *Miss Bardahl* driven by young Billy Schumacher, a new *Notre Dame* with veteran Jack Regas, and Chuck Hickling in the *Harrah's Club*.

When the starter's gun fired, Schumacher and the *Bardahl* grabbed lane one and the lead, with the *Notre Dame* in lane three charging hard. As the boats headed toward the first turn at over 160 mph, the *Notre Dame* hit a roller, made a couple of big hops, and buried her nose in the water with a terrific explosion that looked eerily similar to Mira's accident in 1963. Chuck Hickling in the *Harrah's Club* had made an awful start and was trailing the field by several seconds. Hickling, frustrated with himself and trying hard to make up time, came screaming into the accident scene at full throttle. The *Harrah's Club* hit the sinking wreck of the *Notre Dame* and was launched 20 feet into the air. Hydroplanes don't fly well, and after sailing almost a hundred feet, *Harrah's Club* slammed back into the lake nose first, pitching Hickling out and tumbling end over end, landing upside down with a huge splash. Red flares and smoke bombs shut down the racing. Within seconds, a Coast Guard helicopter set down next to Regas and loaded him onboard while a rescue boat rushed to aide Hickling. Neither driver was seriously hurt, but once again, fans and drivers were reminded of just how dangerous the sport had become.

When the wreckage was cleared away, Billy Schumacher and the *Miss Bardahl* won the restart of the heat and went on to win race. It was a difficult day for Mira. The *Chrysler Crew* only finished one of the three heats she started, earning Mira a disappointing tenth place.

Before Mira left the race course, he stopped at Harrah's pits. The boat was still on the bottom of Lake Washington and Mira thought the sight of the empty trailer was one of the saddest things he had ever seen. Harry Vopli took a break from loading up the race team's truck and walked over to Mira. The two men embraced and Volpi said, "I think we're looking for a driver. Do you want to come back next season?"

Mira nodded and said, "Yah, I'd like that." The men shook hands and Mira would be back driving for Harrah for the 1968 season.

Susan's plans for her Moscow flight had fallen behind schedule. She needed to take the plane to Florida to have long-range fuel tanks installed. There was no way the tanks could be fitted in time to meet the Soviet deadline, but her requests for an extension had gone unanswered. She was continuing to plan for the trip and hoped that details with the Soviets could be resolved before she had to leave.

Mira had a race in the *Chrysler Crew* in Kelowna, BC, on August 19, where he nabbed fourth place, followed by several straight days of flying for Continental. Ernest Gann's offer to buy his Bücker had been weighing on Mira's mind. He had been thinking about changing his aerobatic act anyway. He wanted to try acrobatics with a glider. It was much more challenging in a glider than a biplane, and acrobatic glider acts were not nearly as common as biplane acts, so it would be easier to book shows. He scoured the flying magazines, learning all he could about gliders. Eventually, he identified one that he wanted to buy—a Fournier RF-4 powered glider built by Sportavia in Schmidtheim, West Germany. The unique powered glider used a 36-hp Volkswagen engine and looked like a fun plane to fly cross-country. Yet Mira, ever the showman and entrepreneur, had bigger plans. He wanted to open up a Sportavia dealership and figured that to promote the plane he would buy it in Germany and then fly it home across the Atlantic, in what would surely be the world's first solo transatlantic glider flight. This amazing world record flight would give his dealership loads of publicity and start his new business off with a bang. On August 24, Mira sent a letter to Sportavia ordering his new glider, telling them that he would pick the plane up in Germany and fly it home to California.

When his flying schedule slowed down and he had a day off, Mira returned to Los Angeles to help Susan fly her Aero Commander to Miami to get the new fuel tanks installed. At 3 p.m. on August 28, Mira and Susan took off together in her tiny plane for the first leg of the trip to Miami. They would go 750 miles east to El Paso, Texas. That was as far as Mira could go before having to catch a flight back to LAX to resume flying for Continental. It was his first chance to fly cross country with Susan and get a feel for how prepared she was. To her complete surprise, Mira made her turn off all her fancy electronic navigational aids and fly with just a compass, airspeed indicator, and chronometer.

"But that's not fair! I've never done any dead reckoning navigation before." Susan protested.

"The Atlantic Ocean doesn't care anything about fair or not fair. If your nice electronics break down while you are out over the ocean, you will have to dead reckon, and would you rather your first time was at night, alone over the cold Atlantic or here, over dry land with an experienced pilot next to you?"

Susan reluctantly agreed, but she was not happy about it. She did a fair job, but there were plenty of tears and disagreements before she located the lights of El Paso in the darkness of the Texas desert. Mira only had twenty minutes to catch a deadhead ride on a Continental flight back to LAX, so there was not time for a "mission debrief," but Mira was having significant doubts about Susan's ability to complete the flight safely. On his way home, he sat in the dim light of the passenger cabin surrounded by sleeping businessmen and tried to figure out a way to explain his position to Susan. He believed that 99.9 percent of the time, flying was easy and beautiful and joyful, but 0.1 percent of the time, things could go wrong suddenly, and flying turned dark and deadly. There were a million things that could go wrong, and when an engine died, a hydraulic system failed, the windscreen iced up, or a battery exploded, the only thing that kept the plane from crashing was the pilot's experience and ability to stay calm and solve the problem. Mira knew that Susan had the basic knowledge, motor skills, and reflexes to fly the plane safely, but he knew in his heart of hearts that she did not have the experience necessary to handle even the most basic emergencies that could arise on a single-engine transatlantic crossing. There was also still something about the whole project that did not feel right. He felt like she was borrowing against his reputation as a flyer to get some of the help and publicity she was getting. He could not figure out how to express it, but he wondered how Susan would feel if he were to use his relationship with her to get a big role in a movie that he clearly was not qualified for. He kept all of his doubts to himself, but he was becoming convinced that the trip to Moscow was a bad idea.

Susan continued on to Florida alone. When she arrived in Miami at International Aircraft Deliveries (IAD), the company that would install the long-range fuel tanks, she was met with more bad news. The tanks were ready, but the FAA paperwork to approve the instillation was not. She spent the night at the Key Biscayne Hotel making phone calls, trying to rearrange her schedule to accommodate this delay. The next morning, she decided to fly back to Los Angeles, and return to Miami in September to have the tanks installed. Before she headed home, IAD convinced her to spend some time in its simulator, where she could practice some of the "unusual attitudes" that she was likely to experience on her Atlantic crossing. She proceeded to "crash" the simulator a couple of times before finally making a safe crossing. As she left Miami to fly back to Los Angeles, the simulator operator told the IAD staff that he did not think that Susan was qualified to make the transatlantic flight.

The first leg of Susan's trip home took her to Houston, where she was joined by Mira, who give her more instructions as they flew home. He arrived early and was on the ground watching Susan land. She did a fine job landing but got lost in the maze of taxiways trying to find Continental's area, where Mira was waiting. She was flustered and near tears when Mira climbed into the right seat to talk her through her next takeoff and the flight to San Antonio. Again, Susan took a wrong turn and got lost taxiing to the departure runway. Mira took over and got her back on track, but there were more tears. The flight to San Antonio was uneventful except that Susan turned the wrong way on the downwind leg of the landing pattern and entered the pattern going head on into traffic. Luckily, the pattern was empty, but it was as serious a mistake as trying to merge onto a freeway by driving the wrong way up the exit ramp. Mira helped Susan get turned around and was able to bite his tongue long enough to keep from telling her that there is no way that she should attempt the trip to Moscow. They spent the night in a small motel near the airport. Neither one was able to sleep well, but they were up again early the next morning, September 2. A light rain came down as they took off from San Antonio, and visibility was limited. They would be flying under instrument flight rules for the next several hours.

As they flew through the clouds, Mira decided to quiz Susan on her problem-solving skills. "Let's say that you take off from San Antonio and you see a wall of thunderstorms. You check with the weather station and they tell you that it is band of storms that stretches from the Gulf of Mexico up to Wyoming. What do you do?"

"I'll fly around it, I'll head north until I get to the end and then I'll turn back toward California."

"That will add over 1,000 miles to your trip. Your range is only 1,080 miles, so you would have to land somewhere to refuel. Is there a better answer?"

"I could try to climb over them. How tall did you say they were?"

Mira sighed with exasperation, "You should know this. Cumulonimbus clouds can be as high as 70,000 feet. This plane can't climb that high. What's a better solution?"

"I suppose I could just sort of fly along the front until I saw a break and follow it in, like I'm looking for a pass through the mountains."

Mira interrupted angrily, "No! You can't fly a light plane through a thunderstorm. You can't fly over a thunderstorm, and you can't fly around a thunderstorm. The only sensible solution is that you return to your field and wait it out. That is the only way you can stay alive as a pilot. My old instructor used to say, 'When it comes to weather, there are only two types of pilots: patient pilots and dead pilots.'" Susan sulked as they flew on to Los Angeles in silence.

After arriving back in LA, Susan spent Sunday the 3rd making preparations for her trip. She and Rockwell had selected September 14 as her departure date and there was still much to do. Late in the day, she received a phone call from Washington, D.C. The Soviets have given their permission, but only if she agreed to leave on the 11th.

On Monday morning, Susan jumped on the phone and began to try to move up her departure. She needed to head back to Florida to pick up the new tanks, which had now been approved by the FAA. She had to cancel several navigational training sessions as well as a few interviews. She ended the busy day with a quiet dinner with her mother, and once she was home, she called Mira to tell him of her change in plans. She tried to be cute on the phone, "Well I've got good news and bad news. The good news is, the Russians say I can come; the bad news is they are insisting that I leave three days early. So I'm going to be heading back to Florida tomorrow."

"This is madness!" Mira interrupted. "You can't do this!"

"But I have to! The Russians say ..."

"I don't care what the Russians say." All of Mira's built up doubts and frustrations spilled out in an angry torrent of words. "The Russians shouldn't even figure into this. When you asked me for help, I told you I would help, but only if you would listen to me, and if I didn't think you were ready to go, you wouldn't go. Well I'm telling you now, you aren't ready to go!"

"I have to! Don't you understand? There are so many people counting on me."

"You aren't prepared! You aren't ready yet!"

"But they tell me I have to come east now!"

"Then I wash my hands of the whole thing! Go kill yourself by yourself!" Mira slammed down the telephone.

Mira understood that relationships were almost living things. They were born, they grew, and they matured. They got hurt and they healed, but if the hurt was too deep, the relationship would die. Mira knew that this wound was mortal and the relationship could never recover. Susan went ahead and made the trip. She flew successfully across the Atlantic and got as far as Copenhagen, and then the Soviets changed their minds again and she was not allowed to enter the country. She waited for several days while Rockwell explored all the diplomatic options that they could; eventually, she returned home on a commercial flight, and Rockwell shipped her plane back.

Mira completed the unlimited season in San Diego, securing second place in National High Points for the *Chrysler Crew*, at the exact same time Susan was flying across Greenland on her way to Europe. In the aftermath of the broken relationship, Mira tried to stay busy cleaning and re-cleaning his hangar and working on his Bücker until every nut and bolt shinned. Shortly before Halloween, Ernest Gann walked into Mira's hangar and called out, "Anybody home?"

Mira popped up from behind the engine where he had been working on clearing up a small oil leak. "Hello, Mr. Gann. What brings you to Santa Paula?"

"Damn it Mira, why the devil can't you just call me Ernie? Everyone else does."

Mira wiped his hands on a rag as he approached Gann and said, "I don't know how to explain this in English, but in Czechoslovakia we call everyone "Mister" unless we have fed the geese together."

"What the hell does it mean 'to feed the geese together?'"

"Well in my country, feeding the geese is a job for children. So if you feed the geese together, it means you grew up working side by side and are equals and you can use each other's first names. For everyone else, I must show respect and call them 'Mister.'"

Gann nodded and said, "I understand, but I still want you to call me Ernie."

"Yes Mr. Gann, I would be happy to call you Ernie."

Gann dismissed the topic with a shake of his head and said, "That's not what I came down here to talk about. I still want to buy your Bücker and I'm not going to take no for an answer."

Mira figured that if he asked enough, he could replace the Bücker and pay for the new RF-4 glider that was on order, so he threw out a wild price. To his surprise, Gann pulled out his checkbook and said, "Will you take a check?" Mira said yes, Gann wrote the check, and Mira was ready to start a new chapter in his career. He did not think that Gann should fly an unfamiliar plane cross country, so he offered to help fly the Bücker to Gann's home field, Friday Harbor, in the picturesque San Juan Islands north of Seattle. Neither man had the time to leave right away, so two weeks later, on November 12, they flew together as far as Oakland, with Gann in the forward cockpit and Mira in the rear giving advice and instructions. They left the plane in Oakland for a week while Mira returned to LA to fly for Continental and Gann attended to other pressing business. Mira came back on the 19th and flew the plane on to Roseburg, Oregon, spent the night, and flew on to Friday Harbor the next day.

Friday Harbor sits in a horseshoe-shaped bay on the eastern side of San Juan Island, the largest of over 170 islands that make up the San Juan Archipelago, which straddles the U.S. and Canadian border in northwestern Washington. The rugged islands are covered with ancient old-growth evergreen trees and rock-strewn craggy beaches. Orcas, bald eagles, and seals are frequent sights. Gann had been introduced to the majestic beauty of the islands when he had sailed through them with his good friend actor John Wayne, on Wayne's yacht, the *Wild Goose*. Smitten by the serenity of island life, Gann soon bought an 800-acre ranch outside of the rustic port of Friday Harbor.

Mira arrived late in the day at Friday Harbor's tiny airport with grass runways and surplus military Quonset huts for hangers. The deep-blue sky was dotted with billowing clouds that caught the gold rays of the setting sun. Mira could not resist, and he made one last pass low and fast over the field, with the plane inverted as he waved to Gann, who was standing on the apron awaiting the delivery. By the time he was on the ground and the plane was tied down, it was dark. They climbed into the front seat of a rugged old station wagon to ride to Gann's ranch, where his wife, Dodie, was waiting. The dirt road was lined with tall grass and barbed-wire fences. The clouds obscured the moon and the headlights cut two bright cones of light into the night. When Gann found a particularly dark stretch of road, he pulled off onto the shoulder. He left the car idling and the headlights pointed out into a field. Gann opened his door and said, "Come on, Mira, follow me."

Mira was confused by the stop, but wanted to be polite, "Of course, Mr. Gann."[2]

As he got out of the car, he could smell the dry dust that had been kicked up by the car's tires. Gann scrambled across the road and over the barbed-wire fence. He was not a young man, nor was he very athletic. Mira had to choke back a laugh as he watched the great author stumble over the top of the fence. Once they were in the field, Mira could see that they were standing in a flock of sheep. Gann ran towards the nearest one and tackled it while the other sheep scattered in confusion. The sheep wriggled free of Gann's grasp and skittered away. "Come on, Slovak, help me catch this damn sheep."

The two men chased the bewildered sheep around the field until Gann was able to tackle it around the neck. He held it down while Mira caught up. "Grab his hind legs and help me carry him."

"What are we doing?"

"We're stealing this sheep!" Mira had no idea what was going on, but he grabbed the hind legs of the sheep while Gann grabbed the front and they headed back toward the car. The fence proved to be quite an obstacle. The sheep, weighing over 100 pounds, was not happy about being kidnapped, and it struggled as Mira and Gann half-lifted and half-rolled the poor thing over the top of the fence.

They were both filthy and soaked with sweat when they arrived at the back of Gann's station wagon. Gann swung the tailgate open and the interior dome light came on to silhouette the two sheep rustlers as they tried to force the struggling animal into the back of the station wagon. Just then, another car appeared on the road. The new car slowed and a flashing red light blinked on its roof. The police car pulled in behind the rustlers and Gann and Slovak stood motionless in the police car's headlights.

"Damn it." Gann whispered under his breath.

The officer opened his door, stepped out cautiously and asked, "Okay what's going on here?"

Gann confessed immediately, "We're stealing sheep, officer!"

The officer squinted into the night trying to see better and said, "Ernie? Is that you?"

Gann answered, "Yes, Jake."

"What the hell are you doing, Ernie?"

"I told you Jake. We're stealing sheep."

"Dang it, Ernie," the officer said, pointing toward the field, "We're on your land. Aren't all of these sheep yours already? How can you be stealing your own sheep?"

"I'm doing it for Slovak."

Mira raised his hands and said, "How did I get dragged into this?"

The officer said, "Slovak? Are you Mira Slovak? I've been a fan of yours for a long time."

Ernie's arms were getting tired and the poor struggling sheep found an opportunity to make a break for it. He wriggled free and ran back to the field. "Darn it Jake, now look what you made me do."

Mira was beginning to lose patience and said, "Mr. Gann, would you please tell me what is going on?"

Gann turned to the officer and said, "This is really all Mira's fault. I keep asking him to call me 'Ernie.' But he won't. He insists on calling me 'Mr. Gann,' because there is some old Czechoslovakian tradition that says you can't call someone by their first name unless you used to steal sheep together. So I'm out here stealing sheep with Mira so that he will finally start calling me Ernie!"

Officer Jake laughed at the explanation, and then pointed out that Dodie was probably getting worried, so why didn't they all just go home. Mira stayed silent until he and Gann were back in the car and Jake had driven away. Gann slipped the station wagon into gear and pulled back on to the road.

"Mr. Gann," Mira said calmly trying hard to hold back his laughter, "The expression is 'We never fed geese together.' It has nothing to do with stealing sheep."

"God damn it!" Gann said as he slammed his hand against the wheel. "Will you please call me Ernie?"

"Yes sir, Mr. Gann, I would be happy to call you Ernie, Mr. Gann."

"Slovak, you're a stubborn SOB."

"Yes, Mr. Gann, I've been told that before."

30

50 Feet Short: Santa Paula, 1968

When Mira returned to Los Angeles, he found a letter waiting for him from Sportavia telling him that his new glider, with the registration number N 1700, would be ready to be picked up in mid-April. He spent the next several months reading everything he could find on transatlantic crossings. He learned that the smallest plane to make the trip successfully had a 120-hp engine. Charles Lindbergh, the first person to solo the Atlantic, had 220 hp in his Spirit of St. Louis. Mira was going to try it with 36 hp. He studied maps, plotted routes, and purchased survival gear, including a skin diver's wet suit and an inflatable raft. He asked Continental for two weeks of vacation and flew to Germany. When he arrived, he was surprised to see that his plane was not finished. The fuel tanks need to be installed, the cockpit was missing the long-range radio, and the engine was not complete. Mira changed his vacation to an indefinite leave of absence, and rolled up his sleeves and went to work to get the plane ready. By May 7, 1968, the fragile plane was complete, flight tested, and ready to go. Mira named her the *Spirit of Santa Paula* and stuck an American flag decal on the fuselage right behind the Plexiglas bubble of the cockpit. Back in the States, newspapers from Seattle, Los Angeles, and Reno reported on Mira's preparations as if he were getting ready for a hydroplane race.[1]

The RF-4 looked like most other gliders, with long tapered wings and streamlined fuselage. The only difference was the tiny 36-hp Volkswagen engine nestled beneath the fiberglass nose cowling. The RF-4 normally carried 10 gallons of fuel; Mira, a firm believer that "the only time an airplane has too much fuel on board is when it's on fire," added extra tanks, extending her range to almost 1,500 miles. Mira taxied his tiny glider into takeoff position. The RF-4 is 19 feet long with a 36-foot wing span. Normally, it weighs 860 pounds when fully loaded. With the extra fuel and rescue supplies on board, the *Spirit of Santa Paula* was over 1,200 pounds.

At 10.15 a.m., Mira advanced the throttle to 3,600 rpm. In a throwback to the days when gliders did not have radios, an airport worker at the far end of the runway fired off a flare to signal that the runway was clear. Mira released the brake and began his takeoff roll. Overweight by more than 340 pounds, the *Spirit of Santa Paula* struggled to fly. With each bump in the grass field she bounced a few inches off the ground before settling back to earth. The first bounce was 6 inches, the next was 8 inches, and eventually, it was 12 inches. Mira was running out of runway when the plane took a final bounce and stayed in the air. He pulled back gently on the stick and headed north. He backed off the throttle to 3,200 rpm and made a quick scan of his instrument panel. All his temperatures and pressures were good, so he settled back in the cramped cockpit to enjoy his journey. Keeping the plane below 1,000 feet, he headed north. He saw gentle rolling hills and the shattered remains of concrete bunkers left behind by World War II. After a few minutes, he crossed into Belgium. It took three hours to fly from one end of Belgium to the other. He entered France and crossed over Dunkirk, and flew easily across the Channel towards the legendary white cliffs of Dover.[2]

Mira passed London by and landed 30 miles north, in Luton, to spend the night, having traveled 400 miles on his first day. The next morning it was raining and Mira spent hours waiting for the weather to improve. Late in the afternoon, he took off into wet skies and flew 400 miles to Glasgow, where he ran into heavy rain that cut his visibility down to almost zero and made it difficult to find the airport. The rain kept him grounded for five days. The puddles on the runway grew as Mira's time and money dwindled. Back home, the newspapers carried stories about the long delay, and he was just about to give up when he received a short telegram from three young boys in Santa Paula. They were John Miller, Mark Hanson, and Harrison Jerome. Mira had taken the boys under his wing at Santa Paula and was teaching them to fly. The telegram said, "We love the Spirit of Santa Paula—We love Mira Slovak." Mira knew then that he had to go on. He could not let these young pilots down.

The next morning, Mira looked out his hotel window to see that the sun had broken through and the runway was drying up. Before putting on his flight suit, he got into his skin diver's wet suit, in case something happened and he had to ditch into the frigid Atlantic. He took off from Glasgow and headed for the tiny airport of Stornoway, on the Isle of Lewis, off the coast of Scotland. After a quick stop to refuel, he was back in the air, heading for his first long flight over water, to the Faroe Islands.

As Mira headed out over the cold water toward a stark empty horizon, he was reminded of his decision to escape from Czechoslovakia. He had left home, heading toward an unknown future, trusting that his skill and courage would help him find his way to a better life. Today, he was doing the same thing, leaving safety and security to fly out over a cold ocean toward an island he had never seen.[3] The Faroe Islands are a craggy, windswept group of eighteen small islands in the North Atlantic, halfway between Norway and Iceland. They are ruled by the Danish, but were occupied by the English during World War II, so most of their 30,000 inhabitants can speak Danish and English.

After three-and-a-half hours of flying over the unforgiving ocean, Mira saw a dark stain on the horizon that grew into towering black cliffs of volcanic rock sticking out of the ocean at odd angles. He had reached the Faroes, but they were surrounded by dense clouds, and as he flew toward Vágar, he ran into heavy snow. As the thick flakes hit his windshield, they melted quickly, but the snow hitting his wings was turning to ice, making the plane harder to fly. He radioed Vágar, asking for permission to land, and was shocked when permission was denied. The airport was closed because the runway was being resurfaced. Mira called the tower again and told them it was an emergency. The tower responded that one side of the runway could be cleared in fifteen to twenty minutes, or he could proceed on to Reykjavik, Iceland, which was the next nearest airport and only 480 miles away. He told the tower that with as much ice as he was building, the only way he could get to Iceland would be to swim, so he decided he would continue to circle the airport until they were ready for him. He watched nervously as the snow continued to build on his wings and the glider got harder and harder to fly. Finally, he was given clearance to land, but the tower reminded him that the runway was under repair and told him to expect a bumpy touchdown. They were right. The runway was full of holes, and the poor *Spirit of Santa Paula* bounced and wobbled over every bump until Mira was finally able to get her stopped.

After a night in a hotel, Mira woke to a clear morning. He refueled and set out toward Reykjavik, Iceland. He had heard that the weather in Iceland was unpredictable. As he approached the island nation, he saw a black cloud billowing over the water. It looked thick and solid. Mira knew that it was a cloud of volcanic ash from one of Iceland's volcanoes. The abrasive ash can damage engines, so he made a wide detour to the south, away from the dangerous cloud. No sooner had he escaped the ash when he ran into a fierce snowstorm. Luckily, the plane quickly flew out of the snow and into warm spring sunshine, but it only lasted a few minutes before being replaced by a driving rain. In less than ten minutes, Mira had encountered rain, snow, sun, and ash, proving the old adage that if you do not like the weather in Iceland, just wait five minutes and it will change. It was late in the day when he side-slipped the plane down to a gentle landing on Reykjavik's long, smooth runway.

Mira felt a sense of pride and accomplishment as he prepared for the next day's journey. He was halfway across the Atlantic, but the longest and most difficult leg of his trip was ahead of him. The first faint rays of gold were tinting the eastern horizon when Mira began wiping the dew off the *Spirit of Santa Paula*. His breath hung in the air in white clouds as he started the tiny Volkswagen engine with a one-handed spin of the propeller. He lifted off into the thin light of morning at 4 a.m., bound for the tiny island of Kulusuk, just off the east coast of Greenland. He estimated it would take him six hours and fifteen minutes to get there. As the sun rose, the sky turned a deep peaceful blue and was reflected in the ocean. The *Spirit of Santa Paula* was fully loaded with fuel for the long flight over water, and Mira had trouble getting the overweight plane to gain much altitude. He brought her down to just a few feet above the water to skim along in the thick, dense air that pilots call "the ground effect." With the sun behind him, the tiny glider's shadow danced on the water just ahead of his right wing tip. He spent most of the morning chasing his shadow west. Once he was a few hours into the flight and had burned off enough fuel, he climbed to 3,000 feet. From this altitude, he enjoyed watching the peaceful rollers that seemed to lead him gently toward Greenland. Then he saw a massive cargo ship being tossed and battered by the waves and realized that the rollers were huge and neither peaceful nor gentle. With a shiver, he understood that if he had to make an emergency landing, his fragile plane would be smashed to match sticks before he even had a chance to inflate his life raft.

After three hours in the air, he estimated that he must be above the Arctic Circle. Almost on cue, the blue sky started to give way to ominous clouds. It was not raining, but as Mira flew through the clouds, they left thick droplets of condensation on his windscreen that made him worry about ice. So he took the plane down below the clouds into the warmer air near the ocean's surface. As soon as he broke out of the clouds, he saw that the weather had changed. The long, sloping rollers he had seen earlier had been replaced by sharp, angry waves that broke into foam, which blew across the water in streaks. Mira knew that he was now flying head on into gale force winds of more than 40 mph. Powerful gusts buffeted the tiny glider, and the wings rocked back and forth. He was reminded of being a young boy walking along railroad tracks with his arms stretched out from his sides, trying to stay balanced. Yet now, his arms had turned into wings and if he lost his balance, he would face an icy death. He also knew that the headwinds would dramatically slow his speed over the water, and he was probably traveling at under 50 mph. That would change his estimated time of arrival at Kulusuk. To let the airport know that he was going to be late, he keyed his microphone and said, "Atlantic Radio Control, this is glider November one seven zero zero, come in please." There was no answer. Trying again, he heard only silence in response. Mira figured that he was too low for his radio transmission to travel far enough to reach Kulusuk. He scrunched a little further down into his seat to avoid seeing the angry water beneath his wings and tried not to think about all of the countless things that could go wrong. Yet trying not to think about problems just made his mind fixate on the exact thoughts he was trying to avoid. "I have never seen so much nothingness in my life. Here I am, hours from anybody. In case I have to go down it would be a long time before they found me. They say that if something goes wrong, you can survive for four minutes in the cold water. My rubber suit will give me maybe three hours. If I can inflate the dingy, and get into it, it would give me two days. But the icy wind and bitter cold make it impossible to say if I could even survive that long."[4]

The little Volkswagen engine kept putt-putting along, and the silver disc of the propeller kept turning as the tiny *Spirit of Santa Paula* fought through the storm. Mira tried to raise Kulusuk again. There was no response. He had been in the air for four hours. He ought to be halfway to Greenland and within easy radio range. He tuned his automatic direction finder (ADF) to the USAF's radio "Big Gun" beacon in Kulusuk. Mira spent several minutes turning the dial one way, then the next, hoping to hear the reassuring buzzing tone when the ADF picked up the Big Gun signal, but it remained silent. Maybe the headwind was so strong that he was still out of range, but there was a faint tingling in the back of his mind telling him that something must be wrong.

With Mira's high-tech navigation equipment acting sullen and silent, he had to depend on his old-fashioned magnetic compass. The problem was that compasses do not actually point to true north; they point to magnetic north. For most places in the world, magnetic north and true north are close enough that the few degrees of difference does not matter and can be easily accounted for with a variation and deviation chart. However, flying above the Arctic Circle can put a pilot almost in between true north and magnetic north, which will cause huge variations in the compass headings.

Adding to the problem are large deposits of iron ore underneath the Arctic ice that cause the compass needle to move even further off course. Mira had two compasses on board and the needles on both were swinging wildly back and forth in a 40-degree arc. By watching the swing, and guessing that the midpoint of the swing was probably magnetic north, Mira continue to fly towards where he hoped to find Kulusuk.

The tiny engine kept running for another hour as the cloud cover thickened and descended to the ocean's surface. Now, when Mira caught a glimpse of the ocean, it was covered with chunks of jagged ice that where so close together that there was not enough open water to even try a water landing.

Another hour went by in silence. He had now been airborne for six-and-a-half hours without radio contact. He was surrounded by clouds and fifteen minutes past his ETA and still was not able to pick up the signal from Big Gun. Mira reasoned that since Big Gun's signal reached out 200 miles into the Atlantic, and he was still unable to pick up the signal, he must be at least 200 miles off course. Somehow, he must have missed Greenland completely, but was he north of Greenland, flying blindly into the icy Arctic, or was he south, sailing out into the middle of the Atlantic Ocean? His mind wrestled with the heartbreakingly obvious fact that he had made a huge mistake and would probably end up paying for it with his life. He went over the details again and again and could not figure out what had gone wrong. Within his thoughts, he berated himself for the unknown error that was leading him towards disaster. He keyed the microphone and announced, "This is glider November one seven zero zero declaring mayday, mayday, mayday."

He flew on in silence. Fifteen minutes later, he tried again. Suddenly, a voice boomed in his headset, "Glider November one seven zero zero. This is Icelandic Air flight three zero zero, I read you loud and clear. What is your emergency?"

"I am unable to receive my ADF. Requesting position from Kulusuk, Greenland."

"Glider November one seven zero zero your radar fix is: six five degrees two zero minutes north and three four degrees three zero minutes west. Your heading to Kulusuk is three two zero degrees."

"Roger, my heading to Kulusuk Greenland is three two zero degrees."[5]

Mira was elated. He was right on course, just two hours delayed because of the fierce headwinds. A few minutes later, a break in the clouds revealed the rugged coast of Greenland fewer than 40 miles ahead, and just a few degrees to the right were the huge radar antennas of the USAF base on Kulusuk.

Mira's headset crackled, "Glider November one seven zero zero, this is Kulusuk tower. Where have you been? You are two hours past your ETA. We were just about to send a search party for you."

"I ran into stronger than expected head winds. What happened to your radio beacon?

"Two days ago we turned it off for maintenance."

Mira heaved a sigh of relief. There was nothing wrong with his plane or his navigation skills. Mira only stayed in Kulusuk long enough to refuel his plane and grab a quick lunch. Then he took off to fly over the icecap on his way to Sondrestrom, on the west coast of Greenland. During this whole trip, the highest that Mira had been able to coax the over laden *Spirit of Santa Paula* had been 6,000 feet. Greenland's icecap was 10,000 feet tall, and the Kulusuk tower recommended that Mira climb to at least 12,500 feet to cross it. After an hour and a half in the air, Mira was able to persuade the *Spirit of Santa Paula* to climb to 10,500 feet and with 500 feet to spare he headed over the icy plateau. Many pilots consider flying the Greenland icecap the most difficult route they have ever flown. The endless white of the ice, stretching out for hundreds of miles in every direction to seamlessly meet a white sky with absolutely no horizon, makes it easy for a pilot to become disoriented and succumb to vertigo. Three planes, all bigger, stronger, and with better navigational equipment than the *Spirit of Santa Paula*, had crashed, killing their entire crews, in the two weeks just before Mira's attempt. With the lightweight, primitive instruments in Mira's glider, the only way he could be sure to keep his balance was to watch the sun and its reflection on the ice below. For four tense hours, Mira and the tiny RF-4 flew over the Greenland Plateau. He was exhausted when he arrived at the USAF base in Sondrestrom and he slept well, confident that the most dangerous part of his trip was behind him.

The next day, he flew across Davis Strait and made landfall in North America at Cape Dyer. He headed south through Canada's Northwest Territories and landed at Frobisher Bay Airport, where he was greeted by 100 Eskimo children in authentic costumes. From Frobisher Bay, he flew south across the Hudson Strait to Fort Chimo, Quebec, then a quick jump to Sept-Iles and over Montreal to pass into the U.S. As he crossed over the border into New York State, Mira sang "America the Beautiful" and did an impromptu victory loop.

Back in the States, Mira made a beeline to Las Vegas, where he met Harry Volpi on Friday, May 24. Volpi drove him to Lake Mead so he could get in a few practice laps with the new Griffon engines that had been installed in the *Harrah's Club*. Mira could not help but notice the irony of jumping out of a slow 36-hp glider to drive a 3,000-hp race boat. The new Griffon engines had amazing horsepower, and Mira declared the *Harrah's Club* ready to race. After the test, the crew, including Jarda, headed across country to Guntersville, Alabama for the first race of the 1968 season.

Mira left Las Vegas and flew to Reno for a press conference with Bill and Sherry Harrah. They talked about the glider trip across the Atlantic as well as his plans to drive for Harrah in the coming season. In Reno, Mira heard that his friends Perry Schreffler and Bob Van Ausdal were at an antique aircraft show in Watsonville, CA. Both were TWA captains and owned antique Curtiss Robins that they were exhibiting at the show. Mira decided to fly to Watsonville and surprise his friends.

After spending Saturday night in Watsonville, Mira, Schreffler, and Van Ausdal decided to fly to Santa Paula together. They took off Sunday morning, May 26, and flew in a "V" formation. Mira took the lead, with Schreffler on his left wing and Van Ausdal on his right. The three planes sailed over green hills and ocean beaches on the way to Santa Paula. Once they arrived, they flew a low pass over the runway in tight formation. On the ground, there was a huge barbecue and welcome party planned. Champagne was cooling in buckets of ice. A large sheet cake decorated with a plastic model of the *Spirit of Santa Paula* sat on a table in Mira's hangar, while hot dogs and hamburgers sizzled on open grills. The *Associated Press* reported that over 2,000 people were on hand to welcome Mira home.

Van Ausdal peeled away from the formation as Mira prepared to land. Schreffler, in his bright red Curtiss Robin, stayed on Mira's wing. The two planes sank toward the runway and the waiting crowd. Mira lowered the RF-4's single landing gear. Some 100 feet from the runway, Schreffler pulled ahead of Mira, wiggled his wings, and pulled up dramatically to leave Mira to land by himself. The unexpected prop wash hit Mira's left wing, causing the glider to tip violently to the left and fall from the sky.[6] Mira applied full power and almost got the plane under control, but he was too low and heading directly at a small trailer home. He banked to avoid the house but a wing tip touched the ground and the plane cart wheeled, slamming nose-first into a dry drainage ditch 50 feet east of the airport. The engine broke off as the fragile plane ripped apart. Mira was thrown face-first into the dirt and lost consciousness.

For a moment, the crowd of well-wishers stood in stunned silence. The first person to regain his wits was fifteen-year-old Mark Hanson. He jumped on his bike and pedaled as fast as he could to the crash scene. He found Mira face down in the rubble, unable to breathe from all the dirt in his mouth. Hanson turned Mira over and began to clear his airway.

A sudden gasp from Mira let Mark know he was alive. Moments later, the fire department arrived and took over the rescue. As Mira was carried from the accident on a stretcher, people heard him moaning "my plane, my plane." On his way to Santa Paula Community Hospital, he lost consciousness and hovered between life and death for seven days. His injuries included four broken vertebrae, seven broken ribs, a collapsed left lung, a lacerated stomach and kidney, a broken left arm, a gash on his head that was so deep it damaged an optic nerve, and both hips cut clean to the bone. The plane was destroyed. Across the country, newspaper headlines announced Slovak's crash.[7] A local television station tracked down Earnest Gann to talk about the accident. The reporter asked Gann, "Do you believe in fate?" Gann answered:

> Yes I do. He flew the Atlantic, 9,000 miles, through lots of isolated country, miserable weather, over places if he went down nobody would ever find him. He came home, he conquered the difficult trip; he was 50 feet from his destination when he ran out of speed, altitude, and luck. Yes, I believe in fate.[8]

31

$23.65: London, 1969

While Mira was in intensive care, his doctors kept him sedated so he could tolerate all the tubes and wires hooked up to him. After a week, his condition improved enough that the doctors began to wean him off his medications. He slowly returned to consciousness like a swimmer coming up from the depths of the ocean. While his eyes were still closed and his mind clouded from the haze of medication, he heard a soft familiar voice saying, "Mira *miláčik, ako sa máte*?" This was Slovakian for, "Mira darling, how are you?" He smiled but was too sleepy to open his eyes. The voice continued in Slovakian: "*Ľubim Ťa*" (I love you.) The warm, comforting voice sounded like his mother's, but that was impossible as his mother was still in Czechoslovakia. As he lay drifting between sleep and consciousness, trying to decide if he should open his eyes, he felt a soft hand stroke his forehead and brush his hair to one side. The familiar voice asked again "*Kako se počutim*?" (How do you feel?)

Mira responded with, "*Slabo se počutim*." (I feel terrible.)

"*Rożumien*." (I understand.)

Finally, enough of the fog cleared from Mira's brain that he recognized the voice. He opened his eyes to see his mother standing next to his bed. "*Dobrē rano*, Mira," she whispered. (Good morning, Mira.)

Mira tried to sit up to hug her, but she whispered, "Shhh, don't move, you'll pull out the tubes."

"How did you get here?"

"I got on a plane as soon as I heard about the crash."

"You didn't have to wait for government approval?"

"No! We have a new president. He is changing everything. I was able to fly out right away."

"How long have I been knocked out?"

"They tell me it's been a week."

Later that day, Mira's doctors upgraded his condition from serious to satisfactory and moved him out of intensive care, but it was another few weeks before he was allowed visitors other than his mother. Maria came to see him every day, sitting next to his bed, holding his hand and talking for hours. She was sorry to hear that Mira and Susan had broken up, but assured him that the right girl would come along. Mira quipped that he couldn't get married because "I'm already married to flying."

Mira was anxious to hear about the changes taking place in Czechoslovakia. Maria told him about Alexander Dubček, who became First Secretary of the Communist Party in 1968. His plans for "Socialism with a human face" promised sweeping reforms, including lifting all travel bans and restoring freedom of the press. The reforms were being called the "Prague Spring." Maria and Jan were hopeful that even their farm and grain silos would be returned soon. Mira said that he did not think that "a leopard could change its spots," and that he doubted that the reforms would last.

On June 10, fifteen days after the accident, while still confined to the hospital, Mira wrote a letter to Sportavia in Schmidtheim ordering a brand-new plane to replace the damaged N 1700.

In mid-July, after more than seven weeks in the hospital, Mira went home. Maria stayed with him, making huge home-cooked meals to "fatten him up" after almost two months of hospital food.

When Mira was injured, the *Harrah's Club* quickly found a replacement driver, but that did not mean Mira was done with hydroplane racing. KIRO TV, the CBS affiliate in Seattle, hired him to assist with its live race coverage. In early August, Mira and Maria flew to Seattle together and stayed at the Cechs' house, overlooking the racecourse. Mira did such a great job announcing the race that he was hired by ABC Sports to assist with its coverage of the Unlimited Air Races in Reno the following month.

With Mira well on his way to recovery, Maria allowed herself to daydream about what life could be like if the reforms at home continued and both her boys returned to Czechoslovakia.

Soviet General Secretary Leonid Brezhnev and other hardline communists in the Kremlin had been watching in dismay as Dubček tried to reform the Czechoslovak government. By mid-August, they had had enough. On August 20, in the largest use of military force in Europe since the end of World War II, 200,000 Soviet combat troops and 5,000 tanks roared into Czechoslovakia from Poland, taking control of the country and arresting Dubček. The Soviet Union's willingness to use its massive military to crush resistance in its communist satellites quickly became known as the "Brezhnev Doctrine."

Maria's dream quickly turned into a nightmare. She was in America with her sons and her husband was back in Czechoslovakia while Soviet troops overran the country. She could stay with her sons in America and live as a free woman but abandon her husband, or she could abandon her sons and freedom to return to her husband and live under harsh new communist oppression.

Mira was heartbroken to watch his mother struggle with the same awful decision he had faced when forced to choose between freedom and family. Mira had been allowed to make the difficult choice in private, but because of his fame, Maria had to make the decision in public. *Seattle Post-Intelligencer* reporter Maribeth Morris came to the Cechs' house on August 22 to interview Maria about the Soviet crackdown. Maria said that she was "frightened and afraid." She pleaded with Morris, "I am afraid to speak. I hope you will be careful. My husband is in Czechoslovakia." She went on to say, "When I left home we had such hopes under the new regime. We were certain we would get back the property taken from us so long ago when the communists took over."[1] In the end, Maria could not abandon her husband, and she returned to Czechoslovakia. Once more, Mira cursed the evil system that continued to come between him and the people he loved.

Mira could not pass his FAA physical until December 19, and Continental Airlines did not reinstate him as a captain until January 31, 1969. By the time he was back in the cockpit of a 707, Sportavia had delivered his new plane to Los Angeles and he was already planning another transatlantic flight.

On June 14, 1919, a pair of intrepid British fliers named John Alcock and Arthur Brown had taken off from Newfoundland in a fragile Vickers Vimy twin-engine biplane and flown to Ireland, to claim the *Daily Mail's* £10,000 prize for being the first people to fly nonstop between North America and Europe. To honor the fiftieth anniversary of this historic event, the *Daily Mail*, one of England's biggest newspapers, was sponsoring the *Daily Mail* Trans-Atlantic Air Race. The race would be held between May 4 and May 11 and was open to planes in twenty-one different categories, determined by such things as the size of the plane and national origin of the pilot. With $144,000 in prizes, the race attracted more than 300 contestants. While billed as an airplane race, it was in fact a runners' race, with the runners starting from the eighty-sixth floor of the Empire State Building in New York and finishing on the thirty-fourth floor of the Post Office Tower in London. Contestants were allowed to travel in either direction, but with the prevailing winds blowing from west to east, most contestants traveled from New York to London. Mira entered his *Spirit of Santa Paula* II in the category for "Light Aircraft weighing less than 5,000 pounds." Contestants would check in on the eighty-sixth floor of the Empire State Building and complete some paperwork. They would then be given a punch card and then time-stamp it. Next, they took an express elevator to the ground floor, and rushed out of the building to a waiting ride to the nearest airport. They would then fly across the Atlantic, land near London, and race to the Post Office Tower. On the thirty-fourth floor, there was another punch clock where the contestants would get their cards time-stamped again and turn them in at the reception desk. The lowest elapsed time in any given class was declared the winner. The fiercest competition was between the Royal Navy and Royal Air Force. Both branches of the military pulled out all the stops to claim bragging rights. The RAF used a Hawker Harrier Jump Jet that could take off vertically and was able to land in an empty lot near the Empire State Building so the pilot could get on the back of a waiting motorcycle that sped him to the finish line. The Navy won with an F-4 Phantom that made the crossing in four hours, fifty-three minutes, and ten seconds.[2]

When Mira arrived at the Empire State Building, he wore a bright orange flight suit and a heavy brown leather bomber's jacket. With his collar turned up and his black hair slicked back, he looked like a World War I ace straight out of central casting. He flirted easily with the three well-dressed middle-aged women working at the registration desk, making them laugh and blush. Once he was checked in and had his time card punched, he walked slowly to the elevator. When the bell dinged and the doors slid open, he waited patiently for his turn as the other racers jostled and pushed to be the first ones in. He rode to the ground floor, walked through the lobby, stopping at the newsstand to give the clerk a quarter for a 15 cent Nestlé chocolate bar. He waited quietly while the clerk gave him his dime change. He turned to the photographers that were following him, held up the candy bar and said, "Sustenance," and walked out the door to a chauffeur-driven Volkswagen Beetle. He stopped in front of the flashing cameras and said that he was going to "Take Volkswagen all the way."

The VW took Mira into the Holland Tunnel and across to New Jersey's Teterboro airport. At 9.45 a.m. Sunday, May 4, he took off to fly back to Europe. While he had mugged it up in front of the cameras, he looked at this trip it as a way to make amends for crashing at the end of his last transatlantic flight.

On the first day, Mira flew 756 miles and made it to Sept-Îles, Quebec. The following morning, he woke to wind and rain, so he stayed on the ground all day. On Tuesday, the storm broke and he got as far Goose Bay, Labrador before he ran into snow. He stopped again, waiting several more days for the snow to clear before he flew on to Frobisher Bay.[3] Then, in his longest single day's flight, he went from Frobisher Bay across the frigid Davis Strait and the Greenland icecap, all the way to Kulusuk. This time, the ADF beacon was turned on and he had no difficulty finding the airport. The following day, he flew to Reykjavik, then Stornoway, Glasgow, and finally London, where he was met by another chauffeur-driven VW Bug, which took him to the Post Office Tower. Mira rode the elevator to the top and clocked in with a time of 175 hours, forty-two minutes, and seven seconds. It was far and away the slowest time of the entire race, but when the prizes were awarded, Mira received the "Evening News Prize" of £1,000 for the best performance by a light plane under 5,000 pounds. Later that week, he took his glider to the Biggin Hill Air Fair where he displayed his tiny RF-4 alongside the Royal Navy Phantom that had made the fastest crossing. He charmed the English media even further when he announced that with gasoline at 30 cents a gallon, the whole trip had only cost him $23.65.[4]

Some 175 hours, forty-two minutes, and seven seconds is long time to be alone, and Mira used the solitude to do some thinking. He was thirty-nine years old and a few months shy of his tenth anniversary at Continental. He had been in three serious hydroplane accidents and one plane crash. He had missed over twelve months of work for emergency medical leave. He wondered how much longer Continental would put up with his adventurous lifestyle. He was not ready to slow down, but he did decide to put his career first.

Mira began studying to upgrade from 707s to Boeing's new 747 jumbo jets that would be coming on line in June 1970. Unfortunately, he ran into three distractions that kept him from being able to give as much attention as he had planned to the new 747.

The first was another Bücker biplane. Mira had learned through a Czechoslovakian aviation magazine that the original Bücker that he had learned to fly in, OK-BIH, was in storage at the Prague National Museum. During the easing of communist rule in 1968, under the assumed name of John Pernell, Mira had begun to correspond with a young man at the museum about the prospect of buying the plane. Negotiations were well underway when the Russian tanks rolled in and the hardliners took over. Mira was sure that he would never hear from his museum contact again. Yet on March 17, 1969, he received a letter telling him that the plane was ready to ship and giving him instructions on where to send the money. Mira sent the payment, half expecting the money to disappear, but to his utter amazement, a few months later he got a call from U.S. Customs in Los Angeles telling him that they had a container of airplane parts for him to pick up. Mira had the old Bücker trucked to Santa Paula to be restored and painted white, black, and gold, just like the plane he had sold to Gann. Soon, he was back on the airshow circuit, performing in front of huge crowds.

The second distraction was a young flight attendant named Mary Opat. She was twenty-five years old and very pretty. Mira was forty years old, and she stole his heart in a whirlwind romance. They were married on Valentine's Day, 1970. Predictably, the marriage ran into many of the problems that could have been expected with a fifteen-year age difference, and they divorced a little over a year later, in May 1971. A few months after his divorce, Mira asked Ingrid Bondi out again; he had now been pursuing her for more than ten years. She told Mira that she was married, with a baby, and he should stop trying.

The third distraction was a P-39 Airacobra, a World War II fighter. During Mira's time in the air force, he had gotten to know a number of Soviet pilots who had flown the P-39 on the Eastern Front. The mid-engine Airacobra, with its Allison engine mounted behind the pilot and a powerful cannon in its nose, was a devastatingly effective low-level "tank killer." Mira often heard Soviet pilots praise it with the same reverent attitude that RAF pilots used when talking about the Spitfire.

The Soviets were not the only ones to think highly of the Airacobra. When the National Air Races returned to Cleveland in 1946, the first winner was Bell Aircraft test pilot Alvin "Tex" Johnston, flying a yellow-and-black P-39 named *Cobra II*. The P-39 in racing configuration proved treacherous to fly. Johnston's teammate, Jack Woolams, was killed when his plane, *Cobra I*, crashed during a test flight a few days before the race. Several years later, Johnston's plane, which had been sold and renamed *Cobra III*, crashed, killing its new owner, Mike Carroll. In spite of its deadly record, Mira was fascinated by the P-39 and began corresponding with Johnston about building his own racing P-39. In a letter to Mira, Johnston wrote, "The P-39, properly modified, results in probably the fastest propeller-driven airplane in the world."

Mira was making good money as a pilot for Continental, but he did not have the type of money needed to fund a successful unlimited air racing team. Fellow Continental captain Bill Arcamuzi had a Messerschmitt Bf 108 that he needed ferried from Morristown, New Jersey to California. Mira offered to make the flight for him. When he was in Morristown to pick up the plane, Mira had a chance encounter with a pleasant middle-aged man in his fifties, wearing a green bowtie and a short-sleeved white shirt.

The two chatted pleasantly about aviation. The bowtie man was knowledgeable about flying and knew quite a bit about Mira's career. Eventually, Mira said, "I apologize. You know who I am, but I don't know who you are. What is your name?"

The bowtie man smiled and held out his hand, "My name is George. George Mennen."

George Mennen was president of the Mennen Corporation, a large cosmetics manufacturer headquartered in Morristown. Mr. Mennen was an aviation buff and spent a lot of time at the airport. He also owned and flew a vintage Spartan Executive. The plane sported highly polished aluminum skin with green trim and was named *Mrs. Mennen* in honor of his wife, Kay. When Mira was back in Santa Paula, he wrote Mennen a letter asking for help on the P-39 project. Mennen agreed because "I have always liked the P-39," and Mira "is such a wonderful fellow."

With Mennen's backing, Mira bought the last airworthy P-39 in America and sent it to Dick Martin at Van Nuys Airport to prepare the plane for racing. Martin put the already-light plane on a diet and got it down to 5,222 pounds. He also made a number of changes to the brakes, flaps, and fuel tanks. The biggest change was replacing the original 1,200-hp Allison with a 2,000-hp, souped-up G-6 Allison similar to the engine in the *Tahoe Miss* (but without the auxiliary blower). In homage to Mennen's Spartan Executive *Mrs. Mennen*, Mira named the plane *Mr. Mennen* and painted it white, gold, and green. He also installed a massive four-bladed propeller from a P-51 Mustang.

During *Mr. Mennen*'s first test flight, the P-51 propeller proved to be too big, causing *Mr. Mennen* to snap-roll violently to the right immediately after takeoff. Mira got the plane under control but then noticed that the engine was overheating. He quickly returned to the airport and landed. That night, Mira took his crew to dinner at Johnny's Skytrails restaurant at the south end of the Van Nuys Airport for what had been planned as a celebration dinner. The plane's dangerous tendency to snap-roll, along with the engine troubles, had a sobering effect on Mira. He told the somber crew that flying the plane was "like trying to stand on a beach ball."

The second test flight later that week was also cut short by an overheating problem when a cooling line popped off the engine during takeoff and filled the cockpit with steaming hot glycol. Mira declared "mayday" and landed safely. The next time they scheduled a test flight, a Van Nuys Airport fire truck pulled up in front of the hanger and one of the firemen, wearing his bunker gear, lumbered into the hanger and teased, "We just want you to know that if you guys are going to fly today, we're ready!" After a few more test flights, Mira announced that there was no way he could race with the four-blade propeller, so he arranged to have three of the big P-51 blades installed on a three-bladed hub.

The first race for *Mr. Mennen* was scheduled for September 15–17 at Reno. When Mira learned that the new propeller could not be finished in time, he decided to skip the race. If he ran the P-51 propeller, he could not control the plane in a high-speed racing formation. "If I try it, I'll kill someone. Probably me!" The normal P-39 propeller was too thin to take advantage of all the horsepower from the G-6 Allison, and Mira did not want to debut the plane if he could not be competitive.

On September 13, Mira got a visit from the president of the Professional Race Pilots Association, who convinced him to take the plane to Reno with the stock P-39 propeller. Mira knew he was well past the entry deadline, but the president assured him that if he showed up he could race. With the sudden change in plans, Mira's crew scrambled to get ready, loading tools and spare parts into a couple of pickup trucks and hitting the highway for the all-night drive to Reno. Mira and *Mr. Mennen* flew out the next morning.

When *Mr. Mennen* arrived at Stead Field in Reno, the unique plane was surrounded by fans. As his crew worked to get the plane prepared to qualify, Mira signed a few autographs and then headed to the pilots' meeting to get the waiver he needed to compete. Much to Mira's surprise, and contrary to the president's assurances, the competition committee refused to give Mira a waiver and told him that if he had been serious about racing, he should have shown up before the deadline, like all the other pilots.

Mira stormed back to the plane, telling the crew to "Pack it all up. We're going home."

Jerry Duty, the race director, hurried over to Mira and explained that he could not overrule the competition committee, but that he would be happy to let Mira fly some demonstration laps as part of the opening ceremony. That way, the Mennen Company would still get some publicity from the race, and the fans who were excited about seeing Mira's new plane would get a chance to watch him fly. Mira calmed down and agreed to fly the exhibition laps. The local newspaper announced Slovak's disqualification from the race with banner headlines that said, "Slovak scratched!"

On the Friday morning, the skies were deep blue and crystal clear. The crowd was the largest to ever attend a Reno Air Race up to that time, and it was officially "Bob Hoover Day." Hoover performed several flawless aerobatic routines, first in his familiar yellow-and-black Mustang, followed by a twin-engine Rockwell Shrike Commander and then a custom yellow

F-86 jet. As the Shrike Commander act ended with Hoover shutting off both engines and doing a series of aerobatic maneuvers without power, then landing in front of the grandstands, he had asked for and received permission to take off and land from the apron, which was a couple hundred feet closer to the fans in the bleachers than the main runway.

As soon as Hoover's show was done, Mira was given permission to take up *Mr. Mennen*. He flew three fast laps, skimming the ground on the straightaways and banking the plane 90 degrees to roar through the turns. Midway into the third lap, Mira saw the temperature gauge climb into the red. Mira figured that he had blown another cooling hose off the engine. He knew that with no coolant in the engine, he would not be able to fly all the way to the end of the airport, enter the landing pattern, and bring *Mr. Mennen* back around for a normal landing. Thinking fast, he chopped the throttle, lowered his landing gear, and put the plane down safely on the apron in front of the bleachers where just a short while earlier Bob Hoover had landed his Shrike Commander. Mira brought the plane to a stop and his crew drove out with a white pickup truck to pull him back to the pits to examine the engine.

As Mira waited for his crew to diagnose the overheating problem, he was approached by James Leecke, the Federal Aviation Administration's inspector from the General Aviation District Office for Reno. Leecke informed Mira that because he had "recklessly" landed on the apron instead of the runway, he was suspending Mira's pilot's license for thirty days. Mira was incredulous. He explained that he had had an emergency and had no choice but to land on the apron. Leecke pointed out that Mira had never declared an emergency or called mayday on the radio. He had also failed to ask for permission to land. Therefore, he was in violation of FAA regulations and he had to surrender his license immediately. Mira angrily pointed out that Bob Hoover had been landing on the apron all weekend. Leecke countered, saying that Hoover had asked for and received prior approval but that Mira had not.

Mira turned in his license and served his suspension. Notice of the violation was sent to Continental, and its VP of flight operations angrily told Mira he could race planes or he could fly for Continental, but not both. Reluctantly, Mira sold *Mr. Mennen* without ever flying a lap in competition.

Shortly after *Mr. Mennen* sold, Mira learned that that his father had died. The news hit him hard. Maria had come to the U.S. to visit Mira a few times, and of course, his brother was living in the U.S. working for Harrah, but Mira had not seen his father since March 1953. Jan was scared to fly and after his one flight to Prague with Mira in 1946, he refused to get on a plane again, so of course he had never been able to come to the U.S. Of all Mira's relatives, his father had suffered the most at the hands of the Communists. He had his business seized and his home taken away. He alone had been sent to a re-education camp. Mira was caught off guard by the profound sense of guilt that washed over him.

Losing his father caused Mira to reflect on his life and what he had accomplished. He was overcome by the need to grow up, settle down, and act like a man. He soon married again, this time to a woman seventeen years younger than him named Linda Johnson. His second marriage lasted longer than his first, but it eventually succumbed to many of the same problems as his first, and Mira and Linda were divorced.

Mira threw himself into work, picking up more flights on Continental, eventually flying from Los Angeles to Honolulu more than 800 times. He used his free time to expand Mira Slovak Aviation, adding several more lines of aircraft, including the Great Lakes 180 and the Italian-built Partenavia P.68. He also continued to fly air shows across the country, alternating between his well-known Bücker act and a new glider show with a Czech-built Lunak glider, an aerial ballet choreographed to the music of "Born Free," where the silent plane danced across the sky trailing red and blue smoke while Andy Williams singing "Born free, as free as the wind blows, as free as the grass grows" came from speakers lining the flight line.[5]

In 1978, Continental Airlines decided to phase out its entire fleet of Boeing 747s and convert its long-distance, wide-body business to McDonnell Douglas DC-10s. Mira moved into the new DC-10s. At about the same time, President Jimmy Carter signed the Airline Deregulation Act of 1978. After deregulation, Continental expanded dramatically. Robert Six had been a legend in the aviation world, building Continental Airlines from a tiny airmail service in 1936 into one of the world's largest airlines by the 1970s. Success in business is often attributed to skill and courage, but in truth, there is also a good deal of luck involved. Unfortunately for Six, his luck was about to turn against him. By early 1979, Continental was heavily leveraged to pay for its expansion in the wake of deregulation. It had also borrowed huge sums to replace all its Boeing 747s with DC-10s.

On May 25, 1979, American Airlines Flight 191 pushed back from the gate at Chicago's O'Hare Airport to fly to Los Angeles. There were 271 people on board the DC-10—thirteen crew members and 258 passengers. As the plane took off, the left engine inexplicably ripped off the wing, causing the plane to roll violently to the left and crash into a nearby field. In the deadliest aviation accident to ever take place on U.S. soil, everyone on board was killed. In the immediate aftermath of the accident, all DC-10s were grounded for five-and-a-half weeks while the NTSB tried to determine why the engine had come off the plane.

Continental was forced to cancel almost all its long-range, wide-body service. It was a crippling blow. The DC-10s came back into service in mid-July, but before the airline could recover, the U.S. economy went into a recession and revenue dropped. In 1980, Continental lost $27 million. Stock prices fell, and on January 1, 1981, Frank Lorenzo, of Texas Air Corporation, announced his plans to buy enough stock to take over Continental Airlines. Continental employees fought back, buying as much stock as they could afford, but by the end of August 1981, the hostile takeover was complete and Lorenzo was in charge, eventually controlling 65 percent of all Continental stock. He forced Robert Six into retirement and demanded that his union pilots, mechanics, and flight attendants take a 50 percent pay cut.

Sunday, October 18, 1981 was a warm day with light winds and no rain in Santa Paula. Autumn was taking hold of the tiny town. The reader board outside the Safeway store advertised a sale on Halloween candy. Around town, hand-lettered signs saying "U-Pick Pumpkin Patch" directed tourists to the old-fashioned red barn of a quaint family farm where laughing children struggled to load huge orange pumpkins into muddy red wheelbarrows. Mira spent the morning puttering around the hangar working on his Bücker. He went flying in the late afternoon. At this time of year, he liked to fly alone over the Los Padres National Forest, admiring the beauty of the changing leaves. It was after 7 p.m. when he landed and returned to his hangar. The radio chatted softly in the background as he cleaned his plane. The LA Rams were playing the Dallas Cowboys in a late game. Mira was not much of a football fan, but the noise of the game kept him company as he worked. Mira lost interest in the game and was just about to turn it off when he heard a name that sounded like "Bill Muncey." An inexplicable chill ran down his back as he faced the radio to better hear what was being said.

"Legendary hydroplane racer Bill Muncey, the winningest driver in the history of powerboat racing, was killed today when his hydroplane, *Atlas Van Lines,* crashed while leading the World Championship race in Acapulco, Mexico." The news hit Mira like a punch to the stomach. For a moment, he could not breathe. He went into his office and leaned against the corner of his desk. His walls were covered with photos and trophies from his racing career. He picked a black and white 8 × 10-inch photo in a cheap plastic frame from the wall. It showed Muncey and Mira sitting side by side on a dock in Coeur d'Alene. They were both young and smiling. It seemed impossibly long ago, but at the same time it seemed like yesterday.

Mira knew that Muncey had continued to race and he knew that the sport was still deadly, but somehow, he felt that after all Muncey's crashes and near missies, he was invincible. Mira needed to talk to someone, but he did not know who to call. It had been fourteen years since he had had retired from driving and so many of his friends were gone, retired or dead. Finally, he found a phone number and called Russ Schleeh. "Did you hear about Muncey?"

"Yes. I was searching for your number. I was going to call you."

"It's hard to believe. Somehow I thought he would live forever."

"Me too," Schleeh agreed. "That's exactly what I was thinking. But you know, this is probably how he would have wanted to go, out in front, leading the race."

"Yes, but it still doesn't seem possible," Mira said, looking at the old photo in his hand.

Mira had a difficult time sleeping that night. It was not just the loss of his friend and rival, but he also felt cut off and left behind by the whole hydroplane world. For years, he had been a big part of the racing community and now he was so removed that he could not even come up with the phone number of someone to call who could tell him what had happened.

The next morning, a plane from Mexico carrying Muncey's body landed in San Diego. Lee Schoenith, who had been at the race, called Mira from an airport pay phone and told him about the accident. This was the first unlimited race in Mexico and Muncey had been involved in promoting it. He was committed to putting on a great show for the locals. In the final heat, he made a perfect start, stole the inside lane from the *Miss Budweiser*, powered through the first turn, and had a huge lead going up the backstretch. It was late in the day and the low angle of the sun, glaring right into the drivers' eyes, made it tough for them to read the water conditions. A guest of wind caught the *Atlas*. It rocked precariously back and forth and then blew over in a spectacular back flip that threw Muncey out at 170 mph. His neck broke when he hit the water and there was nothing anyone could do to save him. Schoenith told Mira that the funeral would be Saturday the 24th, at the Glen Abbey Memorial Park, south of San Diego.

On the Saturday morning, Mira dressed up in his best black suit, tucked his tie into his pocket so it would not whip around in the wind, strapped on his leather flying helmet, and got into his Bücker to head 185 miles south to San Diego for Muncey's funeral. As he climbed into the clear autumn sky, he thought about that day twenty-four years ago when he flew Muncey's battered body from Madison to Chicago after *Miss Thriftway* disintegrated. He wondered if he could have helped if he had been in Acapulco.

Maybe he could have flown Muncey home to an American hospital? The Bücker's engine purred as the Southern California landscape slipped beneath Mira's wings and a whirlwind of memories circled through his mind—the first time they met, the way Bill always called him "Slim," their great duels on the water that were often followed by a brotherly hug on the beach, standing side by side signing autographs until their hands grew tired, and visiting each other in hushed hospital rooms after their many crashes.

Mira was approaching Lindbergh Field. Suddenly, as clear as day, he could imagine Bill's bright gap-toothed smile after the air show they had flown together over Moses Lake in 1958. In an instant, Mira understood what a special relationship he had shared with Bill and he knew that standing silently beside an open grave was not the right way to honor Bill. He pushed the Bücker's throttle forward, gave her hard right rudder, and headed out over the Pacific Ocean. Once he was out of sight of land, he pulled back on the stick and the spry little Bücker flew straight up into the cloudless October sky. When he was high enough, Mira pushed the nose over and dove toward the water in a hammer-head dive, pulling out in a long series of snap rolls just a few feet above the surface of the ocean. The rolls were followed by a Cuban Eight, then loops, stall turns, and tail slides. Mira flew the most challenging, intense, and beautiful aerobatic show of his life, with only Bill Muncey's memory to keep him company. When the show was done, Mira brought the plane low over the water, flipped into inverted flight and skimmed the waves, waving good bye to his dear friend. Mira knew in his heart that somewhere Bill was smiling that big friendly gap-toothed grin and waving back.

Continental's problems continued to mount. By September 23, 1983, the airline was over $100 million in debt and Lorenzo filed for Chapter 11 bankruptcy protection, a move that allowed him to void all his existing contracts with union employees. On October 1, Continental's 2,000 pilots, represented by the Air Line Pilots Association, went on strike. At first, Mira was reluctant to support the strike. He felt that "organized workers" telling management what to do sounded like communism. After several visits from union organizers who explained to Mira that the American labor movement was a big part of what made America work and that being a "scab" and crossing picket lines would be seen as unpatriotic, Mira reversed his position and agree to support the strike. It was a hard-fought strike that ended with a defeat of the union and Mira, along with the rest of the striking pilots, was fired.

Meanwhile, Mira Slovak Aviation was doing well. He was representing several new lines of planes and added half a dozen hangars in Santa Paula to house the growing collection.

32

Nuclear Power Plants and Candles: Soviet Union, 1986

Throughout history, grand empires have risen to power, flourished, and eventually died. The causes of any empire's crumble and decay are complex and difficult to pinpoint, except for the Soviet Union. Mikhail Gorbachev, its eighth and last leader, says that its fall started at exactly 1.06 a.m. on April 25, 1986 when a worker at the number four reactor of the Chernobyl Nuclear Power Plant pushed a button to begin a test of the plant's emergency cooling system.

Gorbachev became general secretary of the Soviet Union on March 11, 1985. Prior to Gorbachev taking power, the Soviets were struggling under the weight of a costly and unpopular war in Afghanistan, and large swaths of the population were dissatisfied with their standard of living. After taking over the reins of the government, Gorbachev instituted new polices of "*Glasnost*" (openness) and "*Perestroika*" (restructuring.) The goal of Glasnost was to acknowledge the shortcomings of the Soviet system in order to find viable solutions. The goal of *perestroika* was to persuade unhappy people to work to reform the government and enable it to solve the country's problems rather than working against the government.

Chernobyl's operators lost control of the reactor during the system test. An explosion blew the reactor apart, set the complex on fire, and released forty times more radiation than the atomic bomb at Hiroshima. It was a catastrophe of monstrous proportions. The fires were put out in a few hours, but over 3,600,000 acres were contaminated with enough radiation that they were uninhabitable, requiring more than 300,000 people to be permanently relocated. The estimated death toll ranged from a few dozen workers killed in the explosion and fighting the fire, to hundreds of thousands of increased cancer deaths in the years since the explosion. The Soviet government, already running low on cash because of its long and costly war in Afghanistan, was driven to the brink of bankruptcy by the billions of dollars needed to pay for the Chernobyl clean up.

In the immediate aftermath of Chernobyl, the Soviet government used lies, denials, and half-truths to try to cover up the disaster. Within a few days, honest reports were published on the massive scope of the accident and the avoidable mistakes that led to it. Prior to Gorbachev, such open criticism would never have been allowed. The people responded by stepping up their protests and demanding to know more about the government. "*Glasnost*" was proving to be more than just a hollow party slogan but a new reality of Soviet life. Reporters, inspired by the anger of the people and emboldened by *glasnost*, began to print more stories critical of other aspects of the Soviet government. Freedom of the press, coupled with an angry population, led to many of the Soviet Union's dark secrets spilling out into the press—Stalin's purges, Siberian death camps, persecution of dissidents, and costly blunders in Afghanistan were soon public knowledge.

One of the first changes to come after the Chernobyl disaster was the abandonment of the Brezhnev Doctrine. Gorbachev said that philosophically, he disagreed with Soviet intervention in other communist countries, but by that time, after years of war in Afghanistan and the cost of the Chernobyl cleanup, it was unlikely that the Soviet Union had the resources to interfere even if Gorbachev had wanted.

Dissidents in Czechoslovakia cautiously watched events unfolding in Russia. On March 25, 1988, Roman Catholics in Bratislava held a candlelight vigil in Hviezdoslav Square, demanding religious freedom. Rain and sleet were whipped across the city by bitter winds. Still, 5,000 peaceful protesters, many of them school teachers, nuns, or grandmothers carrying umbrellas in one hand and candles in the other, crowded into the square. Thousands more jammed the side streets leading to the protest. It was the largest protest in Czechoslovakia since the Russian tanks had crushed the Prague Spring twenty years earlier. At first, the police tried to break up the demonstrations by driving their cruisers, with sirens blaring and lights flashing, through the crowd. The good-natured protesters pirouetted out of the way of the charging cars like matadors waving umbrellas instead of capes. The police lost their patience and sent in tanker trucks with water cannons. The demonstrators, already soaking wet from the awful weather, huddled together in small phalanxes and shielded themselves with their umbrellas. Eventually, the angry police resorted to clubbing the protesters with nightsticks. There were minor injuries and a few arrests but Gorbachev stayed true to his word and there was no Soviet interference. The protest became known as the Candle Demonstration.

In the weeks that followed, anti-government demonstrations spread to Poland and other East-European communist nations. In December 1988, Gorbachev told the United Nations that he would soon be withdrawing all Soviet troops from Eastern Europe.

Events unfolded quickly. The Communist party in Hungary called for an end to single-party rule. Latvia, Estonia, and Lithuania declared themselves independent from the Soviet Union. Solidarity claimed victory in the Polish parliamentary elections. Refugees from the Soviet Bloc streamed into Hungary and across the now-open border into Austria and Western Europe. On November 8, 1989, the Berlin wall was opened and thousands of Germans were reunited with friends and family for the first time in over forty years.

Students in Prague planned a demonstration for "International Students Day," November 17, to solemnize the fiftieth anniversary of the Nazis storming the major universities in Czechoslovakia, closing the schools, and sending countless students to the concentration camps. Some 15,000 students marched into downtown Prague, carrying banners and chanting anti-communist slogans. They were met by armed police, who violently broke up the peaceful demonstrations.

Protests grew in Prague and spread to other cities. On November 24, the entire executive committee of Czechoslovakia resigned and was replaced by new, more liberal members. A non-communist government was sworn in on December 10, 1989, and on the 29th, the Federal Assembly elected Vaclav Havel, a spokesman for the protesters and successful playwright, as the new president of a free and democratic Czechoslovakia.

Mira watched the events in Eastern Europe unfold with a mixture of excitement and fear. He was thrilled that his former country was finally throwing off the oppressive bounds of communism, but his distrust and suspicion of the Soviets ran so deep that he kept expecting to see Gorbachev change his mind and send the tanks rolling back into Prague.

By October 1990, convinced that the reforms were real, Mira decided to go home. He landed at Prague Airport on the afternoon of October 5. The day was clear and brisk, with no rain. As his plane pulled up to the Prague terminal, he was stunned by how unchanged the airport was. It looked exactly the way it had on that night in 1953 when he had waited at the controls of his DC-3 for the tower to give him clearance to start his engines. The terminal building was the same long, two-story white building with blue trim and red neon letters saying "*Letiště Praha*" (Prague Airport).

The only difference was that the propeller driven DC-3s and Ju 52s waiting on the apron had been replaced with modern Russian-built Tupolev and Ilyushin jets.[1]

Once the plane was parked, a ground crew in white coveralls rolled up a set of portable stairs. As the doors opened, passengers anxious to make their connections or meet a loved one rushed to the exit. Mira waited patiently, collecting his thoughts, thinking of all he had experienced since he left Czechoslovakia. He walked to the door and stepped out into the sunshine. He had been in exile for 13,712 days, but now he was home.

He walked to the terminal and cleared customs with a dozen other tourists. The customs officer stamped his passport without even looking up. As he walked across the worn linoleum floor toward the exit, he passed the restroom where thirty-seven years earlier, he had changed out of his pilot's uniform into civilian clothes to try blend into the crowd the night before his escape. It did not even feel like these were his own memories. He felt as if he were remembering a scene from a movie he had seen long ago. He left the terminal and hailed a taxi to take him into the city. He was only spending one night in Prague before catching a train to Leopoldov. He could have changed planes and flown to Bratislava, but a powerful sense of nostalgia pulled him to Prague. He needed to walk across the Charles Bridge, lean against the rail and watch the Vltava River flow by, then wander aimlessly through Wenceslaus Square. Prague's beauty and charm were timeless. The city did not seem changed, but the people seemed worn, tired, timid, and drab. Compared to the vibrant red, purple, blue, or green coats and scarves he had seen on the streets of New York and Paris, everyone in Prague seemed dull, wearing only black or gray. The air smelled different too. Mira had forgotten the unique way that coal smoke, diesel exhaust, and the scent of baking rye bread seemed to mingle together and hang in the air near the river.

He checked into a small hotel and climbed a narrow set of stairs to his room, letting himself in with an old-fashioned skeleton key. He sat on the single bed with a faded blue chintz comforter; he looked nervously at the phone. He had told himself that the reason he came to Prague was to see the sights and relive old memories, but that was a lie. He came to make two phone calls.

Mira slid open the drawer of a small wooden desk and pulled out a tattered Prague phone directory. He looked up the two numbers and wrote them on the desk pad. He held the pad in his hands for a long time, trying to decide which number to call first. He wished that this hotel had adopted the American fashion of providing a private mini bar, because a nice gin and tonic would calm his nerves and make the phone calls a lot easier. Outside the second-story window, it was growing dark. He could hear horns honk, truck engines growl, and an occasional siren from a faraway police car. He picked up the old-fashioned black phone. He had not seen one like this in America in twenty years. He dialed zero to reach the front desk. Mira gave the desk clerk the number and waited. The phone buzzed again and after a few moments, a woman answered. It was Jiřinka's sister. Mira did not want to cause trouble or interfere in Jiřinka's life, but they had dated for so many years, when he was a young flight cadet and learning to become a man, that he needed to know how she was doing and how her life had turned out. It was a brief, disappointing conversation that ended with her sister slamming down the receiver, but Mira learned that Jiřinka was happily married to a CSA navigator; she had several children and was now a grandmother. It was enough. Mira was able to let go of a little bit of the guilt he had carried with him for so many years. He had never believed that he had "ruined Jiřinka's life," but he often felt guilty over the way he had hurt her and how callously he had acted when he left.

The next phone call was tougher. He gave the desk clerk the second number and paced back and forth in the tiny room while the earpiece of the phone buzzed with the low, flat sound of a Czech phone ringing. Finally, there was a click and a gravely male voice answered saying, "*Dobrý den.*" (Hello.)

Mira responded, "*Dobrý den. Můžu, mulvit na* Honza?" (Hello. May I please speak to Honza?)

"*To je* Honza" (This is Honza.)

Suddenly, Mira choked up. His mouth went dry and his eyes stared to water. "*To je* Mira." (This is Mira.)

There was a moment of silence. "I wondered when I would hear from you."

"How have you been, Honza?"

"Good, Mira, very good, but not as good as you."

"What do you mean?"

"Oh, even in the communist years, we still heard about you. Your racing, your victories. You even met the president. You've done well."

"Honza, you could have had all of that too."

"No! Don't start down that path. I've been happy. I got married, I had children and I continued to fly. I was given the Prague to Havana route, so I've gotten to spend time in the warm sunshine on sandy beaches too, just like you."

"Can I see you?"

There was another long pause. "No. I lied. I'm not doing that well. I have cancer. I'm going through chemotherapy treatments. My hair is falling out and I'm sick all of the time. No, you shouldn't see me."

"I don't care. I just want to see you,"

"You might not care Mira, but I care. I don't want you to see me like this; thin, frail, old. You'll be back and maybe we can see each other next time."

Mira paused. "Okay, but may I ask you a question?"

"No." There was something that sounded like fear in Honza's voice.

"You don't even know what it is," Mira protested.

"Yes I do, and I won't answer it. I can't answer it."

"Honza, please I need to know. Were you working for the StB?"

On the other end of the phone, Mira could hear Honza draw a deep breath, sigh heavily, and finally say, "I told you I wouldn't answer, Mira. It's pointless for you to ask a question when you already know the answer. We were friends. I did what I had to do, but I always made sure you were safe."

"Honza, please, yes or no. Were you with the StB?"

"Goodbye Mira." The phone clicked dead.

The next day, clouds moved in and an autumn rain washed the streets of Prague. Mira caught the train to Piešťany, where his mother was now living. Along the way, he planned to stop in Leopoldov. Alone on the train, he watched the ravaged countryside slip by the windows and was reminded of an old black-and-white photo he had seen in a magazine. It showed a once-beautiful movie star from the 1920s who was now almost ninety years old. Her lovely face was lined and wrinkled. Her lips were thin and her body frail. Her hair was sparse and wiry but she still tried to wear makeup and dress as if she were young and provocative. The effect was sad, almost pitiful. The photo was disturbing, and so was the view from the rain-streaked window. The beautiful land he had loved was fallow and ruined. The fields were bare, fences were falling down, and many buildings were empty. It broke his heart. He worried that he had done the wrong thing. Maybe he should have stayed, defended his people, made sure that his parents lived a better life. He felt a rush of guilt. He had been living in a fantasy world of jet planes, fast boats, and beautiful women while his homeland had suffered under the heel of a brutal regime. What would his life have been like had he stayed and married Jiřinka? Could he have had children, raised a family, and fought the communists? Ghosts of what could have been rose up in his mind and filled him with worry and regret.

The train arrived in Leopoldov. It was strange to get off the train with no one to meet him; his family was long gone. His father was dead, his brother was living in Las Vegas, and his mother had moved north to Piešťany. He would be catching a train to see her in an hour, but there was something he needed to do first. Walking out of the station, he turned his collar up against the October damp. At a flower stall, he bought a bouquet of red carnations. He walked toward the church. The trees were taller now, but the yellow stucco building with its steep red tile roof seemed unchanged from Christmas night in 1940, when Mira's father had played the trumpet solo of "Oh Holy Night." Inside the church's open door, he could hear the organist practicing. He walked to the small graveyard to the left of the cloister. He wandered through the tall, wet grass, looking at tombstones as the rain dripped from a low-hanging grey sky. So many of the names were familiar—friends he had gone to school with, families he had grown up alongside. Eventually, he found the stone he was looking for. There was a long, white granite slab that covered the grave. Perched on top of the slab was a black marble tombstone engraved with gold letters that said "Jan Slovak 1903–1973."

Mira knelt and placed the flowers on the grave. "I came home, Dad," he whispered with tears in his eyes. He thought of his father sick and dying while Mira and Jarda were away in a foreign land. He was suddenly hit by the pain and loneliness Jan must have felt. The guilt multiplied in Mira's imagination. He was just about to whisper an apology to his father when something caught his attention. He looked to his left and saw a tombstone that listed several generations of the same family—fathers, sons, and grandsons; he looked to his right and saw the same thing. Then he looked back at his father's tombstone and saw just Jan's name and a large blank space where there was room for many more names. Suddenly, Mira understood. The blank spot was for his name. If he had stayed, he would have died. His spirit was too strong. His desire for freedom was too great. It was never a choice between life under the communists and life as a free man; it had always been a choice between life as a free man or death at the hands of the communists. He never could have stayed and married Jiřinka and become one of the countless soulless men slaving under the yoke. He would have rebelled like Roberto and died like Roberto, and he would have been buried right here next to his father. The realizations hit him like a shaft of warm summer sunlight. He knew with certainty that he had done not just the right thing but he had done the only thing that was possible. The confirmation lifted a weight from his soul. He looked to the right, toward the yellow stucco church. He had been raised in this church and had been taught to pray in this church and had learned to ask for God's protection and blessing for the people he loved. Now, more than ever, he felt an overwhelming sense of gratitude, but wasn't sure how to express it.

He began the way he did as a child when he lay in bed during the long nights of Allied bombings during World War II. "God Bless Mother and Father and …." He paused, not quite sure what to say next. He was so grateful for the marvelous, miraculous life he had led, the freedoms he had enjoyed, and the riches and acclaim he had won. A simple thought came to him. It was the way he ended every one of the hundreds of speeches he had given in America when he talked about the dangers of communism. During his speeches, it had almost felt like a political slogan, or just a catch phrase to pander to the audience's patriotism, but here, back in Czechoslovakia, kneeling in front of his father's grave as he faced the reality of the awful death that had awaited him if he had stayed in the communist world, the words came back to him in a sincere and reverent prayer. He started again, "God bless Mother, God bless Father, and God bless the USA."

Epilogue: Seattle, Washington, 2017

Shortly after Mira returned to the US, he ran into his friend Ingrid Bondi at an arts and crafts store in Santa Barbara. She was single again, and as he had done each time he saw her for the previous twenty-six years, Mira asked her out, but much to his surprise, this time she said yes. The two quickly fell in love, moved in together, and became inseparable for the rest of Mira's life.

After the Continental strike, Mira never returned to airline flying, but continued to do air shows and run Mira Slovak Aviation. By the time he flew his last plane in 2013, he had a total of 38,585 hours of flying in almost 200 different airplanes—everything from big four-engine jets like a Boeing 747 to tiny single engine gliders.

Mira had one last fling with hydroplane racing. Dave Knowlen, who Mira met and befriended in the Gold Cup pits in 1958, grew up to become a successful hydroplane designer, but Dave also went on to become a special projects manager for Boeing Commercial Airplanes and was instrumental in convincing BCA President Scott Carson and three of his closest friends to underwrite the *Miss Wahoo* replica that was built by the Hydroplane Museum in 2009.

When the replica was launched, I was lucky enough to take her out for its first run, and even though Mira was seventy-nine years old, I made sure that he was the first person I would give a ride to.

I felt like a bit of a fraud as Mira and I changed into our driving gear. I told him that he should be the one giving me the ride, but insurance requirements would not allow me to turn over a 160-mph race boat to a seventy-nine-year-old man who had not been in a hydroplane cockpit for over forty years. Mira laughed and said he was just grateful to have a chance to be in a boat again.

The *Wahoo's* engine started easily, and as we pulled away from the pits, I saw Mira affectionately pat the deck with his hand. I have given a number of rides over the years and always try to make sure that the first few laps are easy and comfortable, especially when the rider is someone in their late seventies. We motored through the first two laps at three-quarters throttle, hitting about 120 mph and making sure that I kept the boat out in lane three, where I could slide easily through the corners without giving Mira too rough a ride. As I started lap three, I tapped Mira's shoulder and pointed at the steering wheel, hoping he would take it over. He reached out and two things happened at once. First, I felt his foot stomp down hard on top of my foot and smash the accelerator to the floor. Instantly, the boat leapt forward as the speedometer needle climbed toward 160 mph. Next, even though we were in the middle of the straightaway, he took a hard left turn. For a moment, I was panicked, not knowing what was happening, but as we shot in from lane three, Mira slammed the boat in to a hard right turn in lane one, and there we stayed for the next few laps, running hard and fast in lane one, skimming the buoys with fewer than six inches to spare. I let Mira drive the rest of the way. We finished and headed back to the dock. When he shut off the motor and the lake fell silent, the only sound was the two of us laughing like little kids. Mira passed his check ride in flying colors and we let him take the boat out by himself a couple years later at eighty-one years old to give him the official world record as the oldest person ever to drive an unlimited hydroplane.

An adventurer to the very end, Mira was busy planning a transatlantic flight in his Bücher when he was diagnosed with the stomach cancer that would eventually claim his life. Mira and I had talked for years about writing his biography, but he was always too busy to sit in front of a computer and get it done. It was not until February 2014 that we started in earnest. We would email daily, and when it became apparent that we could not get the job done with just emails, I flew to his beautiful home in Fallbrook, California to spend a pleasant week with Mira. During the day, we dug through the mounds of records and papers in his office. In the evenings, we sat sipping cocktails on a patio next to his pool. By the time I left, we had recorded hours of interviews and collected hundreds of pages of photos, notes, and documents.

A few weeks later, Mira succumbed to cancer. An aviator to the last, he died at exactly 7.47 a.m. on the morning of May 16, 2014. His remains were cremated and sprinkled in the warm Pacific waters in front of the Palapala Ho'omau Church where famed aviator Charles Lindberg is buried.

I could not have written this book without the help of Ingrid Bondi, the late William E. Boeing Jr, and the entire Boeing Family, Frank Danes, Brad Haskin, the late Ron Jones, David Knowlen, the late Chuck Lyford, Wil Muncey, Will Raddamaker, Bill Thompson, and my amazing wife Linda Williams.

I want to extend a special thank you to my friend and editor, Roger Lippman. His guidance and assistance throughout this entire project was indispensable.

Endnotes

Introduction

1. The four partners that donated money to the Hydroplane Museum to build the Miss Wahoo replica were: Scott Carson, Joe Clark, Bruce McCaw, and Bill Boeing Jr. Scott Carson, who was President of Boeing Commercial Airplanes at the time of the donation, was careful to make sure that all involved knew that these were personal donations and did not come from the Boeing Company.
2. Personal interview with Mira Slovak (2014).

Chapter 2

1. Anicka and Petr were not the real names of the married couple in this story, but for reasons that will become obvious as the story unfolds, false names were used to disguise their identity.
2. Personal interview with Mira Slovak (2014).
3. *Ibid.*

Chapter 3

1. Personal interview with Mira Slovak (2014).
2. *Ibid.*
3. Shaw, *World War II Day by Day*, (2010), p. 145.
4. Both the Weiss and Engels families survived World War II and left Europe. The Weisses moved to Australia and the Engels to Asuncion, Paraguay. Higman, *My Boyhood Heroes* (2014), p. 71.

Chapter 4

1. Personal interview with Mira Slovak (2010).
2. The Russian engineering battalion that rebuilt the bridge in Leopoldov was commanded by a woman, but for reasons that will become obvious as the story unfolds, her real name was not Nina Kominski.
3. Personal interview with Mira Slovak (2014).

Chapter 5

1. Kovaly, *Under a Cruel Star A life in Prague 1941–1968* (2010), p. 76.
2. Hanak, *V Pilotnim Vycviku 1947 az 1949* (2006), p. 11.
3. Hanak, *V Pilotnim Vycviku 1947 az 1949* (2006), p. 33.

Chapter 6

1. Personal interview with Mira Slovak (2014).
2. *Ibid.*

Chapter 7

1. Personal interview with Mira Slovak (2014).
2. *Ibid.*

Chapter 8

1. The description of Roberto's imprisonment and integration come directly from personal interviews with Mira, but are corroborated by frighteningly similar descriptions in Charles Novacek's *Border Crossing, Coming of Age in the Czech Resistance* (Detroit, MI, Ten21 Press, 2012).
2. *Ibid.*
3. *Ibid.*

Chapter 10

1. Personal interview with Mira Slovak (2014).

Chapter 11

1. Kovaly, *Under a Cruel Star A life in Prague 1941–1968* (2010), p. 101.

Chapter 12

1. Personal interview with Mira Slovak (2014).
2. In the late 1960s, the Soviet newspaper *Pravda* claimed that Mira had flown Gottwald to Stalin's funeral "in Gottwald's jet." This story was debunked when it was proved that at the time of Stalin's death, neither the Soviet nor Czech Air Forces had operational jet transports.
3. In the late 1960s, the Soviet newspaper *Pravda* clained that Mira was part of the honour guard at Gottwald's funeral. Mira vehemently denied this and I have been unable to find any evidence to support *Pravda*'s claim.

4. *Ibid.*
5. *Unpublished Collected Writings of Mira Slovak.*

Chapter 13

1. "Six Czechs Claim Asylum, Airliner Diverted to West," *The Post—Standard Syracuse NY*, March 25, 1953, p. 1.
2. Quigley, J., "Czechs Tell of Unrest, Flight Plot," *Stars and Stripes—European Edition*, March 26, 1953, p. 1.
3. "Czechs Ask Return of Escape Plane. Claim Two Who Engineered Escape Must Be Punished," *The Lowell Sun, Lowell MA.27*, March 1953, p. 1.
4. "23 Are Returned to Czechoslovakia," *The Lowell Sun, Lowell MA.31*, March 1953, p. 1.
5. One of the most improbable aspects of Mira's escape story is the mysterious box of plans that the Czech Air Force placed on board CZ flight 300. Multiple Freedom of Information requests to the CIA were all met with the same cryptic response, "The CIA can neither confirm nor deny the existence or nonexistence of records responsive to your request. The fact of the existence or nonexistence of requested records is currently and properly classified." Mira was told of the contents of the box by Nicky Morris of the U.S. Army's Counter Intelligence Corp., and Bill Boeing Jr. was told about the contents of the box by Wayne Richardson of the U.S. Counter Intelligence Agency. Personal interviews with Bill Boeing Jr. and Mira Slovak (both 2014).

Chapter 14

1. "Czechs Convict 5 As 'Plotters' of Freedom Flight," *Stars and Stripes*, September 28, 1953, p. 3.
2. Personal interview with Mira Slovak (2014).
3. *Ibid.*
4. *Ibid.*
5. *Ibid.*
6. "Fleeing Czechs Win Asylum," Record *Eagle, Traverse City MI*, December 19, 1953.
7. In 1953, the Soviet Embassy in Washington D.C. was located on 1125 16th St. It did not move to its current location on Wisconsin Ave. until 1995.
8. Wayne Richardson's role with the CIA was well documented in the media. In 1952, Wayne had the bad luck of finding himself in a feud with Federal Judge William Lindberg. Richardson was called to testify in the espionage trial of Owen Lattimore. Richardson refused, claiming a national security exemption. Judge Lindberg disagreed and threatened Richardson with contempt of court charges. CIA Director Walter Smith got involved in the case, ordering Richardson not to testify believing that the judge would not risk defying the head of the CIA. Judge Lindberg responded on October 2, 1952 by having Richardson arrested and thrown into jail. After spending eight weeks in jail, Richardson was pardoned by President Harry Truman on Christmas Day. "Two Pardoned in Lattimore Case," *Humboldt Standard*, December 26, 1952, p. 4.

Chapter 15

1. Personal interview with Mira Slovak (2014).

2. "Czech Escapee Now Flying Crop Dusting Planes," *Union-Bulletin*, April 19, 1954, p. 8.
3. Hartley, M., "Winging It," *Ukiah Daily Journal*, February 18, 1979, p. 6.
4. Personal interview with Mira Slovak (2014).
5. *Ibid.*
6. *Ibid.*

Chapter 16

1. Sayre, M., "Boeing, Jr., Plans Racing Hydroplane," *Seattle Times*, November 11, 1955, p. 21.
2. Personal interview with Mira Slovak (2010).
3. Sayre, M., "Boeing and Waggoner Hulls Arrive," *Seattle Times*, May 10, 1956.
4. "Czech Named Boat Driver," *Union Bulletin Walla Walla WA*, May 11, 1956.
5. "U.S. Radio Permit Granted Refugee," *Nevada State Journal, Reno NV*, May 12, 1956, p. 4.
6. "Miss Wahoo Launched," *Seattle Post-Intelligencer*, July 19, 1956.
7. Harrison, C., "Miss Wahoo Shows Class," *Seattle Post-Intelligencer*, July 27, 1956.

Chapter 17

1. Personal interview with Russ Schleeh (August 2, 1996).
2. Personal interview with Mira Slovak (2014).
3. Personal interview with Bill Boeing Jr. (2014).
4. Race coverage for the 1956 Seafair comes from a variety of sources including the *1956 Seafair Trophy* coverage from KING-TV; the *1956 Seafair Trophy* film by the Hydro Museum; personal interviews from Bill Boeing Jr., Russ Schleeh, Jack Regas Ted Jones, and Mira Slovak; and several stories from the *Seattle Times* and *Seattle Post-Intelligencer*.
5. "President Signs Bill so Slovak can Stay," *Seattle Times*, August 6, 1956.
6. Personal interview with Bill Boeing Jr. (2014).
7. Personal interview with Mira Slovak (2014).
8. *Ibid.*

Chapter 18

1. Personal interview with Mira Slovak (2014).
2. Race coverage for the 1957 Mapes Mile High Gold Cup comes from a variety of sources including the *1957 Mapes Mill High Regatta* coverage from KING-TV; the *1957 Mapes Mill High Regatta in Color* film by the Hydro Museum; personal interviews from Bill Boeing Jr., Russ Schleeh, Jack Regas, and Mira Slovak; and several stories from the *Seattle Times* and *Seattle Post-Intelligencer*.
3. Personal interview with Les Edie (2014).
4. Personal interview with David Knowlen (2014).
5. "Easy Does it," *Seattle Times*, October 2, 1957.

Chapter 19

1 Zimmerman, H.,"Slovak Say's He'll Drive Miss Burien or Miss Spokane," *Seattle Times*, April 15,1958.
2 Sheppard, S. *Hydromania, A History of the Diamond Cup*, (2013) p.45
3 Harley Beards was not the real name of the backup driver that accompanied Mira to Detroit in 1959
4. Personal interviews with Russ Schleeh (1996) and Mira Slovak (2014).
5. Personal interview with Mira Slovak (2014).

6. *Sahara Cup Lake Mead*, KING-TV, 1958.
7. Personal interview with Mira Slovak (2014).

Chapter 21

1. *Presidents Cup*, WAML-TV, 1959.
2. *This is Your Life*, "Mira Slovak," A Ralph Edwards Production, 1959.
3. *Ibid.*
4. *Ibid.*

Chapter 22

1. *The President's Appointments Thursday, March 17, 1960*, The Eisenhower Library.
2. *The Roaring 50's*, KING-TV, 1960.

Chapter 23

1. *1960 Apple Cup*, KING-TV.
2. Watson, E., "I Will Drive Like I Drive," *Sports Illustrated*, August 8, 1960.
3. *Ibid.*
4. Harrison, C., "Boeing Calls It Quits," *Seattle Post-Intelligencer*, August 9, 1960.

Chapter 24

1 "Special Case: Slovak, of Hydro Fame, Now Citizen," *Seattle Times*, January 5, 1961.
2 "Affidavit of Witness, Oath of Allegiance" *U.S. Government Printing Office*, January 4, 1961.
3 Private papers of Mira Slovak

Chapter 26

1. The description of the 1964 Reno Air Races come primarily from personal interviews with Chuck Lyford (2014–2016) and Mira Slovak (2014).
2. "1964 Reno Air Races," *Wide World of Sports*, ABC, 1964.
3. *Ibid.*
4. Slovak, M. "Thoughts From a Poor Refugee" *Flying Magazine*, January, 1965

5. *Ibid.*
6. "Just a Dry Run," *Time*, October 2, 1964.

Chapter 27

1. "Letters to the Editor," *Flying*, May 1965.
2. Gilbert, J., "Rumble at Rockford," *Flying*, January 1966.
3. Tegler, *Gentlemen, You Have A Race,* (1984), p. 59–76.

Chapter 28

1. "7 Killed as 2 Planes Crash," *Chicago Tribune*, March 9, 1966.
2. Livesley, B., "Stead, Stout-Hearted Pilot, Started Young, Died Young," *Seattle Times*, April 29, 1966.
3. Kirby, B., "Hydroplanes Seek Shelter," *Tampa Tribune*, June 10, 1966.
4. "Muncey by 2 Ticks, Refs Nod," *Seattle Post-Intelligencer*, June 13, 1966.
5. Personal interview with Eileen Crimmin (1999).
6. Personal interview with Mira Slovak (2014).
7. Zimmerman, H. "It's Time for a Second Look at Hydroplane Racing." *Seattle Times*, June 21,1966
8. Green, J. "There Was No Room, Says Stunned Slovak" *Detroit Free Press*, July 5,1966.
9. Halls, J. "Nobody Shakes - Drivers are Pros" *Detroit Free Press* July 6,1966.
10. "1966 Detroit Gold Cup," *Wide World of Sports*, ABC 1966.
11. Zimmerman, H. "And Now Four Are Dead" *Seattle Times*, July 5, 1966
12. Oliver, S., *Odyssey: A Daring Transatlantic Journey* (1983), p. 5.
13. *Ibid.*
14. *Ibid.*
15. Personal Interview with Mira Slovak (2008-2014).
16. Oliver, S. *Odyssey: A Daring Transatlantic Journey* (1983) p. 8.
17. The details of Mira's relationship with Susan Oliver take up a large portion Susan's autobiographical book, *Odyssey: A Daring Transatlantic Journey* (1983).
18. Oliver, S. *Odyssey: A Daring Transatlantic Journey* (1983) P.82
19. Slovak, M., "We Try for the Mile Record," *Hot Boat Magazine*, February 1967.
20. Zimmerman, H. "Enough is Enough" *Seattle Times*, October 24, 1966

Chapter 29

1. The details of Susan Oliver's effort to fly across the Atlantic are contained in her book, *Odyssey: A Daring Transatlantic Journey* (1983).
2. Personal interview with Mira Slovak (2014).

Chapter 30

1. Owen, J., "The W-I-L-D Blue Yonder," *Seattle Post-Intelligencer*, 10 May 1968.
2. Slovak, M., "Thirty-Six Horsepower Over the Atlantic," *Unpublished Collected writings of Mira Slovak.*
3. *Ibid.*

4 *Ibid.*
5. *Freedom Flyer*, Freedom Flyer Productions, 1975.
6. Throughout Mira's life, he steadfastly denied that his good friend Perry Schreffler had anything to do with the RF-4 crash and always described that accident as pilot error. However, two pilots I interviewed who witnessed the crash said it was clearly the unexpected prop wash from Perry's Curtis Robin that sent Mira out of control. When I wrote this section, I struggled with conflicting promises—to always tell the truth and also to respect Mira's friends and not muddy their reputations. Eventually, my commitment to tell the truth won out.
7. McCormick, J., "Santa Paula Crash Ends Czech's Flight," *The Press-Courier, Venture County*, May 30, 1968.
8. Slovak, M., "Thirty-Six Horsepower Over the Atlantic," *Unpublished Collected writings of Mira Slovak*.

Chapter 31

1. Morris, M. "Mira Slovak's Mother Worried by Russian Invasion" *Seattle Times* August 22, 1968
2. "Slovak Begins New Adventure," *The Press-Courier, Venture County*, May 1969.
3. "Hare Trails Tortoise in Wild Atlantic Race," *Kingsport Times News*, 11 May 1969.
4. "Achter een VW 1200-motor de Oceaan over," *deVW*, June 1969.
5 Black, D., *Born Free*, Columbia Records, 1966.

Chapter 32

1. Personal interview with Mira Slovak (2014).

Bibliography

Books

Albright, M., *Prague Winter A Personal Story of Remembrance and War 1937–1948* (New York, NY HarperCollins, 2012)

Alsip, J., *Artistry of the Great Flyer* (North Charleston, SC CreateSpace, 2013)

Churchill, W., *The Gathering Storm* (New York, NY, Houghton Miffin Company, 1948)

Crumpton, H. A., *The Art of Intelligence Lessons from a Life in the CIA's Clandestine Service* (New York, NY, Penguin Press, 2012)

Ford, D., *The Wizards of Speed on Water* (Denver, CO Doug Ford, 2015)

Gann, E. K., *Fate is the Hunter* (New York, NY, Simon & Schuster, 1961)

Halberstam, D., *The Fifties* (New York, NY, Open Road Books, 1993)

Hanak, M., *V Pilotnim Vycviku 1947 az 1949* (Bucovice, CZ Jakab, 2006)

Higman, P., *My Boyhood Heroes in the Pacific Northwest* (Anacortes, WA High Peaks Books, 2014)

Kovaly, H. M. *Under a Cruel Star A life in Prague 1941–1968* (Lexington, MA Plunkett Lake Press, 2010)

Mailloux, C. (ed.), *Aviation in Santa Paula 1930–2015* (Santa Paula, CA, The Aviation Museum of Santa Paula, 2016)

Matthews, B., *Wet Wings and Drop Tanks* (Atglen. PA Sciffler Aviation History, 1993)

McCullough, D., *The Wright Brothers* (New York, NY Simon & Schuster, 2015)

Muncey, W., *Winningest, The Bill Muncey Chronicles* (Honolulu, HI, Wil Muncey, 2012)

Muntz, A. J., *At the Ragged Edge* (Edmonds, WA Scribewerx, 2013)

Novacek, C., *Border Crossing, Coming of Age in the Czech Resistance* (Detroit, MI ten21 Press, 2012)

Oliver, S., *Odyssey A Daring Transatlantic Journey* (New York, NY Macmillan Publishing, 1983)

Osterberg, J., *Dragon Days* (Seattle, WA Peoh Publishing, 2007)

Lowney, P., *This is Hydroplaning* (Seattle, WA Paul B. Lowney, 1959)

Serling, R. J., *Maverick: The story of Robert Six and Continental Airlines* (Garden City, NJ Doubleday, 1974)

Sharkey, J., *Hydro Who's Who 1946 to 2000* (Seattle, WA Jim Sharkey, 2000)

Shaw, A. J., *World War II Day by Day* (New York, NY Chartwell Books, 2000)

Sheppard, S., *Hydromania A History of the Diamond Cup* (Coeur d' Alene, ID, The Museum of North Idaho, 2013)
Tegler, J., *Gentlemen, You Have A Race* (Maryland Wings Publishing, 1984)
Thompson, R., *Contrails* (Lincolin, NE Iuniverse, 2004)
Williams, D., *Hydroplane Racing in Seattle* (Charleston, SC Arcadia, 2006)
Williams, D., *Hydroplane Racing in Detroit* (Charleston, SC Arcadia, 2009)
Wilmont, H. P., *World War II* (New York, NY, DK, 2004)
Zycie, W., *Eyewitness Travel, Czech & Slovak Republics* (New York, NY, DK, 2009)

Interviews

Alter, F. (2011, August 4). Personal interview.
Boeing, B. (2016, April 2). Personal interview.
Boeing, Bill Jr. (2009–2015, various dates). Personal interview.
Boeing, G. (2016, April 2). Personal interview.
Bondi, I. (2014, May 20). Personal interview.
Carson, S. (2009, various dates). Personal interview.
Cech, B. (2016, April 2). Personal interview.
Cech, Frank IV. (2016, April 2). Personal interview.
Crimmin, E. (1999, April). Personal interview.
Dickenson, B. (2016, May 13). Personal interview.
Dickenson, C. (2016, May 13). Personal interview.
Edie, L. (1996, various dates). Personal interview.
Evans, M. (2000–2016, various dates). Personal interview.
Ford, D. (2016, various dates). Personal interview.
Foster, D. (1996, August 2). Personal interview.
Hanson, M. (2014). Telephone interview.
Haskin, B. (1993–2016, various dates). Personal interview.
Jackson, K. (2006, October 6). Personal interview.
Jones, R. (2000–2016, various dates). Personal interview.
Jones, T. (1995, various dates). Personal interview.
Karelsen, E. (1996–2016, various dates). Personal interview.
Knowlen, D. (2000–2016, various dates). Personal interview.
Link, J. (2016, February 9). Personal interview.
Lyford, C III. (2014–2016, various dates). Personal interview.
Lyford, G. (2016, May 6). Email interview.
Moski, G. (2014, May 20). Telephone interview.
Muncey, W. (2000–2016, various dates). Personal interview.
Pascal, D. (2016, April 2). Personal interview.
Regas, J. (2011, August 4). Personal interview.
Schafhausen, M. (2015, May 15). Telephone interview.
Schleeh, R. (1996, August 2). Personal interview.
Schroder, B. (1999, various dates). Personal interview.
Smith, David. (2000–2014, various dates). Personal interview.
Smith, Dixon. (1996–2016, various dates). Personal interview.
Shepperd, S. (2012–2016, various dates). Telephone interview.
Slovak, M. (2008–2014, various dates). Personal interview.
Vance, D. (2014, May 20). Telephone interview.

Films and Videos

1956 Sahara Cup Lake Mead, Dir. Kenneth Schwedop, KING-TV, 1956. Film.
1956 Seafair Race, Dir. Doug Hall, Hydro Museum, 1996. Film.
1956 Seafair Race, Dir. Kenneth Schwedop, KING-TV, 1956. Film.
1957 Apple Cup, Dir. Kenneth Schwedop, KING-TV, 1957. Film.
1957 Hydro Hilites, Dir. Kenneth Schwedop, KING-TV, 1957. Film.
1957 Mile High Regatta, Lake Tahoe, Dir. Kenneth Schwedop, KING-TV, 1957. Film.
1957 Mile High Regatta in Color, Dir. Don Mock, Hydro Museum, 1957. DVD.
1957 Silver Cup Detroit, Dir. Kenneth Schwedop, KING-TV, 1957. Film.
1958 Apple Cup, Dir. Kenneth Schwedop, KING-TV, 1958. Film.
1958 Gold Cup, Dir. Kenneth Schwedop, KING-TV, 1958. Film.
1958 Gold Cup Time Trials, Dir. Kenneth Schwedop, KING-TV, 1958. Film.
1958 Mile High Regatta, Lake Tahoe, Dir. Kenneth Schwedop, KING-TV, 1958. Film.
1958 Sahara Cup Lake Mead, Dir. Kenneth Schwedop, KING-TV, 1958. Film.
1958 Silver Cup Detroit, Dir. Kenneth Schwedop, KING-TV, 1958. Film.
1958 Thriftway/Coast Guard incident, Dir. Don Mock, Hydro Museum, 2010. DVD.
1959 Gold Cup, Dir. Kenneth Schwedop, KING-TV, 1959. Film.
1959 Presidents Cup, Dir. unknown, WAML-TV, 1959. Film
1960 Apple Cup, Dir. Don Mock, Hydro Museum, 2015. DVD.
1960 Apple Cup, Dir. Kenneth Schwedop, KING-TV, 1960. Film.
1960 Seafair, Dir. Kenneth Schwedop, KING-TV, 1960. Film.
1963 Diamond Cup, Dir. Kenneth Schwedop, KING-TV, 1963. Film.
1964 Reno Air Races, Dir. Roone Arledge, ABC, 1964. Film.
1966 Atomic Cup Tri Cities, Dir. Don Mock, Hydro Museum, 2015. DVD.
1966 Gold Cup Detroit, Dir. Roone Arledge, ABC, 1966. Film.
1966 Sacramento, Dir. Don Mock, Hydro Museum, 2015. DVD.
1967 Atomic Cup Tri Cities, Dir. Don Mock, Hydro Museum, 2015. DVD.
1967 Gold Cup Seattle, Dir. Roone Arledge, ABC, 1967. Film.
1967 Kelowna, Dir. Don Mock, Hydro Museum, 2015. DVD.
Black Sunday 1966, Dir. Don Mock, Hydro Museum, 2015. DVD.
Echoes of Thunder Vol. I, Dir. Doug Hall, Hydro Museum, 1996. DVD.
Echoes of Thunder Vol. II, Dir. Doug Hall, Hydro Museum, 1997. DVD.
Freedom Flyer, Dir. Merl Dodry, Freedom Flyer Productions, 1975. Film.
Hydros Up Close—The 1963 Exide, Dir. Don Mock, Hydro Museum, 2015. DVD.
Mira Slovak Home Movies, Dir. Mira Slovak, Mira Slovak, 1969. Film.
This is Your Life: "Mira Slovak," Dir. Richard Gottlieb, A Ralph Edwards Production, 1959. Film.
The Bill Muncey Story, Dir. Don Mock, Mock One Productions, 2005. DVD.
The Green Girl, Dir. Gregory Pappy Jr., Green Girl Productions, 2014. Film.
The Roaring 50's, Dir. Kenneth Schwedop, KING-TV, 1960. Film.
The Wahoo Story, Dir. Don Mock, Mock One Productions, 2010. DVD.
Unos, Dir J. Kadar, Stani Films, 1953. Film.

Select Sources from the Hydroplane Museum Archives

APBA Propeller (multiple issues, 1956–1967)
Boating News (September 1966)
Coeur d' Alene Press (multiple issues, 1958–1966)
Detroit Free Press (multiple issues, 1957–1966)

Detroit News (multiple issues, 1957–1966)
Flying (January 1965)
Homboldt Standard (December 1952)
Hot Boat (multiple issues, 1965–1967)
Life (multiple issues, 1954–1969)
Los Angeles Times (multiple issues, 1965–1975)
The Lowell Sun (March 1953)
Madison Courier (multiple issues, 1957–1976)
Motor Boating (multiple issues, 1957–1966)
National Champion Air Races Program (1964)
Nevada State Journal (May 12, 1956)
Newsweek (multiple issues, 1964–1966)
Pacific Motor Boat (multiple issues, 1956–1963)
Powerboat (multiple issues, 1961–1967)
San Francisco Chronicle (multiple issues, 1958–1967)
San Jose Mercury News (multiple issues, 1964–1969)
Santa Barbara News Press (multiple issues, 1969–2014)
Santa Paula Chronicle (multiple issues, 1969–1978)
Sea (multiple issues, 1964–1967)
Seattle Post-Intelligencer (multiple issues, 1955–1969)
Seattle Times (multiple issues, 1955–1969)
Small World for Volkswagen owners in the US (Fall issue, 1969)
Spokesman Review (multiple issues, 1958–1969)
Sports Illustrated (multiple issues, 1957–1966)
The Orange County Register (multiple issues, 1969–2015)
The Post—Standard (March 25, 1953)
Record Eagle (December 19, 1953)
Rudder (multiple issues, 1956–1967)
The Santa Paula Times (multiple issues, 1969–2014)
The Stars and Stripes (multiple issues, 1953–1954)
Thunderboat (multiple issues, 1970–2017)
Time (multiple issues, 1953–1969)
Tri Cities Herald (multiple issues, 1966–1967)
Ukiah Daily Journal (February 18, 1979)
Union Bulletin (multiple issues, 1954–1956)
Unlimited Hydroplane News (multiple issues, 1957–1960)
Unlimited News Journal (multiple issues, 1966–2014)
Unpublished Collected writings of Mira Slovak (1967–2014)
Washington Post (multiple issues, 1953–1969)
Yachting (multiple issues, 1956–1967)